DOWRY PROHIBITION AND LAW: A SOCIO-LEGAL STUDY

Dixit, Shaifali

ACKNOWLEDGEMENT

This thesis is dedicated to Prof. (Dr.) Nishtha Jaswal who is a true blessing and benediction of almighty 'Lord Shiva'. Undertaking this Ph.D has been a truly life-changing experience for me and it would not have been possible to do without the grace of God and support as well as guidance that I received from many people.

To commence with, I pay my sincere gratitude and profound respect to my supervisor Prof. (Dr.) Nishtha Jaswal, Vice Chancellor, Himachal Pradesh National Law University, Shimla and Former Professor, Department of Laws, Panjab University, Chandigarh. Her enduring motivation, unfailing support, invaluable insights, precision and clarity of each and every law point has not only helped to widen the ambit of my thoughts but also inspired me to develop a more rational approach over the area of study. She has been as affectionate as mother, as motivational as an inspiration, as guiding as a true leader and as helping as 'God', throughout this journey of my study. Despite her ever increasing academic responsibilities and extremely busy schedule, she has always provided me her precious time and priceless guidance.

I am most blessed and fortunate to have Dr. Shipra Gupta as my co-supervisor in this study. I pay my humble thanks and overwhelming obeisance to my co-supervisor Dr. Shipra Gupta, Associate Professor, Department of Laws, Panjab University, Chandigarh. Her valuable guidance, immense knowledge, positive and loving attitude, constructive and undoubtedly crucial criticism has enabled me to work and achieve up to the best of my ability. She gave me her valuable time, constant co-operation and unfailing support at each and every step of not only my Ph.D but throughout my academic life at Department of Laws, Panjab University, Chandigarh.

My profound thanks to Prof. (Dr.) Meenu Paul, Chairperson, Department of Laws, Panjab University, Chandigarh for her kind co-operation in the completion of this study.

For me, it is a proud privilege and a matter of honour to pay my overwhelming gratitude to Prof.(Dr.) Paramjit Singh Jaswal, Vice Chancellor, Rajiv Gandhi National

i

University of Law, Patiala who encouraged me with his massive words and blessings throughout the study.

From the core of my heart and soul, I pay my overwhelming gratitude and thanks to Dr. Rakesh Kumar Jaswal for the indispensible help, valuable support, immense co-operation and motivation in initiating, pursuing as well as completing this study. I also pay my humble thanks to Dr. Rakesh Kumar Jaswal and Dr. Ritu Jaswal for their constant love, affection and motivation.

I pay my sincere thanks to Dr. Rajesh Sharma and Mrs. Meena Sharma, for their great help and support at each and every step of this study and conducting empirical survey in District Kangra and Shimla. This work could not have been possible without their contribution, motivation and abundant love that they have showered on me.

My humble thanks to Dr Tejinder Kaur, Principal Army Institute of Law for her most needed support, constant encouragement and cooperative attitude for the completion and submission of my work on time.

My sincere thanks to Dr. Jayanti Dutta, Deputy Director, Human Resource Development Centre, Panjab University, Chandigarh who has put her valuable experience and wisdom at my disposal. She provided critical analysis of my work and suggested many important additions and improvements.

I am also extremely indebted to Mr. Madan Kumar Sharma, Secretary Law, Himachal Pradesh, Secretariat, Shimla, who has contributed through his valuable experience, wisdom and kind co-operation to conduct the survey in the remote areas of Rohru, District Shimla.

I am highly thankful to Mr. Ajay Sharma, Senior Advocate, Himachal Pradesh High Court, Shimla, Mr. Bhuvanesh Sharma, Senior Advocate, Himachal Pradesh High Court, Shimla and Prof.(Dr.) Kamal Jeet Singh, Professor, Department of Laws, Himachal Pradesh University, Shimla for providing their immense co-operation and valuable information in conducting empirical survey among Police, Lawyers, Judges and Academicians in the field of law.

I am highly thankful to Mrs. Pawna Sharma, Dr. Nidhi Raina IGMC, Shimla, Mrs. Pratibha Chauhan, Principal, GSS, Junga, Shimla for their immense support in conducting empirical survey among married women and general public and providing valuable information on this topic. I am also thankful to Dr Kulbhushan Sood, Dr. Pranpreet Singh for their help and support in completing my work.

I also appreciate the co-operation extended by the staff of the library of Army Institute of Law, Mohali, Library of School of Law, LPU, Phagwara, Library of Department of Laws, Panjab University, Chandigarh, A.C. Joshi Library, Panjab University, Chandigarh, Library of Indian Institute of Advanced Study, Shimla, State Library, Shimla, British Library, Chandigarh for their ever readiness and rendering every help as and when required.

My heartfelt thanks to the manager and staff of hotel Apple Blossom, Shimla and Nau Nabh Heritage hotel, Rampur Bushehar for extending their support and co-operation in conducting the empirical survey in district Shimla.

The words fail to express my gratitude and appreciation for my father-in-law Colonel (Dr.) S. S. Parmar (Retd.) for providing me constant motivation, unfailing support and effort in achieving this goal as well as conducting empirical survey in District Kangra. This work could not have been possible without the co-operation, immense love and sacrificing approach of my parents-in-law Colonel (Dr.) S. S. Parmar (Retd.) and Mrs. Manju Parmar.

I am extremely fortunate to gratefully acknowledge the immense support and love of my father Advocate B.K. Dixit, who provided each and every help, assistance and guidance required in conducting the empirical study in Himachal Pradesh and my mother Dolly Dixit for her selfless love, constant prayers and many sacrifices of those long awaited months of my absence on several occasions of her life. I cannot express in the words, my gratitude and tribute to my beloved *Nana Ji*, Late Shri. D.V. Dharmani and *Nani ji*, Late Smt. Santosh Dharmani, who had always showered immense love and everlasting blessings on me.

I also want to say thanks to little flowers of my family Anahita and Rihu for their unwavering cuteness and humor that helped me to survive all the stress after the long hours of work. I cannot forget to thank my dear friends and well wishers Mrs. Rinky, Mrs. Jessica Vij, Dr. Bhupinder Kaur, Mrs. Anmolpreet Kaur, Dr. Anju Chaudhary, Dr. Priya Singla for providing me help whenever I needed it.

In the end I would like to thank 'God' who has constantly made me realize his presence through the presence of my husband Mr. Ashish Parmar, like a true companion, at each and every step of this work. I do not have words to express my gratitude for his constant encouragement, huge moral support, intense efforts, uncountable sacrifices, unmatchable patience, unfailing co-operation and that too without a single expectation, throughout the entire journey of my thesis. So, I will only quote it in the words of Winston Churchill, "Now this is not the end. It is not even the beginning of the end. But it is, perhaps, the end of the beginning".

CONTENTS

TABLE OF CASES

Saburannessa v. *Sabdu Sheikh*, AIR 1934 Cal 693.	75
Sallial Kotakkat Manakkal Narayana Nambudiri v. *Patticharavoor alias Charavoor Manakkal*, 1945 MLJR 145.	116
Satbir Singh v. *State of Punjab*, AIR 2001 SC 2828.	74,85
Satya Narayan Tiwari v. *State of U.P*, (2010)13 SCC 689.	142
Shanti and Anr v. *State of Haryana*, (1991) 1 SCC 371.	83,133
Shobha Rani v. *Madhukar Reddi*, (1988) SCC 105.	94,132
Shyam M. Sachdev v. *State*, 1991 (97) Cr LJ 300.	73
Smt. Laxmi v. *Om Parkash & Ors.*, (2001) 6 SCC 118.	131
Social Action Forum for Manav Adhikar and Anr. v. *Union of India Ministry of Law and Justice and others*, (*2018*) 10 SCC 443.	147
State of Andhra Prades v. *Raj Gopal Asawa*, (2004) 4 SCC470.	183
State of Himachal Pradesh v. *Nikku Ram and Ors.*,1995 (6) SCC 219.	134
State of Karnataka v. *Choudegowda*, 2007 Cri L J 2812.	101
State of Karnataka v. *M.V.Manjunathegowda*, AIR 2003 SC 809.	101
State of Punjab v. *Anil Kumar*, 1992 Cr LJ 3131(P&H).	87
State of Punjab v. *Dal Jit Singh*, 1999 Cr LJ 2723 (P&H).	92
State of Punjab v. *Iqbal Singh*, AIR 1991 SC 1532.	87
State v. *Shivappa Bhimappa Pathat*, 2003 (2) Kar LJ 171.	76
Stree Atyachar Virodhi Parishad v. *Dilip Nathumal Chordia & Anr*, 1989 SCC (1) 715.	124
Sushil Kumar Sharma v. *Union of India, AIR* 2005 (6) SC 266.	113
Suvetha v. *State*, 2009 Cr LJ 2974.	90
Tarsem Singh v. *State of Punjab*, AIR 2009 SC 1454.	96
Tekait Mon Mohini Jemadai v. *Basanta Kumar Singh*, ILR (1901) 28 Cal 751.	115
Trimukh Maroti Kirkan v. *State of Maharashtra*, (2008) 8 SCC 456.	100,101
Uday Chakraboty v. *State of West Bengal*, AIR 2010 SC 3506.	86

CHAPTER 1

INTRODUCTION

Marriage has been considered as the most sacred, pious and indispensable institution in Indian society. The most common endeavour of the mankind is an inherent instinct for companionship. Since ages, the underlying aim behind the institution of marriage has been the fulfillment of the need of companionship and lineage. As the institution of marriage came into existence, it gave rise to several marriage related rituals, customs, ceremonies and traditions. In many communities, gifts and valuables were given to the bride by her parents and relatives at the time of wedding while she had to leave her parental home and become part of her husband's family. It was considered as an auspicious custom that also served as a support to establish and arrange newly required household amenities. In those times, women were neither employed nor had any personal source of income. Hence the economical value of brides was considered to be lower in comparison to her bridegroom. Therefore the custom of dowry also originated as a compensation for this lower economic value of bride to her bridegroom and in-laws who were supposed to bear all her financial expenses after marriage. Dowry was also looked upon as a compensation paid by the father of the bride to his son-in-law for the maintenance of his daughter as well as to the parents of groom for the expense they had borne while in educating and upbringing their son. Moreover, the daughters were not given any share in the parental property therefore dowry was impliedly a kind of share in their father's wealth given to them at the time of their marriage.

With the passage of time, several rituals and customs came and gradually vanished with the passage of time, however, the practice of dowry has not only continued, rather flourished over the years. The perspective of people towards the prevalence of this custom is neither same nor predictable. Hypothetically, a large number of people among the educated class verbally condemn it, but in actual conduct they themselves follow this evil practice under the veil of certain cultural and social legitimization. Finding and getting a suitable partner for the daughter has always been another significant reason for the acceptance of dowry system by the parents of bride.

1

It is a common perspective that payment of huge dowry ensures or helps in fetching a suitable match of desired caste and social status. For the bridegrooms and their families, dowry system has turned out to be perhaps the most easy and quick method for securing wealth and gaining high financial status. It has lead to a very difficult and unavoidable situation for the present generation. On one side the extremely rich class has made it a status symbol to perform most expensive marriages of their daughters by giving flats, expensive cars, most expensive ornaments etc and on the other side the middle class and poor people are getting choked under the inevitable burden of giving dowry. Dowry that was voluntarily given as a token of love and blessings has now turned into a budgetary snag to marriage. Dowry demands have inflated, even leading to extortionate payments.

The social scientists differ widely in interpreting the concept of dowry reflecting the specific features of the societies which they have studied. It seems complicated to give a universal definition to dowry in terms of social perspective. The sociologists who have studied dowry system in north India emphasize the 'gift' aspect of dowry and it is variously called *'Daaj'* or *'Dahej'*. In middle India, the *'daan'* or 'donation' aspect of dowry is more prominent and it is generally called as *'Daan Dahej'* (in Bihar) and 'Dayaj' (in Awadh region). On the other hand, south Indian societies define dowry as 'female inheritance' and very often is termed as *'Stree Dhanam'*.[1] The dowry has emerged as a social problem which has disturbed the behavioural as well as social order of society. Following were the factors that converted the socio-religious nature of dowry into a social evil.

Dowry as a fake status symbol: With the passage of time, the economic conditions of the people have improved. Therefore, the people have started spending more lavishly on weddings in their struggle for social recognition. As a result dowry is glamorised and has created a delusion that giving dowry in abundance is a measure to upgrade the status and self esteem in the community.

Psychological pressure of giving dowry for the happiness of daughter: Dowry has become a fearful psychological compulsion in the mind of the parents that if adequate dowry is not given, their daughter may be mal-treated and tortured. The feeling that

---

[1]   Arunima Baruah, *The Soft Target-Crime Against Women 149* (Kilaso Books, New Delhi, 2004).

their daughter cannot be happy without giving dowry has deep rooted this evil more firmly in the society.[2]

Changing role of women with changing times: In the beginning, the role of women was religious and spiritual. Then, there was a time when most of the people used to work in the fields to earn their livelihood, women also used to work on fields. Thereafter, the society took a leap and it became prestige issue for the wealthier people that their women would not work on the land. With the passage of time, spiritualism changed into materialism and the society started looking at the women from the economic angle. Thereby, the women who were formerly an economic asset in the past had become a liability. So it was expected by the groom's family to be paid for taking the responsibility of bride.

Compulsiveness of marriage and expectation of well-settled bride-groom: In *Manava Grhya Sutra,* five qualities of groom were mentioned i.e. wealth, handsomeness, knowledge, intelligence and relatives.[3] Educated and well settled grooms became able to fetch huge dowry because parents of girls want their daughters to get married with decent salaried men. Thus the pre-meditated choice of bridegroom gave a boost to the evil of dowry.

The orthodox mentality and rigid caste system: The custom of dowry originated from *Brahmins. Brahmins* were the reference group for village, so it became a general tendency to imitate *Brahmin* customs with a hope of raising one's social status.[4] Secondly the strictness of caste system and an urge to find out a 'same caste suitable match' has decreased the availability of suitable match. Therefore, the parents of the bride started surrendering to the unreasonable demands of dowry.

Predominance of parents in taking decisions regarding marriage: In olden days the upper most authority of marriage of the children exclusively rested with the parents but gradually the younger generation started making their own choice. The changing trend was accepted by the parents provided with the condition that although the consent of the boy and the girl was taken but the authority to negotiate the matrimonial alliance should remain with the parents.

---

[2] Suman Nalwa and Hari Dev Kohli, *Law Relating to Dowry, Dowry Death, Cruelty to Women & Domestic Violence* 534(Universal Law Publication Co., New Delhi, 2013).

[3] *Id at* 535

[4] S. Gokilavani, *Marriage, Dowry, Practice and Divorce* 61 (Regal Publications, New Delhi, 2008).

The menace of Dowry has become a social menace in modern India leading to the oppression on women, physical violence on the bride, causing a financial and emotional stress on the parents of the bride, marital conflict and so on[5]. It is a deep rooted evil and subsisting since ages. The phenomenon of dowry deaths and bride burning has started occupying a leading position yet for years it was considered an aberration of certain north Indian communities. Earlier, cases of bride burning and dowry death were camouflaged by the police as accidents or suicides.[6] By 1977-78, it could be realized that most of the deaths of married women which were registered as accidental deaths or cases of suicides were, in fact, murder or induced suicides[7]. It took more than a decade for the legislature to make dowry death a crime under the Penal Code and to prescribe sentence for the offendors[8].The form in which dowry exists since last quarter has no roots that can be traced to traditional marriage rituals.[9]

This changed scenario has not only created a social and financial concern to the prospective brides and their parents rather it has resulted into many offences related to the demand of dowry. The non-fulfillment of such illegitimate demands often lead to even some more severe forms such as; cruelty, domestic violence, abetment of suicide and dowry deaths etc. Now the custom of dowry which was once a beautiful practice to shower love and blessing on bride and bridegroom has now become one of the major concerns of law to control violence against married women. It has not only engulfed the piousness and sacredness of marital bond rather has indirectly given birth to other social evils like female feticide etc. As soon as the legislations have been made to prohibit the custom of dowry and to provide a shield for the women against dowry related offences, another major concern has been emerged regarding the misuse and abuse of such legislations in certain cases. It has witnessed that at certain instances, these laws have been proved to be incapable of curbing the menace of dowry and at some other point they are abused as weapon

[5] Gurudev, "The Origin of Dowry System – British Policies convert Gifts to Bride into an instrument of oppression against women" *available at* http://www.hitxp.com/articles/history/origin-dowry-system-bride-woman-india-british/ (Visited on July 29, 2017).

[6] Shobha Saxena, *Crimes Against Women and Protective Laws* 114 (Deep and Deep Publications Pvt Ltd, New Delhi, 2008).

[7] *Id at* 115.

[8] *Virbhan* v. *State of U. P.* (1983) 4 SCC 197.

[9] *Id at* 198.

against innocent husbands and in-laws. Therefore there is an intense need to examine the efficacy of laws related to dowry prohibition and analyze the social paradigm on acceptability and implementation of these laws.

1.1 Problem Profile

Marriage ceremonies and customs range across cultures and it is good to perform these customs until and unless any custom becomes a social evil as has happened in the case of dowry. In the early days gifts and presents were given to the bride at the time of her marriage as an auspicious custom. But, in course of time, it became a crude institution resulting in female infanticide, suicide, bride-burning and other indignities and cruelties. In the last few decades, India has witnessed the evils of the dowry system in a more acute form than the past. Recently in Kolkata, a husband has been alleged of blackmailing his wife for dowry by clicking her nude pictures and making objectionable videos. He extorted and assaulted his wife that he would upload these pictures and videos on porn sites in case of non-fulfillment of his dowry demands.[10] A 27 year old woman died as she has been forcefully starved by her husband and mother-in-law for dowry in Kerala. The case resulted into public outrage, as it was revealed that at the time of her death, she weighed just 20 kg and was in extreme illness and uneasiness.[11] Another woman and her three month old daughter were allegedly burnt alive by her in-laws over demand of dowry in Rampur. On the complaint of victim's brother a case was registered against the deceased's husband, her father-in-law and five other family members, all of whom were absconding.[12] Unfortunately, 21dowry deaths are reported in India, every day.[13] The NCRB recorded that in the year 2015, as many as 7,634 women died in the country due to dowry harassment. Their deaths were caused either as a result of being burnt alive or they were compelled to commit suicide for non fulfillment of dowry demand.

---

[10] Times of India, "West Bengal: Hubby uploads wife's private pictures, video for dowry" *available at:* https://timesofindia.indiatimes.com/city/kolkata/west-bengal-hubby-uploads-wifes-private-pictures-video-for-dowry/articleshow/72176774.cms (Last Modified on Nov 22, 2019).

[11] Indian Express, "Weighed just 20 kg': Kerala woman starved to death over dowry, husband, mother-in-law held", *available at:* https://indianexpress.com/article/india/starved-death-dowry-kerala-woman-weighed-5650755/ (Last Modified on March 30, 2019).

[12] Hindustan Times, "Woman, with her 3-month-old child, locked and burnt alive by in-laws in UP" *available at:* https://www.hindustantimes.com/india-news/woman-with-her-3-month-old-child-locked-and-burnt-alive-by-in-laws-in-up/story-zwHbDJhnn211edGm24cIbO.html (Last Modified on Sep 19, 2019).

[13] Chayyanika Nigam, "21 lives lost to dowry every day across India; conviction rate less than 35 per cent", *India Today,* April 22, 2017 *available at:* https://www.indiatoday.in/mail-today/story/dowry-deaths-national-crime-records-bureau-conviction-rate-972874-2017-04-22 (Visited on April 22, 2019).

5

NCRB has reported 4668 dowry deaths in the year 1995. The numbers increased to 6787 in the year 2005 and further witnessed a huge rise as7634 in 2015.[14]

There has been a huge rise in the number of cases related to dowry in last two decades.[15]There were 8,093 cases of Dowry Death in the year 2007, in the year 2008 the number increased to 8172, in the year 2009 it further went to 8383, thereafter in the year 2010 it reached to 8391 and then in the year 2011 it was 8618. Similarly, there were 75930 cases of cruelty by husband and relatives in the year 2007, in the year 2008 the number increased to 81344, in the year 2009 it further went to 89546, thereafter in the year 2010 it reached to 94041 and then in the year 2011 it was 99135. The number of incidents reported under Dowry Prohibition Act, 1961 were 5623, 5555, 5650, 5182 and 6619 in the years 2007, 2008, 2009, 2010 and 2011 respectively.[16]Around 8,233 young females, most of whom were newly wedded brides, became victim of dowry deaths in 2012. The incidences of cruelty by husbands and their relatives also witnessed a huge increase from 99,135 to 106,527 in the year 2012. Most of the cases of cruelty were dowry related, but the biggest irony is that however the charges were brought in 94 per cent of dowry death cases, but the conviction rate was only 32 % in dowry death cases and merely 15 % in the cases of cruelty.[17]

However, dowry alone is not the sole cause of violence or cruelty done to the married women, but it can't be denied that dowry demands and increasing pressure of pomp and show in the marriages has contributed to considering daughters as a liability or burden and consequent demeaning of valuation of females in society. The custom of dowry has even spread to those communities, which had no such custom in their previous generations. It is a gross failure of anti dowry laws and a sign of their poor implementation. Many legal experts strongly point out the loopholes in the

---

[14] Vageshwari Deswal, "Dowry deaths: An Ominuous Ignominy for India", *The Times of India*, Apr. 3, 2019 *available at:* https://timesofindia.indiatimes.com/blogs/legally-speaking/dowry-deaths-an-ominuous-ignominy-for-india/ (Visited on Sept 15, 2019).

[15] Rukmini S., "Dowry, What the Data Says and What it Doesn't", *The Hindu, available at:* https://www.thehindu.com/opinion/blogs/blog-datadelve/article6186330.ece (visited on Oct 15, 2016).

[16] NCRB Report, Chapter 5, *available at:* http://ncrb.gov.in/StatPublications/CII/CII2011/cii-2011/Chapter%205.pdf (Visited on Sept 20, 2019).

[17] Dean Nelson, "Woman killed over Dowry 'Every Hour' in India", Jul.7, 2014 *available at:* https://www.telegraph.co.uk/news/worldnews/asia/india/10280802/Woman-killed-over-dowry-every-hour-in-India.html (Visited on Aug 25, 2017).

existing laws related to dowry prohibition. Improper investigations in the beginning stage of such case are also another factor that delays the process of judicial proceedings.[18]

Dowry is such a custom of society which is consistently prevailing but no educated Indian would expressly accept or own up it with pride, although most of the people still adhere to this disreputable practice. Besides huge condemnation the dowry system continues to be given and taken in all forms of societies; educated or uneducated, rich or poor, rural or urban etc. Apparently, the educated and high class people flaunt their eminence by discarding this social evil in their verbal and public discussions but practically the practice of dowry persists to be an integral part of the negotiations that are done in their family marriages. A former bureaucrat of Central government, his wife and son were convicted and sentenced of imprisonment ranging of three to ten years by a court in Noida for causing death of his pregnant daughter-in-law over dowry pressure.[19] A Famous actor of a bollywood movie 'Bahubali', has been accused of harassing and beating his wife for dowry, which eventually abetted her to commit suicide.[20] It is commonly practiced across the country and in almost all the sections of society. The rich people with their accounted and unaccounted wealth have indulged in the practice of giving and taking dowry as a status symbol. The middle class people of the society are also somehow stretching their economic capacity to perform marriages with great pomp and show as giving and taking of dowry is considered as a matter of prestige and social status. Even the economically backward people are also indulged in performing this custom merely because of a wrong belief of social obligation or the helpless situation of their daughter not getting married without giving Dowry.

The menace and evil impact of the practice of dowry has turned into a social hazard in present day India, prompting the maltreatment of women and physical

---

[18] Chayyanika Nigam, "21 Lives Lost to Dowry Every day Across India; Conviction Rate Less than 35Percent", *India Today*, Apr. 22, 2017 *available at:* https://www.indiatoday.in/mail-today/story/dowry-deaths-national-crime-records-bureau-conviction-rate-972874-2017-04-22 (Visited on Oct 11, 2019).

[19] News 18, "Noida Court Sends Former Bureaucrat, Wife and Son to Jail for Dowry Death", *available at:* https://www.news18.com/news/india/noida-court-sends-former-bureaucrat-wife-and-son-to-jail-for-dowry-death-2253519.html (Last Modified on July 31, 2019).

[20] News 18 "Actor Madhu Prakash Booked for Dowry Death After Wife's Suicide", *available at:* https://www.news18.com/news/movies/baahubali-actor-madhu-prakash-booked-for-dowry-death-after-wifes-suicide-2262917.html (Last Modified on August 8, 2019).

violence on the newly wedded females. In Chandigarh, a husband along with his five other family members had been booked for abetment of suicide of his wife for alleged demands of dowry. She has consumed poison after allegedly bearing harassment and battering several times for continuous demands of dowry.[21] In another case, an FIR has been filled under Sections 304B, 498 A of Indian Penal Code and Sections 3 and 4 of Dowry Act against a husband, his brother, mother and father who have allegedly strangulated, killed his wife for dowry. They had abandoned her body in a hospital in Greater Noida and ran away.[22] At present, the act of giving dowry is widespread and profoundly established in the Indian culture. Giving dowry in the marriage is mostly considered and viewed as a universal principle and that is why the demands and expectations for dowry are rising every day. However the ancient dowry system had a humble beginning but now at present scenario, the modern dowry system has to reached to such massive proportions that occasionally bridegrooms decline to continue with the rest half of the marriage ceremonies part of the way through except if the interest of dowry has not been met according to their expectations.[23] It is causing a monetary and psychological burden on the parents of the brides, conjugal clash, etc.

A Patriarchal set up is still prevalent in most of the regions of India, where the women are not in a position to stand up for themselves. Their voice stays unheard in the public arena. Absence of political cooperation because of social-monetary limitations is another motivation behind why woman had not possessed the capacity to stand up for herself and secure against this evil practice. This is likewise viewed as the disappointment of male-arranged polity by a few specialists. Because of such disadvantageous condition of women, we neglect to take care of this serious dowry issue even after all consideration and focus on it[24].

---

[21] Times of India,"Husband booked for dowry death in Chandigarh", *The Times of India*, Sep. 18, 2019 *available at:* https://timesofindia.indiatimes.com/city/chandigarh/husband-booked-for-dowry-death-in-chandigarh/articleshow/71177155.cms (Last Modified on Sep 18, 2019).

[22] Abhishek Awasthi, "Noida: Woman strangled; husband, in-laws booked for dowry" *The Times of India*, Jul 25, 2019 *available at:* https://timesofindia.indiatimes.com/city/noida/woman-strangled-husband-in-laws-booked-for-dowry/articleshow/70370675.cms (Last Modified on Jul 25, 2019).

[23] *Supra* note 6 at 116

[24] Reshma and A. Ramegowda, "Dowry – The Cancer of Society" 17 *IOSR-JHSS* 38(2013) *available at:* http://www.iosrjournals.org/iosr-jhss/papers/Vol17-issue4/H01743545.pdf (Visited on Oct 11, 2018).

1.2 Review of Literature

Literature is the essence of a good research. A study cannot be carried without referring commentaries, books, research papers, statutes, lexicons, websites and articles etc on the relevant topic. It is the foremost step to initiate a research on a topic that the prevailing literature on the subject has to be thoroughly analyzed in depth. The review of already existing literature and research on the related topics has not only provided the clarity of thoughts but also contributed in an in depth and thorough understand of the subject. It helped in identifying the key problem areas which are still untouched in terms of research or needed to be examined and studied in more detail. Following sources have been reviewed thoroughly to understand the concept:

Concept of Dowry

P.S. Narayana in his book *"Laws Relating to Dowry Prohibition"* [25] has covered the meaning, nature of dowry and various laws related to dowry prohibition. The author has aptly remarked upon a significant hurdle in the smooth functioning of laws related to dowry prohibition i.e. the social conditions in India are not favourable for effective implementation of such laws.[26] The author has critically analyzed the efficacy of presumptions taken in Indian Evidence Act in the cases related to dowry.

Madan C. Paul in his book *"Dowry and Position of Women in India"*[27] has discussed 'dowry' as a modern phenomenon. A conceptual perspective of dowry has been taken by the author and a field study of Delhi Metropolis has been conducted. A social survey on dowry has been conducted on the basis of cast, religion, educational level, occupation, economic status and quantum of dowry given or taken. It has been observed that there is a close correlation between the different factors such as income of family, educational status, social obligation in giving and taking of dowry.

S. Gokilwani in his book *"Marriage, Dowry Practice and Divorce"* [28], has given a comprehensive exposition of dowry and various laws related to dowry

---

[25] P.S. Narayana, *Laws relating to Dowry Prohibition* (Gogia Law Agency, Hyderabad, 2001).
[26] *Id. at 19.*
[27] Madan C. Paul, *Dowry and Position of Women in India* (Inter-India Publications, New Delhi, 1986).
[28] S. Gokilavani, *Marriage, Dowry, Practice and Divorce* (Regal Publications, New Delhi, 2008).

prohibition. It also deals with the changing dimensions of law related to dowry with the changing needs of society.

The Shift of 'Bride Price' to '*Stridhan*' and 'Dowry'

Lionel Caplan in his article "Bridegroom Price in Urban India: Class, Cast, And Dowry Evil among Christens in Madras"[29] has discussed that the classical notion of dowry as *stridhan* no more exists in contemporary urban India. The author has pointed out the harsh truth of materialistic world and mentioned that although dowry system is widely criticized as an evil but practically it is widely spreading among the urban well-to-do families. The author has described it as 'bridegroom price' and remarked that it has lost its significance as *stridhan* because neither it serves the purpose of giving daughter's portion, since it is alienated from her to the husband; nor is utilized by her as it is passed to the bridegroom's parents who use it to acquire their son-in-law. He has thoroughly analysed the changing dimensions of the customer of 'bride price' to *stridhan* and its further shift to 'bridegroom price'. Now days, the dowry system is not serving even a single positive purpose which was attached to it in the traditional times. It was used to serve the purpose of giving daughter's share of property and ensuring her financial security in terms of her *stridhan* but in present scenario the benefit of dowry remains no more in the hands of bride rather it passes to her husband and in-laws.

Veena Talwar Oldenburg in her book "*Dowry Murder*"[30], had pointed out the difference in the states of North India and South India with regard to the impact of the customs of bride-price and dowry on disturbed sex ratio in these states. The author has critically described the shift of custom of '*Mul*' (a kind of bride price) to '*Daj*' (a custom like dowry) in North India. She has also examined the views of other authors on the emergence of dowry and its connection with female infanticide.

---

[29] Lionel Caplan, "Bridegroom Price in Urban India: Class, Caste and 'Dowry Evil' Among Christians in Madras" 19 *TJRAIGBI(MAN)* 216-233 *available at:* http://www.jstor.org/stable/2802278 (Visited on July 22, 2017).

[30] Veena Talwar Oldenburg, "*Dowry Murder*"54(Oxford University Press, New York, 2002), available at:https://books.google.co.in/books?id=BSjVgCpc5p4C&pg=PA67&lpg= PA67&dq= less +successful.+The+British+also+passed+Infanticide+Act+in+1870+to+abolish+this+practice+to+fe male+infanticide&source=bl&ots=sd3YH2mzfl&sig=ACfU3U1NxBGQoJYkJmmywxurA2BthkO BEg&hl=en&sa=X&ved=2ahUKEwj034mcur7mAhXvwzgGHQjtAcwQ6AEwD3oECAoQAQ#v= onepage&q=less%20successful.%20The%20British%20also%20passed%20Infanticide%20Act%20 in%201870%20to%20abolish%20this%20practice%20to%20female%20infanticide&f=false (Visited on November 22, 2019).

Junsen Zhang and William Chan, in their paper "Dowry and Wife's Welfare: A Theoretical and Empirical Analysis" [31] have thoroughly analyzed the co-existence of the customs of dowry and bride-price. The authors have taken a very strange view point by putting forward an argument that dowry improves the wealth of bride and her new family and therefore contributes in the welfare of bride whereas bride-price has no such effect. The dowry has been considered as a form of pre-mortem inheritance gifted by selfless parents to their daughter for her welfare. The dowry results in the welfare of the bride as it increases the wealth of her new family and enhances her supremacy and position in that family. But on the other side, the bride-price is given to the bride's parents and therefore it could not contribute in the welfare of bride or her groom in the new matrimonial setup.

History and Evolution of the Custom of Dowry

Dalbir Bharti in his book *"Women and the Law"*, [32] has discussed evolutions of custom of dowry and related laws. The author has fairly analyzed the close connection between dowry, cruelty and domestic violence. He has examined all the offences related to dowry, cruelty and domestic violence and the initiatives of Government to take remedial steps along with the judiciary to curb these offences.

Mahamahopadhyaya Pandurang Vaman Kane, in his work *"History of Dharamsastra"*, [33] has precisely quoted the rules prescribed by *Dharamsastras* regarding the property rights of inheritance of daughters. The author has very well quoted, translated and explained that in ancient Vedas the sons were always preferred over daughters and their rights were of paramount consideration. The author has also explained the concept of *'Stridhana'* in the Vedic literature. The existence of dowry has been traced in the hymns of verses of *Rig Veda.*

Anjani Kant in her book *"Women and the Law"*[34], has done a historical study of position of Indian women. The author has examined the status of women in all the

---

[31] Junsen Zhang & William Chan, "Dowry and Wife's Welfare: A Theoretical and Empirical Analysis" 107 *JPE* 786-808 (1999), pp. 786-808 available at: http://www.jstor.org/stable/ 10. 1086/250079 (Visited on July 22, 2017).
[32] Dalbir Bharti, *Women and the Law* (A.P.H. Publishing Corp., New Delhi, 2002).
[33] Mahamahopadhyaya Pandurang Vaman Kane, *History of Dharamsastra* (Bhandarkar Oriental Research Institute, Poona, 1946).
[34] Anjani Kant, *Women and the Law* (A.P.H. Publishing Corp., New Delhi, 2008).

phases i.e. from Vedic era to modern India. The changing status of women with the changing era of society has also been discussed.[35] It has been used to identify the causes of gradual increase in the offences related to dowry, to determine the impact of declining status of women on increasing crime rate against her in her marital home and to arrive on a solution to combat with these social evils and regain the previous status of women.

Ranjana Sheel in her book *"The Political Economy of Dowry"*[36], has traced the historic origin of the system of dowry as an integral part of marriage among Hindus of north India.[37] She has taken an unusual vistas to explain that how the codification of Hindu laws has established dowry as an integral part of marriage. The author has mentioned that although a number of women's movement took place to resolve the issue of widespread practice of dowry but was of no good use. The author has critically considered the Dowry Prohibition Act and its subsequent amendments to be totally ineffective and flouted with impunity every day.

Mamta Rao in her book *"Law Relating to Women and Children"*[38], has elucidated the gradual change of sacred customs of *Kanyadan* and *Vardakshina* into the evil of dowry. The author has further remarked upon increasing rate of dowry deaths. She has thoroughly discussed the historical background of dowry. Moreover the study tends to analyze the reasons behind increase in dowry deaths and measures to control it.

Ranjana Sheel in her article "Institutionalization and Expansion of Dowry System in Colonial North India[39]" has thrived to depict that how growing *'Brahmanisation'* of the society has affected the various forms of the marriage and what is its role in arousal and spreading of practice of dowry. She has explained the eight forms of marriage and origin and evolution of dowry system in these various forms. The various forms of the marriage had a strong impact on origin and growth of dowry system in the ancient India.

---

[35] *Id. at 338.*
[36] Ranjana Sheel, *The Political Economy of Dowry* (Manohar Publishers, New Delhi, 1999).
[37] *Id. at 40.*
[38] Mamta Rao, *Law Relating to Woman and Children* (Eastern Book Company, Lucknow, 2012).
[39] Ranjana Sheel, "Institutionalisation and Expansion of Dowry System in Colonial North India" 32 *EPW* 1709-1718, *available at*: http://www.jstor.org/stable/4405621 (Visited on July 22, 2017).

H. A. Rose, in his article, "The Development of Bride-Price and of Dowry"[40] has compared the code of Hammurabi and the code of Manu in context to the customs of dowry and bride-price. The author has remarked that the code of Hammurabi has not permitted a father to sell his daughter however he was permitted to give her in concubinage with or without dowry. It has considered marriage as contract and no marriage was valid without dowry. The custom of dowry was firmly established but it was not clear that whether it was secured by the contract or not. There were some more rules regarding the entitlement of dowry likewise; on a divorce for misconduct of wife, the husband was entitled to keep the dowry with him. However, if the wife was divorced for infertility, she had complete right over her dowry. The code of Manu also prohibits the selling of daughters. It has not even allowed the concubinage of daughter. Dowry was considered to be a part of a woman's *'Stridhan'* and she had full entitlement over the same.

Stephanie Dalley in his Article, "Old Babylonian Dowries"[41] have described the age old Hammurabi's Code of Laws related to dowry, prevailing in Babylon. The custom of dowry was well accepted in the law code of Hammurabi. But it was well ensured that the dowry brought by a woman from her father's house must not be dishonestly snatched or misappropriated by her husband and in laws. On the failure of marriage, she was well entitled to take back the dowry and use it for her subsequent marriage. On the death of her husband, her in-laws were bound to return each and every article of dowry to her in the same condition as it was brought by her at the time of her marriage. If she died, the right of inheriting her dowry persisted with her sons, father or her parental family and not with her husband.

Offences related to Dowry

P.K Majumdar and R.P. Kataria in their commentary *"Law Relating to Dowry Prohibition, Cruelty and Harassment"* [42], have deeply analyzed the offence of dowry. The authors have thoroughly discussed the provisions of The Dowry Prohibition Act,

---

[40] H. A. Rose, "The Development of Bride-Price and of Dowry" 36 *FOLKLORE* 189-193 (1925) *available at:* http://www.jstor.org/stable/1256331 (Visited on July 22, 2017).

[41] Stephanie Dalley , "Old Babylonian Dowries" 42 *IRAQ* 53-74 (1980) *available at:* http://www.jstor.org/stable/4200115 (Visited on July 22, 2017).

[42] P.K. Majumdar and R.P. Kataria, *Law Relating to Dowry Prohibition Cruelty & Harassment* (Orient Publishing Company. New Delhi, 2014).

1961 and all the provisions related to dowry in other statutes. In this commentary, the deep rooted history of dowry in India as well as in Europe, South Asia and Africa is summarized. The gradual increase in the menace of this social evil and its disastrous consequences on the society are the major concern. The laws enacted to eradicate the evil system of dowry and their effectiveness is evaluated. There is an emerging need to identify the root cause of existing dowry system besides the stringent laws and to find out the means of controlling and combating this menace. The procedural aspect in the cases of dowry and dowry deaths has been minutely observed, analyzed and the much needed changes have been suggested.

Paras Diwan and Peeyushi Diwan in their book "*Dowry, Dowry Deaths, Bride Burning, Rape and Related Offences*" [43], have dealt with different aspects of law related to dowry and its prohibition, offences related to dowry with a special reference to bride burning. It also deals with the origin of the concept of dowry in ancient, medieval and British India. The origin and history of dowry and related offences as well as their punishments in law are broadly examined. The prime focus of the authors is inclined towards the increasing rate of such offences despite the stringent laws.

K.D. Gaur in his commentary on the *"Indian Penal Code"* [44], has deeply analyzed the agony of the victim of dowry death since these crimes are always committed in the safe four walls of victim's own house. Since these offences are always committed in the four walls of the house henceforth there is always a challenge to get sufficient evidence and eye witnesses.

Dowry Prohibition Act, 1961

R.L Anand and Gargi Sethi in their book "*The Prohibition of Dowry Act, 1961*"[45], have scrutinized the scope and applicability of Dowry Prohibition Act. The authors have pointed out the possibilities for scheming minds to find ways and means of destroying the utility of the Act. The suggestions have been made for some necessary amendments to overcome these grey areas. The possibilities to incorporate

---

[43] Paras Diwan, *Law relating to Dowry, Dowry Deaths, Bride Burning, Rape and Related Offences* (Universal Law Publishing co. Pvt. Ltd.,Delhi, 2002).
[44] K. D. Gaur, *Commentary on the Indian Penal Code* (Universal Law Publishing, 2013).
[45] *Supra* note 38.

these amendments have been audited in reference to the decided case laws and the probabilities of misinterpretation of the Act. The authors have also come up with the suggestive measures to enhance the efficacy of the Act by substantive changes and procedural means.

Suman Nalwa and Hari Dev Kohli in their book *"Law relating to Dowry, Dowry Death, Cruelty to Women & Domestic Violence"*[46], have made a sincere venture in highlighting the cruelty on women under the garb of dowry and its horrible consequences leading to a disturbed life of women as well as of family. The authors have boldly described the failure of Dowry Prohibition Act and overshadow of criminal provisions over this social enactment. Their critical study is enriched by copious references to leading judgments. The authors have discussed the cruelty and domestic violence on women and its impact to shatter the stability of marriage resulting in battered and devastated wives groaning with pain and agony. They have thoroughly reviewed the reasons behind the failure of the Dowry Prohibition Act, 1961 in combating the menace of dowry. The merciless cases of dowry death, bride burning and suicide of wife have also been mentioned and the failure of statutory and administrative mechanism in preventing such cases has been critically analyzed. The equation between the Domestic Violence Act, 2005, The Dowry Prohibition Act, 1961 and the penal laws related to dowry prohibition is derived and the procedural improvements to make these statutes practically compatible and effective have been suggested.

B.K. Sharma and Vijay Nagpal in their book *"Treatise on Economic and Social Offences"*[47], have thoroughly commented upon The Dowry Prohibition Act, 1961. The authors have examined the need, objective and substance of the various provisions of this Act. They have critically examined The Dowry Prohibition Act, 1961 as well as the various amendments that took place to make it more stringent and effective in implementation.

---

[46] Suman Nalwa and Hari Dev Kohli, *Law Relating to Dowry, Dowry Death, Cruelty to Women & Domestic Violence* (Universal Law Publication Co., New Delhi, 2013).
[47] B.K Sharma and Dr.Vijay Nagpal, *Treatise on Economic & Social Offences* (Allahabad Law Agency, Faridabad, 2010).

Crimes against Women and Dowry

Arunima Baruah in her work *"The Soft Target-Crime against Women"* [48], has categorized and described various species of crimes against women. The author has remarked that the women are vulnerable to all sorts of exploitation, molestation, violence and even fatal assaults. The author has also attempted to identify the precipitating factors, which ultimately lead to violent relationship between the marital partners. The author has pointed out a true factual obstacle in implementation of laws that in most of the cases, women do not approach for a legal support at all and leave apart fighting a case in the court against their husband or in-laws. She has focused specifically on the crimes against women related to dowry and comparatively analyzed all the aspects of these crimes and their increasing ratio in comparison to other crimes. The author has also suggested certain solutions to combat the issue.

R.C. Goel and Rajiv Raheja in their commentary *"Hints and Tricks on Criminal Law"*[49], have discussed Dowry related offences, Cruelty and Harassment in light of landmark judgments of various High Courts and Supreme Court of India. The authors have elucidated it that how the requirement of nexus between the demand of dowry and the harassment done to the victims is closely monitored by the judiciary. To bring home the guilt in such cases, there must be a demand of dowry and as a consequence the further maltreatment.

Dowry Death and Bride Burning

Dorothy Stein, in her article "Burning Widows, Burning Brides: The perils of Daughterhood in India[50]" has elucidated the danger of taking birth as a daughter in India. The author has sadly remarked that neither the legislation of female inheritance laws in Hindus, nor its prohibition among Muslims and nor even its weakness among Christens and *Parsis* has prevented the wide spread of the evil of dowry in most of the Indian communities. The transition and barbaric transformation of a pious custom of *kanyadana* to a life taking evil of dowry and bride burning has been well explained.

---

[48] Arunima Baruah, *The Soft Target - Crime Against Women* (Kilaso Books, New Delhi, 2004).
[49] R.C. Goel and Rajiv Raheja, *Hints and Tricks on Criminal Law* (Capital Publishing House, Delhi, 2010)
[50] Dorothy Stein, " Burning Widows, Burning Brides: The Perils of Daughterhood in India" 61 *PA* 465-485, *available at* : http://www.jstor.org/stable/2760461 (Visited on July 22, 2017).

She has examined the factors responsible for the changing dimension of a nuptial custom to a social evil. The impact of urbanization, industrialization and modernization has been examined on dowry system as well as marriage system.

Geetanjali Mukharjee, in her book *"Dowry Death in India"*[51], has remarked that the existence of dowry is a major social issue existing in India. It is a significant cause of violence against women and the most dramatic and brutal violence is bride burning. The author has discussed the growing number of bride burning cases in 1970s and 1980s. The author has termed dowry system as a prime motive for two other crimes i.e. female foeticide and infanticide.

Wanda Teays in his work "The Burning Bride: The Dowry Problem in India"[52], has sadly described that how a bride is set ablaze by her husband and in-laws for a dissatisfaction of not getting ample money, valuable articles or wealth in the form of dowry from her parents. This vulnerable condition of society and continuously deteriorating institution of marriage are of great concern. The author's perspective is to find out the connections between education and dowry, tradition and dowry and the role of legislature, and Courts in dealing the incidents of bride burning for dowry.

Significance of Forensic Evidence in Dowry Death

Pragnesh Parmar in his article "Dowry Death and Law– Indian Scenario", deals with the role of investigating officers, forensic experts, magistrates to bring out justice in the cases of dowry deaths.[53] The major challenge in the application of procedural laws is the lack of expertise in collecting, examining and investigating the forensic evidence in the cases of dowry deaths. India is neither having highly advanced forensic laboratories nor the adequately employed forensic experts to collect forensic evidence properly in the cases of dowry deaths.

B.R. Sharma in his book *"Forensic Science in Criminal Investigation & Trials"*[54] has comprehensively illustrated the identification, collection, and evaluation

---

[51] Geetanjali Mukharjee, *Dowry Death in India* (Indian Publishers Distributers, Delhi, 1999)

[52] Wanda Teays, "The Burning Bride: The Dowry Problem in India" 7(2) *JFSR* 29-52, *available at*: http://www.jstor.org/stable/25002154 (Visited on July 22, 2017).

[53] Pragnesh Parmar, "Dowry Death and Law– Indian Scenario" *IAIM* (2014) *available at:* http://iaimjournal.com/wp-content/uploads/2014/10/6-dowry-death-and-law-indian-scenario.pdf (Visited on December 31, 2016).

[54] B.R. Sharma, *Forensic Science in Criminal Investigation & Trials* (Universal Law Publishing, New Delhi, 2014).

of forensic clues in determining the dowry death by various means. The author has described that how an effective investigation can be achieved with the help of forensic expertise. Forensic evidence play a major role in investigation of dowry deaths that occur due to burns, bodily injuries or death caused in unnatural circumstances like poisoning, hanging, drowning, suffocation due to strangulation, starvation or fatal wounds etc.

Vinod Nijhavan in his book *"Police Law and Crimes"* [55] has overviewed the medico-legal aspects in death by burning. The author has examined the competence of these provisions to absorb and adapt itself to the forensic advances and their evidentiary value. There is a huge impact of shifting the burden of proof on accused in the offences of 'dowry death' and 'cruelty'. There is a major significance of judicial attitude upon burden of proof in the cases where the offence took place within the matrimonial home and practically there is no direct evidence available to nab the guilty. The practical efficacy of the provisions is assessed where the victims are left with little evidence and are driven from police stations to the Courts to seek justice.

Role of Police in Dowry Related Cases

Aparna Srivastava in her book *"Role of Police in Changing Society"*[56], and James Vadackumchery in his book *"Police, Women and Gender Justice"*[57], had thrown light on various aspects of police functioning and the arising needs to redefine the role of police in the contemporary context. The authors have examined the sensitivity, precautions and seriousness by which Police is expected to deal with while investigating the crimes against women. The role of Police in crime against women has critically examined in light of the action taken by Police in registering, investigating and filing the charge sheet in the cases related to dowry.

Arvind Verma and KS Subramanian in their book *"Understanding the Police in India"*[58], have well explained the role and responsibility of investigation officer

---

[55] Vinod Nijhavan, *Police Law and Crimes* (Vinod Publications, Delhi, 2016).
[56] Aparna Srivastava, *Role of Police in Changing Society* (A.P.H. Publishing Corp., New Delhi, 1999).
[57] James Vadackumchery, *Police, Women and Gender Justice* (A.P.H. Publishing Corp., New Delhi, 2000).
[58] Arvind Verma and KS Subramanian, *Understanding the Police in India* (Lexis Nexis, New Delhi, 2009)

after occurrence of crime, the rules governing search and seizure and the arrest of the suspects. The authors have further explained that how the police play a crucial role in presenting the evidence in the court. The police must take the dowry related offences with the same seriousness as they take up the other crimes rather than adopting a lenient approach by considering such cases as internal family matters. It takes a lot of courage for dowry victims and their parents to take a stand against own family members and relatives while registering such cases. The situation becomes more uncomfortable and vulnerable for these victims if they fail to get seriousness and support in the attitude of police.

A.B. Srivastava in the commentary *"Mitter's Police Dairies"* [59], has outlined the general principles of cognizance and investigation of offences under The Dowry Prohibition Act. The author has described the material difficulties of police investigation in obtaining independent witnesses in dowry death cases. The principles regarding registering an FIR, police report etc are again well explained by the author.

Dowry and Domestic Violence

D.K Ganguly in his commentary on *"The Protection of Women from Domestic Violence Act, 2005"* [60], has examined in detail that how the demand of dowry acts as a root cause in ill treatment of the women in their matrimonial home. The author has thoroughly examined the interpretation of Section (b) of Domestic Violence Act in relation to the unlawful demand of dowry. It has been aptly remarked by the author that the victims of dowry related offences are likely to face harassment, harms and injuries in the form of domestic violence.

Suman Rai in her commentary on *"Law relating to Protection of Women from Domestic Violence"*,[61] has mentioned the reasons for Domestic violence. She has critically examined that whether the demand of dowry or the non-fulfillment of demand of dowry could be a significant cause of domestic violence done to women in their matrimonial home.

---

[59] A.B. Srivastava, *Mitter's Police Dairies* (Law Publisher's India, Allahabad, 2010)
[60] D.K Ganguly, *Ganguly's Commentory on The Protection of Women from Domestic Violence Act, 2005* (Dwivedi Publishing Company, Allahabad, 2014)
[61] Suman Rai, *Law Relating to Protection of Women from Domestic Violence* (Orient Publishing Company, New Delhi, 2011)

R. Revathi in her book *"Law Relating to Domestic Violence"* [62], deals with the dowry related offences in relation to the domestic violence. She has discussed the provisions under The Protection of Women from Domestic Violence Act, 2005 and the way in which it regulates the offences related to dowry. The need to broaden these provisions in their scope and ambit is also observed.

Mehak Singh in his article "Dowry as a factor of violence in Marriage: A study of Women seeking help in Family Counseling Centers in Chandigarh"[63], deals with the dowry related domestic violence and the case study of such women who have undergone through such violence. The cases of domestic violence for dowry are reviewed and the measures to overcome this violence are suggested.

S.C. Tripathi and Vibha Arora in their book *"Law Relating to Women and Children"* [64], has quoted recent judicial pronouncements made by the S.C. and H.C. on protection of women from Domestic Violence Act, 2005. The authors have critically remarked that dowry death will not *ipso facto* suck husband into net of Section 304B. The position of women in pre independence period and British period has also been thoroughly discussed and elaborate synthesis has been drawn on the dowry related provisions in Indian Penal Code and significance of evidence to prove such charges. This work has overviewed the provisions of Domestic Violence Act, 2005 in relation to dowry related offences.

Anjani Kant in her book *"Law Relating to Women and Children"*[65], has discussed that whether these constitutional safeguards are sufficient enough to protect the women from domestic violence, dowry related crimes or not. The effect of social and legal position of women on increase or decrease in the offences committed against her is further discussed.

---

[62] R. Revathi, *Law Relating to Domestic Violence* (Asia Law House, Hyderabad, 2004).

[63] Mahek Singh, "Dowry as a factor of violence in Marriage: A study of Women seeking help in Family Counseling Centers in Chandigarh" 2 *IJOAIRT* (2013) *available at:* http://www.ijoart.org/docs/Dowry-as-a-factor-of-violence-in-Marriage-A-study-of-Women-seeking-help-in-Family-Counseling-Centers-in-Chandigarh.pdf (visited on January 11, 2017).

[64] S. C. Tripathi and Mrs. Vibha Arora, *Law Relating to Women and Children* (Central Law Publications, Allahabad, 2015).

[65] *Supra* note 34.

Francis Bloch and Vijendra Rao in their paper "Terror as a Bargaining Instrument: A Case Study of Dowry Violence in Rural India"[66], have focused on domestic violence and wife battering as a tool of bargaining and blackmailing the parents of wife to extract more and more dowry. The authors have given a unique perspective by stating that marital violence is not only connected to low dowry payments rather the women from rich family are more likely to be beaten by their husbands in an effort to extract higher transfers from their parents. There is a consistency between income of bride's parents and crimes, violence related to dowry committed to those brides. It has been further discussed that whether more violence towards results in getting more payment of dowry or not.

International Perspective on Dowry

Madame Adam in her research paper, "The Dowries of Women in France"[67] has described the prevalence of dowry culture in France. The author has claimed that dowry is a significant word for each and every French girl, which enters in her life from her childhood. The young girls in France are brought up with an ideology that the more dowries if their parents give in their marriage, the better would be their chances of getting a best suitable match. Those parents who are not in sound financial position to give huge dowries, they brought up their daughters in such a way to take great pain and put maximum efforts to somehow attract an eligible man. The main factor behind the widespread of the custom of dowry in France is that it has become a fast way of raising financial status. The author has claimed that unfortunately the main driving force behind marriage has been emerged as a desire of getting dowry rather than attraction for one another. The author had shown a great concern over the prevailing conditions where the money is depreciating day by day as it has decreased the ability of parents to give huge dowries. It may lead to a downfall in number of marriages and thereafter decrease in population.

---

[66] Francis Bloch and Vijayendra Rao, "Terror as a Bargaining Instrument: A Case Study of Dowry Violence in Rural India" 92(4) *TAER* 1029-1043, *available at*: http://www.jstor.org/stable/3083293 (Visited on July 22, 2017).

[67] Madame Adam, "The Dowries of Women in France"152 *TNAR* 37-46 (1891) *available at*: http://www.jstor.org/stable/25102113 (Visited on July 22, 2017)

Siwan Anderson in his Article, "Why Dowry Payments Declined with Modernization in Europe but Are Rising in India"[68] has marked a comparison between Europe and India in the context of prevalence of dowry culture. The author has pointed out the constant increase in the custom of dowry in India which is contrary to the most of other modernizing societies where this custom has seen a decline. The author has identified the caste system as a major phenomenon behind the rise of dowry payments in India unlikely the modernized European countries where there are no caste-based societies. The author has claimed that, "in caste based societies, the increases in wealth dispersion that accompany modernization necessarily lead to increases in dowry payments, whereas in non-caste-based societies, increased dispersion has no real effect on dowry payments and increasing average wealth causes the payments to decline."[69] The author has shown a major concern over the devastating consequences of increasing dowry payments. The huge sum of cash and articles often destroys the whole economical equilibrium of bride's family. In many cases, the girls remain unmarried and considered as a burden on their family due to incapability to fulfill the dowry demands of suitable grooms. It has even led to many offences like female infanticide, dowry death, physical torture and bride burning etc. The author has remarked that in medieval Europe dowry was a common practice, it was prevalent in Italy, China and even Rome. But with modernization, the practice of dowry has seen a gradual decrease in all these regions. However in India, dowry culture has seen a constant increase irrespective of modernization. In fact, increased dispersion of wealth in modernization has increased the dowry payments. The author has claimed that "a low income high-caste groom will have no effect on the dowry as a lower-caste bride would be willing to pay for him. Brides of his caste, however, value him less and therefore wish to pay less, but because brides of his caste will forfeit their caste ranking if they marry into a lower caste, they are willing to match the higher payments he is offered from brides in the lower caste."The author has suggested that the government in India must take essential steps to break down the

---

[68] Siwan Anderson "Why Dowry Payments Declined with Modernization in Europe but Are Rising in India" 111 *JPE* 269-310 (2003) *available at:* http://www.jstor.org/stable/10.1086/367679 (Visited on July 22, 2017)

[69] *Ibid.*

cast system by providing educational and occupational opportunities for lower caste groups. It will gradually and automatically decline the custom of dowry.

Eugene H. Korth & Della M. Flusche in their research paper, "Dowry and Inheritance in Colonial Spanish America: Peninsular Law and Chilean Practice"[70] have clarified the concept laws and procedures related to dowry in Colonial Spanish America, prevailing in 18th century. The authors have primarily emphasized on the control and custody of dowry which had been brought by the wife at a time of marriage. According to the authors, the role of a husband was of legal custodian of the dowry of wife. He had no right to sell, mortgage, transfer, dispose off or donate the dowry of his wife. The primary function which he was supposed to perform was of a prudent manager to manage the assets gathered by the way of dowry. In case if the wife had misfortune to get a husband possessing bad habits like gambling, spendthrift ; the wife had legal right to drag him to court and compel him to surrender an entrustment of dowry.

John L. McCreery in his Article, "Women's Property Rights and Dowry in China and South Asia"[71] has marked the fundamental distinction between inheritenc and dowry. He had completely rejected the idea that dowry can he considered like a pre-mortem inheritance given to the daughters. He has admitted that the women in China have not been given the property rights in the Ching's Code. But it would be unreasonable to equate them with dowry. Dowry is not a definite legal right and whether it would be given or not and the amount to be given is on the complete discretion of the father and brothers of bride, whereas the property rights are definite and legally enforceable. It would be unreasonable to compensate the inheritance rights of daughters by giving them dowry. The amount of dowry may vary for two or more sisters, depending upon the status of their prospective grooms, the amount is rarely equal to their share in parental property and it is not just an atonement of their father for depriving them of inheritance rather also a means of show oof of their wealth in the society.

---

[70] Eugene H. Korth & Della M. Flusche "Dowry and Inheritance in Colonial Spanish America: Peninsular Law and Chilean Practice" 43, *TA* 395-410 (1987) *available at:* http://www.jstor.org/stable/1007185 (Visited on July 22, 2017).

[71] John L. McCreery, "Women's Property Rights and Dowry in China and South Asia" 15, No. pp. 163-174 (1976) *available at:* http://www.jstor.org/stable/3773327 (Visited on July 22, 2017).

Anjani Kant in her book *"Law Relating to Women and Children"* [72], has discussed various U.N. declarations and conventions on women rights. The author has widely covered the constitutional safeguards to protect the women in India. The position of women has been briefly discussed in their respective personal laws. The author has emphasized upon women's empowerment and gender justice. She tends to figure out the impact of such U.N. initiatives on decreasing the rate of offences related to dowry. Mohammad Abu Taher in his article "The Role of Law Enforcement Agencies in Preventing Dowry-Related Crimes in Bangladesh and India" [73], has compared the role of law enforcement agencies in preventing dowry related crimes in Bangladesh and India. The custom of dowry and dowry related laws prevailing in Bangladesh have been compared with Indian scenario.

John L. Mc Creery in his paper "Women's Property Rights and Dowry in China and South Asia"[74], has described women's property rights and their relation with the custom of dowry in the statutory Law of China's imperial dynasty (Ch'ing Code). The author has compared the property right of women in Indian Law and Chinese Law. The custom of dowry in Ceylon in relation to property rights of women has also been studied. He has compared the custom of dowry prevailing in India with the custom of dowry in the statutory Law of China's imperial dynasty and Ceylon.

Judicial Discourse on Dowry Related Cases

Reshma and A. Ramegowda in their article "Dowry – The Cancer of Society"[75], make a critical analysis of judicial activism and thereby effectiveness of law in curbing dowry. The role of judiciary in imparting justice to the victims of dowry is the most crucial. The authors have critically examined the impact of judicial activism on dowry prohibition.

---

[72] *Supra* note 34.
[73] Mohammad Abu Taher and Siti Zaharah Jamaluddin, "The Role of Law Enforcement Agencies in Preventing Dowry-Related Crimes in Bangladesh and India" 23 (3) *IIUMLJ* (2015) *available at:* http://journals.iium.edu.my/iiumlj/index.php/iiumlj/article/view/172/173 (Visited on January 1, 2017).
[74] John L. McCreery, "Women's Property Rights and Dowry in China and South Asia" 15, No. pp. 163-174 (1976) *available at:* http://www.jstor.org/stable/3773327 (Visited on July 22, 2017).
[75] See *supra* note 24.

S.P. Tyagi in his commentary *"Criminal Trial"* [76] has elucidated various principles of appreciation of prosecution and defence evidence, which are kept in mind by the Courts while deciding dowry death cases. It has also elaborated the significant considerations regarding the conduct of accused which have to be taken in due care in such cases. The relevance of dying declaration, its admissibility and corroboration are also analyzed by the author.

Offences Related to Dowry and Law of Evidence

V. Nageshwara Rao in the commentary *"The Indian Evidence Act"* [77] has critically analyzed the burden of proof in the offences of 'dowry death' and 'cruelty' under The Indian Evidence Act, 1872. The author has elucidated the role played by the Indian judiciary in interpreting the provisions of the Indian Evidence Act in the context of presumptions taken in dowry death and abetment of suicide.

Avtar Singh in his book *"Principles of the Law of Evidence"* [78] has asserted a serious concern over the increasing number of dowry deaths. The shift taken by the judiciary in certain provisions have also been discussed likewise, in a case of multiple dying declarations, the version that seems to be more compatible with the circumstances is now been accepted. The retrospective nature of section 113A has been critically examined. He has reviewed the latest judgments related to evidentiary value of dying declaration and its corroborative aspect. The retrospective applicability of the provisions has also been discussed.

M. Monir in his book *"The Law of Evidence"* [79], as well as M.C. Sarkar and S.C. Sarkar, in their commentary *"Sarkar's Law of Evidence"* [80], have brought together the legal aspects of theory structure and procedural practice of provisions related to dowry in Law of Evidence in India. The developments of Law of Evidence with respect to circumstantial evidence, effect of presumptions in cases of dowry deaths or the softening of the rule of corroboration in dying declaration has been dealt with clarity and precision.

---

[76] S.P. Tyagi, *Criminal Trial* (Vinod Publications, Delhi, 2006).
[77] V. Nageshwara Rao, *The Indian Evidence Act, A Critical Commentary* (Lexis Nexis, Gurgaun, 2015).
[78] Avtar Singh, *Principles of The Law of Evidence* (Central Law Publications, Allahabad, 2016).
[79] M. Monir, *Textbook on The Law of Evidence* (Lexis Nexis, Gurgaon, 2015).
[80] M.C. Sarkar, S.C. Sarkar, et.al., *Sarkar's Law of Evidence* (Wadhwa and Company, Nagpur, 2004).

Procedure in Dealing with the Offences of Dowry

B.M. Gandhi in his book *"Indian Penal Code"* and R.P.Kathuria, *"Law of Crimes and Criminology"[81]* has elaborately explained the offences related to dowry under I.P.C, the ingredients of such offences and their punishments.[82] B.M.Prasad and Manish Mohan in their book *"Ratanlal and Dhirajlal, The Code of Criminal Procedure"* [83], have commented upon the dowry death, cruelty and other offences, their essentials and the different views that have been taken by Supreme Court in deciding such matter. Ratanlal Ranchhoddas and Dhirajlal Keshavlal Thakore, in their commentary, *"The Code of Criminal Procedure"[84]*, as well as K.N Chandrasekharan Pillai in his commentary *"R.V. Kelkar's Criminal Procedure"[85]*, have discussed various postulates of criminal procedure adopted in Indian legal system to deal with the offences related to dowry.

Y.H Rao and Y.R. Rao in their commentary *"Criminal Trial"[86]*, have thoroughly examined all the probabilities which are worth consideration in the dowry related offences for establishing the guilt of accused. The authors have discussed in the light of various judgments that the major challenge that comes before the Court across the trial is the reliance upon the statements of victim's family. As the relation becomes sour between the families, there are chances that the parents of bride may try to implicate most of the people in her in-laws. Such a situation requires a judicious implication of mind and thorough scrutiny by the Courts while deciding such matters.

Surendra Malik and Sudeep Malik in their commentary, *"Supreme Court on Criminal Procedure Code & Criminal Trial"* [87], have examined the basis of deciding sentence and quantum of punishment to be given to the offenders of dowry death. The authors have also elaborated the impact of mitigating and aggravating circumstances

---

[81] R.P.Kathuria, *Law of Crimes and Criminology* (Vinod Publications, Delhi, 2001).
[82] B.M. Gandhi, *Indian Penal Code* (Eastern Book Company, Lucknow, 2014).
[83] B.M. Prasad Manish Mohan, *RatanLal & DhirajLal The code of Criminal Procedure* (Lexis Nexis, Gurgaun 2013).
[84] Ratanlal Ranchhoddas and Dhirajlal Keshavlal Thakore, *The Code of Criminal Procedure* (Wadhwa and Company, Nagpur, 2002).
[85] K.N Chandrasekharan Pillai, *R.V. Kelkar's Criminal Procedure* (Eastern Book Company,Lucknow, 2014).
[86] Y.H Rao &Y.R. Rao, *Criminal Trial* (Wadhwa and Company, Agra, 2008).
[87] Surendra Malik and Sudeep Malik, *Supreme Court on Criminal Procedure Code & Criminal Trial* (Eastrn Book Company, Lucknow, 2011).

on determining the quantum of sentence in dowry related cases. The authors of discussed it in the light of various judicial pronouncements that what are the factors which are kept in mind by the Courts while deciding the punishments in Dowry Death Cases.

Misuse of Anti-Dowry Laws

Malik and Raval in their work *"Law and Social Transformation in India"*,[88] deal with the offences relating to dowry. The authors remark upon the increase in these offences every year. They have also commented upon the misuse of the dowry prohibition provisions against the husband due to the non-bailable and non-cognizable nature of certain offences. They have further suggested some changes in law that need to be brought to combat with such kind of misuse.

Prashanti in the article "Dowry laws: Loopholes and Possibilities of Misuse" [89], has covered the incidents and consequences of misuse of Anti- Dowry laws. He has commented upon the other side of current situation in which the misuse of Anti-Dowry laws has imbibed a negative terror in the minds of the husband and in-laws.

Madhu Kishwar in the article "Laws against Domestic Violence: Underused or Abused?[90]" has shown a great concern over the misuse and abuse of laws relating to dowry prohibition. Very often the policemen and lawyers encourage complainants to add dowry demands as the main cause of cruelty. Sometimes the family members of the bride, who, at the time of marriage have given voluntary gifts to the groom and his family, do not hesitate to attribute all their gifts giving to forceful demands of dowry, once the marital relations turns sour and ready for the breakdown. The author has vigilantly examined the other side of the coin through case studies on misuse of anti dowry laws. The question that whether that the dowry prohibition laws should be more stringent and women centric to curb the menace of dowry or such laws should be more logical and gender neutral to stop the misuse, has been elaborately answered.

---

[88] Krishna Pal Malik and Dr. Kaushik C. Raval, *Law and Social Transformation in India* (Allahabad Law Agency, Faridabad, 2011).

[89] Prashanti, Dowry laws: Loopholes and Possibilities of misuse *Available at:* http://www.legalservicesindia.com/article/article/dowry-laws-loopholes-and-possibilities-of-misuse-2034-1.html (Visited on January 19, 2017).

[90] Madhu Kishwar, "Laws against Domestic Violence: Underused or Abused? from Manushi" A Journal aboutWomen and Society," 15 *NWSA* 111-122 (2003).

Dowry as a Social Custom

Nithya N.R. in the article *"Dowry in India: Social Custom or Modern Malaise"* [91], has examined the complex social and cultural practice of dowry in India. The author argues that this menace of Dowry leads to the oppression on women, physical violence on the bride, causing a financial and emotional stress on the parents of the bride, marital conflict and so on. It has been explained that how the custom abiding behavioural pattern of society has hampered the effective implementation of dowry prohibition laws.

Padma Srinivasan and Gary R.Lee in their article "The Dowry System in Northern India: Women's Attitudes and Social Change"[92], have studied attitudes towards the dowry system among married women in North India. The authors have documented the adverse consequences of the dowry system, particularly for women.

Sonia Dalmia and Pareena G. Lawrence in their work "The Institution of Dowry in India: Why it Continues to Prevail"[93], has theoretically linked the practice of dowry with the other factors like inheritance system, status of women, relative availability of potential spouses and social stratification etc. The authors have taken up the institutional and economic reasons behind the prevailing dowry system.

Steven J. C. Gaulin & James S. Boster "Dowry and Female Competition: A Reply to Dickemann" [94], have described the custom of dowry with an entirely different perspective. The author has remarked that dowry is a kind of wealth transfer by only one gender to another and therefore it is a kind of gender bias. It has inculcated a disproportionate competition for marriage partners among wives in polygynous societies. The author has compared it with other mammals where generally the competition is in between male species for females. He opines that

---

[91] Nithya N.R., "Institutionalization of Dowry in India: Social Custom or Modern Malaise?"2 *IJSR* (2013) *available at:* www.ijsr.net/archive (Visited on January 14, 2017).

[92] Padma Srinivasan and Gary R. Lee, "The Dowry System in Northern India: Women's Attitudes and Social Change", 66(5) *JMF* 1108-1117, *available at:* http://www.jstor.org/stable/3600328 (Visited on July 22, 2017).

[93] Sonia Dalmia and Pareena G. Lawrence, "The Institution of Dowry in India: Why It Continues to Prevail" 38(2) TJDA 71-93, *available at:* http://www.jstor.org/stable/4192976 (Visited on July 7, 2017)

[94] Steven J. C. Gaulin & James S. Boster "Dowry and Female Competition: A Reply to Dickemann", 93 *AA* 946-948 (1991) available at http://www.jstor.org/stable/680974 (Visited on July 22, 2017)

wherever the custom of dowry is prevalent, it clearly indicates the competition between females for husbands.

Dowry and Female Foeticide

Nadia Diamond-Smith, Nancy Luke and Stephen Mc Garvey in their article " Too Many Girls, Too Much Dowry"[95] has reported the reasons behind increasing son preference and the adverse consequences of such preference. The authors expressed that disliking for giving birth to daughters is due to perceived economic burden of daughters because of dowry. There is a significant impact of dowry system on female foeticide and female infanticide. The burden of dowry is one of the main reasons for not wanting the birth of a girl child in the family.

Veena Talwar Oldenburg in her book *"Dowry Murder"* [96], had precisely correlated the offence of female foeticide, female infanticide and the custom of dowry. The author has discussed that how the practices like bride-price and dowry have put an impact on the rate of female infanticide.

Shipra Kaushal in her book *"Gender Inequality Illustrated through A Legal Perspective on Female Foeticide"* [97], has summarized the rights of women since the inception of civilization to contemporary times. The author has described emergence and growth of dowry system along with the legal developments that took place to curb the menace of this evil practice. The author has discussed the overlapping of the terms dowry and *stridhan* and marked a clear distinction between the two. Besides dowry, the prime focus of this work is on female foeticide, its causes, effects and remedies. The feeling of birth of a girl child make the parents anxious to make future arrangements for the dowry to be given in her marriage whereas a boy child brings a hope of getting monetary benefit by taking dowry at the marriage of their son.

Wayne Ingalls in his research paper "Demography and Dowries: Perspectives on Female Infanticide in Classical Greece", has critically examined the impact of

---

[95] Diamond-Smith, Nancy Luke and Stephen McGarvey, "Too Many Girls, Too Much Dowry': Son Preference and Daughter Aversion in Rural TamilNadu, India" 10(7) CHS 697-708, *available at:* http://www.jstor.org/stable/20461054 (Visited on July 22, 2017).

[96] *Supra* note 30.

[97] Shipra Kaushal, *Gender Inequality Illustrated through A Legal Perspective on Female Foeticide* (Satyam Law International, New Delhi, 2014)

dowry custom on the selective female infanticides done in Greece.[98] The author has critiqued some prominent scholars in considering dowry as a significant factor for the rise in female infanticides in Greece. The author has put an argument that that dowry to the daughters was given by the fathers for three prime reasons; firstly to give it as an alternate of giving share in the property, secondly to find a best possible match for their daughter and thirdly to show off their wealth. It had been nowhere seen evidently that the fathers had ever shown reluctance to pay any dowry. This is an entirely different point of view from the other authors who have mostly considered dowry as a significant factor for the rise in female infanticide.

Burden of Dowry on the Family of Bride

Bharat Dogra in his work "Burden of Dowry System[99]" has described the growing burden of the oppressive dowry system and its dangerous consequences in the form of financial pressure on the father of daughter, disturbance in the equilibrium of the families and huge number of suicides and attempts to suicide committed by the young girls. The author has sensitively explained the desperation of the family members of young girls to arrange dowry for their marriages. Very often failure to arrange the dowry results in broken engagements, hopelessness and ultimately drives the girls to take their own life. He has examined the impact of this evil system on the families of young girls. Through various case studies and attitudinal surveys, the author tends to ascertain the pressure, hopelessness and dire consequences in the form of suicides faced by the girl and her family.

Francis Bloch, Vijayendra Rao and Sonalde Desai in their article "Wedding Celebrations as Conspicuous Consumption: Signalling Social Status in Rural India[100]" the authors have examined the factors affecting the expenditures on wedding celebrations organized by rural Indians. The authors have strived to derive the

---

[98] Wayne Ingalls, "Demography and Dowries: Perspectives on Female Infanticide in Classical Greece" 56 *PHOENIX* 246-254 (2017) *available at:* http://www.jstor.org/stable/1192599 (Visited on July 22, 2017)

[99] Bharat Dogra, "Burden of Dowry System" 32, *EPW* 2855, *available at:* http://www.jstor.org/stable/4406035 (Visited on July 22, 2017).

[100] Bloch, Vijayendra Rao and Sonalde Desai, "Wedding Celebrations as Conspicuous Consumption: Signaling Social Status in Rural India" 39(3) *JHR 675-695, available at:* http://www.jstor.org/stable/3558992 (Visited on July 22, 2017).

connection between social status of people, the expenditure done on marriage celebration and its impact on increasing menace of dowry system.

Empirical Survey on the Custom of Dowry

Ursula Sharma in her book *"Dowry in North India: Its Consequences for Women"*[101], has mentioned her fieldwork research, which was done by her in 1970s. The research work is based upon comparative studies of Punjabi and Himachal villages. She became daughter in-law in a Brahmin family in Himachal and then she noted down that many families were complaining about the increasing expenses in the marriage of daughters, in their day to day conversation. She has observed that earlier, the dowry items given in Himachal Pradesh were very limited to some conventional items like clothes, ornaments, household items etc but after World War I, the amount of dowry began to rise. The value of dowries given in marriages in those times had been escalated far more than the olden times. During that time period, the offences like 'bride burning', 'dowry murders' and 'abetment of suicide of bride for dowry' were neither common nor prevalent. While conducting her research she has found a surprising fact in her study that rather than in-law, the brides were more complaining in regard to any disparity done between the '*daaj*' given to them and the '*daaj*' 'given to their sisters. The Author strongly disagrees with the idea that the dowry was given as a compensation for the expense to be borne by husband and in-laws on the bride after marriage. The author has contended that there was a complete shift of 'bride price' to 'daaj' in the villages of Punjab. However the women's labour at home and fields had not at all changed considerably. Therefore the author had put an argument that those brides who were earlier brought after paying a sum to their father could how become a burden without any change in their contribution and role in family and agriculture.[102]

Junsen Zhang and William Chan, in their paper "Dowry and Wife's Welfare: A Theoretical and Empirical Analysis" [103] have conducted an empirical survey in Taiwan, China and concluded that the custom of dowry is far more beneficial than the custom of bride-price. The empirical survey was based upon a data collected in 1989 in Taiwan in a women and family survey. The respondents were around 964 women

---

[101] Ursula Sharma "Dowry in North India: Its Consequences for Women" 32-33, 35 (St Martins Press, London, 1984)[101]
[102] *Supra* note 30.
[103] *Supra* note 31.

aged between 25-60 years. Surprisingly all the women reported the transfers on dowry or bride-price in their marriage. The bride-price given in Taiwan was usually cash and other valuable items given by bridegroom's side to the bride's parents. The dowry items popular in Taiwan were mostly cash, ornaments, furniture, bedding and other household items. A large dowry has benefitted the bride in several ways likewise increasing the financial status, providing an upper hand to the bride in her new family and it was even observed that it has increased the probability of husbands of doing more household chores.

Government Documents and Reports on Laws related to Dowry

The researcher has also reviewed certain reports of Law Commission of India. The 91st report of Law Commission of India dealt with the recommendations to amend law so as to reduce the number of dowry deaths.[104] The major concern behind formulating this report was the alarming rise in the incidents of death of married women in the highly suspicious circumstances. It was mentioned in the report that such deaths seemed to be closely associated with dowry and very often were the cases of bride burning. Unfortunately, there was not only an unusual increase in the number of such deaths but also many cases of deaths were unreported. There has been an unusual increase in dowry deaths and therefore it was realized that the existing criminal law has to be resorted for bringing up the reform. Despite stringent laws to punish the offenders of dowry death, there is no evident decline in the number of dowry deaths occurring every year.

The 202nd report of Law Commission of India gives an answer to the demand for death sentence for the offence of dowry death. The commission has take has taken a very deep thought and concluded that the death penalty as a punishment for dowry death is not a solution rather it may lead to commission of more offences.[105] But the issue was that whether the addition of the death penalty for the offence of dowry deaths is certainly most despicable. It was found that the offence of murder cannot be considered equivalent to the offence of dowry death. Therefore,

---

[104] Law Commission of India, 91st Report on Dowry Deaths and Law Reform: Amending The Hindu Marriage Act, 1955, The Indian Penal Code 1860 and The Indian Evidence Act, 1872, (August, 1983) *available at:* http://lawcommissionofindia.nic.in/51-100/Report91.pdf (Visited on January 11, 2017).

[105] Law Commission of India, 202nd Report on Proposal to Amend Section 304-B of Indian Penal Code, 1860 (October, 2003) *available at:* http://lawcommissionofindia.nic.in/reports/report202.pdf (Visited on January 11, 2017).

there was no recommendation by the Law Commission to amend Section 304B of IPC in order to provide capital punishment as the maximum punishment for the offence of dowry death. There can be a huge impact of death penalty for such offence upon the offenders and related consequences.

The 243rd report of Law Commission covers the suggestions to amend Section 498A as to keep a check on its misuse and abuse.[106] The commission has done a thorough research and identified certain provisions including Sec. 498A which should be made compoundable. It was recommended in this report to make Sec. 498A compoundable however with the permission of the court. The commission has further suggested some preventive measures and safeguards to rule out the apprehension that after making this provision compoundable, there might be coercion on the wife to opt for a compromise. There are numerous required changes and solutions for making this provision more effective, practical and various ways of its implementation.

The Civil Services (Conduct) Rules, 1964 specifically prohibits government servants for giving and taking Dowry or abetting the giving and taking of Dowry.[107]A similar provision has also been enacted in the Indian Services (Conduct) Rules, 1968.[108]It is mentioned in these rules that the Public Servants must lead an agenda against this social evil and start a movement because they are holding the offices of utmost responsibility.

The researcher has further reviewed the report of Malimath Committee. The Committee has submitted its report in 2003 with an objective to bring reforms in

---

[106] Law Commission of India, 243rd Report on Section 498A IPC (August, 2012) *available at:* http://lawcommissionofindia.nic.in/reports/report243.pdf (Visited on January 11, 2017).

[107] Rule 13A The Civil Services (Conduct) Rules, 1964 No government servant shall –
(i) Give or take or abet the giving and taking of Dowry or
(ii) Demand directly or indirectly, from the parents or guardians of a bride or bridegroom, as the case may be, any Dowry.
Explanation – For the purpose of this rule, dowry has the same meaning as in the Dowry Prohibition Act, 1961, *available at:* www.persmin.gov.in (visited on January 11, 2017).

[108] The All India Services (Conduct) Rules, 1968, Rule11A Giving or taking of dowry.— No member of the Service shall—
(i) give or take or abet the giving or taking of dowry; or
(ii) demand, directly or indirectly, from the parents or guardian of a bride or bridegroom, as the case may be, any dowry.
Explanation.— For the purpose of the rule, "dowry" has the same meaning as in the Dowry Prohibition Act, 1961 (28 of 1961) *available at:* ipr.ias.nic.in/Docs/AIS_ConductRules1968.pdf (Visited on January 11, 2017).

administration of criminal justice.[109] It has strongly favoured the proposal to modify the nature of Section 498 A by making it a compoundable offence.

1.3 Objectives of the Research

1. To ascertain the extent of existence and prevalence of dowry system.
2. To identify the factors responsible for continuous prevalence of dowry despite stringent laws.
3. To enquire whether there is any gap between actual and the reported incidence of dowry.
4. To examine the efficacy of laws relating to dowry prohibition.
5. To enquire the reasons behind the non- compliance of society towards the laws relating to dowry prohibition.
6. To analyze the connection between the prevalence of dowry system and other offences against women.
7. To assess the efficacy of legal and police machinery in dealing with dowry related offences.
8. To identify the reasons for the abuse and misuse of the dowry prohibition laws.

1.4 Research Hypothesis

The custom of dowry and offences related to dowry are an age old concept. The increasing number of dowry related offences has been a constant area of concern for not only to the law and judiciary but it is also affecting the society. But with the passage of time, instead of getting diminished and therefore loosing the significance, this social evil has deep rooted in the society. The present study is based on the hypothesis that:

Lack of social will is an impediment in the effective implementation of laws relating to dowry prohibition and as well leads to the misuse of the laws.

---

[109] Government of India, Report: *Committee on Reforms of Criminal Justice System* (Ministry of Home Affairs, 2003), available at: https://mha.gov.in/sites/default/files/criminal_justice_ system.pdf (Visited on January 13, 2017).

1.5 Research Methodology

The present research work required both doctrinal and non-doctrinal study. The doctrinal work deals with the analysis of literature relating to dowry prohibition, legal provisions, legislative policies/measures and the judicial pronouncements dealing with the issue. For theoretical work the reliance has been kept on various statutes, books, commentaries, journals etc. The reports and recommendations by Law Commission, National Commission for Women, National Crime Record Bureau, as well as the committees that have been formulated so far for curbing the menace of dowry are thoroughly analyzed.

For empirical research both qualitative and quantitative methods have been adopted. An effort has been made to understand the attitude of the people including various stake holders like the boys and girls of marriageable age, ever married men and women, advocates, judges and police officials. The empirical work has been done by means of questionnaires/interview schedules specifically designed to ascertain the social and practical perspective of the evil of dowry. With regard to the objectives of empirical work and the informational needs, separate questionnaires were prepared for different categories of respondents to have in-depth view of the situation and the associated perceptions. One category of questionnaire was circulated among general public to capture their views, opinion, perception and awareness regarding the custom of dowry and the offences related to dowry. Second category of questionnaire was circulated among married women to assess their experience, perception, opinion and awareness regarding the custom of dowry and the offences related to dowry. Third category of questionnaire was circulated among Judges/Lawyers/ Police/Law Academicians to enquire about their practical experience and opinion regarding major challenges in dealing with the offences related to dowry and the lacunas in the law, societal behaviour and legal machinery to overcome the problem of widespread of this evil. The study is based on the sample of 400 respondents, including 200 people from general public comprising of 100 respondents each from district Kangra and Shimla, 100 married women respondents, 50 each from district Kangra and Shimla and 100 respondents from Judges/Lawyers/ Police/Law Academicians comprising of 50 respondents from district Kangra and 50 respondents from district Shimla. Data in the present study was collected through questionnaires, thereafter it was systematically arranged in SPSS (Statistical Package for Social Sciences) for statistical analysis.

1.6 Universe of study

There has been a constant rise in the number of cases related to dowry, cruelty and dowry deaths in recent decades. A series of laws have been enacted from time to time to eradicate this social evil from the society. But for the effective implementation of such laws, there must be coherence between the social will to adhere such laws and the viability of legislations to achieve such acceptability in the society. The socio-cultural reasons are undoubtedly responsible for the failure of any law and the lack of social will in accepting the laws over the customs has created a major obstacle in implementation of laws relating to dowry prohibition.

The empirical survey was conducted in district Kangra and Shimla of Himachal Pradesh. Although these two districts lie in the same state but some customs related to marriage prevailing in these districts are different. Earlier, the whole region of district Kangra was in Punjab and was transferred to Himachal Pradesh in the year 1966. Therefore the region is influenced by patriarchal mindset as well as many customs which were prevalent in the state of Punjab. The giving and taking of dowry by the parents of the bride was common in district Kangra. The Shimla town was also transferred from Punjab to Himachal Pradesh but most of the areas of district Shimla consist of old Himachal like Rampur Bushr, Rohru, Jubbal, Kotkhai etc which were part of Himachal Pradesh since its establishment. There was a prevalence of matriarchal mindset in old Himachal region of district Shimla and even the custom of reverse dowry system known as *'dhari'* was also practiced in some parts of these regions. Therefore the empirical study has been conducted in these two districts to examine the perspective of society towards the custom of Dowry and the acceptability of people towards Dowry Prohibition Laws. The number of reported cases of offences related to dowry is low in Himachal Pradesh in comparison to some other states in India. The survey aims to examine that whether due to socio-cultural factors, the dowry related offences are less prevalent in this region or there is a difference in actual and the reported incidences of dowry. The survey further aims to examine the efficacy of laws in creating preventive and deterrent effects on the offences related to

36

dowry and to analyze that whether the people consider giving and taking of dowry as a purely personal family affair or they report such matters to the police station.

1.7 Plan of Study

Chapter 1 deals with the basic introduction of the concept of dowry as a custom and its degradation to a social evil. It is discussed that how the custom of dowry originated with the institution of marriage and ultimately changed to an evil practice which gave birth to several dowry related offences. It has even resulted to some severe forms of violence against women in the form of cruelty, abetment to suicide and dowry killings etc. This chapter contains a thorough review of literature of all the books, commentaries, research articles, reports and government documents which have been read and examined for the doctrinal study. The chapter further contains object of study, hypothesis, research methodology and universe of study.

Chapter 2 deals with the historical perspective on the origin, growth and evolution of the custom of dowry and the laws related to dowry prohibition. It discusses the custom of dowry in different countries and under various civilizations since inception. It also discusses the origin of dowry system in ancient India, its prevalence in medieval India, growth of dowry culture in Mughal as well as British Empire and the rise of dowry related offences after independence. The enactment of dowry prohibition laws since its beginning is also discussed and analyzed.

Chapter 3 primarily deals with the legislative measures taken in India to curb the menace of dowry and offences related to dowry. It thoroughly discusses the various postulates of The Dowry Prohibition Act, 1961 and amendments related to dowry. It also discusses various provisions related to dowry in the Indian Penal Code, Criminal Procedure Code, The Indian Evidence Act, Hindu Law and Domestic Violence Act. The offences like dowry death, cruelty and abetment to suicide are discussed in detail. Apart from that, the relevance of dying declaration and forensic evidence in dowry death is also discussed. This chapter also deals with the UN initiatives, CEDAW and ICCPR provisions which are directly or indirectly deal with dowry prohibition.

Chapter 4 deals with the judicial pronouncements and the attitude of judiciary while dealing with the cases of dowry related offences. The various landmark judgments related to the initial use of the term dowry, the cases of bride burning before the insertion of the offence of dowry death in the Indian Penal Code and the position thereafter have been discussed. The significance of circumstantial evidence, forensic evidence and dying declaration in the cases of dowry death is also discussed. The recent landmark judgments on the misuse and abuse of anti dowry laws and the non compoundable nature of the offence of cruelty are also thorouly analysed.

Chapter 5 deals with the various policies and schemes of state governments, central government and their efficacy in curbing the menace of dowry. It also analyses the recent data of National Crime Record Beruo in offences related to dowry, cruelty, dowry death, domestic violence and abetment to suicide. It further discusses the time to time recommendations of various reports of Law Commission of India, National Commission for Women, Malimath Committee etc. for the prevention as well as control on dowry related crimes in dowry related laws.

Chapter 6 deals with the empirical survey on dowry prohibition and laws in district Kangra and district Shimla of Himachal Pradesh. It elucidates the findings of the empirical study in detail. The three types questionnaires distributed in the three different categories of the respondents are analysed along with the interviews and narratives of victims of dowry related offences.

Chapter 7 deals with the discussion, conclusion and suggestions upon the various findings of study. It discusses the various factors responsible for the origin, growth and prevalence of the deep rooted evil of dowry. The lacunas and loopholes present in the dowry prohibition laws, societal set up, police machinery as well as procedural shortcomings in dealing with the dowry related offences are figured out. The various suggestions to eradicate this menace of dowry from the society are also analysed and discussed in detail.

CHAPTER 2
HISTORY, EVOLUTION AND GROWTH OF DOWRY

History of a civilization is the foundation of its upcoming social values, traditions, customs and legal structure. The reflections of the age old experiences and cultural values have although contributed in our ideological advancement in various aspects, yet some of the customary shackles had degenerated the equilibrium of society. Some problems and evils have gradually emerged by turning wrong from the right course, wresting the genuine importance of the causes prompting the rise of numerous traditions and customs which are striking defiling blows against our social and religious beliefs. Despite strong and efficient legal system, such evils had disturbed the peace of society, destroyed the pious objectives of ancient customs and even lead to occurrence of offences[1]. Although some of the dirty evils have been eradicated by legislative measures and adoption of modern education, yet some of them are still adequately harming our general public.

Marriage had been considered as one of the most significant institutions of human beings since ages. It had been a very old social institution that laid a foundation upon which the entire structure of civilization, family and kinship has been built.[2] In Indian history, the institution of marriage had been seen as a pious union of two hearts, body as well as soul. In ideal situations, where everything runs smooth in relationships, marriage would culminate in happiness for both men and women. Even for women, the institution of marriage had been considered by many as the ultimate goal to be achieved in their life. But with the passage of time, the ancient genre of marriage got transformed into modern form.[3] Now all the marriages do not begin or end on a 'happy note'. Gradually some factors got associated with marriage that brought a misery not only to the couple but also to their families, communities and even societies. Dowry has been one such factor.[4] The tradition of dowry was closely

---

[1] Veena Talwar Oldenburg, *Dowry Murder: The Imperial Origins of a Cultural Crime,* 13(Oxford University Press New York, 2002)

[2] Elizabeth Abbott, *A History of Marriage: From Same Sex Unions to Private Vows and Common Law, the Surprising Diversity of a Tradition,* 22 (Seven Stories Press, New York, 2011) *available at:* https://books.google.co.in/books?id=o2e7 D2CQBJMC&printsec=frontcover&source=gbs_ge_summary_r&cad=0#v=onepage&q&f=false

[3] *Ibid.*

[4] P.K. Majumdar & R.P. Kataria, *Law Relating to Dowry Prohibition Cruelty & Harassment* 7 (Orient Publishing Company, New Delhi, 3rd edn., 2014).

connected with the paramount institution of marriage and the status of women in ancient history.

2.1 Concept of Marriage and Dowry under Various Civilizations

The institution of marriage has been an integral part of most of the civilizations since ages. The custom of dowry and bride price had originated as age old tradition associated with the institution of marriage in several parts of the world. Dowry culture had long histories mainly in parts of Asia, Northern Africa , Europe etc.[5] Dowry had been most common in the cultures that are strongly patrilineal and that expect women to reside with or near their husband's family like India. The dowry culture was even existed in Rome, China, Colonial Spanish America. The custom of payments to grooms was prevalent in Polenesia, ancient Greece, Rome and in ancient Babylone.[6]

2.1.1 Roman Concept of Dowry

One of the essential components of Roman marriage was "Dos". No claim of any sort arose upon the property of wife in the favour of husband. But at the same time, there was no obligation upon the husband to maintain his wife. Because Romans were of the opinion that it was the duty of a father to maintain his daughter even though if she is living under the husband's roof. Therefore, there was a custom of giving a sum as a lump sum compounded amount which was termed as "Dos".[7] It was a contribution made usually by the father of bride or the bride herself or by any other person on her behalf for the sake of joint household.

2.1.2 Greek Law of Dowry

Originally there was a Patriarchal set up in Greek families. The head of the family or the overall authority was named as '*Pater Familias*'. An unmarried girl was under the power of her father and a married woman was under the power of her

---

[5] Patrick Heady and Lale Yalcin Heckmann, Implications of Endogamy in the Southwest Eurasian Highlands: another look at Jack Goody's Theory of Production, Property and Kinship *available at:* https://www.tandfonline.com/doi/full/10.1080/02757206.2019.1640693 (Visited on 30, December, 2019)

[6] M. Cary and T.J. Haarhoof, *Life and Thought in the Greek and Roman World* 142 (Methuen & Co., London, 1959).

[7] A.M. Richard, *Leage's Roman Private Law,* 1961(P. 108.) at Suman Nalwa and Hari Dev Kohli, *Law Relating to Dowry, Dowry Death, Cruelty to Women & Domestic Violence* 3 (Universal Law Publication Co., New Delhi, 2013).

husband. The match making was done by her father and the bridegroom and a sum was paid to her family as a consideration. The system of payments to grooms existed in Polenesia, ancient Greece, Rome and in ancient Babylone.[8]

Some prominent scholars have also considered dowry as a significant factor for the rise in female infanticides in Greece. However some had argued that dowry to the daughters was given by the fathers for three prime reasons; firstly to give it as an alternate of giving share in the property, secondly to find a best possible match for their daughter and thirdly to show off their wealth.[9] It had been nowhere seen evidently that the fathers had ever shown reluctance to pay any dowry rather it was practically more convenient to them to give a small share in the form of dowry to the daughters rather than to give an entire share of property to their sons. Moreover it had paved a way to establish their supremacy over their son-in-laws and society by flaunting huge payment of dowry.

2.1.3 Dowry and Inheritance in Colonial Spanish America

The concept of Dowry and laws related to dowry also existed in Colonial Spanish America in 18th century.[10] The control and custody of dowry which had been brought by the wife at a time of marriage was with her husband. The role of a husband was of legal custodian of the dowry of wife. He had no right to sell, mortgage, transfer, dispose off or donate the dowry of his wife. The primary function which he was supposed to perform was of a prudent manager to manage the assets gathered by the way of dowry. In case if the wife had misfortune to get a husband possessing bad habits like gambling, spendthrift ; the wife had legal right to drag him to court and compel him to surrender an entrustment of dowry.

2.1.4 Jewish Concept of Dowry

The marriage was considered as the significant essence of family life. It was seen as an institution created by the God himself. There was a formal marriage

---

[8] *Supra* note 6.

[9] Wayne Ingalls, "Demography and Dowries: Perspectives on Female Infanticide in Classical Greece" 56 *PHOENIX* 246-254 (2017) available at: http://www.jstor.org/stable/1192599 (Visited on July 22, 2017)

[10] Eugene H. Korth & Della M. Flusche "Dowry and Inheritance in Colonial Spanish America: Peninsular Law and Chilean Practice" 43, *TA* 395-410 (1987) available at: http://www.jstor.org/stable/1007185 (Visited on July 22, 2017)

document termed as *'Ketubah'* in which the willingness of both parties to enter into the contract of marriage was expressed, and the duties specified followed by *'mohar'* which was known as *'Ketubah'* money. Therefore, the traces of custom of dowry amongst the Jews are seen in the form of *'Ketubah'* money.[11]

2.1.5 Dowry under Christian Civilization

Some of the western Christian countries regarded marriage as a sacrament and the others as a civil contract. In Europe the custom of dowry was prevalent predominately. It was a general perspective that marriage was related to family economy and a prospective couple was required to find out the means of supporting themselves and their children. It was usually felt that the wives must have a dowry as a means of contributing to the household. In old English Law, dowry is the portion given to the wife by the husband at the church door in consideration of marriage. However the changes to social and economic conditions have resulted into the minimization of the custom of the dowry in Europe.

2.1.6 The Custom of Dowry in Old Babylon

The age old Hammurabi's Code also contained several laws related to dowry, prevailing in Babylon. [12] The custom of dowry was well accepted in the law code of Hammurabi. But it was well ensured that the dowry brought by a woman from her father's house must not be dishonestly snatched or misappropriated by her husband and in laws. On the failure of marriage, she was well entitled to take back the dowry and use it for her subsequent marriage. On the death of her husband, her in-laws were bound to return each and every article of dowry to her in the same condition as it was brought by her at the time of her marriage. If she died, the right of inheriting her dowry persisted with her sons, father or her parental family and not with her husband. However, the code of Hammurabi has not permitted a father to sell his daughter however he was permitted to give her in concubinage with or without dowry.[13] It has considered marriage as contract and no marriage was valid without dowry. The

[11] Suman Nalwa and Hari Dev Kohli, *Law Relating to Dowry, Dowry Death, Cruelty to Women & Domestic Violence*, 4 (Universal Law Publication Co., New Delhi, 2013).

[12] Stephanie Dalley , "Old Babylonian Dowries" 42 *IRAQ* 53-74 (1980) available at: http://www.jstor.org/stable/4200115 (Visited on July 22, 2017)

[13] H. A. Rose, "The Development of Bride-Price and of Dowry" 36 *FOLKLORE* 189-193 (1925) available at: http://www.jstor.org/stable/1256331 (Visited on July 22, 2017)

custom of dowry was firmly established but it was not clear that whether it was secured by the contract or not. There were some more rules regarding the entitlement of dowry likewise; on a divorce for misconduct of wife, the husband was entitled to keep the dowry with him. However, if the wife was divorced for infertility, she had complete right over her dowry.

2.1.7 Marriage and Dowry in Islam

The term '*Dower*' and 'Dowry' are often confused with each other however these are distinct in their inclination. The concept of *Dower* in Arabic is also known as '*Mahr*'. *Dower* is an obligation imposed by the law on the husband as mark of respect or as a consideration of marriage for the wife. In pre-Islamic period, there was no such concept of *Dower*. Prophet Muhammad initiated the custom of *Dower* to be given to wife as a token of respect.

However, dowry system was unknown to the Muslim Society and it cannot be traced in Islamic '*Shariah*'. But the fact was not denied that the newly wedded couple needs to establish a new home and henceforth the parents of the bride or bridegroom used to help them through cash or household articles. The earlier instances clearly indicate that such presents or money were merely a token of love and affection and not a result of demand or compulsion. But now, dowry among Muslims has taken an ugly form and the quantum of dowry depends upon the socio-economic status of the bridegroom.

2.1.8 Dowry Culture in France

There was a widespread prevalence of dowry culture in France. The young girls in France were brought up with an ideology that more the dowries their parents give in their marriage, the better would be their chances of getting a best suitable match. Those parents who were not in sound financial position to give huge dowries, they tamed their daughters in such a way to take great pain and put maximum efforts to somehow attract an eligible man. The main factor behind the widespread of the custom of dowry in France was that it had become a fast way of raising financial status. Even a situation had arisen where the main driving force behind marriage had been emerged as a desire of getting dowry rather than attraction for one another.[14]

---

[14] Madame Adam, "The Dowries of Women in France"152 *TNAR* 37-46 (1891) available at: http://www.jstor.org/stable/25102113 (Visited on July 22, 2017)

2.1.9 Property Rights and Dowry in China

The women in China have not been given the property rights in the Ching's Code.[15] The dowry was impliedly considered like a pre-mortem inheritance given to the daughters. However it was unjustified to equate property rights of inheritance with dowry. Dowry was neither a definite legal right and nor was legally enforceable. The inheritance rights of daughters were compensated by giving them dowry. The amount of dowry varied, depending upon the status of their prospective grooms, the amount was rarely equal to their share in parental property and it was not just an atonement of their father for depriving them of inheritance rather it was also a means of show off their wealth in the society. There was a co-existence of the customs of dowry and bride-price in China. The dowry has been considered as a form of pre-mortem inheritance gifted by selfless parents to their daughter for her welfare. [16] The custom of dowry was considered as a welfare of the bride as it used to increase the wealth of her new family and enhanced her supremacy and position in that family. But on the other side, the bride-price was given to the bride's parents and therefore it had never been considered to contribute in the welfare of bride or her groom in the new matrimonial setup.

2.2 Concept of Marriage and Dowry under Indian Civilization

During Vedic period the institution of marriage was treated as one of the sacred sacraments[17]. In ancient times, marriage was considered as a mode of uniting the two distinct halves of life, male and female. During those times the individual was regarded as the social and political unit and subsequently marriage was viewed as a pious ceremony or sacrament. Marriage was a pious and religious union achieved by divine dispensation. While choosing a husband for the bride; intellect, high character, adequate wealth and good health were the several factors to be taken into the consideration. However, criteria for selecting a bride were undeniably more intricate

---

[15] John L. McCreery, "Women's Property Rights and Dowry in China and South Asia" 15, No. pp. 163-174 (1976) available at: http://www.jstor.org/stable/3773327 (Visited on July 22, 2017)

[16] Junsen Zhang & William Chan, "Dowry and Wife's Welfare: A Theoretical and Empirical Analysis" 107 *JPE* 786-808 (1999), pp. 786-808 available at: http://www.jstor.org/stable/10.1086/250079 (Visited on July 22, 2017)

[17] Pradyot Kumar Maity, *Human Fertility Cults and Rituals of Bengal: A Comparative Study*, 29 (Abhinav publications, New Delhi, 1989) *available at:* https://books.google.co.in/books?isbn=8170172632

than those of choosing a husband. In certain prehistoric Indian communities, women were viewed as property thus it was the father of the bride and not the father of the bridegroom, who was entitled to ask or demand any payment from the bridegroom side at the time of marriage[18]. It was opined that since the bridegroom had taken away daughter of the family as his bride and deprived them from the benefit of her services and hence he should not be entitled to any other wealth or donation.[19]

2.2.1 Marriage Practices in Indian History

Marriage in the Vedic tradition was a religious necessity rather than a mere physical luxury. According to Manu and other ancient law makers, eight forms of the marriages are recognized. The four form of marriages were approved and were named as; *Daiva, Brahma, Arsha, Prajapatya.* The other four kinds of marriages were unapproved and were known as; *Gandharva, Asura, Rakshasa* and *Paishaca.*[20]

Dowry, in some or other form was prevalent in *Brahma* form of marriage. The girl was given as a gift known as *Kanyadan* to the groom, the gifts in cash or kind were given to the bride as her *Stridhan* and the gifts, transaction of wealth in the favour of bridegroom were offered as *Varadakshina.*[21] However, this form of dowry was entirely based on love and affection unlikely to the modern form of dowry which is based on expectation, demand and compulsion.[22]

The *Daiva* form of marriage was marked by gifting of a daughter who has been embellished with precious ornaments, to a priest who duly administers at a sacrifice throughout the course of its performance.[23] In *Arsha* type of marriage, there used to be a custom in which the bride's father used to receive a cow and a bull or two pairs of cattle from the bridegroom. In return, he gave away his daughter to the bridegroom. However, receiving the cattle from the bridegroom by the bride's father

---

[18] Anant Sadashiv Altekar, *The Position of Women in Hindu Civilization,* 69 (Motilal Banarasidas, New Delhi, 1987)

[19] P. N. Mari Bhat and Shiva S. Halli, *Demography of Brideprice and Dowry: Causes and Consequences of the Indian Marriage Squeeze,129 (53)PS* 129-148 (1999) *available at:* https://www.jstor.org/stable/2584672?seq=1(Visited on July 22, 2017)

[20] Monica Chawla, *Gender Justice: Women and Law in India,* 40(Deep and Deep Publications, New Delhi, 2006)

[21] Kavya CN, Pavan Kumar, "A Sociological Study on Religious Aspects in Hindu Marriage System" 1(13) IJAR 544 (2015) *available at:* http://www.allresearchjournal.com/archives/2015/vol1issue 13/PartH/1-13-67.pdf

[22] Madan C. Paul, *Dowry and Position of Women in India* 3 (Inter-India Publications, New Delhi, 1986).

[23] Ranjana Sheel, *The Political Economy of Dowry* 40 (Manohar Publishers, New Delhi, 1999).

has been strongly condemned by Manu.[24]*Samriti* has defined *Prajapatya* form of marriage in which the father gifted his daughter, and thereby used to address the couple with the quotes "may both of you perform together your duties" and had shown respect to the groom[25].

These four forms of marriages were socio-culturally acceptable and were known as *dharmya* marriages. There was a significance of gift giving by the father of bride to groom and his family in such form marriages which can comprehend the linkages of dowry with *dharmya* marriages. [26]

The other four forms of marriages were known as *adharmya* marriages and were against the socio-cultural norms.[27] Where the bridegroom received a bride, after gifting as much wealth as he could afford to the family and his bride, it was as called *Asura* rite. The *Gandharva* rite was a voluntary union of bride and her lover for desire and sexual intimacy. The *Rakshasa* rite was the forceful abduction of a bride from her house, whereby her family member was wounded, house was broken while she was crying and weeping. Where a man seduced a sleeping, intoxicated or disordered girl was known as *Pisachas* rite.[28]

Evidences of the historical roots of dowry can be seen in all forms of marriages. It was, however, more predominant in *Dharmaya* form of marriages requiring the father to bestow the daughter in marriage with gifts, property, wealth, etc[29]. This prompted the institution of the dowry system and facilitated its evolution as an all pervading part of the modern marriage system.[30]

2.2.2 Status of Women in the Institution of Marriage in India

The women of our country were described with a high respect in our ancient scriptures. Many female Goddesses acquired powerful position than male Gods in

---

[24] *Supra* note13.
[25] Ludwik Sternbach, "A Sociological Study of the Forms of Marriage in Ancient India"22 *ABORI* 205 (1941) *available at*: https://www.jstor.org/stable/43975949?seq=1
[26] Lokesh Ramnath Maharajh & Nyna Amin, "A Gender Critique of the Eight Forms of Hindu Marriages" 21 *JGRA* 84 *available at*: https://www.researchgate.net/publication/298789343_A _Gender_Critique_of_the_Eight_ Forms_of_Hindu_Marriages(Visited on February 21, 2019).
[27] *Id. at 86.*
[28] *Supra* note 23.
[29] *Supra* note 26.
[30] *Supra* note 28 at 45.

Hindu religion. *'Maa Saraswati'* possessed more significance as Goddess of knowledge than *'Lord Brahma'*.[31] *'Maa Lakshmi'* signified more dominance as Goddess of wealth than *'Lord Vishnu'*. Even *'Maa Parvati'* was revered as Goddess of power and energy even before *'Lord Shiva'*.[32] In almost all spheres of life, the women in ancient India were given equivalent status and position as men.

The refrains of *RigVeda* recommend that women married at an adult age were quite free to select companion of their own choice in a ceremonial practice known as *Swayamvar* and were even free to adopt a *Gandharva* marriage which was almost a kind of live-in relationship.[33] In the ancient Hindu marriage traditions, only the concept of *'Swayamvar'* was popular.[34] It was a ceremonial practice in which the bride was free to choose her bridegroom, out of a group of eligible men who used to come in the ceremony to exhibit their talent and compassion for her. There used to be no such contests named as *'Swayamvadhu'*, where the bridegroom could not hold beauty contests to select the bride to whom he would marry. It was evident in the historical instances that the women were on upper hand to put all the competing potential bridegrooms in various competitions or contests and then choose the bridegroom of their liking. In *Ramayana*, even the Lord *Rama* who is worshipped as a God had to lift the bow of Lord Shiva in the *Swayamvar* to prove his eligibility to marry *Sita*. In *Mahabharatha*, Arjuna had to won his wife *Draupadi* by hitting the eye of an above rotating fish rotating by only looking at the fish's reflection in a pool of oil below[35].

Undoubtedly, it was clearly evident in the historical references that the women in ancient India enjoyed an equal or superior position as to men in terms of decision making in marriage and selecting the bridegroom of their own choice. But it nowhere

[31] Mark Cartwright, "Ancient History Encyclopedia- Saraswati", *available at: https://www.ancient.eu /Sarasvati/* (Visited on July 22, 2019)

[32] Gurudev, "The Origin of Dowry System – British Policies Convert Gifts to Bride into an Instrument of Oppression Against Women", *Available at*: http://www.hitxp.com/articles/history/ origin-dowry-system-bride-woman-india-british/ (Visited on July 27, 2017)

[33] M. L. Agarwal, *Transcendental Vision of Sri Ram*, 55 (Indra Publishing House, Bhopal, 2006) *availableat*:https://books.google.co.in/books?id=FS9LxDkVOUC&pg=PA53&source=gbs_toc_r& cad=4#v=onepage&q&=false (Visited on April 08, 2018).

[34] Anindita Basu, Ramayana, Ancient History Encyclopedia, available at: https://www.ancient.eu/ The_Ramayana/(Visited on January 30, 2019).

[35] Shinde Sweety, *Arjun: Without a Doubt*, 12 (Leadstart Publishing Pvt. Ltd, 2015) *available at*: https://www.goodreads.com/book/show/24466957-arjun (Visited on October 25, 2017).

assured that because of this status, there was absence of suppression or crime against them in the history. *Sita* was abducted by the *Ravana* and was mercilessly taken away by him and was kept in *Lanka*, the *Draupadi* was brutally insulted and humiliated by the *Kauravas* in the full view of their *Raj Darbar*.[36] Draupadi was shamelessly put as a pawn by her own husband *Yudhishter* in gamble and as a result *Dushashan* had tried to denude her in front of all the respectable elders. Her agonized supplications for justice remained unheard by the deaf ears of all the elders, who were present in the *Raj Darbar*. Not a single voice was perhaps raised against that injustice that was being accomplished[37].The women had been victims of various crimes and atrocities since as old as the human civilizations originated and equally ancient were the various efforts to combat these crimes and protect the women against them. There were records of women being raped, abducted, mercilessly tortured, beaten and subjected to humiliating maltreatment. [38] However the offences related to dowry like bride burning, dowry death, cruelty etc were not evident in those times. The present form of dowry culture was quite absent in the antiquated India.[39]

However the custom of giving gifts to bridegrooms by the parents of bride, at marriage among the rich and royal families was prevalent. Such gifts or wealth were voluntarily and happily given out of mere love and affection. The custom of dowry practice was connected with the notion of marriage to be closely associated with *dana* or gift.[40] A sacramental gift in general was usually accompanied by cash, ornaments of gold or silver. So as a custom, the gifts of the bride were also accompanied with cash or gold ornaments etc[41].Evolution of dowry was closely related to the inheritance rights of women and their rights to the *Stridhana*, i.e. wealth transferred to them by their parents, at the time of their marriage.

---

[36] *Supra* note 32.
[37] Shobha Saxena, *Crimes against Women and Protective Laws* 21 (Deep and Deep Publications Pvt. Ltd., New Delhi, 2008).
[38] *Ibid.*
[39] Richa Gupta, The Evil of Dowry in India: A Legal Insight, 3 IJ L ISSN 57-64 (2017) available at: http://www.lawjournals.org/archives/2017/vol3/issue4/3-4-21(Visited on March 24, 2019).
[40] Zeba Hasan, "Blasphemy of Dowry in India and an Insurgence of an Artist: Neelima Sheikh Against the System", 2 *ESJ* 400 (2014) *available at*: https://eujournal.org/index.php/esj/article/viewFile/3734/3587(Visited on October 12, 2016).
[41] Indira Sharma, "Hinduism, Marriage and Mental Illness", 55 *IJP* 243-249 (2013) *available at*: https://www.ncbi.nlm.nih.gov/pmc/articles/PMC3705690/ (Visited on December 19, 2016).

2.2.3 The Inheritance Rights of Women and *Stridhana* in Ancient India

The Vedas strongly disapproved the inheritance of property by daughters. Since the daughters were regarded incompetent to inherit the property of their father, henceforth, a custom was evolved in which they were gifted away by the father while their brothers were not. Kautilya was of the opinion that the unmarried daughters shall be paid adequate dowry, payable to them on the occasion of their marriage. Some share of property or wealth was given by the father in lieu of complete absence of any kind of inheritance of the rights of property of women. [42]

Generally the right of women to S*tridhana* was equated with her right to property and inheritance.[43] It was the earliest recognized form of women's own wealth and property. There is another opinion that the concept of *Stridhana* has been originated from the practice of bride-price or *kanyashulka* given to the bride by the family of bridegroom. Under the belief of denouncing gifts received from groom's family, the girl's parents transferred the *shulka* amount to the girl as her *Stridhana* and dowry.[44]

The term *Stridhan* was originally derived from two words; *stri* means female and *dhan* means property, therefore as a whole the term stands for 'female's property'. Any movable property like utensils, adornments and attire that was given at the time of marriage, to the bride, was counted as *Stridhan*.[45] It was mentioned in *Manusmriti* as well as in *Yajnavalkya*, *Stridhan* was a rule comprised of blessings received from close relations in connection to the marriage.[46] By 1100 A.D. observers like *Vijneshwara* having a place with the *Mitakshara* School started to argue that all properties obtained by a female like property procured by inheritance or family partition and so on ought to be considered as *Stridhan*.[47] The females were however

---

[42] *Supra* note 23 at 43-47.
[43] Debarati Halder & K. Jaishankar, "Property Rights of Hindu Women: A Feminist Review of Succession Laws of Ancient, Medieval, and Modern India" 24 (2) *JLR* 669 (2009), *available at*: https://www.jstor.org/stable/25654333?seq=1 (Visited on May 20, 2017).
[44] *Supra* note 23 at 48.
[45] Anjani Kant, *Women and Law* 338(A.P.H. Publishing Co., New Delhi, 2008)
[46] *Debi Mangal Prasad Singh* v. *Mahadeo Prasad Singh*, (1912) ILR 34 All 234 *available at*: https://indiankanoon.org/doc/1286600/?type=print (Visited on November 05, 2016).
[47] Leepakshi Rajpal and Mayank Vats, "Stridhana: A Critical Approach" 7 IJRSSH 89 (2017) *available at*: http://www.ijrssh.com/images/short_pdf/1501650266_Leepakshi_9.pdf (Visited on February 15, 2019).

not permitted the privilege of transfer over this property and could just make the most of its income. The *Dayabhaga* School of Bengal did not acknowledge this enhancement of *Stridhan*, rather it permitted the women for the privilege of disposing off the *Stridhan* in a narrower sense of the term.[48]

2.2.4 Custom of Dowry in Indian Civilization

During the origin and beginning of dowry system, the brides were given some wealth as a gift from their parents at the time of marriage. It served as a tool of financial independence for the bride even after marriage. It was a common practice to take gifts, valuables etc by the family of bride and was treated as a major aspect in the before conversation and settlement[49]. In a few sections of India it has been pervasive over the hundreds of years in a destructive form, frequently including bartering and negotiating over the value and constituents of the dowry, cash and kind segments of it[50].

The "bride groom price" ascended with the present and potential wealth earning capability of the husband and the richness of the parents of the bride. History offered the instances of dowry practice in a not the same as somewhere else too. For example, in Britain, Henry II gained Aquitaine as "dowry" when he tied nuptial knot with Eleanor, both Henry VIII and Charles I acknowledged gigantic sum of money from their in-laws[51]. The British reinforced their dependable balance in India through a "dowry" when Charles II got at the port of Bombay from his Portuguese father in-law[52].

Customarily, the dowry was viewed as a vital transaction of marriage by the father of the bride, for two major reasons. The prime reason was that the marriage ceremonies in the vedic period were closely related with the rites of *kanyadaan*.[53] The

---

[48] Shreeparna Dutta, "Property Rights of Hindu Women in India – A Reflection of Social Change 1(2) *JLAR* 72 (2014) available at: http://www.ijlp.in/ijlp/imageS/Volume-1,%20Issue-2,%20June-14.pdf

[49] Subham Chatterjee, "Stridhan: A Study on Women's Property under Hindu Law" available at: https://lawcorner.in/stridhan-womens-property-under-hindu-law/(Visited on April 08, 2018).

[50] Mamta Rao, "Law relating to 'Women and Children'", 346, (Eastern Book Company, Lucknow, 2008)

[51] *Ibid.*

[52] *Supra* note 20 at 186.

[53] Rajni Devi, "Marriage among Hindus with Special reference to Dowry" 20 (7) IOSR-JHSS 5(2015) *available at*: http://www.iosrjournals.org/iosr-jhss/papers/Vol20-issue7/Version-6/A020760109.pdf (Visited on December 30, 2016).

second reason for giving the gifts in dowry was that it was additionally given on the grounds that the girl was not given any share in the joint family properties as it was given to her brothers. The privilege of the father to give a little part of even the family property as blessing to the girl at the occasion of her marriage was recognized. It was set down in *dharamshastra* that the commendable act of *kanyadan* could not be accomplished till the groom was given a *dakshina*.[54] Therefore, when the bride was offered to the groom, he had to be offered and given some cash or valuable amount which comprised of the *vardakshina*, ie; the money or blessings in kind by the guardians or parents of the bride to their son-in-law.[55] The *vardakshina* was offered out of fondness and did not comprise of any sort of impulse or any marriage consideration. It was a voluntary practice which was willingly done by family of bride without any force or coercion shown by bridegroom side. Over the span of the time, the intentional component in dowry had vanished and the coercive component has sneaked in. It had taken profound roots in wedding ceremonies as well as after marriage relationship. The valuables and gifts which were initially proposed to be a token *dakshina* for the husband had thereafter gone out of proportions and had transformed to the terminology 'dowry'[56].

2.2.5 Evolution and Growth of Dowry in Ancient, Vedic and Classical Era (1500 BC – 500 BC)

Dowry is not a new phenomenon in ancient times. Before the 20th century Indian societies had bride price, *Dakshina*, *Kanyadhan* and *Streedhana*.[57] Dowry, as a social practice did not come into vogue only in the modern times. Dowry has been in practice right from the time, the ancient socialistic pattern of society changed into a society of male domination and female suppression. The traces of age old custom 'dowry' were very often seen in the Hindu scriptures and sacred books.[58] The *Rig Veda* has referred to the marriage of Sun's daughter *Surya* and *Soma* (Moon) and

---

[54] Kanai L. Mukherjee & Bibhas Bandyopadhyay, Hindu Marriage 64 (Eagle Book Bindery, USA, 2018) *available at*: http://www.agiivideo.com/books/Book-6-Hindu-Marriage.pdf (Visited on November 12, 2019).

[55] *Supra* note 40 at 401.

[56] *Supra* note 53.

[57] Stevan Harrell and Sara A. Dickey, "Dowry Systems in Complex Societies" 24 *ETHNOLOGY* 105 (1985) *available at*: https://www.jstor.org/stable/3773553?seq=1(Visited on April 08, 2018).

[58] Mahamahopadhyaya Pandurang Vaman Kane, *History of Dharamsastra*, (Bhandarkar Oriental Research Institute, Poona, 1946)

quoted; "The bride, wearing a beautiful robe and coverlet, eyes dunked with unguents started for the house of her intended lord in a canopied chariot accompanied by bridal friends. Her treasure chest, containing her dowry, was also placed in her chariot."[59]In 1500 B.C., in another reference of *Atharva Veda,* it was remarked that the parents should give a dowry of intellect and knowledge to their daughter as she leaves for her in-law's house. There was mentioned a royal bride who took along hundreds of elephants, horses and jewels in her dowry. [60] Even in *Mahabharata,* there was an instance of dowries given in the marriages of *Draupadi* and *Subhadra* to *Arjuna* as well as *Uttara* and *Abhimanyu.* [61]

Besides the Hindu scriptures and sacred books the great Sanskrit poet *'Kalidasa',* also testified the prevalence of the dowry system in 400 A.D. In *Raghuvansa,* he referred that a good dowry was given by *Vidharba* in his sister's marriage. Again in *Abhigyan Shakuntalam,* there was a verse stating that *Shakuntala's* father regretted his incapability to give his daughter, a handsome dowry. [62]Therefore, as she fell in love with King *Dushyanta,* trees, flowers, bees etc. were given to her as dowry.[63]

2.2.5.1 Ancient Notions about Dowry

Continuous practice of traditions and customs gave birth, to many new sub-traditions and sub-customs that applied on the customs related to the marriage too. At first, financial contemplations and considerations did not form the part of marriage but later on the customs, related to marriage could not stay unaffected by the money related considerations. The sacred texts bear many propounding directives with

[59] Ralph T.H. Griffith, The Hymns of the Rig Veda, *available at:* http://www.sacred-texts.com/hin/rigveda/rv10085.html(Visited on January 20, 2018).

[60] Sanjeev Newar, Women in Vedas, *available at: http://agniveer.com/women-in-vedas/* (Visited on August 03, 2017).

[61] Arun R. Kumbhare, Women of India: Their Status since the Vedic Times, 130 (IUniverse, New York, 2009) *available at: https://books.google.co.in/books?id=A2dUR4mwBBAC &printsec= frontcover&source=gbs_ge_summary_ r&cad=0#v=onepage&q&f=false*(Visited on May 03, 2017).

[62] Arundhati Hoskeri, Projection and Contribution of Women in Literature, *available at:* https://oceanofknowledgeweb.wordpress.com/2018/03/13/projection-and-contribution-of-women-in-literature/ (Visited on January 20, 2019).

[63] Ashok Kaushik, Abhigyan Shakuntalam 98(Diamond Pocket Books Pvt Ltd, 2014) *available at:* https://books.google.co.in/books?id=Qp_QAgAAQBAJ&source=gbs_navlinks_s (Visited on December 30, 2016).

respect to marriage that stated that the dowry has existed in *Shastric* and *Smritic* periods.

2.2.5.2 Dowry under Dharama-Shastras

The word 'dowry' had not been used directly in the *Shastras* but impliedly, through the description of the customs or kinds of marriage, an impression was given that certain gifts or valuable presents had to be made at marriage.[64] During the period before and after the composition of *Manusmriti,* custom of giving some specific gifts or presents were essential in the *Brahma, Devya, Arsh and Asura* form of marriages either from the side of bride or from the side of bridegroom. The gifts that were made to a bridegroom were called as *'Varadakshina'* symbolizing the token of honour and respect to him.[65]

Such were not at all compulsory, but were voluntary. Manu had clearly remarked that the bride's father must not take any money in consideration of the bride otherwise it amounted to selling one's own child.[66] He never preached for performing monetary negotiations either to get a husband or a wife, therefore the system of dowry was not an outcome *shastric* periods.

2.2.5.3 'Saudayika' reflects the Positive Characteristics of Dowry

In the ancient Sanskrit scripts and literature, *'Saudayika'* has been used for *'dowry'.*[67] Whatever was obtained at the time of marriage along with the girl was known as property obtained with the girl, whatever was obtained by the married or unmarried woman, at her parent's house or at her husband's house, was called *Saudayika.* After having obtained the same she was free to us it or dispose it in whatever way she liked. Since the property given as *'Saudayika'* was given as love, affection or sympathy, the woman was to be considered its free owner.[68]

---

[64] Urusa Mohsin & Pooja Singh, "Disastrous Consequences of Dowry in Ind ian Sub-Continent" *7 VIDHIGYA* 56 (2012) *available at*: https://eujournal.org/index.php/esj/article/view File/3734/3587 (Visited on April 19, 2018).

[65] *Supra* note 40 at 401.

[66] Paras Diwan, "The Dowry Prohibition Law" 27 *JILI 565(1985) available at*: https://www.jstor.org/stable/43953016?seq=1(Visited on October 15, 2017).

[67] Amoolya, "Streedhan – The Right of Woman" *available at*: https://www.lawctopus.com/academike/streedhan-right-woman/(Visited on December 30, 2018).

[68] Sukumari Bhattacharji, "Economic Rights of Ancient Indian Women" 26 EPW 507-512 (1991) *available at*: https://www.jstor.org/stable/4397402?seq=1#page_scan_tab_contents (Visited on December 30, 2018).

2.2.5.4 Arthashastra and Apastamba-Dharamsutra on the Custom of Dowry

In the patriarchal societies, there were very scarce and negligible rights of daughters in the parental property. They only had right to maintenance and at the most, their marriage expenses including dowry. It was written in *Apastamba-Dharamashastra* that the daughters should be given that much of share in their father's property, as much as would be required for their dowry.[69] Among the patrilineal families of the Dharamashastra *'Sidanam'* was given at the time of marriage which was a bit different from *Saudayika* 'but still had certain similarities.[70]

In the Vedic era, women had a commended position and they were treated with a decent measure of individual freedom and equal status with men. Both young men and young ladies were given same opportunities for gaining knowledge and education. The foundation of marriage was a holy observance joining the gatherings in an inseparable and everlasting union of two souls. The couple remained on an equivalent footing. The condition of the bride was a respected one in the family. She was viewed as a significant as well as indispensable member in the family, without whom, the culmination of human life was impossible. [71]

However the culture of modern notion of dowry as an evil was obscure at that time. In rich and lavish families a few presents were given by the parents of bride to the bridegroom at the occasion of marriage. These presents, nonetheless, could barely be termed as dowry as those were intentionally given after marriage out of adoration and love.

Dowry which was given according to the individual's financial status, started as a financial problem in the beginning, and transformed into a social problem today. In the beginning of the production, both men and women were involved in all kind of works. In that context, a woman usually went to live in her husband's house after marriage. So a working force or a working member was lost in the girl's house. To compensate for the loss of the working girl, it was customary for the bridegroom to

---

[69] *Supra* note 58.
[70] Apastamba-Dharamasutra 2.14.6, *The Classical Hindu Law,* available at: https://maghaa.com/the-classical-hindu-law-chapter-05/(Visited on May 22, 2019).
[71] R. Revathi, *Law Relating to Domestic Violence* 1 (Asia Law House Publications, Hyderabad, New edn., 2004).

give money or the means of earning money like cattle, land etc. This economic exchange on the basis of the girl was the beginning of the dowry. [72]

2.2.6 Prevalence of Dowry System in Medieval India (500 BC – 1526 AD)

Although the beginning and origin of the custom of dowry that was prevailing in India had lost in antiquity, but still there had been few evidentiary clues to determine that it was practiced even before 300 B.C. among upper castes of the society such as the *Brahmins* and *Kshatriyas*.[73] However it was not known that whether it was brought along with the conquering armies and mass marriages of Alexander the Great, or if it was practiced even prior to those times. Usually the land was given as dowry in the initial stage. The emergence of Buddhism culture in India began with the great ruler *Ashoka*, the empathy began an era of the strong influence of Buddhist law on a huge part of India. The women had rights in the property and they could even own the property, under Buddhist law and henceforth therefore it minimized the chances of giving and taking of dowry.[74]

In case of the *Brahmin* women there was no general trend of their working outside the home especially for earning wages. Hence these people practiced Dowry of Kanyadhan instead of Bride-price.[75] From about 13th or 14th century A.D., the dowry system assumed alarming proportions in *Rajputs*. [76] The main reason behind the growth in this evil practice was that the *Rajputanas* took extraordinary pride in their ancestry. However this practice was not prevalent to the same extent in the ordinary families. But gradually, the dowry system became common in all sections of the society and has maligned the religious sacrament of marriage.[77]

---

[72] S. Gokilwani, Dr. S. Gabriel Jelestin, *Marriage, Dowry, Practice and Divorce* (Regal Publications New Delhi, 2008).

[73] The New World Encyclopedia, *"Dowry"* available at: https://www.newworldencyclopedia. org/entry/Dowry

[74] Gregory Schopen , Separate but Equal: Property Rights and the Legal Independence of Buddhist Nuns and Monks in Early North India 128 *JAOS* 630 (2008) available at: https://www.jstor.org /stable/25608448?seq=1

[75] Priya Ranjan Trivedi & Manindra Kumar Tiwari, "Brahman : Philosophy, Origins, Roles, Duties, Responsibilities and Contribution 350(Brahman International, New Delhi, 2017) available at: http://www.info.ind.in/BRAHMAN%20BOOK%20WITH%20COVER%20PAGE%20-%20BRAHMIN.pdf

[76] *Supra* note 39.

[77] Dr. Shipra Kaushal, *Gender Inequality Illustrated through A Legal Perspective on Female Foeticide* 15-16 (Satyam Law International, New Delhi, 2014)

In the southern part of India especially in Kerela and some parts of Tamil Nadu, Stridhana had been practiced because according to Hindu Laws daughters had no right over the properties. [78] This was also practiced among the Tranvancore Christans.[79] Gradually, the practice had changed into dowry and its payment was demanded directly or indirectly.

Later a stage came when women stopped doing productive work and did only the domestic works at home. Since only men were involved in productive work of earning money, women lost their economic importance. Hence, women were pushed to a secondary position in society and were subjected to men. In those circumstances, the head of the family, at the time of his daughter's marriage, used to give part of his wealth to the bridegroom, to show his prosperity and to enable the comfortable living of his daughter. Actually this was the custom of the rich to display their wealth to the society. In imitation of this the poor also started changing hands whatever they had. Dowry becoming a social problem to the poor was the second stage in the history of dowry.[80]

The Medieval India was considered as the 'Dark age' for the women. The Muslims conquerors brought a new culture with them after they had invaded India. During the medieval period, the *Kshatriyas,* who were the ruling class at that time and other dominant castes/classes of the society used to give and take valuable properties, movable as well as immovable, to their daughters in the marriage to raise their status in the society and to impress others with their lavishness. [81]

The declining economic participation of women was one of the reasons for the spread of dowry to the groups which were previously practicing the custom of bride-price.[82] The conversion of the practice of bride price to the custom of dowry was an attempt to enhance and establish the social status of family in the community, as the

---

[78] Kanakalatha Mukund, "Women's Property Rights in South India: A Review" 34 *EPW* 1354 (1999) *available at:* https://www.jstor.org/stable/4408023?seq=1

[79] Sindhu Thulaseedharan, Christian Women and Property Rights in Kerala – Gender Equality in Practice 4 (2004) *available at:* http://www.cds.ac.in/krpcds/report/sindhu.pdf

[80] Dr. S. Gokilwani, Dr. S. Gabriel Jelestin, *Marriage, Dowry, Practice and Divorce* (Regal Publications, New Delhi, 2008)

[81] Prakash Chand Jain, "Women's Property Rights under Traditional Hindu Law and the Hindu Succession Act, 1956: Some Observations" 45 *JILI* 520 (2003) *available at:* https://www.jstor.org/stable/43951878?seq=1

[82] Indira Rajaraman, "Economics of Bride-Price and Dowry" 18 *EPW* 275-279 (1983) available at: https://www.jstor.org/stable/4371875?seq=1

custom of dowry was associated with the higher segment of society in many parts of India.[83] These changing notions had been observed in various regions and indicated the declining status of girl in her father's home. Thereafter the girls started becoming a liability in their parental house rather than an asset. This undoubtedly was an inevitable consequence of withdrawing the role of women in production activities and the loss of their production skills.[84] The custom of giving gifts out of love for daughters during their marriage has now become dowry. This started as a practice because the girl did not inherit any property under the Hindu inheritance law.

2.2.7 The Growth of Dowry System in Mughal Empire (1526-1750)

The invasion of India by Mughals led to the further weakening of the condition of Indian women. The Mughal era left a permanent effect, especially, on the Hindu females in a few different ways. Child marriage was the well known component of the public customs which very often denied the opportunity of children education. The husbands automatically grabbed more dominance and power over wives because of their illiteracy and ignorance, making them an easy target of abuse and oppression. [85]

At the point when Muslims came to control in huge parts of India in the eighth century, they did not support the dowry system. They were not determined, be that as it may, and as Hindu zones expanded, the Brahmin standings progressively detached themselves and proceeded and advocated the custom of dowry indeed. [86]*Mughals* kept females in *purdah* which later turned out to be increasingly common among a wide range of society.[87]The situation of the females further worsened by the evil practices likes child-marriages, female infanticide and sati, which were prevailing in those times.[88]. However, southern India was largely free from such malpractices and was not even a part of Muslim invasion. The daughters moved toward becoming a liability

---

[83] Siwan Anderson, "The Economics of Dowry and Brideprice" 21 TJEP 153 (2007) a*vailable at*: https://www.jstor.org/stable/30033756?seq=1

[84] Siwan Anderson, "Human Capital Effects of Marriage Payments " 77 *IZAWL* 5 (2014) a*vailable at*: https://wol.iza.org/uploads/articles/77/pdfs/human-capital-effects-of-marriage-payments.pdf

[85] *Supra* note 32.

[86] New World Encyclopedia, *available at*: http://www.newworldencyclopedia.org/entry/Dowry (visited on March 7, 2017)

[87] Neerja Ahlawat, "Women and Struggle for Equality", 67 *SOCIOLOGICAL BULLETIN* 110-119 (2018) *available at*: https://journals.sagepub.com/doi/full/10.1177/0038022917752164

[88] India Today, Indian women: Yesterday, today and tomorrow *available at*: https://www.indiatoday.in/magazine/cover-story/story/19760115-indian-women-yesterday-today-and-tomorrow-819610-2015-04-28

on the parents and required additional consideration, while a son would not need such additional consideration, rather would be helping in increasing family income through his earnings.[89] All the factors combined and resulted into degrading status of girls and women in society. This offered ascend to new indecencies, for example, Child Marriage, *Sati-Jauhar* and restricting the opportunities of girl-child education.[90]

The culture of Dowry existed in India even before the advent of British Rule, however not in a way that is common in the society today. In pre-colonial times, dowry was a system overseen by females, for females, to empower them to set up their status and have plan of action in a situation of financial crisis. In this old practice and culture of dowry, the guardians, parents, even her friends and relatives all gave valuables, money or property to her as precious gifts and so on. It was much the same as how guardians used to give wealth to their sons, so did they offer it to their daughters too amid at their marriage. These assets or valuables, money or property were given to their daughter at her marriage, and not to her husband or his family. At the end of the day, the wealth of dowry was kept on being possessed by the bride and not by the husband or his family. This gave the required money related autonomy and independence to those females who even dealt with the agricultural income from their rural land, and so forth. So in the initial culture of dowry which was common in India, daughters were given wealth from their folks amid marriage and this filled in as an instrument of financial autonomy for the women even after their marriage. [91]

Customarily, dowry traditions were a demonstration of affection as guardians would bless their daughter with dowry as she entered into the institution of marriage. These endowments extended from cash to land and entitled a female to be a full individual in her spouse's family, enabling her to enter the conjugal home along with her own wealth. [92] It was viewed as a substitute for legacy and rights of inheritance, offering some financial security to the women and was a blessing from her family. [93]

---

[89] Gadhre, The Socio Economic status of Women in India *available at*: http://www.legalservices-india.com/article/1867/The-Socio-Economic-Status-of-Women-in-India-Ancient-to-Modern-Era.html

[90] *Supra* note 40 at 402.

[91] *Supra* note 32.

[92] *Supra* note 60.

[93] Leigh Seeger, "India's Dowry Culture", *Available at:* https://intpolicydigest.org/2013/07/30/india-s-dowry-culture/ (Visited on March 7, 2017).

2.2.8 The Growing Menace of Dowry during British Regime (1750 – 1947)

In any case, the move which influenced the status of the women in the Indian culture was the standard forced by the British which disallowed the females from owning any property whatsoever. It strengthened the menace of dowry custom in India .At the beginning of the British rule, the situation of ladies in family and society had achieved the most extreme level of crumbling. The situation of wife in the family unit was in a heartbroken situation on account of the malevolent socio-religious practices, vile traditions, nonsensical religious rituals and brutal superstitions obscure in the old time frame which had crawled into the society amid British period. Perhaps, the most noticeably awful part of this social corruption was the horrible sufferings and social degradation of status of women. That is the reason because of which, the movements for liberation of women pulled in the consideration of every single social reformer. The predicament of women, in this way turned into the point of convergence for social reconstruction.[94]

However, when the British disallowed women from the entitlement of any property rights, it implied that the whole wealth that a daughter got from her parents would be claimed by her husband. As this arrangement of husband owning the property of his wife was made, the customary dowry practice got transformed into a menace creating custom of covetousness and greed which mistreated, exploited and stifled women. The greed that kicked into the society in the form of expectation of dowry, made a framework where bridegroom and his family began expecting from would be bride as a means of property and monetary benefits. With this started the trend of demanding dowry from the girl and her family. The social amicability and the holding made by the establishment of marriage were no more. Marriage turned out to be simply one more business bargain, where making money was easier. Sons turned into extra wellsprings of salary, and daughters turned into a monetary burden and liability on the family. This led to the prevalence of social issues like female foeticide and created disproportions in male-female ratio in the society, which further resulted into more offences and atrocities upon women. [95]

---

[94] *Supra* note 71 at 2.
[95] *Supra* note 32.

The spillover effect of dowry drew the attention of British administrators. The British governing heads initiated various efforts for the emancipation of women by formulating various laws to protect women in India. Lord Wiliam Bentinck outlawed the practice of Sati in 1829[96]. Sati had always been an exaggeration of the Hindu ideal, never practiced by the majority, and was therefore successfully eradicated.[97] In 1856, Widow Remarriage Act was passed[98]. It was, however, less successful. The British also passed Infanticide Act in 1870 to abolish this practice to female infanticide.[99] In 1860, following much agitation, the age of consent was raised to ten years and in 1891 it was raised to twelve years.[100] The Sarda Act of 1929 rose the age still further to fifteen. In spite of such legislations there was no visible change in women's status.[101] The first enactment carrying women into the plan of legacy was the Hindu Law of Inheritance Act, 1929. It gave legacy rights on three female beneficiaries i.e. son's daughter, daughter's daughter and sister. [102] Another milestone enactment which gave possession rights on ladies was the Hindu Women's Right to Property Act, 1937. [103] However, the British were unwilling to interfere with Indian customs as per the populous measures to keep their government stable[104].

As times took a new phase, the burden of taxes, under British provincial principle has transformed the custom of dowry as a financial gain to the families of bridegrooms to meet urgent financial needs. Under numerous liabilities, for example, overwhelming land tax, peasants were constrained to get money from wherever they could or they would be deprived of their property. Therefore, the dowry turned into a

---

[96] India Today, "The abolished 'Sati Pratha': Lesser-known facts on the banned practice", *Available at*: https://www.indiatoday.in/education-today/gk-current-affairs/story/sati-pratha-facts-275586-2015-12-04 (Last Modified on December 4, 2015, 11:23 AM)
[97] P.K. Rana, "Critical Analysis on Criminalization against Burning of Widows" 3 *IJL* 19 (2017) *available at*: http://www.lawjournals.org/download/84/3-1-12-944.pdf
[98] Hindu Widows' Remarriage Act, 1856
[99] L. S. Vishwanath, "Efforts of Colonial State to Suppress Female Infanticide: Use of Sacred Texts, Generation of Knowledge" 33 *EPW* 1104 (1998) *available at:* https://www.jstor.org/stable /4406753?seq=1
[100] Selwyn Stanley, Social Problems in India 142 (Allied Publishers Private Ltd, Mumbai 1st edn, 2004)
[101] *Supra* note 1 at 68.
[102] As referred in Dr. Shipra Kaushal, *Gender Inequality Illustrated through A Legal Perspective on Female Foeticide* 165 (Satyam Law International, New Delhi, 2014)
[103] As referred in Dr. Shipra Kaushal, *Gender Inequality Illustrated through A Legal Perspective on Female Foeticide* 165 (Satyam Law International, New Delhi, 2014)
[104] Arunima Baruah, *The Soft Target: Crime Against Women* 126 (Kilaso books publication, New Delhi, 1st edn., 2004)

typical source of getting wealth for the bridegroom's family. It was viewed as a compulsory installment on demand that was the consideration of marriage, likening to a family paying a man to marry their girl, in which the bridegrooms supported their family to demand the maximum possible amount for marriage.[105]Under the Colonial empire of British, the dowry system of India grew as well as became widespread with the development and increase in urbanization. As the poor people were not ready to face this menace which involved huge expenses, they tried to cope up the demand and it gave rise to many social problems. [106]

Several scholars have claimed that the condition of the women deteriorated further with the codification of laws and permanent settlement of land system. The codification of customary laws had resulted into mechanical translation of many Hindi language terms into English terminology and moreover the British adopted their own ideology for defining and interpreting such terms. A term likewise 'local' which implied village in customary law came to be changed to signify 'caste' or 'tribe'. [107] "This change in terminology had implications for women, since people were now identified by patriarchal lineage rather than localities. The whole attempt was to translate social and customary practice, which was flexible, into legal codes from which women were excluded."[108] It promoted patriarchy and thereby further decline in the position of women in family.

Even the laws related to property rights are also considered to be one of the primary factors responsible for growth of deformed dowry system. [109]Before the advent of British rule, the property was under the ownership of king. The British rule had given property rights to individuals but only men. However, some traces of acceptance towards the property rights of female could be seen in *Dayabhaga* School in India. But in those days, no property rights were given to the women in Britain, the same was implemented in India. Many historians have strongly opined that "British revenue system, which put land exclusively in the hands of males, weakened the

---

[105] Leigh Seeger, "India's Dowry Culture", *available at:* https://intpolicydigest.org/2013/07/30/india-s-dowry-culture/ (Visited on March 7, 2017).

[106] New World Encyclopedia, *available at:* http://www.newworldencyclopedia.org/entry/Dowry (Visited on March 7, 2017)

[107] *Supra* note 99.

[108] *Ibid.*

[109] *Supra* note 60.

social and economic position of Indian women and encouraged practices such as dowry and female infanticide".[110]

2.2.8.1 Emergence of Laws on Dowry Prohibition during British Rule

In 19th and the beginning of 20th centaury, various social reforms have taken place and many social reformers had put efforts for eradicating many social evils including the evil of dowry custom. The Hindu Code Bill was introduced in 1930.[111] Two major features of this bill were related to the problem of dowry. Firstly it dealt with the intestate succession and marriage; secondly it sought to provide equal rights of property to women. The state was of opinion that these provisions would contribute in enhancing the status of women and effectively curb the growing menace of dowry[112]. Apart from that the Bill has proposed remarkable amendments in the intestate succession to female property i.e. dowry[113].

A significant reference was made in the bill as to the property given at the time of marriage to the daughter as dowry. It was mentioned that such property shall be treated as 'trust property' and the girl should be entitled to claim and use this property after getting 18 years of age[114]. Few years before the independence of India, in 1939 the provincial government of *Sind* passed '*Sind Deti Leti Act, 1939*' to end dowry system. It was a significant state measure which was directly related to dowry but had failed to curb the menace of dowry. Under this Act, any kind of payments made or agreed to be made, as a part of the contract of betrothal or marriage were prohibited in the province of Sind. However, it was not applicable to Muslims, Parsis, Christians and Jews.[115] This statute was enacted to prohibit any kind of payment made or agreed to be made as a part of the contract of marriage and to prohibit the ritual of *Deti Leti* in the province of Sind. Any kind of payment made by or to a person married or by or to a parent or any other relative of such person made or agreed to be

---

[110] Dowry Murder Veena Talwar Oldenburg, "Dowry Murder" (Oxford University Press, New York, 2002), cited at: Rashme Arora, "Dowry Murder as a Legacy of British Policies" *available at:* http://infochangeindia.org/women/189-women/books-a-reports/5892-dowry-murder-as-a-legacy-of-british-policies.html

[111] G. R. Rajagopaul, "The Story of the Hindu Code"17 *JILI* 537 (1975) *available at:* https://www.jstor.org/stable/43953841

[112] *Supra* note 23 at 151.

[113] *Id at* 153.

[114] *Id at* 154.

[115] *Id at* 162.

made in connection with marriage. It included any kind of gifts or wealth given on any festival or ceremony in the families of the parents or relatives of bride or bridegroom. Section 3 of the Act prohibited such payments and section 8 of the Act provided the punishment for violation of any provision of this Act.[116] Unfortunately, this Act had failed to put any impact or to bring any desired effect on ending the evil of dowry.

2.2.9 The Saga of Dowry System: Post-Independence (After 1947)

After freedom, various endeavors have been made to reform the status of women. The Constitution of India was framed, enacted and commenced.[117] The Constitution of India conceived that all are equal in the eyes of law regardless of their religion, race, station, sex or place of birth. The fundamental rights contained in Article 14, 15, 16 of Indian Constitution ensured that women in India ought not to be treated as mediocre compared to men in any regard. Article 15 (3) engaged the state to make unique arrangements for the welfare of women and children. So Article 15 (3) gave substantive quality by empowering the legislation and enforcement of various Acts and laws securing the rights of women[118]. One of the Directive Principles of state policy under Article 39 likewise ordered the state to equal opportunity and rights of earning livelihood to all the people, irrespective of their gender[119].

During British rule, the women were banned to inherit or own any kind of property in their name. The situation continued even after independence, till 1956 the females in India did not get any right to inherit the property of their parents. Ultimately in 1956, certain amendments were done in Hindu Personal Laws which

---

[116] Paras Diwan, *Law relating to Dowry, Dowry Deaths, Bride Burning, Rape and Related Offences* 11 (Universal Law Publishing co. Pvt. Ltd.,Delhi, 2002).

[117] The Constitution of India, 1949.

[118] Article 15(3) - "Nothing in this article shall prevent the State from making any special provision for women and children." So it states that even though the state will not discriminate anyone, they can make special provisions only for women and children for safeguarding their interests, The Constitution of India.

[119] Article 39 - Certain principles of policy to be followed by the State: The State shall, in particular, direct its policy towards securing-
(a) that the citizens, men and women equally, have the right to an adequate means to livelihood;
(b) that the ownership and control of the material resources of the community are so distributed as best to subserve the common good;
(c) that the operation of the economic system does not result in the concentration of wealth and means of production to the common detriment;
(d) that there is equal pay for equal work for both men and women; The Constitution of India.

entitled the right to women in India to inherit ancestral or parental property[120].Be that as it may, again those rights were not equivalent to those of men. According to law, a son had a distinct and independent share in the hereditary property, whereas the share of daughter was dependent on the share gotten by her father. Thus, a father could successfully exclude a girl by denying his share of the hereditary property, yet in such a situation, the son would still have a share in his own right. Also, wedded daughters, even those confronting conjugal harassment, had no private rights to live in the ancestral home. In 2005, the Hindu laws were altered once more, now furnishing the measures to the women to provide equal rights with men regarding ancestral property.[121] Section 6 of the Hindu Law has been amended in a way to provide same rights to the daughters like sons. The liability of daughters, allotment of shares to the daughters and their obligations were made same as that of a son.[122]

The modern dowry system has reached gargantuan proportions; it however had a humble beginning, as stray incidents show that sometimes groom refuse to proceed with the half marriage rituals halfway through unless the demand of dowry was not met. Usually the parents of the girl surrendered to this hold up because of social and financial burden pressure because in those days, marriage was considered as the prime goal for the women. Parents of girls were in every case too anxious to even think about getting their little girls wedded in case they remain a liability on the family for whatever is left of their lives.[123]

2.2.9.1 Emergence of Laws on Dowry Prohibition Post-Independence

With the passage of time, the evil of dowry had acquired an acute form and had spread across the whole country and in almost all the sections of society. Some states like Andhra Pradesh and Bihar have witnessed the evil consequences of dowry in a more severe form and hence enacted "The Bihar Dowry Restraint Act, 1950", and the "Andhra Pradesh Dowry Prohibition Act, 1958" for the respective states. However, these acts also failed to meet the aim for which they were enacted. The evil

---

[120] *Supra* note 32.
[121] *Ibid.*
[122] Section 6, Hindu Succession Act, 1956, substituted by The Hindu Succession (Amendment) Act, 2005
[123] Shobha Saxena, *Crimes against Women and Protective Laws* 116 (Deep and Deep Publications Pvt. Ltd., New Delhi, 1st edn.,4th reprint, 2008).

of dowry has been a matter of serious concern to everyone in view of its ever-increasing and disturbing propositions. The issue of dowry has been engaging the attention of the government since the inception of Constitution, which is based upon the principle of equality. Realizing the problem correctly, that it is a social problem rather than legal, hence it is to be combated through social change and not through purely technical legislation. In view of this the Hindu Succession Act, 1956 has tried to give equal rights to the women in the joint property of family.

The underlying objective behind this enactment was also to end the custom of giving and taking dowry by inculcating rights of women in their family property. It was somehow speculated that a major reason behind giving dowry to the daughter is an implied compensation for not giving any share to her in the property and lieu of that providing some kind of financial security to her in the form of dowry. But nothing has worked much therefore; there was a constant political as well as social pressure on the government to enact a specific legislation with an objective to legally prohibit any kind of giving and taking dowry. As a result on 24th April, 1959 a Bill was introduced in *Lok Sabha* for dowry prohibition.[124] After many debates and discussions, it was sent to the joint committee of Parliament. The joint committee had suggested certain changes on which it had failed to obtain the consensus of both the houses. After various debates, ultimately in a joint sitting of both the houses in May, 1961, the Bill was passed.[125]

The legislature has tried to maintain the balance between the age old traditions of giving customary gifts to the daughters on the auspicious occasions and if such gifts are made with certain compulsions then the law makes it a penal offence. The law has also provided that such gifts shall be utilized for the benefit of such women only. Making the law more stringent on the recommendation of the Committee on the Status of Women in India, the government issued instructions to the states and Union Territories regarding detailed and compulsory investigations into cases of dowry deaths and stepping up anti-dowry publicity. The joint committee of the houses has made the recommendations to effect the amendments in the Indian Penal Code, 1860,

---

[124] "History of Joint Sessions of Parliament", The Times of India (March 26, 2002) *available at:* https://timesofindia.indiatimes.com/anti-terror-law/History-of-joint-sessions-of Parliament/articleshow/4916708.cms (Visited on May, 6 2017)
[125] *Ibid.*

Indian Evidence Act, 1872 and Cr.Pc, 1973 on receiving the replies from government. In 1983, Indian Penal Code was amended and Section 498-A was added to it. It made cruelty to a wife a cognizable and non-bailable offence, punishable of maximum three years imprisonment and fine. In the year 1986 Indian Penal Code was again amended and Section 304 B was added to it.[126] It provides for punishment of not less than seven years and upto life imprisonment for husband and or his relative if a women's death occurs due to cruelty by such husband or relatives. In the same year Section 113 B was inserted in the Indian Evidence Act, 1872.[127] It provides that the Court can draw an inference of the crime of dowry death of a women if it is shown that soon before her death such woman has been subjected to cruelty by her husband or his relatives.

2.2.9.2 Joint Committee of Parliament on Dowry

After ten to fifteen years of passing of Dowry Prohibition Act, it was grossly realized that many inhuman killings of brides or bride burning were closely connected with the evil of dowry and this Act of 1961 was unable to fulfill its objective. Thereafter, a Parliamentary Committee had been appointed with a purpose to thoroughly study the shortcomings of the Act, to conduct an empirical survey on the same and suggest the required amendments. [128] The committee had thoroughly examined the efficacy and implementation of the Act. It had even suggested various changes and insertions to be made in the existing Act. *[129]* Apart from that, various social organizations, women's group and media were pressurizing to bring preventive measures against inhuman treatment of women for dowry. Keeping in mind all these considerations, the Joint Parliamentary Committee on dowry had submitted its report in August 1982.[130] The Dowry Prohibition Act, 1961 was amended twice i.e. in 1984 and in 1986, on the basis of the recommendations suggested by the Committee.[131]

In order to deal with the cruelty done to the women by their husbands or in-laws for unlawful demands of dowry, the committee had given some important

---

[126] The Dowry Prohibition (Amendment) Act, 1986 *available at:* https://wcd.nic.in/act/dowry-prohibition-act-1961(Visited on January 6 , 2016)

[127] *Ibid.*

[128] Crimes against women and protective laws, Shobha Saxena, Deep and Deep Publications Pvt Ltd, New Delhi, 2008, 1st edn (4th reprint) (page 118)

[129] *Ibid.*

[130] *Supra* note 4 at 8.

[131] Paras Diwan, *Law relating to Dowry, Dowry Deaths, Bride Burning, Rape and Related Offences* 12 (Universal Law Publishing co. Pvt. Ltd.,Delhi, 2002).

recommendations to amend Indian Penal Laws,[132] Procedural Laws,[133] and law related to Evidence[134]. These amendments were regarding the insertion of some new provisions and offences like cruelty[135], dowry death[136] and presumptions related to these offences in law of evidence[137]. Various steps have been taken to strengthen the laws in prohibiting the custom of dowry as well as to curb harassment of women for dowry. Giving and taking of dowry has been made cognizable offences, cruelty to wife including coercing her for dowry has also been made criminal offence. It has been made mandatory to conduct investigation by police and magistrate, every time when the death of any married women has been occurred in the abnormal circumstances within the initial seven years of her marriage. [138] Numerous provisions have been incorporated in the IPC to control the dowry related crimes against women. These provisions have strived hard in mitigating the offences like cruelty by husband and in-laws,[139] dowry murders,[140] abetment to commit suicides[141]. The Dowry Prohibition Act, 1961 was specifically enacted to eradicate the custom of dowry completely from the society. Sections 113A[142] and 113B[143] were incorporated in the Evidence Law

2.3 The Custom of Dowry gradually became the Menace of Society

Dowry which was originally a traditional practice, custom, a way of displaying one's wealth, and a basis for the woman's happy and comfortable life has today reached the position of being a menace to the societies. Historically, dowry has been an integral part of Hindu marriage system. It originated from the concept of *Kanyadana* with gifts, ornaments, expensive clothes and later on accustomed as a social ritual. The modern phenomenon of dowry however reflects a change in this customary system whereby, the presentation of gifts has no longer remained a voluntary process. Gradually a trend was started to coerce the bride's family to

---

[132] The Indian Penal Code, 1860.
[133] The Criminal Procedure Code, 1973.
[134] The Indian Evidence Act, 1872.
[135] Section 498 A, The Indian Code, 1860.
[136] Section 304 B, The Indian Penal Code, 1860.
[137] Section 113 A, Section 113 B, The Indian Evidence Act, 1872.
[138] Crimes against women and protective laws, Shobha Saxena, Deep and Deep Publications Pvt Ltd, New Delhi, 2008, 1st edn (4th reprint) (page 118)
[139] Section 498 A, The Indian Code, 1860.
[140] Section 304 B, The Indian Penal Code, 1860.
[141] Section 306, The Indian Penal Code, 1860.
[142] Section 113 A, The Indian Evidence Act, 1872.
[143] Section 113 B, The Indian Evidence Act, 1872.

provide dowry in the name of gift-giving. More often the bridegroom's family settles the amount of dowry on the basis of its own socio-economic status. Repercussions of this deformed custom of dowry are evident in the agonizing experiences of the bride's family and in the destruction of traditional moral values of society. It has created an imbalance and disturbance in society as inadequate dowry or the failure to meet the demands of dowry often causes humiliation, harassment and even torture and death of brides. Unfortunately, the dowry system has not become a fast disappearing remnant of traditional society but rather it has emerged as an expanding and deep rooted custom in modern Indian society.[144]

In a wider perspective, the studies of the other societies of the world indicate that the custom of dowry is not only confined to Indian society. The traces of dowry as well bride-price are found in various marriage forms in the tribal and urban societies of Africa and Europe.[145] In this way, in olden times in Hindu culture, the kind of sense in which the custom of dowry is taken nowadays was absolutely obscure. Male and female appreciated correspondence of status and society. Women were viewed as living goddesses where women lived in harmony, congruity and with poise and status. Divine beings were believed to meander about in human structures, when a newly wedded bride was brought into the family it was viewed as an incredible occasion and it was viewed as carrying fortune into the family not by bringing dowry but rather by virtue of the elegance and fortune the young woman bore with her.

Female infanticide, dowry harassment, dowry death, matchless marriages and financial burden in the girl's house are not due to the second stage in the history of dowry. It is a social cruelty resulting out of the male mentality to demand dowry compulsorily, the competitive spirit of the girl's family in the name of custom. Since dowry is a chance to enhance their economic position, men try to keep it in practice. Some women support it because they want to create a good impression about them at the time of marriage, to be held in high esteem in the husband's family and they do not like to wait till the last days of their parents for the property right.[146]

---

[144] *Supra* note 23 at 17.
[145] *Id.* at 33.
[146] S. Gokilwani, S. Gabriel Jelestin, *Marriage, Dowry, Practice and Divorce* (Regal Publications New Delhi, 2008).
[146] *Ibid.*

CHAPTER 3
LEGISLATIVE MEASURES ON LAW RELATED TO DOWRY PROHIBITION

Over the most recent couple of decades, women in India have confronted the offences related to domestic violence, wife battering, cruelty, dowry and dowry death in a more intense form than the past[1]. From time to time piecemeal changes have been brought about in the legislative framework in order to deal with issues and offences related to dowry. Numerous laws have been enacted and implemented to curb these dowry related crimes against women as well as to raise the status of women. In spite of such legislative efforts, the women are still being oppressed in the society because of the continuance of the evil of dowry which is somehow directly or indirectly responsible for most of other kinds of violence against women. The dowry prohibition laws aim to keep a check over the custom of giving and demanding dowry in connection to the marriage since this custom has acquired an ugly form of a tool of oppression and harassment of the bride and her parents. In many cases, the failure of bride's parents to meet dowry demands result in occurrence of some severe crimes against the brides like cruelty, dowry death, abetment to suicide etc. The non fulfillment of dowry demands result in coercion, harassment, infliction of mental and physical torture to women and in extreme cases they may be strangulated, poisoned or burnt alive. [2]

3.1 Initial Legislative Attempts related to Dowry Prohibition

Though dowry was in its whispering stage, the first attempt related to dowry prohibition was done with the enactment of "Sindh Deti-Leti Act, 1939".[3] It prohibited

---

[1]   National Crime Records Bureau, Report: *Crime in India, 2016 Statistics* (Ministry of Home Affairs, October, 2017) *available at*: http://ncrb.gov.in/Sta tPublications/CII/CII 2016/pdfs/ NEWPDFs /Crime%20in%20India%20-%202016%20Complete%20PDF%20291117.pdf (Visited on April 21, 2018).

[2]   C.S. Ambili, "Domestic Violence : Problems and Perspectives" *CULR* 129 (2003) *available at*: http://dspace.cusat.ac.in/jspui/bitstream/123456789/10826/1/Domestic%20Violence%20_%20Probl ems%20and%20Perspectives.PDF(Visited on October 12, 2016).

[3]   Vinay Sharma, *Dowry Deaths* 22(Deep and Deep Publications, New Delhi, 2007) *available at*: https://books.google.co.in/books?id=xQM3qauAHncC&pg=PA22&lpg=PA22&dq=Sindh+Deti-Leti+Act,+1939&source=bl&ots=XjUZbccMcP&sig=ACfU3U0-dvH6J4XY5h3wpiyYJKD43fs1jw&hl=en&sa=X&ved=2ahUKEwidz7eU8uHmAhUpxzgGHaofCF

the giving and taking of any valuable article or dowry beyond permissible limit prescribed by the list enumerated by the *panchayats* or provincial governments.[4] The next step was "Bihar Dowry Restraint Act, 1950"[5] and "The Andhra Pradesh Dowry Prohibition Act, 1958"[6]. Although the provincial enactments could not bring the desired results, but they stimulated the general public to raise a voice against dowry as the dowry system started strangulating the peace of society.[7] Perhaps the Central government felt that "The Hindu Succession Act, 1956"[8] may be a suitable alternative to the eradication of dowry system as many provisions in the Act were made with regard to the women. All these enactments appeared to be really pro-women but due to the lack of effective awareness, and proper utilization, most of the Acts merely remained on papers rather than curbing the menace of dowry.[9]

In view of the persistent nature of the problem and thereby adverse consequences of dowry system, "The Dowry Prohibition Bill, 1959" was introduced on 24th April, 1959 with an objective of eradicating the evil of dowry system.[10] The underlying object behind this bill was to prohibit the giving and taking of dowry in connection to the marriage.

3.2 Making of Anti- Dowry Legislation

On 24th April, 1959, "The Dowry Prohibition Bill, 1959" was introduced by the government. After a discussion and introduction of several changes, it was further moved to the joint committee.[11] Finally the bill was taken into the consideration at a joint sitting of *Rajya Sabha* as well as *Lok Sabha* and was passed on 1st July 1961. Therefore after a long awaited time period, "The Dowry Prohibition Act, 1961" was finally enacted to curb the menace of dowry with an objective of eradicating this

---

cQ6AEwEnoECAkQAQ#v=onepage&q=Sindh%20Deti-Leti%20Act%2C%201939&f=false (Visited on February 10, 2019).

[4] The Sindh Deti-Leti Act, 1939 *available at*: http://sindhlaws.gov.pk/setup/publications/PUB-14-000155.pdf(Visited on May 22, 2019).

[5] R. Jaganmohan Rao, "Dowry System in India—a Socio-Legal Approach to the Problem" 15 *JILI* 618 (1973) *available at*: https://www.jstor.org/stable/43950234?seq=1(Visited on May 22, 2019).

[6] *Supra* note 3.

[7] Suman Nalwa and Hari Dev Kohli, *Law Relating to Dowry, Dowry Death, Cruelty to Women & Domestic Violence 26* (Universal Law Publication Co., New Delhi, 2013).

[8] The Hindu Succession Act, 1956 *available at*: http://egazette.nic.in/WriteReadData/1956/E-2173-1956-0038-99150.pdf (Visited on April 24, 2018).

[9] R. Revathi, *Law Relating to Domestic violence* 66 (Asia Law House, Hyderabad, 2004).

[10] *Supra* note 7.

[11] *Id. at 30*

practice[12]. This Act is considered to be a remedial as well as a penal statute simultaneously.[13] Originally, there were ten Sections in the Act and afterwards Sections 4A,[14] 8A[15] and 8B[16] were further added by the Amendment[17]. Section 2 defines the term 'Dowry' and Section 3 prescribes the punishment for giving and taking dowry. Dowry is defined as any property or valuable security given or agreed to be given either directly or indirectly.

(a) By one party to a marriage to the other party to the marriage, or

(b) By the parent of either party to a marriage or by any other person, to either party to the marriage or to any other person, on or before or any time after the marriage in connection with the marriage of the said parties, the definition of Dowry does not include dower or *mahr* in case of persons who are governed by Muslim Personal Law (*Shariat*).

The Amendment Act of 1984 has deleted the Explanation I of Section 2.[18] However Explanation II explains that the meaning of the term "valuable security" is same as given in the Section 30 of I.P.C.[19]

There are generally three types of the traditional presents that can be given to a bride in a Hindu marriage:

---

[12] The Dowry Prohibition Act, 1961
[13] *Gurditta Singh* v. *State of Rajasthan*, 1992 Cri LJ 309.
[14] Section 4A Ban on advertisement.—If any person—
  (a) offers, through any advertisement in any newspaper, periodical, journal or through any other media, any share in his property or of any money or both as a share in any business or other interest as consideration for the marriage of his son or daughter or any other relative,
  (b) prints or publishes or circulates any advertisement referred to in clause (a),
  He shall be punishable with imprisonment for a term which shall not be less than six months, but which may extend to five years, or with fine which may extend to fifteen thousand rupees. Provided that the Court may, for adequate and special reasons to be recorded in the judgment, impose a sentence of imprisonment for a term of less than six months.
[15] Section 8A, The Dowry Prohibition Act, 1961
[16] Section 8B, The Dowry Prohibition Act, 1961
[17] The Dowry Prohibition (Amendment) Act, 1986
[18] *Ibid.*
[19] Section 30 "Valuable security".—The words "valuable security" denote a document which is, or purports to be, a document whereby any legal right is created, extended, transferred, restricted, extinguished or released, or where by any person acknowledges that he lies under legal liability, or has not a certain legal right. Illustration A writes his name on the back of a bill of exchange. As the effect of this endorsement is transfer the right to the bill to any person who may become the lawful holder of it, the endorsement is a "valuable security".

(i)   Property or valuable articles that are given with an intention that those would be exclusively and personally used by the bride like her personal jewellery, clothes etc.

(ii) Articles or property of dowry which may be for common utilization or use by her and the other members living in her matrimonial home.

(iii) Articles or property exclusively given as gifts to her husband or the in-laws and other members of her husband's family. There is no control of the bride on such items and valuable property, once it is gifted.

Consequently, the third type of gifts, property or valuable articles given exclusively to the husband or his relatives after delivery would pass into their ownership and obviously seize to be the property of the bride.[20] The first category of gifts are generally considered as *'Stridhan'*, however the second and third category may fall under the ambit of dowry if the other essentials of Section 2 are fulfilled.

Difference between Dowry and *'Stridhan'*

The word *'Stridhan'* literally means property of a woman. This concept has originated from Hindu *'Smritis'*, the traces of its origin are also found in D*ayabhaga* and *Mitakshara* school of Hindu law.[21] Centuries ago, gifts given to the bride at the nuptial fire, at the bridal procession, gifts given as a token of love by in-laws as well as gifts given by her own parents and relatives were considered to be her *'Stridhan'*. For determining the issue that whether a particular kind of property acquired by a woman is covered under the ambit of *Stridhan* or not the source of acquiring that property has to be scrutinized. However, the gifts made to the bridegroom or his relatives by the parents or relatives of bride during and after marriage are not considered as *stridhan.*[22]

Stridhan is quite often misunderstood or misinterpreted as dowry even though the judiciary has time to time made a clear cut distinction between the two. Dowry

---

[20]   P.K. Majumdar & R.P. Kataria, *Law relating to Dowry Prohibition cruelty & Harassment* 231 (Orient Publishing Company, New Delhi, 3rd Edition).

[21]   Shreeparna Dutta, "Property Rights of Hindu Women in India – A Reflection of Social Change 1(2) *JLAR* 72 (2014) available at: http://www.ijlp.in/ijlp/imageS/Volume-1,%20Issue-2,%20June-14.pdf (Visited on August 12, 2018).

[22]   Mukund Sarda, "Claim of Stridhan Property and Limitation Period: A Study" A*vailable at:* https://papers.ssrn.com/sol3/papers.cfm?abstract_id=2758031(Visited on Sep 22, 2019).

signifies the presents given to the married couple or the bridegroom as well his relatives in connection to the marriage by the bride's side however *Stridhan* is the property or valuables exclusively given to the bride or meant for the bride only.[23]

Dowry is a property or valuable security given or agreed by the bride's side to the bridegroom or his family members before, during or after marriage, by pressurizing or demanding while *Stridhan* is a voluntary gift by the parents or family of the bride which is exclusively given to the bride as a venturing stone to building up her own assets and strengthening her household.[24] "When the wife entrusts her *Stridhan* property with the dominion over that property to her husband or any other member of the family and the husband or such other member of the family dishonestly misappropriates or converts to his own use that property, or willfully suffers and other person to do so, he commits criminal breach of trust".[25] Therefore *stridhan* and dowry are not synonyms as *stridhan* is permitted but dowry is clearly prohibited under the law.[26]

Meaning of the Expression- 'given or agreed to be given'

The legislative intention is clear that there should not be any grey area left in the definition for any manipulation by the people. There is no such loophole left where the people may resort camouflage methods and take dowry articles either before the marriage or after the marriage. Henceforth, the expression "given or agreed to be given" has been incorporated very wisely. This expression is used to give a wide coverage to the demand of dowry and impliedly covers the acceptance to such demand as well.[27]

The scope of the term dowry is widely defined so as to include all kinds of properties, valuable articles, gifts, cash etc., given, taken; agreed to be, agreed to be taken; given directly or indirectly.[28] The word 'dowry' can be any valuable article, cash, and property etc; given or agreed to be given in connection with the

---

[23] *Shyam M. Sachdev* v. *State*, 1991 Cri LJ 300

[24] Leepakshi Rajpal and Mayank Vats, "Stridhana: A Critical Approach"7 *IJRSSH* 89 (2017), 89 *available at:* http://www.ijrssh.com/images/short_pdf/1501650266_Leepakshi_9.pdf (Visited on Sep 22, 2019).

[25] *Rashmi Kumar* v. *Mahesh Kumar Bhada*, (1997) 2 SCC 397.

[26] Section 3, The Dowry Prohibition Act, 1961.

[27] *Supra* note 6 at 34.

[28] *Vemuri Venkateswara Rao* v. *State of Andhra Pradesh*, 1992 Cri LJ 563

marriage.[29]It is within the scope of this Section if such valuables are given exactly at the time of the marriage or even before the time of marriage and even afterwards when the marriage has already occurred.[30]

"Dowry" in the meaning of the expression contemplated by Dowry Act is a fulfillment of demand or a demand for any valuable article, property or security having an inseparable connection with the marriage. It may be understood as a consideration for marriage from the bride's parents or relatives to the bride-groom or his parents or even may be to the other relatives for an agreement to marry the bride and keep the nuptial relation harmonious. However, where there is no connection or nexus with the consideration for the marriage of such a demand, it does not amount to a demand for dowry.[31] The Supreme Court has strictly remarked that "furnishing of a list of ornaments and other household articles such as refrigerator, furniture, electrical appliances, etc., at the time of the settlement of the marriage amounts to demand of dowry within the meaning of Section 2 of the Dowry Prohibition Act, 1961".[32] But in a situation where the legal validity of a marriage cannot be established, a demand of dowry in respect of such a marriage is not legally recognizable[33]

Distinction between *Mahr*, Dower and Dowry

Mahr, dower and dowry are entirely different concepts. While on one side dowry is a social evil against woman and is prohibited by law, on the other side, the object of dower is to provide financial security to a woman during and after her marriage and it is legally well permitted.

Mahr differs from dowry in both legal as well as social aspects. According to the Muslim Personal Law, *'Mahr'* is a predetermined amount of money, assets or benefits that is bestowed with the wife which she is entitled to collect from husband. The underlying object is to provide independence to the wife and enable an indirect check over the husband's arbitrary power of taking divorce.[34]

---

[29] *Satbir Singh* v. *State of Punjab*, AIR 2001 SC 2828.
[30] B.K Sharma and Vijay Nagpal, *Treatise on Economic & Social Offences* 111(Allahabad Law Agency, Faridabad, 2010)
[31] *Arjun Dhondiba Kamble* v. *State of Maharashtra*, 1995 AIHC 273.
[32] *Madhu Sudan Malhotra* v. *K.C. Bhandari*, 1988 SCC 424
[33] *Reena Aggarwal* v. *Anupam*, AIR 2004 SC 1418.
[34] Md Sahabuddin Mondal, "Difference between Mahr and Dowry" *available at:* https://lawcorner.in/difference between-mahr-dowry/(Visited on Sep 22, 2018).

In *Saburannessa* v. *Sabdu Sheikh*, it was clearly held by the Calcutta High Court that "dower is an obligation imposed as a mark of respect for the women and not a consideration for the performance of the contract of marriage"[35]. *'Jahez'* is a term used in Islam for dowry and it is strictly prohibited under the Islamic Law. *'Jahez'* is regarded as a social and cultural evil in Islam and highly condemned. However, the concept of *'Mahr'* is considered to be an epitome of women empowerment under Islamic Law. It is considered as a right which is conferred to the wife/bride unlike the evil of dowry where a wrongful liability is imposed on the wife/bride or her family. *Mahr* is viewed as a tool for providing equality to the women in a different sense and giving a voice to them. *Mahr* has a significant importance in Muslim marriages as it acts as a tool to provide protection to the women against the discretionary abuse of the unlimited power of divorce conferred with the husband.

Punishment for Giving or Taking Dowry

Section 3 and 4 provide punishment for giving or taking dowry as well as demanding dowry which may extend to five years sentence and a minimum fine of fifteen thousand rupees or the fine equal to the amount of the total value of such dowry. Any person directly or indirectly demanding dowry, from the parents or other relatives or guardian of either side, shall be liable for a minimum sentence of six months and a maximum imprisonment of two years along with ten thousand rupees fine. Hence mere demanding any kind of dowry before marriage even without the fulfillment of such a demand is also a punishable offence.[36]

The Punjab and Haryana High Court also opined that if any kind of list of jewellery or any other household item is furnished before marriage as a settlement of conditions of marriage, it amounts to the offence of demanding dowry and the persons involved are liable to be convicted under Section 4.[37] Giving or receiving dowry or even abetment for giving or receiving dowry, after the commencement of this Act is prohibited by Section 3 of the Act[38]. However, there shall not be any retrospective application of the Act.[39]

---

[35] AIR 1934 Cal 693.
[36] *Pandurang Shivram Kawathkar* v. *State of Maharashtra*, 2001 Cri LJ 2792.
[37] *Raksha Devi* v. *Aruna Devi*, I (1991) DMC 46 (P&H).
[38] Section 3, The Dowry Prohibition Act, 1961.
[39] *Supra* note 20 at 246.

Essentials of Section 2 must be satisfied to Invoke Section 3 and 4.

It is essential that to bring a case under the ambit of Section 3 or 4, the ingredients of Section 2 must be fulfilled. It means that there must be a demand of dowry 'or giving or taking of 'dowry'. Precisely, the valuables or property in question must be covered under the definition of 'Dowry' as given in Section 2. Moreover, such a demand must be of the valuables, property or money agreed to be given in relation to the marriage of parties.[40] If the evidence on record is adequate to prove that the accused received a sum of two thousand rupees and ten gram of gold during marriage and same were demanded as dowry and were not accepted as gifts, thereby, conviction under Section 3 and 4 is confirmed.[41]

In a related case, *Bhoora Singh* v. *State of Uttar Pradesh*[42], a letter was produced as evidence which was written by the deceased to her father. The repeated incidents of her ill-treatment, harassments and threats of dire consequences for non-satisfaction of demands of dowry given by her in-laws were clearly mentioned by the deceased in that letter. After some time of writing that letter, she was burnt to death by her in-laws by setting her on fire. The Court held that the evidence was sufficient to hold that an offence of demanding dowry under Section 4 had been committed.

Section 4 A puts a ban on any kind of advertisement on giving or taking of dowry.[43] It penalizes any offering any share in the property or any cash or both or any other interest as consideration in connection to the marriage by any person in the marriage of his son/ daughter or any other relative; by publishing or giving or circulating any advertisement in a newspaper, periodical, journal, or through any means of media. The minimum imprisonment for this offence is six months and the

---

[40] *Id.* at 259.
[41] *State* v. *Shivappa Bhimappa Pathat*, 2003 (2) Kar LJ 171.
[42] 1993 Cri LJ 2636 All.
[43] Section 4A Ban on advertisement.—If any person—
  (a) offers, through any advertisement in any newspaper, periodical, journal or through any other media, any share in his property or of any money or both as a share in any business or other interest as consideration for the marriage of his son or daughter or any other relative,
  (b) prints or publishes or circulates any advertisement referred to in clause (a), he shall be punishable with imprisonment for a term which shall not be less than six months, but which may extend to five years, or with fine which may extend to fifteen thousand rupees.
  Provided that the Court may, for adequate and special reasons to be recorded in the judgment, impose a sentence of imprisonment for a term of less than six months, The Dowry Prohibition Act, 1961.

maximum is five years, or a fine of maximum of fifteen thousand rupees. However, the court may, if finds adequate, then may impose an imprisonment of less than six months after recording special reasons in the judgment.

Section 5 clearly states that any kind of agreement that constitutes giving or receiving dowry is void. Therefore, such kind of agreement is not enforceable under law. In case of void agreements, the law refuses to give effect to it, it means that even if an agreement to give or take dowry is carried out, the person promising to pay dowry cannot be legally forced to pay the dowry which he has promised and therefore if the promisee seeks to enforce it, the Court will not help him.[44]

Section 6 is the result of the Joint Committee Report presented by both houses of Parliament at the time of legislation of "Dowry Prohibition Act, 1961". Consequently, changes were made by virtue of the Amendment Acts of 1984 and 1986. The prime objective was to wipe off the social image of the women of being an economic burden and to improve their financial condition by protecting their material assets.

The Section 6 provides that if dowry is received by any person other than the bride, such a person must transfer it to the woman within a stipulated time and on failure to do so, the person is punishable with imprisonment or fine. Secondly, if the woman/bride entitled to such property dies before receiving it, then the legal heirs of the woman are entitled to claim it. Thirdly, if such woman dies within seven years of her marriage in unnatural circumstances, then such property shall be transferred to her heirs. Failure to do so shall attract imprisonment or fine under Section 6.

Thus, by virtue of this Section, dowry is to be for the benefit of the bride or her legal heirs and any violation for the same amounts to criminality and shall be punishable.[45] Section 6 of the D.P.A. aims at the benefit of such woman/wife/bride whose property has been illegally retained by her husband or any other person receiving such property on her husband's behalf and when they are not ready to return back such property to her.[46] However it is no where mentioned under Section 6 that

---

[44] *Supra* note 6 at 78.
[45] *Id. at 83*
[46] *Aimla Jayaram* v. *State of Andhra Pradesh*, 1992 Cr LJ 2217.

the dowry items can be claimed back by the wife only after the marriage is dissolved.[47] It cannot be assumed that the parents of the bridegroom take dowry from the parents of the bride only for and on behalf of the bridegroom. So they cannot always claim that they do not receive any dowry. In fact, it is being observed very often that the parents of the bridegroom are greedy who actually want to have the dowry and take dowry. Therefore, parents of the bridegroom can be summoned for committing an offence under Section 6.[48]

The person receiving dowry assets is legally liable to transfer these assets to his wife within a prescribed time period. On failing to do the same, the wife may file a complaint against him even at a place where she is residing and the husband can be prosecuted on such complaint.[49]

Criminal Breach of Trust on Illegally Retaining Dowry Articles

Section 406 of I.P.C. is invoked where the husband or in-laws do not transfer the property of dowry to the wife or her legal heirs in the situations mentioned under Section 6. On failure to do so a proceeding under the offence of criminal breach of trust can be initiated at either of the place where the property was received or retained or the place of occurrence of criminal breach of trust.[50]

Section 7 provides for cognizance of offences of dowry and says that, the offence under this provision is only triable in the court of metropolitan magistrate or a judicial magistrate of first class or a court superior to that. The cognizance of this offence can only be taken by the court at its own knowledge or on a police report containing the facts of such offence or on the filing of complaint by the aggrieved person, parents or relatives of aggrieved person or by a recognized welfare organization. The aggrieved person shall not be dragged for the prosecution on the basis of the statement made by him or her. Section 7(3) of D.P.A. bars cognizance of complaint against the person aggrieved.[51] It is not necessary that only the victim

[47] *Joginder Kumar Bansal* v. *Anju*, 1989 All LJ 914.
[48] *Supra* note 6 at 85
[49] *P.T.S. Saibaba* v. *Mangatyara*, 1978 Cri LJ 1362.
[50] *Harjit Kaur* v. *Baldeo Singh*, 1980 HLR 373
[51] *Supra* note 20 at 231.

girl/bride be considered as 'aggrieved person'. Even father of the victim girl, who was compelled to give dowry can be considered as an aggrieved person.[52]

The Act has not defined the meaning of the expression 'to take cognizance' nor is defined in Cr PC. However, the term 'cognizance' indicates the point when the judicial notice of an offence is taken by the Magistrate.[53] The legality of cognizance can be determined at the point of time when the cognizance of an offence is actually taken by the court. [54] Any of these five situations must be fulfilled as a pre-requisite to take cognizance under this provision:

- If a complaint has been made by a person aggrieved by this offence,
- If a complaint has been made by the parent of aggrieved person,
- If a complaint has been made by the relative of aggrieved person,
- If a complaint has been made by any welfare institution or organization,
- The court can take cognizance at its own knowledge.

Section 8 states that every offence prescribed under the Act shall be cognizable for certain purposes, and will be non-bailable as well as non-compoundable in nature. It is to be noted that the offences prescribed under the Act are cognizable for the purposes specified under Section 8(1)(a)(b) and this concept "cognizable" is substituted by the Amendment Act of 1984.[55]

The offences under the Act are non bailable and if the criteria of granting bail are fulfilled and the court is satisfied upon the same, only then the bail can be granted. By making these non bailable, the Legislature has tried to give biting teeth to the provision to curb the evil of dowry.

A very important provision Section 8A was inserted in D.P.A. in the year 1986.[56] It states that if a person is prosecuted under Section 3 of the Act for taking or

---

[52] *Yashpal Kumar* v. *Bhola Nath Khanna, available at:* https://indiankanoon.org/doc/160230226/
[53] *Darshan Singh* v. *State of Maharashtra*, AIR 1971 SC 2372.
[54] *M.L. Sethi* v. *R.P. Kapur*, AIR 1967 SC 528.
[55] Section 8- Offences to be cognizable for certain purposes and to be bailable and non-compoundable.—
(1) The Code of Criminal Procedure, 1973 (2 of 1974) shall apply to offences under this Act as if they were cognizable offences—
(a) for the purposes of investigation of such offences; and
(b) for the purposes of matters other than—
(i) matters referred to in section 42 of that Code; and
(ii) the arrest of a person without a warrant or without an order of a Magistrate, The Dowry Prohibition Act, 1961.
[56] The Dowry Prohibition (Amendment) Act, 1986

abetting to take dowry or demanding dowry under Section 4, the burden of proof shall lie on him to prove that he has not committed any offence.[57]

This provision effectively protects the socio-economic interest of Indian women. It is based on the pattern of Sec 113A and 113B of Evidence Act[58]. By shifting the burden of proof on the accused, the woman is absolved of the burden of establishing the guilt of the accused. However, the initial burden of bringing the accused within the circumference still lies on the prosecution, as essentials of term 'dowry' must be proved to have been fulfilled in accordance with Section 2 of Dowry Prohibition Act. It signifies that Section 8(a) must be read with Section 2 of the Act.[59] This provision has been inserted by the Amendment Act of 1985. The burden to prove is placed on the shoulders of the person himself, against whom allegations of committing an offence of either abetting or taking dowry is made.[60]

The provision has been challenged as constitutionally invalid on the ground of violating fundamental rights provided under Article 20(3)[61], 21[62] and 14[63] of the Constitution of India. But Section 8(a) was not found to be suffering from any constitutional infirmity.[64]

Section 8B was inserted by "Dowry Prohibition (Amendment) Act 1986" that empowers the State to appoint Dowry Prohibition Officers. These officers shall exercise and perform all the powers and functions for the prevention of dowry related offence and to collect evidences for the prosecution of persons committing offences. It further empowers the Dowry Prohibition Officer to file complaint in the cases of dowry.[65] This provision is inserted with an aim to create a social instrument designed to eradicate the dowry practice from the society. The objective of this Section is a

---

[57] Section 8A-Burden of proof in certain cases.—Where any person is prosecuted for taking or abetting the taking of any dowry under section 3, or the demanding of dowry under section 4, the burden of proving that he had not committed an offence under those sections shall be on him, The Dowry Prohibition Act, 1961.

[58] See Sections 113A and 113B, The Indian Evidence Act, 1872

[59] *Supra* note 6 at 122.

[60] *Pawan Kumar* v. *State of Haryana*, 1998 (2) CC Cases SC 12.

[61] Article 20(3) - Protection in respect of conviction for offences- No person accused of any offence shall be compelled to be a witness against himself, The Constitution of India.

[62] Article 21- Protection of life and personal liberty- No person shall be deprived of his life or personal liberty except according to procedure established by law, The Constitution of India.

[63] Article 14- Equality before law.-The State shall not deny to any person equality before the law or the equal protection of the laws within the territory of India. Prohibition of discrimination on grounds of religion, race, caste, sex or place of birth, The Constitution of India.

[64] *Harikumar* v. *State of Karnataka*, ILR 1993 KAR 3035.

[65] *Yogesh Chhibbar* v. *State of U.P.*, 2000 Cri LJ 2849.

conscious step to employ social means to curb this evil but unfortunately the practical implementation of this Section is lingering on. However, it appears that the D.P.A has been over shadowed by the insertion of some provisions of Indian Penal Code.[66]

Section 9 and Section 10 have empowered the Central Government[67] and the State Government to make rules for carrying out the purposes of this Act by making a notification in the respective Official Gazettes.[68]

3.2.1 The Dowry Prohibition (Maintenance of the Lists of Presents to the Bride and Bridegroom) Rules, 1985

With an objective to provide teeth to dowry prohibition laws, the Central Government has decided to make it compulsory for the bride and bridegroom to make a list of gifts and valuable articles given and taken during the wedding ceremonies. These dowry prohibition Rules[69] mandate the listing of gifts to ensure that the gifts given in the form of money, jewellery, clothes, and other articles presented to the bride at, before or after the marriage were exclusively given for her benefit and must be mentioned in the list as well as registered.[70] These lists must be made in writing, shall contain the brief description of the presents and must be duly signed by the bride and bridegroom respectively.[71] The non- compliance of these rules and non-maintenance of such list can result into the imprisonment of up to three years for bride, bride groom and even for their parents.

3.3 Dowry Related Offences Covered under Indian Penal Code

The occurrence of 'dowry offences' is one such manifestation of imbalanced power equations and gender violation, to which the married woman are subjected. [72]There are certain offences related to dowry which are covered under Indian Penal Code.

---

[66] *Supra* note 6 at 124.
[67] Section 9, The Dowry Prohibition Act, 1961.
[68] Section 10, The Dowry Prohibition Act, 1961.
[69] The Dowry Prohibition (Maintenance of the Lists of Presents to the Bride and Bridegroom) Rules, 1985
[70] Mamta Rao, *Law Relating to Woman and Children* 137 (Eastern Book Company, Lucknow, 2012).
[71] Rule 2 (2), The Dowry Prohibition (Maintenance of the Lists of Presents to the Bride and Bridegroom) Rules, 1985.
[72] *Supra* note 9 at V.

In the year 1986, a new provision of 'cruelty' u/sec 498A has been added through an amendment.[73] Under this Section, there is a provision of punishing husband or his relatives for subjecting the wife for any kind of cruelty for demand of dowry or which may drive her to commit suicide.[74] The maximum punishment is three years for committing this offence.[75]

3.3.1 Dowry Death (Section 304B)

In 1980s, the incidents of bride burning were increasing day by day and hence had become a matter of concern for the Law Commission of India as well. After realizing the need of a separate penal procedure, the Law Commission has submitted its 91st Report on "Dowry Deaths and Law Reforms" on 10th August 1983. [76] It has been amply realized that the already the existing laws were facing huge difficulty in getting sufficient evidence to prove guilt in bride burning cases. Hence, the Commission also opined to institute a new provision facilitating a presumption in dowry deaths once several essentials are proved.[77]

Section 304B in penal law and Section 113B in the law of evidence, both were added for curbing the rapid increase in dowry murders, by the amendment of 1986.[78] The main objective behind these two insertions was to overcome the challenges in collecting evidence, by adding presumptions. [79] An unfortunate part of dowry murders is that such crimes occur within the enclosed four walls of matrimonial home of

---

[73] Section 498A, The Indian Penal Code, 1860.

[74] Vijay Pal Singh, "Bride burning and Laws in India", *available at:* http://www.legalserviceindia.com/articles/brbu (Visited on January 01, 2017).

[75] Section 498A Husband or relative of husband of a woman subjecting her to cruelty
Whoever, being the husband or the relative of the husband of a woman, subjects such woman to cruelty shall be punished with imprisonment for a term which may extend to three years and shall also be liable to fine.
Explanation- For the purpose of this section, "cruelty" means-
(a) any willful conduct which is of such a nature as is likely to drive the woman to commit suicide or to cause grave injury or danger to life, limb or health (whether mental or physical) of the woman; or
(b) harassment of the woman where such harassment is with a view to coercing her or any person related to her to meet any unlawful demand for any property or valuable security or is on account of failure by her or any person related to her to meet such demand.

[76] Law Commission of India, 91st Report on Dowry Deaths and Law Reform: Amending The Hindu Marriage Act, 1955, The Indian Penal Code 1860 and The Indian Evidence Act, 1872, (August, 1983) *available at:* http://lawcommissionofindia.nic.in/51-100/Report91.pdf (Visited on January 11, 2017).

[77] *Dhan Singh* v. *State of U.P*, 2012 Cr L J3 136(All).

[78] The Dowry Prohibition (Amendment) Act, 1986

[79] *Kunhiabdulla* v. *State of Kerela*, AIR 2004 SC 1731.

victim. The offenders are often her in-laws, husband who are close relative of each other. [80] Therefore, the chances are very rare that they will act as witness or produce any evidence against each other.

The Meaning of 'Dowry' under Section 304B

The Indian Penal Code has not given any definition of the term 'dowry' in the Act. [81] However it is mentioned in the Section 304B that the term 'dowry' shall be having the same meaning as is given under Section 2(1) of "Dowry Prohibition Act, 1961". [82] Dowry is defined as any kind of property or valuable security which is given or which either of the party agrees to give directly or indirectly to another. [83] It can be given before the marriage, at the marriage or after the marriage. '*Mahr*' and 'Dower' are not included in the term dowry.

Very often it has been remarked by several courts that the term is not confined to an agreement or demand which has been done before the marriage or at the time of marriage, rather any subsequent demand even after the solemnization of marriage is also covered within the ambit of dowry. [84]

The Meaning of 'Otherwise, than in Normal Circumstances'

Another essential of Section 304B is that the death must be occurred under some unnatural or abnormal circumstances. Very often the Apex Court has remarked that it means that the occurrence of death was in an unusual course and suspicious circumstances were present. Even if a woman has committed suicide within 7 years of her marriage, it could not be considered as a death occurred in normal circumstances. [85] The legislative intent behind the insertion of this provision was undoubtedly the protection of women from husband and in-laws against dowry related violence and murder. [86] But it does not mean that the in-laws or relatives of husband of any deceased could be merely roped on the grounds that they are also covered within the meaning of close relatives. It must be proved beyond reasonable doubt that they have

---

[80] K.D.Gaur, *Commentary on the Indian Penal Code* 960 (Universal Law Publishing, 2013).
[81] *Shanti* v. *State of Haryana* AIR 1991, SC 1226.
[82] *Supra* note 80 at 957.
[83] Hari Singh Gour, *Penal Law of India*, (3) 3082 (Law Publishers (India) Pvt. Ltd, Allahabad, 2011)
[84] *State of Andhra Prades* v. *Raj Gopal Asawa*, (2004) 4 SCC 470.
[85] *Rajayyan* v. *State of Kerela*, AIR 1998 SC 1211.
[86] *Supra* note 83.

done some overt act in relation to the offence.[87] However, it is not essential that must be fulfilled under this provision to show that there was an agreement for payment of dowry. [88]

Section 304B besides, its own independent objective, is a synthesis of Sections 2 and 3 of the D.P.A. and Section 498A of I.P.C. Therefore, in order to invoke this Section, invocation of Sections 2 and 3 of D.P.A. and Section 498A of I.P.C. is essential and the ingredients of these Sections are ought to be satisfied.[89]

Essentials to Invoke Section 304B

- Death must be occurred by burning or bodily injury or under abnormal circumstances. The legislature has applied its wisdom and used the phrase "otherwise under normal circumstances", to avoid any kind of ambiguity or confusion. The interpretation is enlarged in such a way that only death under normal conditions is excluded from the ambit of Section 304.

- The death must occur within seven years of marriage.[90] It is the duty of the prosecution to prove that the death was caused within seven years of marriage. [91]

- The women must be subjected to cruelty or harassment, soon before her death. This expression is used in a narrow perspective and in a limited and specific sense as explained in Section 498A of I.P.C.[92] This expression, "cruelty" has to further qualify another condition that it must be in connection with any demand for dowry. Thereby, Sections 2 and 3 of D.P.A are inherently present.

- The cruelty must have been done in connection to any demand of dowry. Dowry has the same meaning as defined under Section 2 of D.P.A. "The term Dowry under Section 2 is wide enough to include all types of properties, valuable securities, etc., given or agreed to be given, directly or indirectly."[93]

---

[87] *Kans Raj* v. *State of Punjab*, 2000 Cr LJ 2993.
[88] *Vidhya Devi* v. *State of Haryana*, AIR 2004 SC 1757.
[89] See B.M. Gandhi, *Indian Penal Code* 436 (Eastern Book Company, Lucknow, 2014).
[90] Surendra Malik and Sudeep Malik, *Supreme Court on Indian Penal Code, 1860*, (3) 159 (Eastern Book Company, Lucknow, 2012)
[91] *Ibid.*
[92] *Supra* note 90 at 165.
[93] *Supra*. Note 28.

Liability under Section 304-B r/w Section 113B of Evidence Act

The provision of dowry death clearly states that liability of a person is attracted if it is shown that a woman has died due to unnatural death, within seven years of her marriage, was subjected to cruelty by her husband or relative of husband, soon before her death, in connection to the demand of dowry. If all these essentials are fulfilled than a presumption shall be taken by the court that such person has caused her dowry death. It will be immaterial that such person is directly responsible for her death or not[94]. So it can be concluded that merely by fulfillment of these essentials, presumption of guilt is taken irrespective of the presence or absence of any direct connection with death[95].

No Conviction under 304B if 'Cruelty' is not proved[96]

If dowry is not demanded before or at the marriage or there is no mention of ill-treatment of the deceased and no evidence of cruelty is produced than even the death of a wife occurred in unnatural circumstances even within the seven years of her wedding cannot attract conviction under Section 304B[97].

It must be proved that the victim was subjected to such cruelty 'Soon Before' her death. 'Soon before the death' is a relative term and there is no strait jacket formula that can be applied to determine the exact period which can be termed as 'soon before' the death[98]. It would depend on the circumstances of each case and may vary from case to case. Normally the interval between the death in question and the concerned cruelty inflicted on the victim must not be much.[99] There must be a proximate link between the effect of cruelty for dowry demand and the concerned death.[100] If the infliction of cruelty has become stale enough which can not disturb the mental set up of woman concerned, it cannot be considered[101]. But the term 'soon

---

[94] *Hem Chand* v. *State of Haryana*, (1994) 6 SCC 727.

[95] K.N. Chandrasekhran Pillai, *General Priciples of Criminal Law* 589-590 (Eastern Book Company, Lucknow, 2011).

[96] *Supra* note 92.

[97] *Meka Ramaswamy* v. *Dasari Mohan*, AIR 1998 SC 774.

[98] K.I. Vibhute, *P S A Pillai's Criminal Law* 606 (Lexis Nexis, Gurgaon, 2014).

[99] *Supra* note 90 at 173.

[100] Ram Jethmalani and D. S. Chopra, *The Indian Penal Code*, (2) 2491 (Thomson Reuters, Legal, New Delhi, 2014)

[101] *Satvir Singh* v. *State of Punjab*, AIR 2001 SC 2828.

before' is not a synonym for 'immediately before'[102]. In a related case of *Uday Chakraboty* v. *State of West Bengal[103]*, where the wife of accused died within two years of marriage as a result of burn injuries inflicted upon her, The Apex Court accepted the whole period of two years as 'soon before' her death and held the husband guilty[104].

The Charge under Section 302 and 304B may Co-exist

Sometimes, a question arises as to whether charge under Section 302, I.P.C. can co-exist with the charge under Section 304B, I.P.C. The gist of the offence punishable under Section 302 or the offence punishable under 304B is the same i.e. the extinction of life in unnatural circumstances. Nothing is mentioned in any of these two Sections to either expressly or impliedly exclude one Section if another of the two is applicable. However, in practice, it is too difficult to prove the ingredients of Section 302 and Section 304B of I.P.C. simultaneously. However, the charge under both the Sections may co-exist, but this view looks improbable. The ingredients of both the Sections are different; therefore, it is advisable to charge the person under either of the Sections. By applying both the Sections simultaneously, a situation may arise that the trial becomes vitiated because the prosecution cannot be allowed to adopt a "two version theory". [105]

3.3.2 Abetment of Suicide (Section 306)

To combat the increasing menace of the dowry deaths, Criminal Law (Second Amendment) Act, 1983 has provided a presumption. It states that where a suicide is committed by a married woman within seven years of marriage, the court may presume that her husband and in-laws had abetted her to commit suicide by virtue of Section 113A of Indian Evidence Act, 1872. [106]

It has been seen often that the victim of offences related to dowry commits suicide due to persistent demands. In such a case, the prosecution has to prove-

- The deceased committed suicide.

---

[102] *Supra* note 92 at 607.
[103] AIR 2010 SC 3506.
[104] *Uday Chakraboty* v. *State of West Bengal*, AIR 2010 SC 3506.
[105] *Supra* note 6 at 26
[106] Surendra Malik and Sudeep Malik, *Supreme Court on Evidence Act*, (2) 433(Eastern Book Company, Lucknow, 2013)

- The accused instigated or abetted for committing suicide.

- Direct involvement of the accused in such abetment or instigation.

In a related case, *Brig Lal* v. *Prem Chand*[107], the husband used to quarrel with his wife and had been constantly demanding dowry and money from her. On one unfortunate day she retaliated on these consistent demands of dowry and said that death would have been a better option than such a miserable life. The husband answered that he would be relieved if she would have died immediately. On listening to this, the wife set her ablaze. The Apex Court convicted him for instigating his wife to commit suicide.

In another case, *State of Punjab* v. *Iqbal Singh.*[108], the husband was persistent with his dowry demands. He would beat his wife, cause all sorts of harassments and would permit her a life only under the shadow of his terror. This ultimately resulted in the wife setting herself and her 3 children ablaze. The trial court held that the husband willfully produced an atmosphere which forced the wife to do what she did and recorded a conviction and sentence under this Section of 7 years of rigorous imprisonment. The Supreme Court up held the conviction and the sentence.

Where a newly wedded wife unable to bear the harassment from her husband to bring money from her parents set her ablaze and the accused husband stood nearby not trying to save her, it was held that the accused was guilty of offence under Section 306. His acquittal was set aside.[109]

In another case, pressure for parting with '*stridhan*' was made on the wife. The accused was forcing his wife to transfer the land to his name which she had received as a part of her '*stridhan*' from her father. He concealed her letters. These facts drove her to commit suicide. He was convicted under Section 498-A for the offence of cruelty. On the same evidence, he was convicted under Section 306 r/w Section 221, Cr PC.[110]

In cases of alleged abetment of suicide, the direct or indirect acts of instigation to commit suicide must be proved. The mere fact that the husband or his relatives

---

[107] AIR 1989 SC 1661.
[108] AIR 1991 SC 1532.
[109] *State of Punjab* v. *Anil Kumar*, 1992 Cr LJ 3131.
[110] *K. Prema S. Rao* v. *Yadla Srinivasa Rao*, AIR 2003 SC 11.

have treated the wife with cruelty would not suffice.[111] If the accused has been charged under Section 498A and 304B of I.P.C. but the evidence on record proved him guilty under Section 306, even if no charge has been framed under Section 306, the accused could still be convicted under Section 306.[112]

Where the wife had never complained to her parents that her husband or in-laws maltreated her or inflicted torture or cruelty on her or even any such evidence was also missing, merely the fact that she committed suicide after a couple of months of her marriage, does not drag her husband or in-laws under Section 306[113]. Some abetment is necessary to invoke this provision.[114]

3.3.3 Misappropriation of Dowry amounts to Criminal Breach of Trust (Section 405)

To attract the penal liability under Section 405 of I.P.C., it must be established that the accused had been entrusted with dominion over property which he is set to have converted to his own use.[115] Criminal breach of trust can be committed in respect of both movable and immovable properties.[116] If the in-laws of the complainant retain her *stridhan* despite demand after death of her husband, Section 406 of I.P.C. and Section 3 and 6 of D.P.A. are attracted.[117] If a woman entrusts her *stridhan* property with her husband and in-laws and they misappropriate it or convert it to their use, they are guilty of criminal breach of trust[118]. If there is no evidence to show that there was entrustment of *stridhan* by wife to husband, mere statement of wife that *stridhan* articles were laying in the house when she was turned out shall not attract liability of husband for criminal breach of trust.[119]

When the husband or his relatives do not handover the gifts and ornaments given to the bride, to her, these provisions are invoked.[120]This offence requires that there must be an entrustment of any individual with property or making a person

---

[111] *Mahender Singh* v. *State of Madhya Pradesh*, 1996 Cri LJ 894.
[112] *Vinod Kumar* v. *State*, 2005 Cri LJ (NOC) 222 (Uttar).
[113] *State of Punjab* v. *Kripal Singh*, 1992 Cr LJ 2472(P&H)
[114] Ratanlal Ranchhoddas & Dhirajlal Keshavlal Thakore, Ratanlal & Dhirajlal's The Indian Penal Code (Wadhwa and Company, Nagpur, 2002).
[115] *Velji Raghavji Patel* v. *State of Maharashtra*, AIR 1965 SC 1433.
[116] *R.K Dalmia* v. *Delhi Administration*, AIR 1962 SC 1821.
[117] *Chancharapu Madhusudhan Reddy* v. *State of A.P.*,2006 Cri LJ2978 (AP).
[118] *Pratibha Rani* v. *Suraj Kumar*, AIR 1985 SC 628.
[119] *Supra* note 20 at 1231.
[120] K.T Thomas and M.A.Rashid, *The Indian Penal Code* 1003 (Lexis Nexis, Gurgaon, 2015).

dominion over some property.[121] The person who has been entrusted over the concerned property has either misappropriated or converted such property dishonestly to his own use, or the person entrusted has used or disposed off such property.[122]

The Supreme Court has held that reading this Section with Section 4 and Section 6 of the "Dowry Prohibition Act, 1961", the gifts, valuables or any ornaments received in the marriage from the in-laws shall be handed over to the wife on being driven out.[123] If the husband fails to give such handover, he will be guilty under this provision. [124]

Where the wife was expelled out of the house by her husband who refused to return the 'stridhan', despite repeated requests and persuasions, it was held that criminal breach of trust is a continuing offence and fresh cause of action accrues to the wife till the return of the property.[125]

If mother-in-law takes away the gifts, valuables or cash which has been given to bride at the time of her marriage, she will be guilty for misappropriation of 'stridhan'. Therefore, the mother-in-law was held to be liable for prosecution under this offence.[126] In a case where twenty five lakhs were offered for taking a divorce by mutual consent, it was held that it does amount to an offence under this Section. Even if any gifts are given to the bridegroom or his family as per any prevailing custom, it would not amount to an offence under this provision.[127]

3.3.4 Cruelty by Husband or his Relatives (Section 498A)

"The Dowry Prohibition Act, 1961" was intended to curb the menace of dowry. However, after few years, it was realized that the act had failed miserably due to its inherent defects. Thus the "Criminal Law (Second Amendment) Act, 1983" amended the Indian Penal Code and added a new Chapter XXA, containing Section 498A to satisfy the felt-needs of the time. [128]

---

[121] *Supra* note 83 at 3996.
[122] *Supra* note 83 at 3950.
[123] *Supra* note 90 at 902.
[124] *Supra* note 32.
[125] *Balram Singh* v. *Sukhwant Kaur*, 1992 Cr LJ 792 (P&H).
[126] *Bhaskar Lal Sharma* v. *Monika*, (2009) 10 SCC 604.
[127] *Supra* note 90 at 903.
[128] *Supra* note 82.

Cruelty as an offence under Section 498A was inserted in the Indian Penal Code by the "Criminal Law (Amendment) Act, 1983". It envisages that where a husband or the relatives of the husband subject the wife to cruelty, they shall be punished with imprisonment for a term of upto 3 three years. The Section itself explains the term "cruelty" in the explanation (b), which states that any kind of harassment of the woman with a view to compel her or any person related to her to meet any unlawful demand of dowry or if such a harassment is done to pursue her to commit suicide is termed as cruelty.[129]

The concept of cruelty and its ambit along with Section 306 varies in accordance with facts and circumstances of each case. It may vary from person to person and also depends upon the social and financial status to which such individual belongs. In many judgments, it has been held by the Apex Court that to attract the culpability under Section 498A it is not essential that such cruelty must be physical. Any kind of psychological torture or abnormality in behavior may attract the guilt of committing cruelty or harassment in a particular case. [130]The only requirements to attract the Section 498A are as follows:

- The victim must be a married female.
- There must be a cruelty or harassment done to her either physical or mental.
- The cruelty or harassment must be connected to a demand of dowry or dangerous to her life, limb or health; or sufficient to drive her to commit suicide.
- She must be subjected to such a cruelty either by her husband or his relatives.[131]

Meaning of Cruelty under Section 498A

No comprehensive definition is given anywhere in the Act for the term cruelty. "The act of cruelty may be subtle, brutal, by words or gestures, by taunt, or by mere silence depending upon the circumstances of a particular case."[132] Cruelty may be physical, emotional or mental harassment beyond endurance[133]. In general, cruelty may be explained as a repressible conduct, which is a deviation from the normal

---

[129] *Supra* note 20 at 1108.
[130] *Gananath Patnaik* v. *State of Orissa*, (2002) 2 SCC 619.
[131] *Suvetha* v. *State*, 2009 Cr LJ 2974.
[132] Shriniwas Gupta & Preeti Mishra, *Textbook on Indian Penal Code, 1860* 483 (Asian Law House, Hydrabad, 2016).
[133] S.N. Mishra, *Indian Penal Code* 915 (Central Law Publications, Allahabad, 2016).

standard of marital relationship that causes an injury to the health and happiness of other spouse.[134]

Constitutional Validity of the Offence of Cruelty

The constitutional validity of Section 498A has been challenged several times on the grounds of violation of fundamental rights.[135] In *Inder Raj Malik* v. *Mrs. Sunita Malik*[136], the contention was taken that Section 498A is a violative of Art 14[137] and Art 20(2)[138] of the Indian Constitution. It was argued that the offence dealt under Section 498A is similar to the offence prescribed in Section 4 of Dowry Prohibition Act. Therefore, it leads to double jeopardy and hence violates Art 20(2) of the Constitution. Another argument put forth in this regard was that Section 498A imparts arbitrary powers to the Courts and police therefore, it is violating Art 14 of the Constitution. The Court has rejected both the contentions and held that there is a difference between Sec 4 and Sec 498A because both the Sections differ in the gravity of offence. Section 4 deals with a situation where there is a mere demand of dowry not necessarily accompanied with cruelty or harassment. On the other hand, Section 498A covers those offences which are more aggravated and where cruelty or harassment is done for demanding dowry.[139]

Therefore, there is no question of double jeopardy or any violation of Art 20(2) of the Constitution. It was further held that discretion to interpret the word, given to the Court cannot be termed as an arbitrary power and hence cannot be considered as *ultra vires* to the Constitution. Again in *Krishan Lal* v. *Union of India*[140] It was held by the Court that husband and relatives of a married woman who treat her with cruelty form a separate class and therefore it a reasonable classification and there is no violation of Art 14 of the Constitution.

---

[134] *Bhagat* v. *Bhagat*, AIR 1994 SC 710.
[135] *Supra* note 92 at 2498.
[136] 1986 Cr LJ 1510.
[137] *Supra* note 63.
[138] *Supra* note 61.
[139] *Supra* note 100.
[140] 1994 Cr LJ 3472.

Cruelty by Persistent Demand of Dowry

It is not at all necessary that the cruelty done to the victim must be physical. Any kind of psychological or mental harassment may attract culpability under Section 498A. In a case where the wife was time and again mentally tortured, taunted and a repeated maltreatment was given to her after the first day of getting married, it was held to be a cruelty against her. A quarrel occurred between the victim and her husband just one day before her death and it drove her to commit suicide. Presumption under Section 113B of Evidence Law was held to be invoked. [141] In a related case of *State of Punjab* v. *Dal Jit Singh*, four years after the marriage, the wife was called upon to bring some dowry from her parents for sending her husband's younger brother abroad. It could not be termed as dowry demand, but because she was harassed for it and on account of this she became compelled to end her life, it was held that an offence under Section 498A was made out.[142]

Section 498A is Attracted even if Acquisition under 304B, I.P.C. Fails.

Several times, the Apex Court has been confronted with question as to whether a case under Section 498A, I.P.C. can be made out even if the acquisition under Section 304B, I.P.C. failed. Both Sections deal with two different offences and cannot be considered to be mutually inclusive.[143] Cruelty is common to both the Sections and must be proved to attract the liability of these offences.

In *K.Prema Rao* v. *Yadla Srinivasa Rao*[144], the accused was charged and prosecuted under Section 304B of I.P.C. for causing dowry death. But in this case, the demand of dowry could not be proved and hence the liability under Section 304B, I.P.C could not be made out. But on the basis of the evidence on record, the court found that the accused had committed the offence of cruelty under Section 498A. Therefore, the accused was convicted for cruelty under Section 498A and the offence of abetting suicide under Section 306 r/w Section 113Aof the Evidence Act.

---

[141] *Pawan Kumar* v. *State of Haryana*, AIR 1998 SC 958.
[142] 1999 Cr LJ 2723.
[143] *Heera Lal* v. *State (Govt. Of N.C.T)*, AIR 2003 SC 2865.
[144] *K.Prema Rao* v. *Yadla Srinivasa Rao*, AIR 2003 SC 11.

Where the wife committed suicide and there were allegations of harassment for dowry but the prosecution witness including parents of the deceased said that they had no information about severity of harassment as could lead to suicide, the conviction under Section 304-B was set aside but under Section 498-A was maintained.

A Need to Revisit the Provision of Cruelty

The legislative intent behind inserting this provision was to save the wives from any mental or physical harassment, torture and violence in their matrimonial home. However, while examining the other side of the coin, it has been sometimes realized by the courts that exaggerated version of the incidents and tendency of over implications are reported in many complaints[145]. Unfortunately, it not only overburdens the courts with huge number of false cases but also results in spoiling social peace, harmony and thereby leads to unrest. It was held in *Preeti Gupta[146]* case, that legislature must take this aspect into the consideration and make required amendments in the current provisions.[147]

3.4 Cruelty related to Dowry as a Ground for Divorce under Hindu Marriage Act, 1955

Section 13(1)(ia) of Hindu Marriage Act prescribes various grounds for divorce and states that any marriage which has taken place either before or after this Act has become operative, may be dissolved on the ground of cruelty. If either spouse has treated the other spouse with cruelty, the aggrieved party may present a petition on this ground for the dissolution of such marriage by seeking a decree of divorce.

The cruelty may be of any kind and any variety. If the facts and circumstances in a case are sufficient to draw an inference that any dowry was demanded in the given case, it amounts to cruelty. There is a prohibition of demanding any kind of dowry under Indian legal system. Even after such prohibition, if any demand of dowry is done from the wife, it is well covered within the ambit of cruelty and thereby, entitles the wife to seek a decree for divorce on the ground of 'cruelty'.[148]

---

[145] M.P. Tandon, *Indian Penal Code* 744 (Allahabad Law Agency, Faridabad, 2015).
[146] Preeti Gupta & anr v. State of Jharkhand, AIR 2010 SC 336.
[147] *Ibid.*
[148] P.S. Narayana, *Laws relating to Dowry Prohibition*, 19 (Gogia Law agency, Hyderabad, 2001).

In *Sobha Rani* v. *Madhukar Reddi*[149], it was held that the harassment done to a wife in order to compel her or persons related to her to fulfill any illegal demand of dowry would constitute cruelty under Section 13(1)(i)(a) of Hindu Marriage Act. Therefore, the appellant had been subjected to cruelty by her husband entitling her to obtain a decree for divorce.

3.5 Law of Evidence and Offences Related to Dowry

It must be remembered that the offences related to dowry usually occur within the enclosed four walls of a house and are committed secretly. Therefore it becomes very difficult to obtain any direct evidence with regard to such offences. Therefore, the legislature has tried to strengthen the hands of prosecution by inserting Sections 113A and 113B in the Evidence Act[150]. Section 113A and 113B permit to raise a presumption if the death of a woman has occurred within the seven years of her marriage and certain facts are established by the prosecution.

3.5.1 Presumption of Abetment of Suicide

In the year 1983, Section 113A was added in the "Indian Evidence Act, 1872" under Section 7 of the "Criminal Law (Second Amendment) Act", to give biting teeth to Section 498A of I.P.C.[151]

The clear legislative intent behind the insertion of this Section was an effective implementation of Section 498A and to achieve desired results of prevention of dowry.[152] Woman has acted as a mute epitome of sufferings since ages. She has been reluctant to pen her mouth against any crime or harassment done to her by her own family members. To protect her from the initial hardships of criminal trial and to honour her dignity, this provision has been introduced ignoring the fundamental principal of "burden of proof" on the prosecution. Section 113A is a boon as it relieves the victimized woman from the complex technicalities of the law. The prime objective behind enacting this provision was to eradicate the evil of dowry and to make sure that married women must lead a dignified life in their matrimonial homes. [153]

---

[149] AIR 1988 SC 121.
[150] Paras Diwan and Peeyushi Diwan, *Law relating to Dowry, Dowry deaths, bride Burning, Rape and related Offences* 116 (Universal Law Publishing Co.Pvt.Ltd, Delhi, 1997).
[151] A.N. Saha, *Supreme Court on Criminal Law*, 2408 (Ashoka Law House, New Delhi, 2011)
[152] *Supra* note 6 at 195.
[153] *Krishan Lal* v. *Union of India*, 1994 Cr LJ 3472

Retrospective Effect of Section 113A

Section 113A of Evidence Act read with Section 498A of Indian Penal Code makes it clear that these two statutes permit to draw the past instances of cruelty by necessary implication. Since it is retrospective in operation even in respect of suicide committed prior to 25th December 1983, presumption of abetment of suicide can be invoked.[154]

The phrase used "within a period of seven years of marriage" and the *"Explanation"* added thereto implies that Section 498A of I.P.C. and Section 113A of the Evidence Act, include the past events taken place before the date of amendment.[155]

There are three pre-requisites for invoking presumption under Section 113A:

- The suicide must be committed within the time period of seven years of the marriage.

- Her husband or her in-laws must have subjected her to cruelty as defined under Section 498A of I.P.C.

- The cruelty shall be established having regard to the other circumstances of the case.

Whenever, there comes a question before the court of law that whether the husband or any of his relative has abetted the suicide of a woman, certain facts must be established to invoke Section 113A. Firstly, it has to be established that the suicide has taken place within a period of 7 years of her marriage. Secondly, she was subjected to cruelty by her husband or his relatives. On establishment of these facts by the prosecution, the court may take a presumption that the husband or such relative of the husband is guilty of abetting the suicide of such woman.[156] Section 113A may apply retrospectively and is also applicable in the cases where the abetment of suicide was done prior to the enactment of this provision in the Evidence Act. [157]

---

[154] *Gurbachan Singh* v. *Satpal Singh* AIR 1990 SC 209.
[155] *Vasanta Tulshiram Bhoyar* v. *State of Maharashtra*, 1987 Cr LJ 901.
[156] *Jagdish Chand* v. *State of Haryana*, 1988 Cr LJ 1048 cited at Batuk Lal, *The Law of Evidence* 451(Central Law Agency, Allahabad, 2010).
[157] *Gurbachan Singh* v. *Satpal Singh*, AIR 1990 SC 209.

3.5.2 Presumption as to Dowry Death

Section 113B of Indian Evidence Act was inserted by the Amendment Act of 1986. The gruesome crime of dowry death is usually committed within the four walls of the house, the act is generally manipulated in such a way that it may seem to be either suicide or accidental death.[158] Therefore, it is almost impossible for the prosecution to produce evidence or witnesses. Thus, the legislature was compelled to introduce such a "presumption" against the accused and therefore Section 113B was inserted simultaneously with Section 304B of I.P.C. .

Under Section 113B when it is shown that soon before the death, the woman had been subjected to cruelty or harassment by the accused for the dowry the court shall presume that the accused had caused the dowry death and the burden is on the accused to rebut the presumption.[159]

Application of Section 113B

Section 113B only applies when the question is whether a person has committed dowry death of a woman and it is further supplemented by two facts[160]:

- That soon before death, the woman has been subjected to cruelty or harassment by such person.

- Such cruelty or harassment was in connection with any demand for dowry.

Whenever these facts are established by evidence, the presumption of Section 113B shall apply on the offence committed under Section 304 of I.P.C. .[161]

In *Tarsem Singh* v. *State of Punjab*[162], the Supreme Court held that presumption under Section 113B is one of law. The presumption under Section 113B shall be raised only on the proof of the essentials given under Section 304B of I.P.C.[163] This presumption can only be raised, once all the ingredients of dowry death are proved.[164]

---

[158] M.Z. Khan and Ramji Ray, "Dowry Death" 45 *TIJSW* 3 (Oct. 1984) *available at:* http://ijsw.tiss.edu/collect/ijsw/archives/HASH019d/50507750.dir/doc.pdf (Visited on July 20, 2017).

[159] Batuk Lal, *The Law of Evidence* 452 (Central Law Agency, Allahabad, 2010).

[160] *Supra* note 151 at 2416.

[161] *Supra* note 6 at 346.

[162] AIR 2009 S C 1454.

[163] S. K. Malik, An Exhaustive Commentary on The Indian Evidence Act, 1872, 1261(Delight Law Publishers, 2009)

[164] B.M. Prasad and Manish Mohan, *Ratanlal and Dhiraj Lal The Law of Evidence* 564 (Lexis Nexis , 2015).

The expression 'soon before' occurring in Section 113B, 304B does not indicate any fixed period but applies promising test. A proximal connection must exist between the effect caused by cruelty for demanding dowry and the death of the victim.[165]

3.5.3 Dying Declaration in Dowry Death

The term 'dying declaration' means a statement given by a dying person at the time of his or her death. It is regarding the cause of that person's death or regarding the chain of circumstances that ultimately resulted in that person's death. A question has been several times raised before the Court of Law that whether a dying declaration can become the sole basis of conviction or not. It may form the sole basis of conviction if there is a complete absence of any doubt and if such a statement has been recorded exactly in the manner prescribed by the law. It must inculcate full confidence regarding its truthfulness and accuracy. It amounts to miscarriage of justice if the dying declaration is recorded if in a case. The major reason is that usually in serious crimes, very often the victim is the sole eye witness and non recording of statement in such cases would result in non availability of significant evidence before the Court of Law. No cross examination is possible of the person who has made such statement or dying declaration as such a person is already dead. Therefore, the court must apply a judicious mind to ascertain the reliability and dependability upon a dying declaration.

In dowry deaths usually the evidence taken into consideration is that of the parents, friends or the close relatives of the deceased. If deceased has made certain statements to her parents or relatives about her harassment, maltreatment or cruelty done to her, such statements also assume significance. Moreover, the events of cruelty or harassment already known to the persons who are related with the deceased are also taken into consideration by the court. Even letters written to friends, relatives, etc. expressing the incidences of harassment or cruelty done to her may be taken as material evidence. There is no presumption in law that the relatives of the deceased would make false statements.[166]

---

[165] Batuk Lal, *Batuk Lal's Law of Evidence* 1217 (Orient Publishing Company, 2004).
[166] *P. Bikshapathi* v. *State of A.P.*, 1989 Cri LJ 1186.

Dying Declaration as a Piece of Evidence

In the cases of dowry death, especially in bride burning, dying declaration has its own sanctity as a piece of evidence. Very often it is the last piece of evidence which is relied upon by the court when submitted by the prosecution in support of charge of bride burning.[167] There is a set notion about dying declaration i.e. "The tongues of dying men enforced attention like deep harmony; where words are scarce, they are seldom spent in vein; for they breathe the truth that breathe their word in pain."[168]

Admissibility of dying declaration of a severely burnt victim

It has been observed many times that the dying declaration and its admissibility is questioned on the ground that the victim who is severely burnt lacks mental stability to give a correct statement. Sometimes it is also argued that such a victim is not able to speak in such a clear manner that can be understood properly and thereby accepted by the court[169]. In a Supreme Court Judgment, medical opinion was brought that due to burn injuries on the vocal cords of the victim; there is possibility of difficulty in speaking clearly.[170] But the Court held that if the recorded statements are consistent and the medical evidence and ocular evidence simultaneously establish the occurrence of torture, then the guilt is proved.[171] Where the defence questioned the admissibility of the dying declaration given by the victim on the ground that since her larynx and trachea were burnt and it was impossible for her to speak anything; the court still accepted the dying declaration on the medical opinion which stated that despite the injuries a patient can be able to speak but it may not be very clear.[172]

3.6 Forensic Investigation Procedure in Dowry Deaths

Most of the dowry deaths occur due to burns, bodily injuries or death caused in unnatural circumstances. Majority of which are poisoning, hanging, drowning, suffocation due to strangulation, starvation or fatal wounds[173]. Since the death is

---

[167] *Supra* note 163 at 1258.
[168] *Supra* note 6 at 557.
[169] *Rajeev Kumar* v. *State of Haryana*, AIR 2014 SC 90.
[170] Sripada Venkata Joga Rao, Sir John Woodroffe &Syed Amir Ali's Law of Evidence, (II) 1802 (Buterworths, New Delhi, 17th Edn)
[171] *Deen Dayal* v. *State of U.P.,* AIR 2009 SC 1238.
[172] *Rajeev Kumar* v. *State of Haryana*, AIR 2014 SC 907.
[173] Radhika. R. H. and Ananda.K, "An Autopsy Study of Socio-Etiological Aspects in Dowry Death Cases" 33 *JIAFM* 3 (2011) *available at: http://medind.nic.in/jal/t11/i3 /jalt11i3p 224.pd* f (Visited on July 20, 2016).

usually caused inside the enclosed four walls of the house, that too a matrimonial house where the witnesses present are either the prime accused, co-accused or the relatives of accused. Therefore, it becomes a challenge for the investigating bodies to collect evidence and find genuine witnesses. Therefore, in such cases, physical evidences, circumstantial evidences as well forensic evidence play a major role in investigation and administration of justice.[174]

In a study conducted by Department of Forensic Medicine in Aligarh, it was found that majority of dowry deaths have occurred within the first 3 years of marriage, most of them were Hindu females and living in rural areas[175]. The main causes of death were burning, poisoning, hanging and strangulation. It was also observed that suicide was the most common manner in such cases[176]. The higher rate of death due to burning was also observed in newly married women and was often attributed with cooking. In the cases of suicide, setting oneself on fire is the most common method for women due to the easy availability of kerosene oil, gas stove, matchsticks etc. The in-laws also prefer to burn the bride in order to hide the torture injuries and destroy the circumstantial evidence[177].

The major essential to prove the offence of dowry death[178] is death caused in abnormal circumstances which factually means suspicious circumstances. In many cases, the cause of death appears to be mysterious and even some times the dead bodies are cremated without medical examination. If the death is proved as merely accidental, no prosecution under Section 304B can be brought. Therefore, it becomes really crucial for the investigating authorities to establish the suspicion or abnormality in the cause of death. Such an effective investigation can be achieved with the help of forensic expertise.

---

[174] O. P. Murty, "Dowry Crimes Investigation"4 *IJLTLM* 13(2002) *available at:* https://www.researchgate.net/publication/260955963_Dowry_crimes_investigation (Visited on August 10, 2017).
[175] Afzal Haroon, "A Study of Epidemiological Profile of Dowry Death Victims in Aligarh" 3 IABMCR 7 (2017) *available at:* https://pdfs.semanticscholar.org/ b1aa/ed70a31e3 cb856b0ee2507c851ed25538a6d.pdf?_ga=2.20997243.1143021006.1578113541-1292684471.1578113541(Visited on March10, 2019).
[176] *Supra* note 173.
[177] *Supra* note 175.
[178] Section 304B, The Indian Penal Code, 1860.

Some of the significant points that need to be thoroughly examined to ascertain the cause of death are as follows:

Death Caused Due to Burn Injuries

The factors which need to be analyzed in the death caused of burn injuries are time and date of occurrence, degree/depth of burn, whether the family members took the victim to the hospital or not, to ascertain that whether any combustible fuel, substance or kerosene was found at the site of occurrence; the burn has occurred before death or after the death[179].

In a related case of *Prem Kanwar* v. *State of Rajasthan* where the husband and in-laws portrayed that the victim had died due to burning but the father of the victim claimed that she was harassed and abused for dowry, medical evidence proved to be a deciding factor. It was found in the medical evidence that although the whole body was burnt but the skull bones were already broken before being burnt. This was sufficient evidence to show that she was killed before being burnt. The Apex Court sensitively relied upon the medical evidence, upheld the accused guilty and observed that the persistent harassment and injuries caused thereby were sufficient to prove the greed of the accused for dowry.[180]

Death Caused by Suffocation/ Hanging

The important factors to be determined in death caused by suffocation/ hanging are bruises/nail marks/any injury around the neck; the condition of eyes, tongue, lips, dripping saliva etc.; marks of physical scuffle, bluish discoloration of the skin, any kind of haemorrhage ; to identify whether the hanging has occurred before death or after the death.

Therefore, in a case where the death was stated to be caused by snake bite but it was contradicted by the medical evidence stating that the victim has died due to asphyxia caused by strangulation of neck, the court upheld the guilt of the accused.[181]

---

[179] Dipa Dube and Mukesh Yadav, "Medical Evidence in Dowry Deaths: An Evaluation by Indian Courts" 37 *JIAFM* 299 available at: https://www.researchgate.net/publication/ 283173205_ Medical_Evidence_in_Dowry_Deaths_An_Evaluation_by_Indian_Courts(Visited on Jan 13, 2017).
[180] AIR 2009 SC 1242
[181] *Trimukh Maroti Kirkan* v. *State of Maharashtra*, (2008) 8 SCC 456

In another case decided by the Karnataka H.C., it was shown by the defence that due to epilepsy she fell from the stairs, sustained injuries and died. But the Court relied upon the medical expert opinion that the brain matter was shrunken, thorax region was congested and thyroid cartilage was broken. Therefore, the death was caused due to asphyxia as a result of hanging.[182]

Death Caused as a Result of Poisoning

The major observations to be examined in death caused by poisoning are; Mouth odour of the victim , bluish discoloration of the skin, condition of eyes, nails, fingers, tongue etc; presence of any form around the lips; substances present in stomach/intestines etc. The medical evidence upon which the court relies must be based on legal material on record.

In the case of *Chhotan Sao*, it was alleged that the victim was beaten up and compelled to consume poison resulting in her death. The court acquitted the accused on the ground that "The non-examination of the doctor who conducted the post-mortem coupled with the failure to produce the Forensic Laboratory Report regarding the examination of viscera of the deceased leaves a gaping hole in the case of prosecution regarding the nature of the death of the deceased." [183] Where the death was claimed to be caused by poisoning but a specific chemical testing had not revealed any poison. However, the medical evidence clearly established strangulation of neck. The Court relied upon the forensic report and convicted the accused[184].

Death Caused by Drowning

Where the victim has died due to drowning; clothes of the victim, any presence of foam inside the mouth and nose, eyes and tongue condition, any existence of mud, weed, etc. causing cataleptic rigidity, bluish discoloration of the skin, presence of any goose bumps on the body, bruises on the body, stiffening of joints and muscles of the body and post mortem staining etc must be examined.[185]

In a related case of *State of Karnataka* v. *M.V.Manjunathegowda*[186], the husband cooked up a story that the wife died due to slipping and thereby drowning into the well, while she went to fetch water. But the medical evidence revealed five

---

[182] *State of Karnataka* v. *Choudegowda,* 2007 Cri L J 2812.
[183] *Chhotan Sao* v. *State of Bihar,* AIR 2014 SC 907.
[184] *Supra* note 181
[185] *Supra* note 179.
[186] AIR 2003 SC 809.

fractures in the skull caused shock and haemorrhage resulting in her death. Along with the medical evidence there were other circumstantial evidences on record which were clearly indicating that she was subjected to cruelty by the husband for the demand of dowry. The Court convicted the husband under the charge of dowry death.[187]

In another case, the husband and in-laws contended that the death of the wife was accidental and caused due to falling down into the well. But the prosecution alleged that the dead body had been thrown into the well due to the non fulfilment of dowry demands. The medical expert opined that the death was caused due to coma occurred by a head injury which was possibly inflicted by some blunt weapon. Such injuries could not possibly have been caused in the well as it was *kuccha* well and there was water in the well. It was further found that no water was present inside the windpipe or lungs. The court relied upon the medical evidence, opined that the body was dumped into the well after the death and therefore confirmed the conviction for dowry death.[188]

3.7 The Protection of Women from Domestic Violence Act, 2005

Wife battering as well as physical or verbal abuse occurs very commonly to the women in India within the four walls of her own house. With an objective to provide a civil law remedy for protecting the women from any kind of domestic violence, The Protection of Women from Domestic Violence Act, 2005 was enacted.[189] This Act includes any kind of abuse or the threat of abuse to the woman. Such an abuse may be physical, sexual, verbal, emotional or economic. Dowry is peculiar to Indian conditions that oppress married and unmarried women, giving altogether newer dimensions to the concept of domestic violence across the globe.[190]

Any kind of act of harassing a woman by unlawfully demanding dowry from her or her relatives is also covered under the definition of 'domestic violence'.

---

[187] *Supra* note 178.
[188] *Deen Dayal* v. *State of U.P.*, AIR 2009 SC 1238.
[189] Anderson, Siwan , *"The Economics of Dowry and Brideprice" TJOEP* 21(2007) *available at:* https://econ.sites.olt.ubc.ca/files/2013/05/pdf_paper_siwan-anderson-economics-dowry-brideprice.pdf (Visited on Jan 13,2017).
[190] See Section 3(b) and Section 31(3), The Protection of Women from Domestic Violence Act, 2005.

Therefore, this act provides an additional protection to the dowry victims besides The Dowry Prohibition Act.[191]

All kinds of abuse may it be physical, psychological, verbal, mental, sexual or economic are covered within the ambit of Domestic Violence Act and forms a subset of the anti-dowry laws to the extent it is one of the reasons for domestic violence.[192]. Depriving the victim from all or any economic resources to which she is entitled by law or custom including, *'stridhan'* amounts to an 'economic abuse'. It further covers any kind of restriction upon the access to resources or facilities of which a victim has right to use or enjoy by virtue of the domestic relationship. Any act of causing bodily pain, injury, threat or any harm to life, limb or health of the victim amounts to 'physical abuse'. Committing any kind of assault, coercion, intimidation or use of criminal force is included in physical abuse.

Section 3 of Domestic Violence Act includes all kinds of harassment, injury or harm caused to a woman to force her to fulfill any unlawful dowry demand within the ambit of domestic violence. [193] Many recent studies suggest close proximity between demands for dowry and domestic violence. There are more common chances of abuse or violence towards a wife when her husband and in-laws believe that the dowry given in her marriage or subsequent to the marriage is inadequate. [194] Following remedies are provided under the Act:

- A person may be prohibited to commit domestic violence by passing protection orders against that person.

- A person committing domestic violence may be dispossessed out of a shared household by passing residence orders.

- Custody of a child may be granted by passing custody orders.

---

[191] What protection does a woman have from domestic violence, *available at*: https://www.kaanoon.com/indian-law/what-protection-does-a-woman-have-from-domestic-violence (Visited on Jan 13, 2017).

[192] *Supra* note 6 at 362.

[193] Section 3, The Protection of Women from Domestic Violence Act, 2005.

[194] Mahek Singh, "Dowry as a factor of violence in Marriage: A study of Women seeking help in Family Counseling Centers in Chandigarh" 2 *IJOAIRT* 41 (2013)) *available at:* http://www.ijoart.org/docs/Dowry-as-a-factor-of-violence-in-Marriage-A-study-of-Women-seeking-help-in-Family-Counseling-Centers-in-Chandigarh.pdf (Visited on January 11, 2017).

- A person who has committed domestic violence may be directed to pay the compensation by passing compensation orders.

Even if a woman is threatened by not giving her food to eat or goods related to her daily needs, it may amount to domestic violence. Moreover, if a husband has harassed his wife for demanding dowry from her or her relatives, it is also covered under domestic violence. [195]

3.8 Procedure of Dowry related Offences to be dealt under Criminal Procedure Code

The offences related to dowry are covered under the provisions of Dowry Prohibition Act, 1961 and Indian Penal Code, 1860. But the procedure to file a complaint and taking cognizance of such offences is dealt under Cr PC. After the insertion of Section 498A of I.P.C., a new provision of Section 198A[196] was added in the "Criminal Law (Amendment) Act, 1983" to ascertain cognizance of the offence of cruelty or harassment of women committed under the newly added Section 498A of I.P.C.

It prescribes that no court shall take cognizance of an offence punishable under Section 498A of I.P.C. except upon a police report of facts which constitute such offence or upon a complaint by the person aggrieved or by her father, mother, brother, sister and other near relatives. It gives *locus standi* to the father, mother and other near relations of the woman who is or has been the victim of such cruelty or harassment to complain. [197]

Another new provision i.e. Section 198B was further inserted by the Criminal Law (Amendment) Act, 2013 on the recommendations of the Justice

---

[195] *Supra* note 191.
[196] Section 198 A, The Code Of Criminal Procedure, 1973.
Section 198A reads as- Prosecution of offences under section 498A of the Indian Penal Code- No Court shall take cognizance of an Offence Punishable section 498A of the Indian Penal Code except upon a police report of facts which constitute such offence or Upon a complaint made by the person aggrieved by the offence or by her father, mother, brother, sister or by her father' s or mother' s brother or sister or, with the leave of the Court, by any other person related to her by blood, marriage or adoption.
[197] After Section 198A of the Code of Criminal Procedure, the following Section shall be inserted, namely— Cognizance of offence
Section198B- No Court shall take cognizance of an offence punishable under section 376B of the Indian Penal Code where the persons are in a marital relationship, except upon prima facie satisfaction of the facts which constitute the offence upon a complaint having been filed or made by the wife against the husband, Criminal Law (Amendment) Act, 2013.

J.S.Verma Committee.[198] A new offence in I.P.C. under Section 376 was created whereby sexual intercourse by a husband upon his wife during separation has been made punishable.[199] Section 482 preserves the inherent powers of the High Court.[200] In *Preeti Gupta* v. *State of Jharkand*[201], a complaint had been lodged by the wife against her husband, in-laws, a married sister-in-law and unmarried brother-in-law on the grounds of harassing her for dowry demand. However, no specific allegations were found or proved against the sister-in-law and unmarried brother-in-law. It was observed that they were implicated in the complaint merely with an objective to unnecessarily rope them, harass and humiliate them. Therefore, the Court had quashed the complaint and considered it as an attempt to abuse the process of law.

3.9 Dowry Prohibition and India's Obligation under International Law

UN has always endeavoured to ensure the equality of women in legal as well as social sphere. Various conventions have been introduced by the United Nations to raise the position of the women and it has also formed the commission on the Status of Women in 1946. Even after that UDHR[202] was adopted in the year 1948. Subsequently, the Convention on the Political Rights of the Women and Convention on the Nationality of Married Women were put forward in the years 1948 and 1953 respectively.

Another significant declaration on Elimination of Discrimination against Women was adopted in 1967. But the major step taken forward for the welfare of women was Convention on the Elimination of All Forms of Discrimination against Women in 1979. After that Declaration on the Elimination of Violence against women came in the year 1993. Another optional protocol which was related to the

---

[198] *Ibid.*
[199] Section 376B Sexual intercourse by husband upon his wife during separation- Whoever has sexual intercourse with his own wife, who is living separately, whether under a decree of separation or otherwise, without her consent, shall be punished with imprisonment of either description for a term which shall not be less than two years but which may extend to seven years, and shall also be liable to fine.
Explanation.— in this section, "sexual intercourse" shall mean any of the acts mentioned in clauses (a) to (d) of section 375.
[200] Section 482- Saving of inherent powers of High Court. Nothing in this Code shall be deemed to limit or affect the inherent powers of the High Court to make such orders as may be necessary to give effect to any order under this Code, or to prevent abuse of the process of any Court or otherwise to secure the ends of justice., The Criminal Procedure Code, 1973.
[201] AIR 2010 S.C. 3363.
[202] Universal Declaration on Human Rights *available at:* https://www.un.org/en/universal-declaration-human-rights/(Visited on 22August, 2017)

CEDAW[203] in the year 1999 along with that UN has also established a commission on the status of the women. The practice of dowry and dowry death is not only violating the subsisting local laws of country but these are also violating the International Human Rights Law.

3.9.1 ICCPR and Dowry Related Violence

The ICCPR[204] was formed with an aim to protect civil rights and political rights of the individuals. ICCPR adjudicates through two means i.e. inter-state complaints and self reporting by member states. Besides that an Optional Protocol is available which provides an individual petition procedure. Unfortunately the remedy for enforcing rights under the ICCPR is not available to the victims of dowry crimes and their families in India because the first two means can only be utilized by the States and the individual petition procedure is not available since India being not a party to the Optional Protocol.

But it does not indicate that the dowry deaths are not the violation of the right to life which is an inherent right given under Article 6(1) of ICCPR. It clearly provides that right to live is the inherent and foremost right of every human being. It also mandates that no human being shall be deprived of one's life arbitrarily. Dowry death is an arbitrary rather criminal deprivation of right to life of a woman; therefore, by depriving her of her right to life, all other human rights will become meaningless. The state has already penalized it by making provision under its own penal laws[205]. Consequently, there is an express right given to the Indian women under Article 6(1) which is to be protected by the Indian state against dowry related murders. While there is no general rule of international law that requires treaties to intervene in domestic law, Article 6(1) requires that the right to life be protected by law. India has enacted the laws prohibiting dowry and penalizing dowry deaths and therefore fulfilled this requirement.

---

[203] Convention on the Elimination of Discrimination against Women *available at:* https://www.ohchr.org/documents/professionalinterest/cedaw.pdf (Visited on 21 January, 2017)

[204] International Covenant on Civil and Political Rights, *available at:* https://treaties.un.org/doc/publication/unts/volume%20999/volume-999-i-14668-english.pdf (Visited on 25 January, 2017)

[205] *Supra* note 178.

But Article 2(1) of the ICCPR further states that the parties to the Covenant are under strict obligation to *respect* and *ensure* the rights recognized in the Covenant. Although India has fulfilled the first obligation to respect the right to life in connection with dowry deaths because government does not perpetrate these crimes but the second obligation to ensure the enjoyment of this right to life in all possible measures is not yet fulfilled. The reason being is that the government has failed ineffectively to curb the increasing number of dowry deaths by taking preventive measures. Henceforth, it can be critically stated that India has failed to protect the right to life of Indian women in respect to dowry death in violation of the obligations of Article 2 under the ICCPR.

Practically we lack effective remedies for the few surviving victims of dowry deaths and their families. The police, prosecutors and courts have failed to create a deterrent effect while enforcing the laws prohibiting dowry or those punishing dowry crimes.[206]

The measures taken under Article 2(1) must be adequate and effective. Thus it requires India to take effective measures to protect life of individuals, including the prevention of killing of wives by husbands or in-laws in the disputes related to dowry. Although India has legislated the laws in this regard and has taken the positive measures but all the possible measures have not been taken nor have such measures been proved to be adequate or effective. According to NCRB data in India, the cases of dowry deaths are on continuous increase every year.

3.9.2 CEDAW and the Impact on Dowry related Violence on Women

UN general assembly has adopted the CEDAW on 18th December 1979. In September 1981, it became an International treaty after the ratification given to it by 20 countries. Within 10 years the convention has spread across the world as almost 100 nations have ratified it and agreed to enforce its provisions. This convention was a remarkable step to monitor the actual prevalence of women's right and their promotion. It has aimed to highlight and introspect those all areas where women are denied equal rights with men. In 1994, India has ratified the CEDAW[207] which aims

---

[206] *Supra* note 20 at 69.
[206] *Id. at 72.*
[207] *Supra* note 203.

at eliminating all kinds of discriminations against the females to give a platform for them of equal participation in public life.

Article 1 defines "discrimination against women" as any kind of distinction or restriction on the basis of sex or on the basis of equality of women with men including human rights of women[208]. The inclusions in the term 'discrimination' are further clarified by recommendation 19, which acknowledges gender based violence as another form of discrimination[209]. It includes any kind of physical, psychological or sexual violence occurring in the family including dowry related violence, wife battering, etc.

Article 2(f)[210] of the convention directs the states to frame policies for eliminating discrimination against women and to modify or abolish every kind of customs and practices which constitute such discrimination. Dowry is also a custom which not only discriminates the women but is also responsible for various kinds of atrocities related to dowry. Therefore, our nation must take due care to abolish and eradicate this evil practice with most effective measures.

Article 5(a)[211] further provides that state must take measures to modify social and cultural patterns of conduct to eliminate all customary practices which are based on the superiority of men over women.

Article 16[212] provides that it is the duty of the state to ensure equality of men and women in marital relations. Article 16(c)[213] further provides same rights and responsibilities of men and women during marital relation and even at its dissolution.

---

[208] Article 1, Convention of the Elimination of all forms of Discrimination Against Women, *available at:* https://www.ohchr.org/documents/professionalinterest/cedaw.pdf (Visited on 21 January, 2017)
[209] Recommendation 19, Convention of the Elimination of all forms of Discrimination against Women, *available at:* https://www.ohchr.org/documents/professionalinterest/cedaw.pdf (Visited on 21 January, 2017).
[210] Article 2(f), Convention of the Elimination of all forms of Discrimination Against Women *available at:* https://www.ohchr.org/documents/professionalinterest/cedaw.pdf (Visited on 21 January, 2017).
[211] Article 5(a), Convention of the Elimination of all forms of Discrimination Against Women *available at:* https://www.ohchr.org/documents/professionalinterest/cedaw.pdf (Visited on 21 January, 2017).
[212] Article 16, Convention of the Elimination of all forms of Discrimination Against Women *available at:* https://www.ohchr.org/documents/professionalinterest/cedaw.pdf (Visited on 21 January, 2017).
[213] Article 16(c), Convention of the Elimination of all forms of Discrimination Against Women *available at:* https://www.ohchr.org/documents/professionalinterest/cedaw.pdf (Visited on 21 January, 2017).

3.9.3 United Nations and India: Combined Efforts on Eradication of Dowry

A special rapporteur Christ of Heyns, who came from U. N, has aptly remarked that a contributing reason behind the persistence of dowry deaths in India is the social sanction behind it. Even sometimes, the police do not bother to treat such murders as crimes. U.N has considered it very common in some regions of patriarchal India that the brides are killed by husbands or in-laws for demanding money and such demands not getting fulfilled. [214]Heyns has quoted the record of NCRB of the year 2010 that 8,391 brides were murdered over dowry-related issues in 2010 which means at least one bride every hour. Despite a legal prohibition on this custom, it is still widely practiced and often leads to such a mental and physical harassment which drives the woman to commit suicide. Very often, the brides are often burnt alive in so-called "stove burnings" after pouring kerosene and set her ablaze.[215]

Again in 2008, a round table was organized between the Ministry of Women and Child Development[216] and the United Nations Development Fund for Women on the redrafting of Section 498A of I.P.C. and its increasing misuse. The discussion was an outcome of various campaigns which have taken place against the misuse of this provision. However, after analyzing the NCRB data of the year 2004-2007, they came to the conclusion that the cases of dowry deaths and dowry related offences were on constant increase. Therefore, there was a consensus on the outcome that such campaigns against the misuse of Section 498A lack substantive basis.

3.10 Need to Reform Laws related to Dowry with Changing Dimensions of Society

The violence and crimes against women have always been a matter of great concern for the legislature. Not only the laws related to gender justice and protection of women, are time to time passed but such laws are also reviewed periodically. Various amendments are suggested and incorporated in the laws affecting women to meet the emerging needs of society as well as nation. The occurrence of 'dowry

---

[214] Nita Bhalla, Cultural killings of women have social sanction in India - U.N., *Available at:* https://in.reuters.com/article/india-women-honour-killing/cultural-killings-of-women-have-social-sanction-in-india-u-n-idINDEE8310GP20120402 (Visited on June 20, 2019)

[215] *Ibid.*

[216] Ministry of Women and Child Development, *available at:* https://wcd.nic.in/(Visited on July 10, 2019)

offences' is one such manifestation of imbalanced power equations and gender violation, to which the married women are subjected. [217]

Section 304B of Dowry Death and Section 498A were added under which any cruelty committed by the husband or in-laws were penalised with a sentence of up to three years by "Criminal Law Amendment Act, 1986".[218] In 1983, the necessity for inserting of these offences had been strongly realized by the Law Commission in its 91st Report.[219] Again Section 113A and Section113B of the Evidence Act were inserted for curbing the increasing rate of dowry murders. The major objective behind these insertions was to overcome the challenges faced by the prosecution to prove the offence by providing a presumption.[220]Section 306 also covers the aspects of abetment of suicide of married women by husband and in-laws. It states that where a suicide is committed by a married woman within seven years of marriage, the court may presume that her husband and in-laws had abetted her to commit suicide by virtue of Section 113A of Evidence Act.

The socio-cultural reasons are undoubtedly responsible for the failure of the law to combat the problem but another aspect is that in the provision of dowry death there are still some drawbacks in drafting the substantive law and procedural aspects like that of difficulty in gathering the evidence for convicting the main culprit. When poor or middle class parents cannot give their daughters an expected dowry in such situations, very often the bride suffers cruelty and harassment after her marriage for not bringing expected dowry. Even many times, such cruelty results in dowry death. In such cases it is evident that no complaints were made in the initial stage of demanding of dowry or even after the marriage of the bride. The cases of dowry deaths or suicide where brides end their lives than reporting such cases to the police clearly question the lack of faith on legal framework for dowry prohibition and failure of Anti-Dowry laws. Again many times the prime accused is acquitted by the courts as the charges are not proved or due to inadequate evidence.

---

[217] *Supra* note 9 at V.
[218] See Section 304B and Section 498A, Indian Penal Code, 1860.
[219] Law Commission of India, 91st Report on Dowry Deaths and Law Reform: Amending The Hindu Marriage Act, 1955, The Indian Penal Code 1860 and The Indian Evidence Act, 1872, (August, 1983).
[219] *Supra* note 178.
[220] *Kunhiabdulla* v. *State of Kerela*, AIR 2004 SC 1731.

It must be remembered that the offences related to dowry usually take place within the enclosed four walls of houses where it is not easy to gather any independent and direct evidence related to the commission of the offence. Therefore, the law makers have tried to strengthen the hands of prosecution by introducing Sections 113A and 113B in the Evidence Act[221]. Section 113A and 113B permit a presumption to be raised if certain foundation facts are established and the death of women has been caused within seven years of marriage.

Section 113B of Indian Evidence Act was inserted by the Amendment Act of 1986. The gruesome crime of dowry death is usually committed within the four walls of the house, the act is generally manipulated in such a way that it may seem to be either suicide or accidental death.[222] Therefore, it is almost impossible for the prosecution to produce evidence or witnesses. Thus, the legislature was compelled to introduce such a "Presumption" against the accused and therefore Section 113B was inserted simultaneously with Section 304B of I.P.C. Under Section 113B when it is shown that soon before the death, the woman had been subjected to cruelty or harassment by the accused for the dowry the court shall presume that the accused had caused the dowry death and the burden is on the accused to rebut the presumption.[223] But still there is a way ahead to legislate and implement such provisions in coherence with practical needs as well as social acceptability.

Amending Anti-Dowry Laws for better Implementation

The threat of Dowry has turned into a social danger in present day India prompting the persecution on women, physical brutality on the brides, causing money related and emotional burden on the family of the bride, conjugal clash, etc[224]. This practice is a deep rooted evil in the society which is persisting since ages and flourishing day by day. Prior, instances of dowry deaths, and burning of brides for dowry demand were registered by the police as mishaps or suicides. By 1977-78, after many decades it was finally understood that the major part of the deaths of married

---

[221] *Supra* note 150.
[222] *Supra* note 158.
[223] *Supra* note 159.
[224] Gurudev, "The Origin of Dowry System – British Policies convert Gifts to Bride into an Instrument of Oppression against Women" *available at:* http://www.hitxp.com/articles/history/origin-dowry-system-bride-woman-india-british/ (Visited on July 29, 2017).

111

females which were enrolled as incidental deaths or instances of suicides were, truth be told, murder or abetted suicides. It took over 10 years for the governing body to make dowry death an offence under the Penal Code and to prescribe sentence for the guilty parties[225]. The form to which the evil custom of dowry has transformed since last twenty five years has no traces in the traditional and age old marriage rituals [226]. The requirement for insertion of the provisions was realized by the Law Commission of India in its 91st report which was submitted on 10th August, 1983 on "Dowry Deaths and Law Reform"[227]. Section 304B, I.P.C. [228] and Section113B Evidence Act[229] were inserted by the "Dowry Prohibition (Amendment) Act, 1986". The occurrence of incidents of bride burning and dowry deaths occupies a prime position yet for years it was considered a digression of certain Indian societies. Each citizen must attempt to be refreshed with the existing Acts and statutes passed by the legislature and should appropriately use them when there is a critical need to practice their rights.

---

[225] Shobha Saxena, *Crimes against Women and Protective Laws* 114-115 (Deep and Deep Publications Pvt Ltd, New Delhi, 2008).

[226] *Virbhan* v. *State of U. P.*, AIR 1983 SC 1002.

[227] Law Commission of India, 91st Report on Dowry Deaths and Law Reform: Amending The Hindu Marriage Act, 1955, The Indian Penal Code 1860 and The Indian Evidence Act, 1872, (August, 1983).

[228] *Supra* note 178.

[229] Section113B Indian Evidence Act, 1872.

CHAPTER 4

JUDICIAL APPROACH ON DOWRY PROHIBITION

Judicial decisions and judgments of a nation affect the enactment and implementation of various legislations as well as play a vital part in planning and execution of national policies. The scope, effectiveness and rationale of the legislative provisions can't be accurately perceived until and unless the judgments and decisions which are time to time delivered by the Courts by enforcing and interpreting such provisions. The judges must keep in mind the political and legal ideologies, thereafter accordingly render observations and deliver judgments. The judicial attitude has evolved as more feminist and gender sensitive with the changing dimensions of status and position of women in the society. As the menace of dowry became more widespread, resulting into tremendous increase in the incidents of dowry related offences against women, the judiciary had to adopt more stringent approach against such havoc. Another leap was observed in the judicial prospective with the emergence of misuse and abuse of Anti-dowry laws[1]. As soon as the provisions made for the protection against harassment of women changed into the tools of illegitimate harassment of husband and in-laws in the hands of women in few cases, the judiciary has come up to maintain an equilibrium[2].

4.1 Acceptance of Marriage as a Paramount Institution

In the 19th century, the courts were much influenced with the sayings of Manu in the *Vedas* and *Dharamshastras*. The significance of marriage as a divine union of two bodies and souls till infinity was acknowledged in the judgments. It was not a period when the marriages were commonly dissolved on the grounds of adultery, domestic violence or cruelty, neither the husband nor in-laws were prosecuted for dowry demands and offences related to dowry. The glory of the institution of marriage and duties of wife were well explained by the courts. In *Binda* v. *Kaunsilia*[3]

---

[1] *Preeti Gupta & Anr* v. *State of Jharkhand* (2010) 7 SCC 667.
[2] *Sushil Kumar Sharma* v. *Union of India* AIR 2005 (6) SC 266.
[3] *Binda* v. *Kaunsilia* (1890) I.L.R. All. 126 at Suman Nalwa and Hari Dev Kohli, *Law Relating to Dowry, Dowry Death, Cruelty to Women & Domestic Violence*, 11 (Universal Law Publication Co., New Delhi, 2013)

where a demand was made by the husband that his wife should return to him and the wife refused to do so, the learned Judge of the lower appellate Court has found that the elopement of the plaintiff's wife and his demand for her return and her refusal took place more than five years before suit. In this case, the significance of marriage has been well explained.

> "The effect of marriage is the union of the bride and bridegroom, upon the performance of the nuptial ceremonies and rites, more especially by the recitation of this text of the Veda: 'Bones (identified) with bones, flesh with flesh and skin with skin,' the husband and wife become as it were one person."[4]

The Court has quoted the duties of a wife very stringently. According to the Court, the duty of the wife was to clean the vessels, sweep the dwelling house, to provide curds, rice, *dhurva* grass, leaves and flowers for worship.[5] The wife must salute her husband's parents and afterwards perform the daily household functions. She must not eat anything before worshiping and serving the guests and her husband.

4.2 Devolution of '*Stridhan*' by the Court

Although the menace of dowry does not exist till antiquity but the concept of *stridhan* and the matters pertaining to it are nonetheless new for the Courts. Several times the judiciary took reference of *Smritis* to adjudicate the matters like dissolution of *Stridhan* etc. In *Manilal Rewadat* v. *Bai Reva*[6] A Hindu wife has obtained a decree of maintenance against her husband. The husband filed an appeal against the decree. However, the wife had died, leaving two daughters behind while the appeal was pending in the court. Thereby, the question arose was that whether her husband or her daughters should represent the deceased wife in the pertaining appeal? The question was directly related to the devolution of '*Stridhan*'. The Court discussed the passages from the *Mitakshara* and *Vyavahara Mayukha* which pertain to the devolution of *stridhan*.[7] The question here was that whether the property should devolve on the last

---

[4] *Id. at* 11.
[5] *Ibid.*
[6] Suman Nalwa and Hari Dev Kohli, *Law Relating to Dowry, Dowry Death, Cruelty to Women & Domestic Violence*, 18 (Universal Law Publication Co., New Delhi, 2013)
[7] *Ibid.*

male owner after the death of a woman. The court held that there is nothing of that sort and *stridhana* is recognized as a fresh source of dissolution. Therefore, the Court decided that the daughters of the deceased wife were the legal heirs for the purpose of such appeal.

4.3 Endocentric Approach of Judiciary in the Initial Judgments

In the beginning of 20th century, the status of wife was considered inferior to her husband. The courts had also taken a similar view point. Likewise in *Tekait Mon Mohini Jemadai* v. *Basanta Kumar Singh*[8], the wife has left her husband's house and was living separately on the account of ill treatment, violence and cruelty. There was another issue of maintenance for living separately.[9] The Court has taken a conservative view and opined that the wife is duty bound to live with her husband, wherever he may choose to reside. The wife has to submit herself to the authority of her husband, she can never separate herself from her husband and the violation of such duty is a great sin at the part of wife which results in terrible punishment in the next world. Another point of view given by the Court was

> "The wife is bound to reside with the husband wherever he may choose
> to live. The foot of the husband having another wife will not relieve
> her from that duty; nothing short of habitual cruelty or ill-treatment
> will justify her to leave her husband's house and reside elsewhere."[10]

It was further mentioned by the Court that according to Hindu Law, if in case there is any refusal at the part of wife to live along with her husband, he can forcefully keeps her under his protection.[11] Under I.P.C., there is no punishment for husband for merely keeping his wife under restraint without using any violence or cruel treatment.

4.4 Judicial Viewpoint on the Custom of Dowry

However the culture of modern notion of dowry as an evil was obscure at that time. In rich and lavish families; wealth, presents, movable or immovable properties

---

[8] *Tekait Mon Mohini Jemadai* v. *Basanta Kumar Singh* ILR (1901) 28 Cal. 751
[9] *Ibid.*
[10] *Id at* 761.
[11] *Ibid.*

were given by the parents of bride to the bridegroom at the occasion of marriage. The act of giving and taking dowry was a voluntary and customary act and was not treated as an offence by the courts. The meaning and definition of dowry was however explained in various judicial pronouncements. In *Venkatakrishayya* v. *Laxminarayana*[12], the issue raised was that whether a suit can be filed by the bridegroom to claim the dowry which was promised by the side of bride at the time of marriage. In this case, it was the first time when the term "Dowry" was used by a Court.[13] The Court held that a suit may not lie to recover the amount or valuables which were promised as dowry. Again in *Jagdishwar Prasad* v. *Sheo Baksh Rai*[14], the dowry paid by the father of the bride was claimed back due to certain disturbances in the nuptial relation. The Court clearly held that once the dowry is paid as a consideration of marriage and the marriage is performed, the dowry cannot be recovered back, hence the appeal was dismissed.[15] Further in *Sallial Kotakkat Manakkal Narayan Nambudiri* v. *Patticharavoor alias Charavoor Manakkal*[16], The issue before the court was whether a promise to pay a particular sum of money or some valuable property in consideration of the promise marring the son or daughter of the promisor is valid and enforceable or is immoral or against public policy. The Court referred *Manu Smriti* and a number of case laws and observed that although *Manu* is against receiving any gift or money by the father or the relatives of the girl for greed which results in selling the girl but there is no expressed prohibition of giving any nuptial gift by the parents of the bride to their daughter or son-in-law at the occasion of marriage.[17] Therefore, it was concluded by the Court that the ancient *Smritis* do not permit receiving of gift by bride's parents from the bridegroom however giving the gift by the parents of the girl (bride) to the groom as well as his

---

[12] *Venkatakrishayya* v. *Laxminarayana* (1908) 18 MLJ 405 *at* Suman Nalwa and Hari Dev Kohli, *Law Relating to Dowry, Dowry Death, Cruelty to Women & Domestic Violence*, 21 (Universal Law Publication Co., New Delhi, 2013)

[13] *Ibid*

[14] *Jagdishwar* Prasad v. Sheo Baksh Rai 1919 SCC OnLine All 75

[15] *Ibid.*

[16] *Sallial Kotakkat Manakkal Narayana* Nambudiri v. *Patticharavoor alias Charavoor Manakkal* 1945 MLJR 145 *at* Suman Nalwa and Hari Dev Kohli, *Law Relating to Dowry, Dowry Death, Cruelty to Women & Domestic Violence*, 20 (Universal Law Publication Co., New Delhi, 2013)

[17] *Ibid.*

relatives is not considered to be bad at all.[18] It was further quoted that Hindu Law requires that the parents of the bride should give gifts to the bride and bridegroom during marriage otherwise the marriage is not considered to be properly solemnized and performed.

4.5 Suits for Recovery of Dowry: Judicial outlook after Independence

With the onset of the custom of dowry in the marriages, a new phase began in the judicial history in which in the instances of any friction or breakdown of nuptial relations, the people started filing suits to recover back the dowry, which was given at the time of marriage.

In the case of *Mohd Siddiq* v. *Mt. Zubeda Khatoon*[19], A Muslim wife left her husband's home and started living with parents. A suit was filed by her husband for the restitution of conjugal rights, a conditional decree was obtained. However, the wife did not obey the Court order and instituted suit for the recovering back the dower debt and which she had received by her parents and was lying at her husband's house. The husband gave an explanation that he had already paid a handsome amount of dower as per court order and as he was expecting that his wife would come back to her matrimonial home therefore he did not hand over the dowry to her. It was held by the Court that the neither filing of suits by wife a sufficient justification for disobeying the court's order of restitution nor anything else justified due to which the wife could refuse to obey the decree. Therefore the order given by court to pay a maintenance allowance of Rs. 10 per month to the wife was set aside.[20]

In *Punukollu Parandhamayya* v. *Punukollu Navarathna Sikhamani*[21], the couple got married in the year 1930. After fourteen years of marriage, disputes arose between them. The wife started living apart and filed a case before subordinate judge, for recovery of money and also the movables which were given in the marriage. The relief was given by the lower court on the basis that the Cash, immovable and

---

[18] *Id. at* 21.
[19] *Mohd Siddiq* v. *Mt. Zubeda Khatoon* AIR 1952 All 616 *available at:* https://indiankanoon.org/doc/1225220/ (Visited on Aug 25, 2017).
[20] *Ibid.*
[21] *Punukollu Parandhamayya* v. *Punukollu Navarathna Sikhamani* (1949) 1 MLJ 467 *available at:* https://indiankanoon.org/doc/424691/(Visited on September 15, 2017).

movable properties were intended as *stridhanam* for the benefit of the plaintiff and her children. There was a custom prvailing from a long time in the *Kamma* community of Andhra Desa that on any kind of estrangement results between husband and wife, any kind of kinds of gifts and presents given by the parents of bride to the bridegroom or his family members as dowry had to be returned back to the bride after providing a complete account with interest by the bride-groom or his family. The three named arbitrators who belonged to the Kamma community and were advocates also. They passed an award that the custom was true, valid, as well as ancient and had been consistently acted upon in the community. Therefore it was directed that the amounts presented and dowry given by the family of bride to the bridegroom or in connection to the marriage to be returned back. This decision was challenged in the high court on the contention that the award was illegal within the meaning of Section 30 of the Indian Arbitration Act. It was argued that such a custom would encourage a wife to get rid of her husband with the greed of getting back the money and dowry that was given at the time of the marriage. Therefore this custom should not be acknowledged as it was against public policy. It was held by the High Court held that such a custom had originated as an effort made by the *Kamma* community to stabilize the condition of those women, who, helplessly for some reasons, had to live apart from their husbands. The custom was conceived to protect the interests of women and to save them from unfavorable hardships and ill-timed miseries. Therefore instead of being against the public policy it was rather in the welfare of an important but unfortunately weaker section of the society. The award was upheld and the appeal was dismissed.

In a related case *Kr. Rajendra Bahadur Singh* v. *Kr. Roshan Singh and Anr.*[22], the daughter of the plaintiff was engaged to a boy. There was no clear negotiation or decision regarding dowry before marriage and both parties were on a mutual consensus that everything would be given according to the wish of bride's father as dowry for the marriage. Few ceremonies of marriage were already performed two months before marriage. The plaintiff had already presented some cash, ornaments,

---

[22] *Kr. Rajendra Bahadur Singh* v. *Kr. Roshan Singh and Anr.* ILR (1952) 2 All 681.

clothes and the elephant as dowry to the defendants. But after another ceremony, the defendants further asked for fifteen thousand rupees as a result of which the plaintiff refused their demand and cancelled the marriage.[23] In the mean while unfortunately the girl died few days before marriage. However, a further effort was made to arrange the marriage of the same bridegroom with the sister of deceased would be bride which ultimately failed due to a disagreement on negotiations of dowry. The plaintiff brought suit against the defendants on the two grounds; firstly, that the defendant had made an unreasonable demand of fifteen thousand rupees, which resulted in ending the contract by him. Secondly, due to the death of the girl the contract had become void.[24] Therefore, the money, elephant and other valuable articles that given by him to the defendants were claimed back by him. The Court held that the plaintiff is entitled to get back the gifts, elephant, articles and cash that were given by him to the defendants as a consideration for the proposed marriage of his daughter with their son.[25] After the death of the would-be-bride the contract stands void on the ground of impossibility of execution. It was also decided that all the disputes that may arise, to identify such articles or any deterioration in the condition of the articles so returned would be settled by the court itself.[26] In *Jowand Singh* v. *Chanda Singh and Ors.*[27], the respondent was the father of two girls and has had gifted about four *kanals* of land situated in Tarn Taran in favour of his both daughters. The real brother of the respondent brought a suit to against his brother to challenge this gift. The gift was held to be valid by the Trial Court and the same decision was upheld by the Senior Subordinate Judge on an appeal. The prime issues raised in this case were; firstly whether a father can validly make a gift out of his moveable/immovable, ancestral/ acquired property to his daughter in the form of dowry or '*Jahez*'? Secondly, whether a father can validly make a gift of his whole or some portion of moveable/immovable, ancestral/ acquired property to his daughter or son-in-law otherwise than the dowry? An instance was referred by the Court in which one of the proprietors had gifted a

---

[23]   *Id. at* 683.
[24]   *Id. at* 689.
[25]   *Id. at* 692.
[26]   *Id. at* 693.
[27]   *Jowand Singh* v. *Chanda Singh And Ors* AIR 1952 P H 291

property to his daughter and those heirs were still having the possession. There was no ral son of this Proprietor. Thereafter, the Court referred English *Riwaj-i-am* custom of Amritsar which has shown that the right to make a gift to one's daughters was a well known custom in that district. The Court has also acknowledged the validation of allowing a father to make gifts to the daughters by the way of dowry. It was further admitted that the father has a power to gift property to his daughter even otherwise than her dowry. It was further held that the four *kanals of land given by* the father as gift was valid under custom of Tehsil Taran. as the parties belonged to that district since 1894 and the unrestricted power of making a gift given to proprietors of Tarn Taran Tehsil had never been held as incorrect in the cases which were subsequently decided.

Another case of *Anjani Dei* v. *Krushna Chandra and Anr.*[28], was one of the earliest cases in which the alleged demand of dowry and offences related to dowry were committed.[29] However, to the surprise it was merely a civil suit for claiming the maintenance and recovery of dowry. The reason being could be that in those times, neither there was any particular statute like Dowry Prohibition Act, 1961, nor the provisions of dowry-related offences like Section 498A of I.P.C. in the other statutes of criminal law. Moreover, the violence related to the Dowry was also not very commonly reported as of today.

The brief facts of the case are discussed to understand the matter properly. The appellant got married to the respondent in 1943. She left the house of her husband in 1944. After that the respondent married another female in 1945. At appellant's marriage, she was given gold and silver jewellery by her father and her husband was also given many valuable articles, wrist watch and gold wrist band etc by her father.[30] At a later stage of marriage the groom's father as well as groom pressurized the father of appellant to make a gift of four acre land to them whereas her father agreed upon

---

[28] Anjani Dei v. Krushna Chandra and Anr. AIR 1954 Ori. 117.
[29] *Id. at* 118
[30] *Ibid.*

gifting one acre only.[31] Thereafter, the husband and his relatives started compelling her to persuade her father for which he refused. After her refusal the friction between husband and wife started. Her husband and in-laws started treating with hatred and neglect. No proper food or drink was given to her, she was forced to do menial like servants and was even physically tortured, slapped as well as brutally kicked very often by her mother-in-law.[32] The husband and her in-laws, all were participating in harassing her and depriving her of all the happiness of married life. After such maltreatment it became intolerable for her to live in her matrimonial home. Therefore, she left their house but her ornaments and valuable articles were forcibly kept by her husband and in-laws. She prayed for past maintenance at the rate of fifty rupees per month amounting to a sum of Rs. 1475 and a future monthly maintenance of Rs. 50. She further claimed for the charges for separate residence at the rate of Rs. 10 and the value of articles given in her dowry of Rs. 4084.

Court held that it was clearly indicated by the circumstances that it was difficult to continue her marital life at her matrimonial home. Due to the second marriage of her husband, it was unbearable for her to live with her husband with the esteem and status of a wife and it had been a cruelty to the wife.[33] The cause being justifiable for demanding a separate residence, she was validly entitled for separate maintenance as well as to recover arrears of maintenance, moreover the ornaments and the furniture which was forcibly, a decree equivalent to its value was also reaffirmed.[34]

4.6 Judicial discourse on the Concept of Bride Price or Reverse Dowry

The custom of giving money consideration by the father of the bride, either at the time of engagement or at the time of marriage, to the bridegroom and his family is well-established throughout India. But in certain communities and areas, there is a reverse custom i.e. the father or relative of bridegroom groom pays money to the father of the bride and is called *'sulka'*. The money paid by the bridegroom to the

---

[31] *Id. at* 119
[32] *Id. at* 119.
[33] *Id. at* 120.
[34] *Id. at* 124.

father of the bride intended as a dower is known as *'kanya sulka'* In *Gopi Tihadi* v. *Gokhei Panda and Anr*[35], the brother of the would-be bridegroom had given Rs. 650 to the father of the bride as a consideration for marriage of his brother with his daughter. The engagement took place and thereafter, the appellant paid the stipulated sum of money. Next day he sent a *'palki'* for bringing the bride. However, the father of the bride denied to send is daughter and further demanded 800 Rs more in lieu of marriage.[36] Therefore the marriage got cancelled and thereafter the father of the bride promised to return the money four days later.[37] But when the actual demand was made, he refused to return back the money.

As a result, suit was filed for recovery. The trial Court passed a decree for recovery but the district Court reversed the judgment. The High Court held that this custom of bride price has been an age old custom, is well established and to invalidate such a marriage after such a long period of existence of this custom on the basis of public policy would be too late. The Court further remarked that such marriage contracts cannot be held illegal in absence of any statute that is prohibiting the custom.

If a marriage had been solemnized with a consideration of bride-price, Court cannot pass an order to recover back the money.[38] But if such an agreement of marriage rests unperformed, the Court will order the recovery to be taken of amount given as bride-price. However, the suit for specific performance cannot be entertained. Therefore, the appeal was held maintainable and the decision of the trial Court of returning back the bride-price was restored. [39]

4.7 Emergence of Dowry Related Cruelty and Beginning of Feminist Jurisprudence

As mentioned earlier that in early judgments of Supreme Court, there has been observed an absence of criminal cases for demanding dowry or dowry-related cruelty because neither there was any particular statute like Dowry Prohibition Act nor the provisions of dowry-related in the other statutes of criminal law. Moreover, the

---

[35] *Gopi Tihadi* v. *Gokhei Panda and Anr* AIR 1954 Ori. 17.
[36] *Id. at* 17
[37] *Ibid.*
[38] *Id. at* 22
[39] *Id. at* 23

violence related to the Dowry was also not very commonly reported as of today. But as the time passed, gradually the emergence of such cases has begun. *Om Parkash Tilak Chand* v. *The State*[40] is one of such cases. In this case, the victim was married to the appellant and was harassed, maltreated by her husband and her health deteriorated in her matrimonial house. She put allegations on her mother-in-law and husband that they had beaten her and expressed their annoyance for not bringing any cash in dowry. Her mother-in-law deliberately starved her and used to say that if her daughter-in-law would die she will marry her son in a rich family. The victim was not even allowed to contact anybody and was denied food for many days. Even she was given water in a utensil used in toilet and merely a gram husk mixed in water after five or six days. Once, she tried to escape from the house but was caught by her brother-in-laws in thereafter, was dragged and locked inside the house. On one fortunate day, she managed to go out of the house and reached a nearby hospital. There she took help of a lady doctor who called her brother and lodged a criminal case against the appellant and his mother under Section 307/34 and Section 342 of Penal Code.

The Court imposed the criminal liability on a husband in such case where he withholds necessities of life from her or where he abandons his wife to destruction when he can save her or criminally neglects to shelter her, he is as much a murderer as if he had assaulted her with a deadly weapon. The court found the accused-appellant guilty under Section 307 of I.P.C. and upheld the conviction for three years of imprisonment.[41] However, the benefit of doubt was given his mother and she was acquitted.[42]

4.8 Judicial Attitude in Dowry-Murder Cases before the Amendments in Criminal Law

As the patriarchal social traditions predominant in the society, the pervasive custom of dowry has affected women of all segments. [43] Although the giving and taking the dowry has become illegal since 1961 but still it continued to be demanded by the parents of bridegroom or bridegroom himself and very often even the brides'

---

[40] *Om Parkash Tilak Chand* v. *The State* 1958 SCC OnLine P&H 104 : PLR (1958) 60 P&H 563
[41] *Id. at* 582.
[42] *Id. at* 583.
[43] Lata Jain, "The Horror of Dowry Deaths" (2014) *available at*: https://www.thehansindia.com/posts/index/Hans/2014-05-26/The-horror-of-dowry-deaths/96418 (Visited on Oct 11, 2019).

parents take it as a matter of social status for their young daughter to be given a handsome dowry.[44] The last few decades have witnessed an alarming rise in the incidents in which married women are harassed, physically tortured, mentally abused and event driven to suicide. Even their death occurred in certain circumstances which were abnormal and highly suspicious. In a case *Stree Atyachar Virodhi Parishad* v. *Dilip Nathumal Chordia & Anr*[45] a newly married bride was found engulfed in the flames merely after few days of her marriage. She was found crying for the help and her screams for help were responded by three of their neighbors. It was evident from the facts that no one from the inmates of the house came to her rescue. The fire was extinguished by neighbours which was engulfing her and she was taken to the hospital immediately where she succumbed to her third degree burns. Before her death, she gave her dying declaration in which she had stated that while making tea in the kitchen, her *saree* suddenly caught fire. When the parents of the deceased were informed about her death, they lodged an FIR alleging her husband and in-laws as culprits for her death due to demand of dowry. The investigation also revealed that she was maltreated in her husband's house for their dissatisfaction on getting insufficient dowry.[46] The trial court framed the charges under Section 302 against her husband, however, the High Court accepted the revision petition of accused and discharged his liability under Sections 302 of I.P.C. The Supreme Court held that the trial court has rightly considered each material on record and given a reasoned judgment that why Dilip ought to be charged under Sec 302, besides the police charged him under Sect 306 of I.P.C. Whereas, the High Court merely relied on the dying declaration and took a very narrow approach by treating it as a conclusive proof to discharge the liability of the accused.[47] However, there is no sufficient ground to frame a charge against the in-laws who neither demanded dowry and nor put her on fire. Therefore, the criminal appeal against Dilip is allowed and the Court was directed to proceed expeditiously with the trial. The Court also acknowledged the

---

[44] Stuart Auerbach, "Dowry-Killings Anger Indian Feminist"(1980) *available at*: https://www.washin-gtonpost.com/archive/politics/1980/04/09/dowry-killings-anger-indian-feminists/7de265bc-9ef4-4234-b583-01dac13c64e5/?noredirect=on&utm_term=.6b312b7f567d (Visited on Oct 11, 2019).

[45] *Stree Atyachar Virodhi Parishad* v. *Dilip Nathumal Chordia & Anr* 1989 SCC (1) 715

[46] *Id. at 718.*

[47] *Id. at 724.*

service rendered by the social welfare organization, *'Stri Atyachar Virodhi Parishad'*.[48] As this cruelty or harassment leads to the deaths associated with dowry demand but till 1986 there was no such provision like Section 304 B i.e Dowry Death. Thereafter, the issue of bride burning or dowry death has become the major issue of India's embryonic women's movement to struggle against the centuries-old tradition of dowry. The judiciary has gone through a long journey of deciding such cases along with the changing dimensions of law as well as of society.

4.9 Judicial Interpretation in Widening the Scope of the Term Dowry

In 1961, Dowry Prohibition Act was the first initiative taken by the Parliament against the custom of dowry. The definition of the term dowry was given in Section 2 of this act but the application of this term was potentially extensive. Therefore, Supreme Court in its several judgements has redefined and clarified the inclusions and exclusions of the term dowry. In *S. Gopal Reddy* v. *State of Andhra Pradesh*[49], the Apex Court has taken a very flexible approach in interpreting the term dowry. Any demand of money, property or valuable security by the bridegroom or his side from bride or her side or vice versa in consideration of marriage is dowry.[50] The Court has clearly held that the word marriage would even include a proposed marriage, especially where such proposed marriage has not taken place due to non fulfilment of dowry demand.[51]

Again in *Reema Aggarwal* v. *Anupam and Ors*[52], the appellant's husband and in-laws were charged for the offence of cruelty as they had forced her to ingest a poisonous substance. The trial court had acquitted them on the ground that the marriage of appellant with the respondent was not legal as it was their second marriage. The Supreme Court has again taken a flexible view in interpreting the terms 'marriage' and 'husband'.[53] It was held that the strict construction of the expression 'husband' would frustrate the legislative intent behind the provision of Section 498A

---

[48] *Ibid.*
[49] *S. Gopal Reddy* v. *State of Andhra Pradesh* (1996) 4 SCC 596.
[50] *Id. at 598.*
[51] *Ibid.*
[52] *Reema Aggarwal* v. *Anupam and Ors.* (2004) 3 SCC 199.
[53] *Id. at 200.*

of IPC.[54] Hence, the Court interpreted the expression 'husband' inclusive of a person who has entered into marital relation under the colour of proclaimed status of husband. In *Ashok Kumar* v. *State of Haryana* [55] and *Bachni Devi* v. *State of Haryana*[56], the Court has confirmed that where a husband was demanding a specific amount of money from his wife's father and on non fulfilment of that demand, has tortured and maltreated his wife, such demand is covered within the ambit of 'demand for dowry'.[57] Further where a motorcycle was demanded from the father of wife for business purpose and on not being given, the wife was tortured and harassed in such a way that led her to commit suicide, such demand was also a demand for dowry.[58]

However, there have been certain Supreme Court judgements where the Court has clarified that what will not be covered under the ambit of 'demand of dowry.' A husband's demand for his wife's share in her ancestral property would not be considered as dowry demand.[59] Similarly, demands for presents/gifts/*shagun*/money etc. after the birth of a child from the parents or relatives of wife were considered different from a dowry demand.[60] Where the demand for money from the parents of wife was actually motivated by financial crisis and there was an urgent need to fulfill some domestic expenses, such demands would not constitute a dowry demand.[61]

4.10 Judicial Attitude upon Lack of Evidence or Improper Investigation in Bride Burning

It was been observed that often, the investigation conducted by the police was materially inadequate. Even sometimes, the police did not bother to collect statement of a number of important witnesses or to make correct entries made in the police case diary. Now such circumstances weakened the case of prosecution and there occurred chances of severe miscarriage of justice. Now the question which had to be

---

[54] Section 498A, Indian Penal Code, 1860
[55] *Ashok Kumar* v. *State of Haryana* (2010) 12 SCC 350
[56] *Bachni Devi* v. *State of Haryana* (2011) 4 SCC 427
[57] *Supra* note 55 at 360.
[58] *Bachni Devi* v. *State of Haryana* (2011) 4 SCC 427p. 435.
[59] *Baldev Singh* v. *State of Punjab* (2008) 13 SCC 233.
[60] *Kamlesh Panjiyar* v. *State of Bihar* (2005) 2 SCC 388.
[61] *Anil Kumar Gupta* v. *State of U.P.* (2011) 3 SCALE 453.

determined was that whether the judiciary was able to come for recourse and prevent miscarriage of justice.

In a similar case of *Bhagwant Singh* v. *Commissioner of Police*, Delhi, the petitioner knocked the doors of Justice by seeking for intervention of Apex Court[62], thereby providing justice in the matter of the brutal death of his married daughter. He alleged that his daughter was murdered in her in-laws house by burning but no proper investigation was conducted by the police.[63] The petitioner has mentioned that he and his daughter were against dowry system therefore he got his daughter married to his friend's son. After marriage, the mother-in-law of his daughter started maltreating the bride for not bringing dowry which resulted in the miscarriage of a child because of oppressive tensions.[64] She even warned the deceased that unless a necklace is presented to her, she would remain childless. After some time, his son-in-law demanded fifty thousand rupees for business from him which was however not being given. Thereafter the deceased was found lying on washroom floor due to third degree burns caused by kerosene fire. She was admitted in hospital by her father-in-law. She was able to speak, even though police has not recorded her statement. Section 4 of D.P.A. and a reference to Section 306 was included very late in the F.I.R. Neither material witnesses were examined and nor material objects were recovered by the police properly.

The petition was admitted by the Court, full details of the investigations were demanded by the I.G. of police and the reason was inquired for non filing of the report under Sec. 173(2) Cr.P.C. It has been held by the Court that the investigation conducted by the police was even considered materially inadequate by the Crime Branch itself. Police did not bother to collect statement of a number of important witnesses likewise: the taxi driver, the neighbor and even the deceased herself. Even the entries made in the police case diary were also erroneous. The court has analyzed each and every aspect of the petition and carefully scrutinized the matter. The court has derived to very significant conclusions: It was held that in such a case where there

---

[62] *Bhagwant Singh* v. *Commissioner of Police* (1983) 3 SCC 344.
[63] *Id .at* 347.
[64] *Id. at* 345.

were suspicious circumstances of death of a young wife there must be an attribution that either some crime has been committed to her or she was kept in some suffocated and mentally torturing atmosphere which compelled her to commit suicide. It was aptly remarked by the court that

> "Young women of education, intelligence and character do not set fire
> to themselves to welcome the embrace of death unless provoked and
> compelled to that desperate step by the intolerance of their misery".[65]

The Court held that the object of the Court was not to decide that whether the wife was murdered or she has committed suicide rather the purpose was to determine the manner in which the investigation was conducted in this case. It was further held that although it may be disappointing for the aggrieved party who was in the hope of the institution of criminal action on the verdict that the offence has been committed but due to the insufficient material, the court cannot decide that far. However the case was transferred from Delhi Police to the C.B.I. and the C.B.I. was requested to complete the investigation within three months and take the necessary action as soon as the investigation is completed.[66]

Such cases of such nature are an evidence of deep-rooted infirmity in our social order. It can be analyzed through these judgments that:

- The demand for dowry, greed of getting more and more dowry as well as the whole dowry system as a part of custom, deserves the severest admonition. Such situations clearly prove the gross failure of dowry prohibition law[67] in achieving its objective.

- The cases where the death occurred due to a crime, the offenders could easily escaped from the grasp of the law as a result of insufficient and inadequate police investigation

- Those cases where the wives died under suspicious circumstances in their matrimonial homes, it became very difficult to understand and ascertain the exact circumstances in which the incident took place.

---

[65] *Id .at* 352.
[66] *Id. at* 354.
[67] The Dowry Prohibition Act, 1961

- Generally these incidents occur in the husband's home; therefore, usually the husband or in-laws were the only witnesses, available in these cases.

In another similar case of *Kundula Bala Subrahmanyam and Anr* v. *State of Andhra Pradesh*[68] , the prosecution witnesses rushed to the appellant's house as they heard screams and cry of the deceased. The husband, mother-in-law and father-in-law of the deceased were hastily coming out from their kitchen while the deceased was engulfed in the high flames and was laid on the floor.[69] The appellants did not bother much to extinguish the fire or helping the deceased, however witnesses tried to save her, gave water to drink and asked her that what had happened. She explained that her mother-in- law poured kerosene over her body and her husband set her to fire. The brother of the deceased reached the house of the appellant as soon as he was informed and was told about the burning of the deceased. As the deceased saw her brother, she asked her brother to tell their parents that her mother-in-law had poured kerosene on her body and her husband had set fire to her. She further instructed him that whatever cash was given in her marriage by her parents, it shall be taken back from her husband and in-laws so that the same could be used to get sisters married to some nice persons. After that, her husband entered in the kitchen and with folded hands he requested her to forgive him and begged that he would never repeat such an act again. A first-aid was given by a local doctor to her in the verandah of the house. The deceased was taken to the govt. hospital where after half an hour, a doctor examined her, declared her dead. Her brother and uncle went to the Police Station, lodged an FIR and a case under Section 302 IPC was registered.

Trial Court acquitted the appellants on the basis that there was no motive for appellants to commit the crime, oral dying declaration could not be relied upon, unexplained delay in lodging F.I.R. and therefore it was a suicide case and not a murder. On an appeal by the state, High Court convicted both the appellants under Section 302/34 of I.P.C. and sentenced life imprisonment. On the basis that chain of circumstantial evidence was sufficient to prove the guilt.[70]

---

[68] *Kundula Bala Subrahmanyam and Anr* v. *State of Andhra Pradesh* 1993 SCC (2) 684.
[69] *Id. at* 685.
[70] *Id. at* 685.

An appeal was filed in the Supreme Court contending that the conviction passed by the High Court is not justified. The Apex Court has remarked that motive is very significant in proving circumstantial evidence. Moreover, to establish circumstantial evidence, there must not be any gap in the chain of circumstances.[71] In regard to the dying declaration when it is only made to the close relatives, it must be scrutinized carefully with the evidence of witnesses to the dying declaration.[72] Mere presence of a relationship is not a sufficient ground to reject the testimony of the trustworthy witness. The medical evidence has fully corroborated the case of the prosecution. Neither the husband nor his mother tried to save the victim or render her any kind of first aid. The conduct of both the appellants is well consistent with the hypothesis of their guilt. The Court has shown a great concern on the rapid rise in the cases of cruelty, torture, abetment of suicides, harassment and dowry deaths of young innocent brides.[73] The Court upheld the conviction and sentence of appellants, cancelled their bail bonds and dismissed the appeal.[74]

Such incidences of physical violence and harassment by own family members send shock waves and dreadful fear to the civilized society. When an elder woman participates as a major role in a crime towards the younger female of her own family and the husband of the victim either acts as a mute spectator or even actively participates in such a crime, it is shameful, disgraceful and disregard of his marital obligations. The laws for dowry prohibition,[75] was enacted with an objective to curb this social evil but unfortunately it has remained more on the papers and lesser in the practical implementation. Where Law is not sufficient to combat this evil, a vast social movement is highly needed to educate the women and make them well aware of their rights. Apart from all, it is the duty of court to be more sensitive and vigilant in deciding the culpability of crime against women.

---

[71] *Ibid*
[72] *Id.at* 686.
[73] *Id. at* 687.
[74] *Id. at* 702.
[75] The Dowry Prohibition Act, 1961.

In another landmark case, *Smt. Laxmi* v. *Om Parkash & Ors*[76] , The deceased was married to the accused and was living with her husband and in-laws. This marriage was suffering under the intense pressure of the dowry and subsequently, the deceased registered a complaint under D.P.A. against her husband, mother and sister-in law. On contrary, her husband filed a divorce case which ended in a compromise and the deceased joined her matrimonial house. Unfortunately, on one morning, the accused informed the Police Control Room that his wife has set herself ablaze by pouring kerosene oil. She was taken to the hospital by the PCR vehicle and on the way to the hospital she made her first dying declaration and therefore, all the three were arrested on the same day. She ultimately succumbed to her injuries and died. After completion of initial investigation, a *challan* under Section 302/34 was filed against the three where they pleaded not guilty. The case was opened with the statements of a witness who was among the first who tried to douse the fire and was a close neighbour. She gave the statement that after revival and come back of the deceased to matrimonial home, the couple apparently seemed to be going well. Moreover, on the day of incidence, the accused was also dousing the fire and covered her with a blanket to extinguish the fire. The witness also made two other significant statements where she told that the deceased used to abuse her in-laws publically and was planning to kill herself and implicate them for her death. In 1985, all the three accused were acquitted with the verdict of not guilty by the trial court.[77]

Thereafter an appeal through SLP was filled by the mother of the victim in the Apex Court. The Apex court had analyzed all the five statements and held that none of them sufficed the worth of being considered as dying declaration.[78] The court has rejected to accept these statements as dying declaration because of the fact that these statements come from the mouth of other witnesses rather than the victim herself.[79] Therefore the acquittal was upheld. It is evident that the judiciary had taken a strict approach in accepting the statements regarding the death of the victim as dying declarations. The judiciary had been vigilant enough to not ruling out the possibility

---

[76] *Smt. Laxmi* v. *Om Parkash & Ors.* (2001) 6 SCC 118.
[77] *Id. at* 125.
[78] *Id. at* 120.
[79] *Id. at* 135.

of revenge by the victim or exaggeration of allegations on the accused while imparting conviction. But on the side it has also increased the difficulties of prosecution to prove its case beyond reasonable doubt due to lack of evidence. In the absence of any special provisions, the cases of bride burning were dealt under the offence of murder and the burden of proof beyond reasonable doubt was on the prosecution.[80]

4.11 Judicial approach on Dowry Death and Cruelty after insertions under 1986 Amendment Act

Before the law commission report of 1983 and amendment passed in 1986 there was no separate provision of dowry death and such cases were dealt with under the offence of Murder u/sec 302 of IPC or Abetment to suicide u/sec 306 of IPC. In the case *of Shobha Rani* v. *Madhukar Reddi*[81], the appellant wife filed a divorce petition on the grounds of cruelty. She alleged that her husband and in-laws demanded dowry. Her case was rejected by the trial court as well as High Court and it was held that she seemed to be hyper sensitive and hyper imaginative.[82] It was held by the Court that the main objective of Parliament to enact the Dowry Prohibition Legislation[83] was to curb the evil practice of dowry. But as the deep rooted practice persisted, therefore, the considerable changes were suggested through the Amendments done in 1984[84]. Moreover, a new offence of cruelty[85] was inserted in the criminal law[86]. The dimension of cruelty has been changed by widening its scope. Cruelty is a ground of divorce even under Hindu Law.[87] However, no specific definition has been given in it. Such cruelty may be mental/ physical, intentional/unintentional. It is easy to determine physical cruelty; however, the court must be more sensitive and assertive in establishing mental cruelty.

---

[80] See Section 302, The Indian Penal Code, 1860.
[81] *Shobha Rani* v. *Madhukar Reddi* (1988) SCC 105.
[82] *Id. at* 106.
[83] *Supra* note 75.
[84] The Dowry Prohibition (Amendment) Act, 1984.
[85] Section 498A, The Indian Penal Code, 1860.
[86] The Indian Penal Code, 1860.
[87] Section 13,The Hindu Marriage Act 1955.

The Court held that, matrimonial conduct which constitutes cruelty as a ground for dissolution of marriage, if not admitted, requires to be proved on the preponderance of probabilities as in civil cases and not beyond a reasonable doubt as in criminal cases. There must be an evidence of harassment done to the wife for fulfillment of any unlawful demand for money to constitute cruelty in criminal law. [88] The requirement of evidence of any unlawful demand for money is only under Section 498A of the I.P.C. [89] but there is no such requirement under Section 13(1)(i)(a) of H.M.A. [90] It was further held that there was sufficient evidence to draw an inference that dowry was demanded in this case. Therefore, the court was satisfied by the inference drawn and opined that it amounts to cruelty, therefore, the wife was entitled to get a decree for dissolution of marriage. [91]

The amendments introduced in the year 1986 inserted Sec 304 B and Sec 498 A in the penal law, Sec 113A and Sec 113B in the Evidence law and thereby provided a tight hand to the prosecution against the defense while dealing with matter. The judicial discourse has also undergone the similar change in certain pronouncements. In the case of *Shanti and Anr* v. *State of Haryana*[92], the accused along with three other co accused were charged for committing a dowry death. The trial under Section 201, 304 B and 498 A of I.P.C. was conducted against them. However, the trial court acquitted the three co accused but convicted two accused. [93] In the appeal, the High Court upheld their convictions under Section 304 B and 201 of I.P.C. whereas they

---

[88] *Supra* note 81 at 111.

[89] Section 498A- Husband or relative of husband of a woman subjecting her to cruelty.—Whoever, being the husband or the relative of the husband of a woman, subjects such woman to cruelty shall be punished with imprisonment for a term which may extend to three years and shall also be liable to fine. Explanation.—For the purpose of this section, "cruelty" means—
    (a) any willful conduct which is of such a nature as is likely to drive the woman to commit suicide or to cause grave injury or danger to life, limb or health (whether mental or physical) of the woman; or
    (b) harassment of the woman where such harassment is with a view to coercing her or any person related to her to meet any unlawful demand for any property or valuable security or is on account of failure by her or any person related to her to meet such demand.

[90] Section13- Divorce—(1) Any marriage solemnised, whether before or after the commencement of this Act, may, on a petition presented by either the husband or the wife, be dissolved by a decree of divorce on the ground that the other party—
    (ia) has, after the solemnisation of the marriage, treated the petitioner with cruelty.

[91] *Supra* note 81 at 115.

[92] *Shanti and Anr* v. *State of Haryana* (1991) 1 SCC 371.

[93] *Id. at* 373.

133

were acquitted under Section 498 A on the ground that "once the cruelty under section 498A culminates in dowry death of the victim, Section 304 B alone is attracted."[94] The appeal was filed in the Supreme Court on two major contentions. Firstly, the acquittal under Section 498A prescribes that cruelty was not proved, therefore, the "death" cannot be considered as dowry death. Secondly, the essentials under Sec. 304 B were not fulfilled and there was no direct evidence against the accused.[95] In the instant case, it was never held by the High Court that prosecution has failed to establish cruelty done by appellants but merely considering it as an essential of Section 304B, has acquitted the appellants under Section 498A. Therefore, the Apex Court accepted it beyond all reasonable doubt that an offence under Section 304-B has been committed.[96] The death occurred in such cases is neither natural nor accidental. These are unnatural deaths, either a suicide or a homicide. For an instance even if it is assumed as a suicide, still it would remain a death which occurred in the circumstances that were not natural and shall attract Section 304B.

In the landmark case of *State of Himachal Pradesh* v. *Nikku Ram and Ors*[97], It was alleged that soon after marriage, the husband, mother- in-law, and sister-in-law started abusing deceased for bringing insufficient dowry. They were further alleged of treating her with cruelty, when their demands for television, electric fan and buffalo etc. were not fulfilled. After three years of marriage, the mother-in-law gave deceased a blow with a sickle causing a wound on her forehead. On the same day, being shattered by the torture, deceased consumed naphthalene balls and succumbed to death due to cardio- respiratory arrest. A sickle was recovered and some letters written by deceased to her father also came into light during police investigation. The aforesaid persons were charged and a trial was conducted against them under Sections 304B, 306 and 498A of I.P.C.

The trial court acquitted all the three accused with a conclusion that the prosecution has failed to establish the charges beyond reasonable doubt and the High

---

[94] *Id. at* 376.
[95] *Ibid.*
[96] *Id. at* 377.
[97] *State of Himachal Pradesh* v. *Nikku Ram and Ors.*1995 (6) SCC 219.

Court refused to grant leave to appeal. The judgment of the Apex Court started with the first three words as 'dowry, dowry and dowry'. The court has explained the painful repetition of the word 'dowry' thrice, because there are generally three occasions, when the dowry is demanded; "(i) before the marriage; (ii) at the time of marriage; and (iii) after the marriage."[98] The Court rejected the view point of trial court that anything given after marriage is only for a happy matrimonial relationship and would not be dowry. The word "dowry" was in a significant way and it was aptly remarked that "it could not have been said that anything given after marriage could not be dowry".[99]

The offence under Section 306 IPC was not even proved as none of the respondents could really be said to have abetted suicide as per the definition of "abetment" in Section 107 IPC. No reliable evidence was found to prove any harassment of deceased under Section 498A, clause (b). Only the offence under Section 324 against the mother-in-law was proved, therefore she was awarded a fine of Rs. 3,000 within a period of two months.

The Court had scrutinized the legislative intent of Dowry Prohibition Act that this fact was very well known to the legislature that the dowry demands are made very often as a consideration for the marriage and such demands are made even after the solemnization of marriage. Since greed is limitless, therefore, the demand of dowry is followed by the torture and harassment of the bride which sometimes lead to suicide or murder of the girl. However, those injuries which are present on the bodies of deceased victims but could not have caused death, despite of the demands of dowry; the offences would not attract Section 304B.[100]

Dowry Prohibition Act, 1961 is soft statute and is not stringent enough to deal such a major evil. These new insertions like Section 498 A[101] and 304 B in I.P.C.[102];

---

[98] *Id. at* 220.
[99] *Id. at* 223.
[100] *Id. at* 222.
[101] Section 498 A, The Indian Penal Code, 1860.
[102] Section 304 B, The Indian Penal Code, 1860.

Section 113A[103] and 113B[104] in the Indian Evidence Act; Dowry Prohibition (Amendment) Act, 1986; and changes in Cr.P.C by making the offence of dowry death cognizable and non-bailable, have been done to increase the efficacy of dowry prohibition laws.

4.12 Judicial Attitude on Invoking Presumption under Law of Evidence

The offences related to dowry are generally committed in the privacy of residential homes and in secrecy, independent and direct evidence is not easy to get. That is why the legislature has tried to strengthen the hands of prosecution by introducing Sections 113A and 113B in the Evidence Act[105]. Section 113A and 113B permit a presumption to be raised if certain foundation facts are established and the death of women has been caused within seven years of marriage. But these presumptions must be invoked after applying a judicious mind so that all the people present the in-law's house must not be unnecessarily harassed. Judiciary has taken a very sensitive approach to invoke presumptions under Law of Evidence in certain judgments.

In *Baijnath and Others* v. *Sate of M.P.*[106], the deceased, was married to the nephew of appellant and was living along with her husband, mother in-law, father in-law, appellant and his wife in a joint family. On one unfortunate night, after the dinner all of them went to their respective rooms for sleeping. On the next morning the deceased was found dead by hanging from the fan. After police investigation, a criminal case against both appellants, deceased husband and in-laws was registered under Section 302, 304B, 498A, 201r/w Section 34 of I.P.C. The prosecution alleged that all the accused had subjected Saroj Bai to harassment and torture in connection to their dowry demands. During the trial, deceased's husband committed suicide on by consuming poison. The trial Court acquitted all of them after elaborate assessment of the evidence produced. The Court absolved the accused from the allegations of dowry demand, cruelty or harassment and thereafter held that Section 113B of Evidence Act

---

[103] Section 113 A, The Indian Evidence Act, 1872.
[104] Section 113 B, The Indian Evidence Act, 1872.
[105] Paras Diwan and Peeyushi Diwan, *Law relating to Dowry, Dowry deaths, bride Burning, Rape and related Offences* 116 (Universal Law Publishing Co.Pvt.Ltd, Delhi, 1997).
[106] Baijnath and Others v. Sate of M.P. (2017) 1 SCC 101

was not available for invocation. However, the High Court accepted the version of prosecution, applied Section 113B of Indian Evidence Act and converted their acquittal to conviction.

The appellants brought an appeal in the Apex Court against this conviction order of High Court and contended that the essentials of Section 498A and 304B were not proved. Therefore, the High Court has erroneously applied the presumption of Section 113B. It was further contended that medical evidence was insufficient to ascertain the cause of death, there was no such incriminating evidence to prove the guilt and there was nothing that proves that the dowry was demanded by husband or his family. Apex Court has thoroughly explained that when, why, where and how the presumption of culpability by Section 113B shall be invoked. [107] The Court has aptly remarked that it can only be activated when there is a proof that for demanding dowry, the deceased was treated with cruelty. If prosecution fails to prove by clear cut evidence that deceased was subjected to cruelty by the accused for demanding dowry, the burden of proof cannot be shifted upon the accused to hold him guilty by taking refuge of presumption under Section 113B. The prosecution had failed to prove the cruelty by direct evidence and therefore, Section 113B cannot be invoked. [108] The conviction and sentence was set aside by the Court and the appellants were given the benefit of doubt.

In another case of *Heera Lal and Anr* v. *State of Rajashthan*[109], the deceased has committed suicide by pouring kerosene and setting herself on fire. An F.I.R. was lodged against her mother-in-law and father-in-law under Section 498A and Section 306 of I.P.C., for harassing her for at least five years and ultimately leading to her suicide. The two witnesses, who were neighbors, attested the harassment done by in-laws. It was also confirmed by the medical evidence that her 90% burns were caused by pouring kerosene and setting herself on fire.[110] There was also a dying declaration made by the deceased before the S.D.M. It stated that her in-laws quarreled with her everyday and asked her to leave the house. Her husband was living in Kuwait and was

---

[107] *Ibid.*
[108] *Id. at 112.*
[109] Heera Lal and Anr. v. State of Rajasthan, (2018) 11 SCC 323
[110] *Ibid.*

not responsible for anything. She started living in a separate house and her husband has come from Kuwait for few days. On the day of incidence, her in-laws came with their luggage and forcefully decided to reside with her. As a result she got angry, went to the kitchen, showered kerosene on her and set herself on fire. Her in-laws did not try to stop her, however, her husband tried to save her. She also claimed that her in-laws were demanding dowry from her. On this evidence, the trial court held that Section 498A was not made out but convicted both the appellants under Section 306 and sentenced 3 years imprisonment. The High Court had dismissed their appeal and upheld the conviction by relying upon the dying declaration.[111] The Supreme Court has held that where the wife has committed suicide but her in-laws or husband are acquitted under Section 498A of I.P.C., there is a bar on the prosecution to use presumption under Section 113A of Indian Evidence Act to prove abetment to suicide under Section 306 of I.P.C.[112] It was also held that harassment is lesser in degree than cruelty and mere finding of harassment would not prove that there is abetment of suicide.[113] Therefore, the decision of the High Court was set aside and appellants were acquitted.

For applying Section 113A, three ingredients are required. Firstly, the woman has committed suicide. Secondly, it has been committed within seven years of marriage. Thirdly, her husband or his relatives subjected her to cruelty. If it is not proved that the in-laws of a deceased had subjected her to cruelty, than it would be a grave miscarriage of justice to drag them unnecessarily under the presumptions of Section 113A and 113B. Even for an instance, if it is assumed that the presumption under Section 113A would apply, even though there must be a link or intention on the part of in-laws to assisting the victim to commit suicide to hold them guilty.

4.13 Reliance of Judiciary on the Evidence in Dowry Death Cases

In the case of *Prem Singh, Smt. Shanti* v. *State of Haryana*[114], the deceased within few days of her marriage, started complaining to her parents that she was

---

[111] *Id. at* 324.
[112] *Id. at* 326.
[113] *Ibid.*
[114] *Prem Singh, Smt. Shanti* v. *State of Haryana* (1998) 8 SCC 70.

maltreated, harassed and humiliated for dowry and for not bringing expensive gifts during and after the marriage ceremony. Efforts of a common friend to mediate the issue of dowry went in vein. The father of the deceased also gifted them a buffalo in order to raise their monthly income. Instead, they made a fresh demand of five thousand rupees which her father could not fulfill. One night, the deceased got admitted to the Civil Hospital with the severe burns on her body. Before she died, she told her father that she would not be allowed to live peacefully in matrimonial home until he gives them five thousand rupees.[115] A police complaint was registered against deceased's husband and parents-in-law. The appellants were acquitted by the trial court, whereas the verdict was reversed by the High Court by convicting them under Section 304B of IPC.[116]

It was opined by the Apex Court that, the trial court relied upon the evidence of the doctor who gave medical treatment for her burn injuries. Another Doctor, failed to preserve the viscera and to get the opinion of chemical analyzer to rule out the possibility of poisonous substance having been swallowed by deceased and held that the death of deceased was not occurred by the act of appellants. The High Court analyzed the prosecution evidence in detail and demonstrated that the acquittal recorded by the trial court is contrary to the evidence on record, therefore, reversed the acquittal. After going through the evidence, the Court held that there was no suspicion that any kind of poison was consumed by the deceased. Therefore, not preserving the viscera to get the opinion of chemical analyzer is immaterial.[117] It was stated that cause of her death was asphyxia which was a result of smothering caused to her before death and which was enough to cause death in an ordinary course of nature. Multiple abrasions and contusions on her body and over her upper and lower lip were also found. Death due to smothering was an unnatural death and had caused within a period of seven years of marriage.

A strong presumption does arise against the husband as he failed to explain that how she sustained several scratches and wounds on the body. Merely taking his

---

[115] *Id. at* 72.
[116] *Id. at* 71.
[117] *Id. at* 75.

wife for treatment to Civil Hospital does not demolish the prosecution case as regards the unnatural death. The Supreme Court upheld the conviction of appellant under Section 304B IPC as it appeared in the face of the evidence, that he has caused ill-treatment and harassment to his wife including beating on various occasions for not getting additional dowry.[118] However, it was observed that the mother-in-law was residing separately from her son and there was no evidence to show that either she was instigating her son, to demand additional dowry or to cause ill-treatment or harassment to the deceased. Therefore, an acquittal was given to her of the charge u/sec 304B IPC by rendering her a benefit of doubt.[119]

In another case of *Manoharan and Others* v. *The State*,[120] the deceased got married in 2001. The dowry demands were also met by giving gold, cash and other household articles to her husband and in-laws. One day, the deceased was restricted to enter her matrimonial house till the further demands of the dowry were met.[121] To sort this issue, a *Panchayat* meeting was held, which could not resolve this issue and thereafter the deceased had even sent a petition to the C.M. office. After the inquiry conducted by the police, her husband gave the undertaking and started living with her. But on the same night, a quarrel broke between the two and her husband stabbed her brutally with a knife and killed her. He himself surrendered before village officer by admitting the guilt of crime. Charges were framed against him and his parents u/sec 498 A, 302 r/w Sec 34 of I.P.C. and u/sec 4-A (1)(2)(i) of the Tamil Nadu Prohibition of Harassment of Women Act, 1998.[122] The Investigating Officer went for search and inspection at the place of occurrence and on the basis of statement given by the accused he recovered a knife there.

The post mortem of deceased revealed some major injuries. One incised injuries on scalp; wounds on the right side forehead; one incised wound just below the left eye and two on lower jaw; missing of the lower teeth left incised and canine; fracture in the left side of mandible, deep lacerated wounds and abrasions on the neck;

---

[118] *Id. at* 76
[119] *Ibid.*
[120] *Manoharan and Others* v. *The State* (2018) 16 SCC 113
[121] *Id. at* 114.
[122] *Id. at* 115.

deep wounds on shoulders, forearms, hands and fingers, abrasions over right knee were found.[123] Sessions found her husband guilty but acquitted the other two appellants of the charges of Sec.302 I.P.C. However they were convicted under Sec. 498A I.P.C. and were awarded a three months rigorous sentence and Rs. 1000/- as fine. The trial court's view was reaffirmed and the conviction of all the three accused was upheld by the High Court. An S.L.P. was filed by the father-in-law and mother-in-law of the deceased. However the conviction of her husband attained finality. The Supreme Court held that it was indicated by the evidence produced that no complaint was made against the in-laws for the demand of dowry or any harassment related to it.[124] Even the couple was living separately. Due to the inadequacy of the evidence produced, the charges against the appellants were not proved. Therefore, the conviction was set aside.

In another case of *A.K. Devaiah* v. *State of Karnataka*[125], some wordy altercations occurred between the appellant and his wife, three months before her death. The prosecution alleged that prior to the marriage the appellant had demanded Rs. 15,000 cash and gold-silver jewels in the form of dowry. The entire dowry was given before and at the time of marriage except a pair of gold bangles which were promised to be given after some time.[126] The appellant used to consume liquor and subjected the deceased to mental and physical torture for the remaining balance of dowry. After three months the deceased committed suicide by setting herself on fire as she was unable to tolerate any more torture done by her husband. The husband himself informed the police about the unnatural death of his wife. 97% ante-mortem burns of second and third degree were found in the post mortem.[127] The appellant was arrested but was acquitted by the trial court due to insufficient evidence against him.[128] On an appeal preferred by the State under Section 378(1) and (3) of Cr.PC, the acquittal was set aside and he was convicted by the High Court under Section 3, 4 and

---

[123] *Id. at* 116.
[124] *Ibid.*
[125] *A.K. Devaiah* v. *State of Karnataka* 2015 (1) SCC 752.
[126] *Id. at* 753.
[127] Ibid
[128] *Id. at* 754.

6 of Dowry Prohibition Act and Section 304B, 498A of I.PC. On an appeal filled by the appellant, it was held by the Apex Court that absence of any burns on the body of the accused clearly indicate that he did not try at all to save the deceased from fire.[129] The evidence has clearly revealed the negotiation, demand as well as taking of dowry before and at the time of marriage. The appellant's habit of consuming liquor, committing cruelty to the wife and continuous demand of dowry has led the deceased to commit the suicide and has well covered the essentials of the offence.[130] Therefore, the judgment and conviction imposed by the High Court was upheld.

4.14 Death Sentence in Dowry Related Cases

The maximum punishment under Section 304 B of IPC is life imprisonment but the question to be determined here is that whether the dowry deaths can be equated with murder and that too fitting under the rarest of the rare category. The Supreme Court has taken a remarkable stand and directed all the trial courts to ordinarily add the charge of murder under Section 302 of IPC to the charge of dowry under Section 304B of IPC. The intent of Court is that the death sentence can also be imposed in such brutal and heinous crimes against women.

In *Satya Narayan Tiwari* v. *State of U.P,*[131] The Court held that the expression "rarest of the rare"[132] does not merely mean that the act is uncommon rather it means that the act is heinous and barbaric. Killing of a bride is undoubtedly brutal and barbaric.[133] Again in *Rajbir* v. *State of Haryana,*[134] the Court has directed all the trial courts to ordinarily add Section 302 along with the charge of Section 304B.[135] The intent of the judiciary behind this mandate was that the offenders who have committed such a heinous and barbaric act against their own wives or daughter-in-laws, such offenders must be punished under the most stringent provisions for their

---

129 *Id. at* 759.
130 *Ibid.*
131 *Satya Narayan Tiwari* v. *State of U.P* (2010)13 SCC 689
132 *Bachan Singh* v. *State of Punjab* AIR 1980 SC 898
133 *Supra* note 131 at 693.
134 *Rajbir* v. *State of Haryana* (2010) 15 SCC 116
135 *Id. at 118.*

brutal acts. However, this view is an endorsement of Justice Katju and does not reflect the collective attitude of judiciary in imposing death penalty in dowry deaths.

4.15 Misuse and Abuse of Anti-Dowry Laws

A huge number of women are every day ill-treated, harassed, killed for dowry and face cruelty behind the four walls of their matrimonial home. For safeguarding their interest, this provision is the utmost need of the hour and so is its stringent nature of being non-bailable and cognizable. Although there was an expressed apprehension of many legal luminaries that it would be misused and lead to a disastrous impact on the society. Unfortunately this apprehension took the face of reality and Supreme Court and High Courts have expressed deep anguish for this result. The Supreme Court, hence, in the landmark case of *Sushil Kumar Sharma* v. *Union of India*[136] condemned this section as 'Legal Terrorism'.

In *State of Andhra Pradesh* v. *M. Madhusudhan Rao*[137] 2008, the complainant sent a report to the additional D.G.P., C.I.D. Hyderabad and alleged that her husband and mother-in-law insisted her father to give one house, sixty thousand rupees cash, six *tolas* of gold and household articles of fifty thousand rupees. All these demands were fulfilled by her father at the time of her marriage.[138] She further alleged that still after marriage her husband beat her up, scold, shout and threatens to kill her for demanding fifty thousand rupees more as dowry. Her mother-in-law, her husband's brother and his wife, her sister-in-law and the youngest brother of her husband also helped her husband in beating and harassing her. Another woman who was somehow connected to her husband also used to threaten her by saying that she has married her husband. She narrated another incidence that one day, her husband and his above mentioned relatives forced her to consume poison and as a result thereof, she was admitted to a hospital in an unconscious state. She has stated that the police took her statement in a semi conscious state so she was not aware that what exactly had been

---

[136] *Supra* note 2.
[137] *Andhra Pradesh* v. *M. Madhusudhan Rao* 2008 (15) SCC 582
[138] *Id. at* 584.

recorded[139]. However, no action was taken against any person and thereafter she went to stay with her parents. An important point to be noted was that the complaint regarding the incident occurred on 19th April 1996 was lodged after more than a month i.e. on 22nd May 1996. All the accused were tried under Sec 498A and Sec 307 r/w Sec 34. Accused 1 was found guilty under Section 498A of I.P.C. and was sentenced for one year imprisonment and a fine of Rs. 8,000/-. However, he was not found guilty under Section 307 and all the other accused were completely acquitted. On an appeal against this conviction in the H.C., the conviction was set aside. The State has filed an appeal in the S.C. against the order of acquittal given by the H.C.

The Apex Court has clearly held that there is a huge time gap between the date of alleged occurrence and the date lodging F.I.R. Once the complainant was discharged from the hospital, after that no reasonable explanation for the delay in filing the complaint has been given.[140] Therefore, such circumstances raised a considerable doubt regarding the truthfulness of the complaint and the genuineness of the evidence produced by the complainant and her father. It was considered unsafe and unjustified to base the conviction of the respondent upon such an unreliable complaint and evidence. Henceforth, the acquittal of the respondent was upheld and the appeal was dismissed.

In another landmark case of *Preeti Gupta & Anr* v. *State of Jharkhand* [141], the appellant was the sister of complainant's husband. The complainant was living in Mumbai with her husband after her marriage. She visited her in-law house at Ranchi, to take part in the festival *gangaur* for a week and after that returned back to Mumbai. After three and a half month, she filed a complaint before the Chief Judicial Magistrate, Ranchi under Section 498A, 406, 341,323, and 120B of I.P.C. r/w Section 3 and 4 of D.P.A. against her husband, mother-in-law, Father-in-law, an unmarried brother-in-law and the her married sister-in-law (Preeti Gupta).The Judicial Magistrate summoned all the appellants and the appellants were aggrieved for being summoned.[142] It was found that allegations of luxury car in dowry and physical

---

[139] *Id. at* 585.
[140] *Id. at* 590.
[141] *Supra* note 1.
[142] *Id. at* 670.

assault by her husband were there in the complaint.[143] It was found by the Court all the allegations were false and baseless against the appellant. The Court quashed the complaint and also directed to send a copy of Judgment to Law Commission and to Union Law Secretary, Government of India who may place it before the Hon'ble Minister for Law and Justice to take steps in public interest as deemed fit to prevent the misuse of Section 498A. There are many genuine cases of dowry but misusing it will lead to insurmountable harassment, agony and pain to the complainant, accused and close relatives.[144]

In a famous case of *Rajesh Sharma* v. *State of UP[145]*, the appellant and his parents were unhappy with the dowry given to them, although the father of complainant had given dowry to his full capacity. Later the appellant started beating and abusing his wife for bringing more dowries and this also led to the termination of her pregnancy. On account of termination of pregnancy, he left his wife to her parental home.[146] Later he was summoned by his wife under Section 498 A and 323 of I.P.C. and was found guilty under Section 498A of I.P.C. by the session court. But his wife also summoned his parents, brother and sister-in law and the session judge also accepted the said petition. Therefore, the appellant moved to the High Court against this petition and High Court rejected this petition as no ground of support was found. This also led to take care of tendency of pulling the entire family in the crime.[147] But after the rejection of petition in H.C., he moved to Supreme Court. The Supreme Court in its judgment prescribed some measures to curb the misuse of Section 498A.The concern was to save the innocent family members of the accused when they are dragged and detained under the Act. Therefore following directions were given by the Supreme Court[148]:

i.   The court directed the District Legal Services Authority to must set up one or more Family Welfare Committees with preferably three members. Such

---

[143] *Ibid.*
[144] *Id. at* 667.
[145] *Rajesh Sharma* v. *State of UP* (2018) 10 SCC 472
[146] *Id. at* 474.
[147] *Id. at* 475.
[148] *Id. at* 480.

committee shall look into every complaint of cruelty, filed under Section 498A. The Court further directed that no arrest shall be made under Section 498A, until and unless the Committee would submit its report on the concerned complaint.

- These committees must be reviewed time to time by the district and session judge in a year.
- Para legal volunteers, retired person, social worker, wives of working officers or other citizens should constitute the committee.
- The Court will not call committee members for witnesses.
- The committee will look into all the complaints received under Section 498A and may probe the parties.
- The committee will submit the report within one month to the authority.
- The committee can submit factual aspects and its opinion in a brief report.
- No arrest should be affected till the time committee submits its report.
- This report will be considered by the investigating officer or the Magistrate.
- The Legal Services Authority must train the committee members from time to time.

ii. An investigating officer should be identified and trained to deal with complaints under Section 498A.

iii. The District and Session Judge or any other nominated senior judicial officer may dispose of the cases where settlement has reached including the closure of criminal case if it primarily relates to matrimonial discord.

iv. The bail application shall be decided on the same day as far as possible. The bail must not be denied merely on the grounds of recovery of disputed dowry items if there is a possibility of protecting maintenance rights of wife and minor children. While dealing with the bail matters, it is very important to carefully scrutinize the individual roles, prima facie truth of the allegations, and actual requirement of further arrest or custody.

v. The issuance of the Red Corner Notice and impounding passports should not be a routine for the people residing out of country.

vi.   The District Judge or designated judicial officer nominated by District Judge will be open to link and club all the cases between the parties of matrimonial dispute to give holistic view to the Court where all such cases are entrusted.

vii. The outstation members of the family may not be required to present physically and trial court may allow their appearance via video conference in such way that it does not affect the Court proceedings adversely.

viii. The offences which involve tangible injuries and death will not be covered under these directions.

This pronouncement became a ground of criticism by various women activists and feminist NGOs. The verdict was also condemned on the ground that the judiciary has encroached upon the area of legislature.

After the judgment of Rajesh Sharma Case, a petition was filed in Social Action Forum for *Manav Adhikar* v. *Union of India & Ministry of Law and Justice*[149]. It had a primary objective to seek directions for the Ministry of Law to create a secure environment for those married women who are subjected to cruelty and to enable them to make informed choices. But it was also contended in this petition that the social intent has been defeated, the intensity of Section 498A is diluted due to the restrictions put forth in the case of Rajesh Sharma.[150] Therefore a uniform system of monitoring and reviewing the cases of violence against women covered under section 498A of I.P.C. was demanded. It was further mentioned in the petition that there must be a uniform policy for lodging an F.I.R., arresting the accused and granting bail in the offence committed under Section 498A of I.P.C. It was further sought that there must be a procedure to immediately register F.I.R. whenever a married woman makes a complaint of cruelty and harassment. The petitioner has contended that the social intent has been defeated, the intensity of Section 498A is diluted and the offence has practically been made available due to the restrictions put forth in the case of *Rajesh*

---

[149] Social Action Forum for Manav Adhikar and Anr. v. Union of India Ministry of Law and Justice and others (2018) 10 SCC 443.
[150] *Id. at* 455.

Sharma and others v. *State of U.P. and another*[151].A Three-Judge Bench of the SC held the constitution of Family Welfare Committee by the District Legal Services Authority and conferring power to the committee as impermissible. [152]

The Apex Court observed that the direction to settle a case by a third agency after registering the case is not a correct expression of law. It was remarked that the Apex Court has a power to issue directions only in the fields where there is an absence of law but regarding this matter the statutory provisions and judgments already exist, therefore, the direction to constitute such a committee by the Court is erroneous. It was further held that only High Court can quash F.I.R./complaint on settlement between the parties. The directions given in the Rajesh Sharma case, empowering the District Judge to quash such F.I.R. or complaint was recalled. Since Section 498A of I.P.C. is a non compoundable offence, therefore, in case of settlement, both parties shall file a petition under Section 482 of Cr.PC and only High Court can quash the case if it considers such a petition bonafide. The other directions given by Apex Court in Rajesh Sharma case remained undisturbed. The Court agreed that impounding passports of accused where they are living outside India should not be done as a matter of daily routine.[153]

---

[151] *Supra* note at 145.
[152] *Supra* note at 149.
[153] *Id. at* 471.

CHAPTER 5

ROLE OF GOVERNMENT AND DOWRY PROHIBITION

The Indian women have traversed a long way in their fight against the patriarchal society, continuous suppression, age old customs like dowry and violence against them. Although, the women have come a long way in uplifting their position and status but still many issue likewise domestic violence, cruelty, increasing rate of dowry deaths, wife battering, female foeticide etc. are still rampant in society. Indian Constitution clearly provides the principles of gender equality, equality of status and opportunity as well as specific laws to provide protection and welfare to the women in its Preamble[1], Fundamental Rights[2] and Directive Principles[3].

Despite constitutional assurance of gender equality and several legislations for the protection of women, widespread discrimination as well as suppression of women persists in India. The dowry death incidents, cruelty, domestic violence with women and other offences related to dowry are regularly published in the newspapers, media and our often highlighted by the organizations working for the women. Undoubtedly, killing a woman for non-fulfillment of a dowry demand by her husband or in-laws is not only an extreme violation of her right to life but also a shameful question mark on the institution of marriage. According to the recent report of 2018 of National Crime Record Bureau, the dowry related violent crimes have seen tremendous growth in past few years[4].

5.1 Observation of National Crime Record Bureau.

Offences related to dowry, dowry death, domestic violence, cruelty etc are certain dowry related violent crimes for which crime statistics are recorded throughout the country.[5] In the year 2018, dowry deaths cover a percentage of 1.1% of the total violent crimes that took place in India. In the year 2017, dowry deaths

---

[1] Preamble, The Constitution of India.

[2] Part III, Fundamental Rights, The Constitution of India (See: Article 14, Article 15 and Article 16)

[3] Article 39, Part IV, Directive Principles Of State Policy, The Constitution of India, (Also see: Article 39A)

[4] Chayyanika Nigam, "21 lives lost to dowry every day across India; conviction rate less than 35 per cent", *India Today*, April 22, 2017 *available at:* https://www.indiatoday.in/mail-today/story/dowry-deaths-national-crime-records-bureau-conviction-rate-972874-2017-04-22 (Visited on April 22, 2019).

[5] Press Note Release of *"Crime in India 2016- Statistics"*(Ministry of Home Affairs, 30th November, 2017) available at: http://ncrb.gov.in/StatPublications/CII/CII2016/Press%20release-Crime%20in%20India%202016.pdf

149

cover a percentage of 1.2% of the total violent crimes that took place in India. In the year 2016, dowry deaths cover a percentage of 1.2% of the total violent crimes that took place in India.[6]

The offence of cruelty by husband or his relatives covers a percentage of 7.8% of total IPC crimes that took place in the year 2018 in India. The offence of cruelty by husband or his relatives covers a percentage of 8.1% of total IPC crimes that took place in the year 2017 in India. The offence of cruelty by husband or his relatives covers a percentage of 8.7% of total IPC crimes that took place in the year 2016 in India.

In 2014, around 8455 dowry deaths took place with the crime rate of 1.4%, in the year 2015, the number of dowry death incidents were reported as 7634 with the crime rate of 1.3%. In 2016, the number was again very high as 7621 dowry death incidents were reported at the crime rate of 1.2%. In 2017, the number of dowry deaths was again very high as 7466 dowry death incidents were reported at the crime rate of 1.2%. In 2018, the number was again very high as 7166 dowry death incidents were reported at the crime rate of 1.1%.[7]

It is a matter of great concern that despite the enactment of stringent laws related to dowry prohibition by legislature, constant efforts of judiciary to curb the menace of dowry deaths and other dowry related offences, there is no significant decrease in the dowry related crimes. However a slight change has been observed from the year 2014 to year 2018 that is from 8455 dowry deaths to 7166 dowry deaths. But a very significant rise has been observed in the crimes related to Dowry Prohibition Act. In the year 2016, the total number of crimes related to Dowry Prohibition Act was 9683 at the crime rate of 1.6%, in the year 2017, 10189 at the crime rate of 1.6%, in the year 2018 it rose to 12826 at the crime rate of 2.0%. The states like Uttar Pradesh, West Bengal, Bihar, Karnataka, and Orissa have shown the occurrence of huge number of dowry related crimes in last five years.

---

[6]   National Crime Records Bureau, Report: *Crime in India, 2016 Statistics* (Ministry of Home Affairs, October, 2017) *available at*: http://ncrb.gov.in/StatPublications/CII/CII2016/pdfs /NEWPDFs/ Crime%20in%20India%20-%202016%20Complete%20PDF%20291117.pdf

[7]   National Crime Records Bureau, Report: *Crime in India, 2018 Statistics* (Ministry of Home Affairs, December, 2019) 4 *available at*: http://ncrb.gov.in/StatPublications/ CII/CII2018/pdfs/Crime% 20in%20India%202018%20-%20Volume%201.pdf (Visited on January 31, 2019).

5.1.1 Dowry Deaths in the 10 Most Affected States[8]

The maximum numbers of dowry death incidents were reported in Uttar Pradesh with a significantly high number of 2444 incidents in 2018. It was followed up by Bihar and Madhya Pradesh with the number of 1107 and 547 incidences respectively in 2018. The number of incidents of dowry death was recorded as 444 in west Bengal, 404 in Rajasthan, 312 in Odisha, 252 in Jharkhand, 216 in Haryana, 200 in Maharashtra and 186 in Telangana in the year 2018.

Table 5.1

State/UT	Incidents	Victims	Crime Rate
Uttar Pradesh	2444	2521	2.3
Bihar	1107	1111	2.0
Madhya Pradesh	547	547	1.4
West Bengal	444	444	0.9
Rajasthan	404	405	1.1
Odisha	312	373	1.1
Jharkhand	252	266	1.4
Haryana	216	216	1.6
Maharashtra	200	205	0.3
Telangana	186	186	1.0

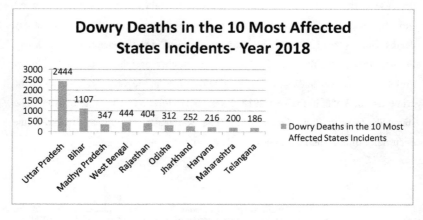

Figure 5.1

---

[8] *Id at* 13.

5.1.2 Crime under Dowry Prohibition Act, 1961 in 10 Most Affected States[9]

In year 2018, the maximum number of crime incidence under Dowry Prohibition Act, 1961 were reported in Uttar Pradesh with a significantly high number of 4371 incidences. Bihar, Odisha, Karnataka and Jharkhand followed with 2094, 1595, 1568 and 1224 incidences respectively which were also quite high. Assam, Andhra Pradesh, Tamil Nadu, Uttarakhand and Maharashtra also reported 1138, 320, 206, 104 and 36 incidences respectively of such crime.

Table 5.2

State	Incidents	Victims	Crime Rate
Uttar Pradesh	4371	4469	4.1
Bihar	2094	2311	3.7
Odisha	1595	1630	7.2
Karnataka	1568	1583	4.9
Jharkhand	1224	1306	6.8
Assam	1138	1138	6.8
Andhra Pradesh	320	321	1.2
Tamil Nadu	206	207	0.5
Uttarakhand	104	104	1.9
Maharashtra	36	36	0.1

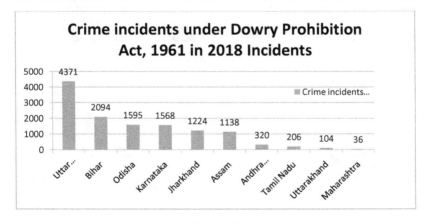

Figure 5.2

---

[9]   Supra note 7 at 32.

5.1.3 Offence of Cruelty by Husband or Relatives Reported in the 10 Most Affected States[10]

In 2018, highest number of offences of cruelty by husband or his relatives were reported from West Bengal with 16951 incidences. Uttar Pradesh and Rajasthan also reported high number of 14233 and 12250 incidences respectively. In east India, Assam topped the number with 11136 incidences. Subsequently, Maharashtra had 6862, Andhra Pradesh- 6831, Telangana- 6286, Madhya Pradesh-4159, Gujarat- 2923 and Bihar-2539 cases of such crime.

Table 5.3

State	Incidents	Victims	Crime Rate
West Bengal	16951	17150	35.9
Uttar Pradesh	14233	14361	13.3
Rajasthan	12250	12363	33.0
Assam	11136	11261	66.7
Maharashtra	6862	6882	11.8
Andhra Pradesh	6831	6889	26.3
Telangana	6286	6286	34.2
Madhya Pradesh	4159	4160	10.6
Gujarat	2923	2928	9.1
Bihar	2539	2603	4.5

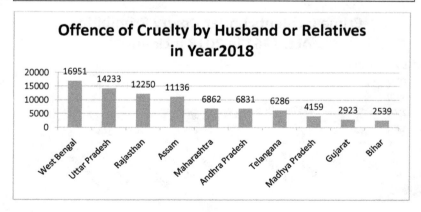

Figure5.3

---

[10]   Supra note 7 at 30.

5.1.4 Incidents of Dowry Deaths in 5 Most Affected Metropolitan Cities[11]

Delhi is the metropolitan city which reported highest number of incidents of dowry deaths in the year 2018. Bangalore, Kanpur, Patna and Lucknow were also among the 5 most affected metropolitan cities with the incidence count of 53, 34, 24 and 20 respectively.

Table 5.4

Cities	Incidents	Victims	Crime Rate
Delhi	133	137	1.8
Bangalore	53	53	1.3
Kanpur	34	85	2.5
Patna	24	24	2.5
Lucknow	20	20	1.4

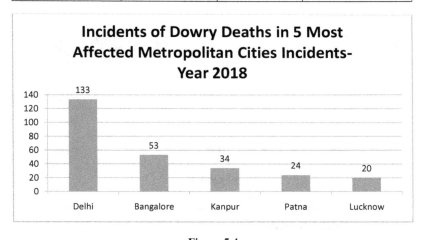

Figure 5.4

5.1.5 Crime under Dowry Prohibition Act, 1961 in 5 Most Affected Metropolitan Cities[12]

In 2018, among the metropolitan cities, the crime cases under Dowry Prohibition Act, 1961 were reported highest from Bangaluru with 692 incidences. It

---

[11] Supra note 7 at 50.
[12] Supra note 7 at 68.

was followed by Lucknow with 66 cases and Patna with 62 cases in the same year. Delhi and Chennai had reported 13 and 4 incidences respectively

Table 5.5

Cities	Incidents	Victims	Crime Rate
Bangaluru	692	693	17
Lucknow	66	66	4.8
Patna	62	62	6.5
Delhi	13	13	0.2
Chennai	4	4	0.1

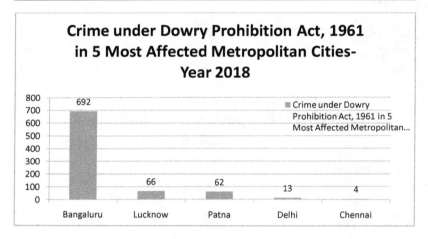

Figure5.5

5.1.6 Offence of Cruelty by Husband or his Relatives Reported in the 5 Most Affected Metropolitan Cities[13]

Among the metropolitan cities, offences of cruelty by husband or his relatives were reported highest from Delhi in year 2018. There were 3128 offence incidences reported in Delhi. Hyderabad reported 1343 and Lucknow had 1212 which were also quite high. Jaipur and Kotkata had slightly lesser cases with 993 and 946 incidences respectively.

---

[13] *Id at 67.*

155

Table 5.6

Cities	Incidents	Victims	Crime Rate
Delhi	3128	3134	41.3
Hyderabad	1343	1346	35.7
Lucknow	1212	1212	87.7
Jaipur	993	993	68.3
Kolkata	946	1099	13.9

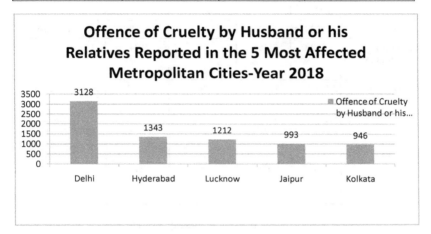

Figure5.6

5.1.7 Police Disposal of Crime against Women Cases [14]

NCRB has recorded the police disposal of crime cases against women in the crimes likewise Dowry death, Abetment of suicide of women, Cruelty by husband or relatives, Dowry Prohibition Act, 1961 and Domestic Violence Act, 1961. In 2016, 7621 cases of dowry death were reported and 4220 similar cases pending in previous year were also carried forward. Out of these cases, 558 cases were observed to be true but could not be proved due to lack of evidence whereas 254 cases were filed wrongly. 66 cases were of mistake of fact and 13 cases were transferred to other PS/Magistrate. The total number of cases related to abetment of suicide of women was recorded as 4466 and similar 2228 cases of previous year were also carried

---

[14] Supra note 6 at 148.

forward. It was observed that 124 cases were true but could not be proved in the absence of evidence but 157 cases were filed wrongly. 34 cases were of mistake of the fact and 4 cases were transferred to other PS/ Magistrate.

Table 5.7

Dowry related Offences	Cases Pending from Previou s Year	Cases Reported During the Year	Cases Transferred to other PS/ Magistrate	True but insufficient Evidence	False	Mistake of Fact
Dowry Death	4220	7621	13	558	254	66
Abetment of Suicides of Women	2228	4466	4	124	157	34
Cruelty by Husband or his Relatives	51807	110378	280	8308	6745	2958
Dowry Prohibition Act, 1961	6090	9683	59	1178	334	148
Domestic Violence Act, 2005	126	437	0	10	8	1

The cases related to the offence of cruelty by husband or relatives were reported as 110378 and similar 51807 cases of previous year were also carried forward. It was observed that 8308 cases were true but could not be proved in the absence of evidence but 6745 false cases were also identified. 2958 cases were mistake of the fact and 280 cases were transferred to other PS/Magistrate. Apart from that, 9683 cases under Dowry Prohibition Act, 1961 were reported and similar 6090 cases of previous year were also carried forward. It was observed that 1178 cases were true but could not be proved in the absence of evidence but 334 false cases were also identified. 148 cases were mistake of the fact and 59 cases were transferred to other PS/Magistrate. It was further recorded that 437 cases under Domestic Violence Act, 2005 were reported and similar 126 cases of previous year were also carried forward. It was observed that 10 cases were true but could not be proved in the absence of evidence but 8 false cases were also identified. 1 case was mistake of the fact.

5.1.8 Disposal of Persons Arrested for Crime against Women [15]

NCRB has recorded the police disposal of persons convicted, acquitted and discharged against the crimes such as Dowry death, Abetment of suicide of women, Cruelty by husband or relatives, Dowry Prohibition Act, 1961 and Domestic Violence Act, 2005 and has also analyzed the data on the basis of gender. In year 2016, 3042 men and 358 women were convicted for dowry death whereas 6131 men and 1088 women were acquitted. 67 people were discharged in 2016. For abetment of suicide of women, 275 men and 30 women were convicted whereas 1912 men and 283 women were acquitted however, 15 people were discharged. For cruelty by husband or his relatives, 11773 men and 1738 women were convicted whereas 69157 men and 12918 women were acquitted however, 2198 people were discharged. In year 2016, 1032 men and 167 women were convicted under Dowry Prohibition Act, 1961 whereas 4946 men and 1038 women were acquitted. 11 people were discharged in 2016. In year 2016, 28 men and no women were convicted under Domestic Violence Act, 2005 whereas 44 men and 2 women were acquitted. 1 person was discharged in 2016.

Table 5.8

Dowry related Offences	Persons Convicted			Persons Acquitted			Persons Discharged		
	Male	Female	Total	Male	Female	Total	Male	Female	Total
Dowry Deaths	3042	358	3400	6131	1088	7219	56	11	67
Abetment of Suicides of Women	275	30	305	1912	283	2195	14	1	15
Cruelty by Husband or his Relatives	11773	1738	13511	69157	12918	82075	1838	360	2198
Dowry Prohibition Act, 1961	1032	167	1199	4946	1038	5984	9	2	11
Domestic Violence Act, 2005	28	0	28	44	2	46	1	0	1

---

[15] Supra note 7 at 156-157

5.2 Suggestions and Recommendations of National Commission for Women

A dire need of NCW was realised due to the lack of effective constitutional machinery to fight against the problems of women of India as well as to strengthen the status of women in the nation and society. Thus a Committee was constituted with an objective of improving the Status of Women in India had further established National Women Commission in the month of January in the year 1992.[16] The NCW has been consistently endeavouring to resolve and decrease the incidents of cruelty against wife done by husband and her in-laws, wife battering, dowry deaths, bride burning, as well as domestic violence.[17] Generally, in the family dispute cases like: cruelty by the husband, the foremost effort of NCW is to settle the dispute by providing counseling to both the parties.[18] Many such matters are successfully resolved through a positive intervention but in severe incidents of domestic violence and cruelty, an enquiry committee is constituted by the commission to look into the matter.

5.2.1 Functioning of NCW in the Complaints Related to Dowry

The complaint and counseling cell of the commission is the main unit and it receives the grievances related to domestic violence, harassment, dowry, torture, bigamy, rape, and cruelty by the husband, sexual harassment at work place etc. It has an authority to process such complaints or to take *suo moto* action under NCW Act.[19] In the year 1999, the complaints received by the commission were 4329.[20]

Many amendments have been proposed by the Commission in the Penal Code,[21] Hindu Laws[22] and Dowry Prohibition related laws[23] to deal with the cruelty and dowry deaths etc offences. In the year 1994, the commission had proposed a bill

---

[16] Annual Report, National Commission for Women, 1996-97, 1-2 referred in Sadhna Arya, "The National Commission for Women: A Study in Performance" 22 available at: http://www.cwds.ac.in/wp-content/uploads/2016/11/NCWreport.pdf.

[17] National Commission for Women, *"Mission- Women" available at:* http://ncw.nic.in/mission-and-vision/mission.

[18] National Commission for Women, "Complaint and Investigation Cell", *available at:* http://ncw.nic.in/ncw-cells/complaint-investigation-cell.

[19] Section 10, The National Commission for Women Act, 1990.

[20] Government of N.C.T of Delhi, *Department of Women and Child Development, available at:* http://wcddel.in/ncfw.html.

[21] Section 304 B and Section 498A, The Indian Penal Code, 1860.

[22] Section 13, The Hindu Marriage Act, 1950.

[23] See also, The Dowry prohibition Act, 1961.

before the Indian Government[24] to provide a civil as well criminal remedy against the domestic violence.[25] The draft legislation also proposed the addition of a new provision, Sec 498B in IPC[26] to punish domestic violence with an imprisonment of 3 years and fine. The scope of the definition of the term 'domestic violence' was also proposed to be widened. In the year 1996-97 Report, it was mentioned that the commission decided to review the legislations regarding the offences related women.[27] Again in 1999-2000 Annual Report, a recommendation was forwarded to enact a comprehensive legislation consisting of civil and criminal remedies for the violence against women at their matrimonial homes. An elaboration in the definition of cruelty[28] was also given.

NCW had organized a convention at Symposia Hall, New Delhi on the matter relating to the eradication of the rampant menace of Dowry on 22nd Nov, 2005.[29] The commission has proposed certain recommendations and amendments to the provisions related to dowry death.

- The offence of dowry death shall be dealt equivalent to murder as it is not less grave than murder.

- The existing legislations related to dowry prohibition in Dowry Prohibition Act and penal laws and have failed to bring any dissuasion in the mindset of culprits. The commission strongly proposed that the weakness of such provisions must be removed by bringing necessary changes and thereby such provisions must be made effective.

---

[24] The Domestic Violence to Women (Prevention) Bill, 1994, drafted by National Commission for Women.

[25] Dr. Khurram Shikoh Qazalbash & Brajesh Kumar Gupta, "Protection of Woman from Domestic Violence" Law, - A Biting Reality: History, Causes and Its Social Impact", 10 *IOSR- JHSS* 42 *available at:* http://www.iosrjournals.org/iosr-jhss/papers/Vol10-issue2/F01024144.pdf?id=6208

[26] Savitri Goonesekere, *Violence, Law and Women's Rights in South Asia* 145 (Sage Publications, New Delhi, 2004) *available at:* https://books.google.co.in/ books?id=5pKHAwAAQ BAJ&pg= PA145&lpg= PA145&dq =National+Commission+for+Women+draft+Sec+498B+in+IPC+ ++to+punish+domestic+violence+with+an+imprisonment+of+3+years+and+fine.&source=bl&ots= MMSuOf83ox&sig=ACfU3U1IWwu3uENqWkpw0NEZX0mlQsjr9g&hl=en&sa=X&ved=2ahUK EwjPwNr1cjmAhVTmuYKHQszBvlQ6AEwDXoECAoQAQ#v=onepage&q=National%20Commi ssion%20for%20Women%20draft%20Sec%20498B%20in%20IPC%20%20%20to%20punish%20 domestic%20violence%20with%20an%20imprisonment%20of%203%20years%20and%20fine.&f =false.

[27] *Supra* note 16.

[28] *Ibid.*

[29] P.K. Majumdar & R.P. Kataria, *Law Relating to Dowry Prohibition Cruelty & Harassment* 49 (Orient Publishing Company New Delhi, 2014).

- A unique recommendation has been proposed that the time limit of presumption of 7 years of marriage may be increased to avoid any pre planned offences.

- It was also proposed to increase the minimum punishment from seven years to ten years. [30]

It was discussed in the convention that the legislation has failed and proved to be ineffective to curb the gradually increasing menace of dowry. All the people attending the convention like, the chairpersons of different state commissions for women, representatives of various NGOs, Public Servants, and Police Officers etc. have unanimously concluded that there was a strong need to make certain amendments in Dowry Prohibition Act so as to make it effective.[31]

As recommended by the National Commission for Women, certain amendments are required in the definition of "dowry":

1. There must be a single provision in which the definition of the word dowry and the exceptions related to it should be provided.

The term "presents" should be replaced by the expression "gifts" to specify the willing nature of giving and taking. There must be an explanation to explain certain terms like "gifts", "voluntary" and "indirectly" etc to remove any kind of ambiguity in the interpretation.

2. Certain amendments were also suggested in the Sec. 3 of the Act[32] likewise;

- There shall be different punishments for the givers of dowry and the people who take dowry.

- There shall be prescribed penalties if no list of gifts are maintained which were received at the marriage.

---

[30] *Ibid.*

[31] *Ibid.*

[32] See also, Section 3- Penalty for giving or taking dowry.— (1) If any person, after the commencement of this Act, gives or takes or abets the giving or taking of dowry, he shall be punishable with imprisonment for a term which shall not be less than five years, and with fine which shall not be less than fifteen thousand rupees or the amount of the value of such dowry, whichever is more.
Provided that the Court may, for adequate and special reasons to be recorded in the judgment, impose a sentence of imprisonment for a term of less than five years, The Dowry Prohibition Act, 1961

- The parents and the family members of the bride shall be included as aggrieved persons under the scope of Sec. 7(3) of the Act.

3. The provision relating to the reversion of dowry in Section 6(3) on the death of the married female in abnormal circumstance shall be omitted. For whatsoever reason, the death of the woman might have been caused, but once the death is caused, whatever was obtained as dowry has to be returned back to her parents or her children. The justification behind this clause is given that receiving any kind of dowry by the husband itself was an illegal act. Therefore, the dowry property which has to be given back during her life time cannot be claimed as inheritance even after her death.

4. A provision related to the jurisdiction is to be added in Section 7 in which the term, "any recognized welfare institution or organization" shall be substituted by "any recognized service provider or protection officer".[33] Usually, in case of any marital friction, wives start residing at their parental home or any place other than their husband's home, such place might be not connected with the place where the marital offences actually occurred to them. Hence, it is essential that the Law must provide an opportunity to such women that they may file cases at any of the place i.e. either where the offence was committed on them or where they have started residing afterwards. This would encourage the victims to come forward against such offences for filing a case as per their convenience. The Domestic Violence Act[34] precisely expresses that the place where the offence has been committed or the place where the woman is temporarily or permanently residing,

---

[33] Section 7(1) reads as: "Cognizance of offences –
(1) Notwithstanding anything contained in the Code of Criminal Procedure, 1973 (2 of 1974),-
(a) No court inferior to that of a Metropolitan Magistrate or a Judicial Magistrate of the first class shall try any offence under this Act.
(b) No court shall take cognizance of an offence under this Act except upon-
(i) Its own knowledge or a police report of the facts which constitute such offence, or
(ii) A complaint by the person aggrieved by the offence or a parent or other relative of such person, or by nay recognized welfare institution or organization.
(c) It shall be lawful for a Metropolitan Magistrate or a Judicial Magistrate of the first class to pass any sentence authorized by this Act on any person convicted of an offence under this Act.
Explanation – For the purpose of this sub section, "recognized welfare institution or organization" means a social welfare institution or organization recognized in this behalf by the Central or State Government."
[34] The Protection of Women from Domestic Violence Act, 2005.

both the courts have jurisdiction over the matter.[35] Similar provisions needs to be inserted in the Dowry Prohibition Act.

In a case, *Y Abraham Ajith & Ors* v. *Inspector of Police Chennai*[36], it was held that "no part of cause of action pertaining to dowry arose in Chennai where the victim was residing, and therefore, the magistrate at Chennai had no jurisdiction to deal with the matter". Therefore, it ordered to quash the proceedings.

5. Insertion of a new section i.e. Section 7A was recommended to provide the mode for getting the orders of relief. This new provision must provide that the victim, or parents or family member of that person, or a protection officer or a service provider may file an application before the Magistrate requesting one or more reliefs under Domestic Violence Act.[37]

It is also recommended that the provisions of Section 31 of DV Act[38] should apply to the provisions of Dowry Prohibition Act. A positive move has been taken by the Domestic Violence Act[39] by going ahead from merely penalties and arrests to the directions of providing necessary protection to the victims. The legislature has to keep in mind that mere punishing the accused will not support the victim to overcome her mental trauma or to improve her economic condition that she has faced due to such violence and harassment. In such situations, it is essential for the legislature to show humanity towards the victim and make such

---

[35] Section27 reads as: Jurisdiction.—
  1. The court of Judicial Magistrate of the first class or the Metropolitan Magistrate, as the case may be, within the local limits of which—
  a. the person aggrieved permanently or temporarily resides or carries on business or is employed; or
  b. the respondent resides or carries on business or is employed; or
  c. the cause of action has arisen, shall be the competent court to grant a protection order and other orders under this Act and to try offences under this Act.
  2. Any order made this Act shall be enforceable throughout India.
[36] *Y Abraham Ajith & Ors* v. *Inspector of Police Chennai* (2004) SCC (Cri.) 2134.
[37] Chapter IV of the Protection of Women from Domestic Violence Act, 2005
[38] Section 31 reads as: Penalty for breach of protection order by respondent.—
  (1) A breach of protection order, or of an interim protection order, by the respondent shall be an offence under this Act and shall be punishable with imprisonment of either description for a term which may extend to one year, or with fine which may extend to twenty thousand rupees, or with both.
  (2) The offence under sub-section (1) shall as far as practicable be tried by the Magistrate who had passed the order, the breach of which has been alleged to have been caused by the accused.
  (3) While framing charges under sub-section (1), the Magistrates may also frame charges under section 498A of the Indian Penal Code (45 of 1860) or any other provision of that Code or the Dowry Prohibition Act, 1961 (28 of 1961), as the case may be, if the facts disclose the commission of an offence under those provisions.
[39] *Supra* note 34.

laws that are capable to provide her the necessary protection. Dowry Prohibition Act merely prescribes the imprisonment or fine for the people who give or take dowry[40] but ignores the insertion of any provisions related to the protection, monetary relief or residential facility for the victim; neither has it authorized the Magistrate to pass any such order. It is therefore, the need of the hour to incorporate the provisions related to the benefit of the victim.

6. The insertion of Section 8B (4) prescribes for appointing advisory board for assistance of Dowry Prohibition Officers in performing their functions. Such appointment must be made as a mandate for the Governments of various states as it ensures the efficiency of protection officers and provides help in performing their duties.

7. Introduction of another Section i.e. 8C is recommended. It shall deal with delegating the responsibility to the Government to provide maximum publicity to the provisions of this Act. The central Government shall be imparted two major responsibilities. Firstly, it has to instruct all the Government and Public Servants; to furnish a declaration after their marriage that they have not received any dowry. Such declaration must contain the signature of his wife, father and father-in-law. Secondly, it must take necessary steps to give huge publicity to the Dowry Prohibition Act through media and news papers at regular intervals.

5.3 Reports of Law Commission of India

Legislative reforms have always been a part of Indian legal history since its inception. To maintain the dynamism of law various reforms have taken place to bring changes in age old customs and customary laws. In the third decade of 19th century, the Government had constituted Law Commissions to consolidate, codify and amend various laws. The Government of India had established first Law Commission of Republic India in the year 1955. The first initiative to curb the evil of dowry and to make more stringent laws was taken by the Law Commission in its 91st report on 10 August 1983.[41]

---

[40] Section 3 and Section 4, The Dowry Prohibition Act, 1961.
[41] Law Commission of India, 91st Report on Dowry Deaths and Law Reform: Amending The Hindu Marriage Act, 1955, The Indian Penal Code 1860 and The Indian Evidence Act, 1872, (August,

5.3.1 91st Report of Law Commission of India[42]

The major concern behind formulating this report was the alarming rise in the incidents of death of married women in the highly suspicious circumstances. It was mentioned in the report that such deaths seemed to be closely associated with dowry and very often were the cases of bride burning. Unfortunately, there was not only an unusual increase in the number of such deaths but also many cases of deaths were unreported. Therefore, there was a dire need to consider and formulate appropriate legislation to overcome the situation.[43]

It recommended bringing certain changes in Hindu Marriage Law[44], Penal Laws[45] and Evidence Act[46]. The main objective behind these recommendations was to bring a law reform to reduce the number of dowry deaths. There has been an unusual increase in dowry deaths and therefore it was realized that the existing criminal law has to be resorted for bringing up the reform.

The first recommendation was regarding the insertion of a presumption in the Indian Evidence Act, 1872. It was proposed that if the death of a married woman occurs within 5 years of marriage, because of burning, or injuries caused to her in her matrimonial home where she was living with her husband, or she dies within the four walls because of some other similar causes, the presumption may be taken that such a death was not of accidental nature. This presumption was based on the factual components of the dowry death. In each case, deceased is a young and married woman who is generally dependent on her husband or her in-laws. The desire to live of such a woman is slowly decreased by the harassing conduct of her husband or in-laws. Very high tension and stressful conditions are built up in her life. Therefore, all such factors would prima facie appear to draw an inference that such incidents which are regularly occurring in same and uniform condition are the grave consequence of some brutal human act and are not the result of an act of God.

1983) *available at:* http://lawcommissionofindia.nic.in/51-100/Report91.pdf (Visited on January 11, 2017).

[42] *Ibid.*
[43] *Id at* 2.
[44] Hindu Marriage Act, 1955
[45] The Indian Penal Code 1860
[46] The Indian Evidence Act, 1872

Another presumption was suggested to be inserted that where the death of the woman is caused within 5 five years of marriage, because of burning or injury caused inside her house where she was living with her husband and there is credible information that there had been persistent demands of dowry, it may be presumed that her death was the result either of suicide to which the woman was driven by such demands or of homicide.

In the Indian Penal Code insertion of a new provision was suggested that where death of the woman is caused within 5 five years of marriage, because of burning or injury caused inside her house where she was living with her husband and her husband, on becoming aware that the woman has so died, does not within a reasonable time, inform the nearest police officer or magistrate about her death, he shall, in the absence of a reasonable excuse be guilty of an offence punishable with sentence of up to three years or with fine or both.

A specific section should be inserted in the Indian Penal Code punishing a person who, by persistent act of cruelty, drives a member of a family to commit suicide. Further it should expressly provide that persistent demands for dowry shall amount to persistent acts of cruelty.

The Hindu Marriage Act 1955 should be amended for the purposes of the sections of that Act providing for the grant of matrimonial relief on the ground of cruelty. Persistent demands for dowry deemed to be the act of cruelty where the demands are made by or with the connivance of the husband. To cope up and effectively control modulation of such situation, it was suggested to amend the definition of 'dowry'[47]. Dowry should be defined as money or anything worth in terms of money, which is demanded from the bride or her family by the husband or his family members, where such demand has no proper legal reference to any recognized entitlement and is merely in connection to the marriage.

5.3.2 202nd Report of Law Commission of India[48]

The subject of 'Dowry Death and Law Reforms' has already been dealt by the Law Commission in 91st Report.[49] Despite various amendments in law as a result of

---

[47] Section 2 The Dowry Prohibition Act, 1961
[48] Law Commission of India, 202nd Report on Proposal to Amend Section 304-B of Indian Penal Code, 1860 (October, 2003) *available at:* http://lawcommissionofindia.nic.in/reports/report202.pdf (Visited on January 11, 2017).

recommendations, there is still alarming increase in dowry death cases. It ultimately led to an arising demand of giving death sentence to the dowry death offenders to create a deterrent effect in the society. This issue has come before the Law Commission pursuant to *Natthu* v. *State of U.P.*[50] While dealing with this bail application Hon'ble Mr. M. Katju J., inter-alia observed. "In my opinion dowry death is worse than murder but surprisingly there is no death penalty for it whereas death penalty can be given for murder. In my opinion the time has come when law is amended and death sentences should also be permitted in cases of dowry deaths".

The Home minister and Law minister were sent a copy of this order by Hon'ble Mr. Katju J. and they were requested to consider and present a bill in Parliament to bring such amendment. In this backdrop, the inadequacy of the prescribed punishments for the offence of dowry death was also considered. The prescribed imprisonment of minimum 7 years and which may extend to life imprisonment was given in the Code.[51] But it was still major concern that whether the addition of the death penalty for the offence of dowry death is certainly most despicable.

Section 304B has been thoroughly reviewed by the Law Commission in the context of various judicial judgments. All the substantive as well as procedural aspects were critically scrutinized. It was found that the offence of murder cannot be considered equivalent to the offence of dowry death. Although, the death of the wife is a common aspect in both of the offenses but the direct link between the husband and the death of the wife is absent. It is a huge mitigating factor and distinguishes the two offences from each other. Apart from that the presumptive nature of offence of dowry death and the fundamental principle of proportionality of the criminal law go in opposition to the prescription of capital punishment for the offence of dowry death. It is relevant to consider that in those cases of dowry death which also fall under the

---

[49] Law Commission of India, 91st Report on Dowry Deaths and Law Reform: Amending The Hindu Marriage Act, 1955, The Indian Penal Code 1860 and The Indian Evidence Act, 1872, (August, 1983) *available at:* http://lawcommissionofindia.nic.in/51-100/Report91.pdf (Visited on January 11, 2017).

[50] *Nathu* v. *State of U.P.* (Criminal Bail Application No.12466 of 2002) *available at:* https://indiankanoon.org/doc/16856996 (Visited on January 11, 2017).

[51] Section 304B(2) Whoever commits dowry death shall be punished with imprisonment for a term which shall not be less than seven years but which may extend to imprisonment for life, Indian Penal Code, 1860

scope of the offence of murder, giving capital punishment is legally permissible. Therefore, there was no recommendation by the Law Commission to amend Section 304B of IPC in order to provide capital punishment as the maximum punishment for the offence of dowry death.

5.3.3 237th Report of Law Commission of India

Law Commission submitted its 237th report on compounding of certain offences in December 2011[52]. The landmark judgment of Preeti Gupta[53], the Apex Court opined for the need to revisit Sec. 498A of IPC. The Law Commission considered the directions of the Honorable Court to re-look the provision in accordance with the changing needs of the society to keep a check on the abuse of law. The commission has done a thorough research and identified certain provisions including Section 498A which should be made compoundable. Again in *Ram Gopal* v. *State of M.P.*[54] case, the Apex Court has reiterated the need to make Section 498A as a compoundable offence. It has directed the commission to examine and send a suitable proposal to the Union Government in this context. The Court further said that "any such step would not only relieve the courts of the burden of deciding cases in which the aggrieved parties have themselves arrived at a settlement, but may also encourage the process of re-conciliation between them[55]."

It was recommended in this report to make Sec. 498A compoundable however with the permission of the court. The commission has further suggested some preventive measures and safeguards to rule out the apprehension that after making this provision compoundable, there might be coercion on the wife to opt for a compromise. There were four major issues which were examined by the commission in this regard. Firstly, when the High Court has an inherent power to quash criminal proceedings/FIR/Complaint in Sec. 482 of Cr. P.C.[56] then what is a need to make Sec.

---

[52] Law Commission of India, 237th Report on Compounding of Certain Offences (December 2011),) *available at:* http://lawcommissionofindia.nic.in/reports/report237.pdf (Visited on January 11, 2017).
[53] *Preeti Gupta* v. *State of Jharkhand* (2010) 8 SCC 131.
[54] *Ram Gopal* v. *State of M.P* 2010 (7) SCALE 711.
[55] *Ibid.*
[56] Section 482- Saving of inherent powers of High Court. Nothing in this Code shall be deemed to limit or affect the inherent powers of the High Court to make such orders as may be necessary to

498A compoundable. This argument was examined in the case of *B S Joshi* v. *State of Haryana* [57], where the HC refused to exercise this inherent power under Sec. 482 and held that this provision cannot be exercised to quash the prosecution for non compoundable offences even if the parties have settled the dispute. However, the Supreme Court has reversed this order. Now the rationale here is that if the wife is ready to forget and forgive the husband for cruelty inflicted upon her then why to drive them to go through this time consuming and expensive process under Sec. 482.Secondly, a social evil like dowry must be strictly curbed by the law and the law must be designed to take its full course instead of putting its approval on the private compromises. Although, no obstacle shall be placed in the effective implementation of law to curb a social evil like dowry but on the other side it must be kept in the mind that there is an equal interest of society in promoting harmony and peace in marital relationships, wherever possible. Thirdly, by making the offense compoundable would be an implied legal acceptance of violence against women by providing an opportunity to legally condone such violence.

The objective of law is not nearly punitive rather the law must endeavour in bringing a genuine reconciliation between husband and estranged wife if it is in the ultimate welfare of the woman. Fourthly, those women who are not independent or less educated might be forced to and pressurized to withdraw the proceedings by their families and in-laws. Such women would be left with no other option except compounding the offence on the necessity of family peace and livelihood. The Commission suggested that the safeguard of Court's permission to compound the offence shall act as a sufficient check against such possible situation. The Judge, while giving such permission is expected to act extra cautiously and may take assistance of a female lawyer or a trained counselor to examine the victim personally in his/her chamber.

Therefore the final recommendation made by the commission in this regard was that "Section 498A IPC should be made compoundable under Section 320(2) of

---

give effect to any order under this Code, or to prevent abuse of the process of any Court or otherwise to secure the ends of justice, The Code Of Criminal Procedure, 1973.

[57] *B S Joshi* v. *State of Haryana* (2003) 4 SCC 675.

CrPC[58] so that it may be compounded with the permission of the Court. However, in order to ensure that the offer of composition is voluntary and free from pressures, it is proposed to introduce sub-section (2A) in Section 320[59] laying down the procedure for dealing with an application for compounding of an offence under Section 498A"[60].

The other aspect which was scrutinized in connection to Sec. 498A was its non bailable nature. However, this matter was left to be considered in a separate report.

5.3.4 243rd Report of Law Commission of India[61]

In the year 2012, it was realized by the Home Ministry on the observations of Supreme Court that the misuse of Section 498A had increased so far. The major concern of the Commission was that whether any amendments are required in section 498A and the related provisions in Cr. P.C. as well as to explore the possible measures needed to be taken to keep a check on the misuse of this provision. The Home Secretary of India kept into consideration the representations by various quarters and the observations given by the Apex Court and the High Courts and thereafter requested the Law Commission to consider the suggested amendments in Section 498A to check the alleged misuse of this provision.

Thereafter, in *Preeti Gupta* v. *State of Jharkhand*[62], the Apex Court has given an observation that the legislature needs to seriously re-look the entire provision of cruelty. It has been commonly seen that a huge number of complaints contain exaggerated versions of the incident. Very often, the tendency of over implication or false implication has been reflected in the complaints. The commission has remarked that the provision of 'cruelty[63]' was inserted to provide protection to the married women against being subjected to cruelty by their husbands or in-laws. The report has submitted that very often the Apex Court as well as the High Courts of many states had pointed out the gross abuse of Section 498A in some cases. However, it is not appropriate to repeal Section 498A on the ground of misuse or to snatch the power and impact of the Section by making some changes. It must be taken care that on one

---

[58] Section 320 (2), The Code Of Criminal Procedure, 1973.
[59] The Code of Criminal Procedure, 1973.
[60] *Supra* note 32.
[61] Law Commission of India, 243rd Report on Section 498A IPC (August, 2012) *available at:* http://lawcommissionofindia.nic.in/reports/report243.pdf (Visited on January 11, 2017).
[62] (2010) 7 SCC 667.
[63] Section 498A , The Indian Penal Code, 1860.

hand the social objective behind enacting this provision i.e. creating deterrence in the society shall not be defeated while on the other hand the false implications, fake complaints or over exaggerated allegations to meet ulterior motives should be discouraged. It has been mentioned in this report that Sec 498A was added in the year 1983 to shield married females from being exposed to cruelty inflicted by the husband or in-laws. A maximum imprisonment of 3 years as well as fine has been added. The term 'cruelty' has been characterized in wide expression in order to incorporate incurring physical or mental injury to the body or health of the victim. Any kind of indulgence in harassing a woman as to compel her or her relatives to satisfy any illegal demand of dowry is also covered under the ambit of cruelty. Dowry harassment is included in the latter half of this provision. Making a circumstance driving the female to end her life is additionally another act covered under the offence of cruelty. It is a cognizable offence as well as non-bailable and non-compoundable in nature.

- It has been aptly remarked in the report that the only ground of 'misuse' or 'abuse' of Sec 498A does not suffice the rationale to omit Sec 498A or to deprive this provision of its sharp teeth. The social objective, legislative intent as well as the necessity of its deterrent behind this provision must be kept in consideration. However it has to be ensured that the complaints filed with fake allegations or exaggerated complaints because of ulterior intention or in a revengeful emotion must not be entertained.

- The report further emphasises on the need of sensitization of the people regarding the laws and available remedies regarding these matters specifically in rural areas and has further recommended the active involvement of District and *Taluka* Legal Services Authorities, media, NGOs as well as law students in creating such awareness. Moreover, efforts must be made for bringing reconciliation in a speedy manner with the help of professional counsellors, mediation and legal aid centres, retired officials/medical and legal professionals or friends and relations in whom the parties have faith.

- The registration of FIR has been another question of concern in the present Report. There is no clear cut legislation to ascertain that whether registration of FIR could be postponed for a particular time or not. Often High Courts have directed in certain cases, that until the preliminary investigation is over as well as

171

reconciliation process is over, no FIR shall be registered under Section 498A. However the cases of visible violence of cruelty might be treated as an exception to it. In this context, the Commission has directed the police to follow the procedure laid down by that High Court which is having the jurisdiction over the matter till the matter is decided by the Apex Court.

- Regarding the nature of the offence, it has been recommended that the offence under section 498-A shall be changed to a compoundable offence, with the due permission of Court and there shall be a cooling off period of 3 months. But it must remain non-bailable as the necessity of custodial interrogation cannot be ignored rather must be carefully scrutinized. Neither there should be an over-reaction nor inaction. Police should take required steps to ensure well being and safety of the victim who has filed the complaint and measures must be taken to protect her from any kind of further harassment.

- There has been another recommendation to add sub-section (3) to Sec 41 Cr. PC in order to keep a check on arbitrary and unreasonable arrests. Moreover there shall be the enhancement five thousand rupees of compensation amount of Sec 358 of Cr. PC to fifteen thousand rupees and the suggested change is not specifically confined only to this Section.

- Some other suggestions were regarding the strengthening of women police stations, hostels and shelter homes both quantitatively and qualitatively. A proposal for separate rooms in the police stations for women complainants as well as accused women involved in Sec 498-A related cases was given. The women who would not be interested in going back to their marital homes should be facilitated hostels and shelter homes maintained in cities and District headquarters and the basic facilities must be provided in such hostels and shelter homes.

- Instead of mechanically impounding the passport of NRI(s) involved in the case of cruelty u/Sec 498-A, they should be insisted upon for bigger amounts of bonds and sureties.

- The prime recommendation of the commission was upon expeditious justice in such cases. The need for speedy disposal of cases was mentioned and it was suggested to the prosecution as well as Judiciary to give special attention to the cases filed u/sec 498A.

5.4 Dowry Prohibition and The Civil Services (Conduct) Rules

The Civil Services (Conduct) Rules, 1964 specifically prohibit government servants from giving and taking Dowry or abetting the giving and taking of Dowry.[64]A similar provision has also been enacted in the Indian Services (Conduct) Rules, 1968.[65]

Currently, there is nothing in the Dowry Prohibition Act to assure the responsibility of Government to create sensitization against the custom of dowry. Therefore, the Public Servants must lead an agenda against this social evil and start a movement because they are holding the offices of utmost responsibility. The addition of some provisions for this purpose might be taken from the Kerala Dowry Prohibition Rules.[66] It has been made compulsory for the Government employees of Kerala to submit a declaration after their marriage that no dowry has been taken by them. [67]

5.4.1 Suspension of Civil Servants in Cases of Dowry Death

Central Civil Services (Classification, Control and Appeal) Rules, 1965 prescribe certain provisions[68] of suspension of government servants in the cases where they are charged of any criminal offence. The order of such suspension may be passed where the disciplinary proceedings against them are pending during investigation, enquiry or trial of such an offence. Rule 10 (2) further provides that a

---

[64]   Rule 13A The Civil Services (Conduct) Rules, 1964 No government servant shall –
(i) Give or take or abet the giving and taking of Dowry or
(ii) Demand directly or indirectly, from the parents or guardians of a bride or bridegroom, as the case may be, any Dowry.
Explanation – For the purpose of this rule, dowry has the same meaning as in the Dowry prohibition Act, 1961, *available at:* www.persmin.gov.in *(visited on January 11, 2017).*

[65]   The All India Services (Conduct) Rules, 1968, Rule11A Giving or taking of dowry.— No member of the Service shall—
(i) give or take or abet the giving or taking of dowry; or
(ii) demand, directly or indirectly, from the parents or guardian of a bride or bridegroom, as the case may be, any dowry.
Explanation.— For the purpose of the rule, "dowry" has the same meaning as in the Dowry Prohibition Act, 1961 (28 of 1961) *available at: ipr.ias.nic.in/Docs/AIS_ConductRules1968.pdf* (Visited on January 11, 2017).

[66]   Kerala Dowry prohibition Rules, 1992 *available at:* www.prd.kerala.gov.in/kdprules.pdf (Visited on January 11, 2017).

[67]   Kerala Dowry prohibition Rules, 1992, Rule7(iv) The Chief Dowry prohibition Officer shall issue instructions to all the Department of the State Government to the following effect:-
(a) Every Government servant shall after his marriage furnish a declaration stating that he has not taken any dowry to the Head of Department. The declaration shall be signed by the wife, father and father-in-law, *available at:* www.prd.kerala.gov.in/kdprules.pdf (Visited on January 11, 2017).

[68]   Rule 10 (1) of the Central Civil Services (Classification, Control and Appeal) Rules, 1965.

detention on a criminal charge of a Government servant for more than 48 hours shall also lead to a deemed suspension once the order of the appointing authority is passed and will be effective by the date of the detention itself.

- The government has taken a serious initiative against the offences related to dowry or dowry death. If a complaint has been filed in the police station and the case is registered against a government employee for 'dowry death'[69], such a public servant has to face suspension orders issued by the competent authority as prescribed by Rule 10 (1).[70] However the suspension will prevail only in the following circumstances:

(i) In case the arrest of such a government servant has taken place in connection with registering of police case against him, his suspension will prevail immediately and not respective to the time period of his detention.

(ii) In case no arrest is made, the suspension shall immediately prevail, once the police report under Sec 173(2) of CrPC[71] is submitted to the Magistrate. But such a report must indicate prima facie that the government servant has committed such offence[72].

Initially the acceptance of dowry was considered as a gift arising out of a custom. Even the government employees were allowed to take such gifts subject to the condition that the gifts must be mentioned and reported properly, either to the government or the designated body. Later on, this matter was reviewed in context to

---

[69] Section 304 B, The Indian Penal Code, 1860.
[70] Central Civil Services (Classification, Control and Appeal) Rules, 1965, *available at:* https://dopt.gov.in/sites/default/files/CCS-CCA-Rules-FINAL.pdf.
[71] Section 173(2) in The Code of Criminal Procedure, 1973.
(2) (i) As soon as it is completed, the officer in charge of the police station shall forward to a Magistrate empowered to take cognizance of the offence on a police report, a report in the form prescribed by the State Government, stating-
(a) the names of the parties;
(b) the nature of the information;
(c) the names of the persons who appear to be acquainted with the circumstances of the case;
(d) whether any offence appears to have been committed and, if so, by whom;
(e) whether the accused has been arrested;
(f) whether he has been released on his bond and, if so, weather with or without sureties;
(g) whether he has been forwarded in custody under section 170.
(ii) The officer shall also communicate, In such manner as may be prescribed by the State Government, the action taken by him, to the person, if any, by whom the information relating to the commission of the offence was first given.
[72] The Central Civil Services Rules, *available at:* https://dopt.gov.in/ccs-cca-rules-1965 (Visited on January 11, 2017).

the provisions of Dowry Prohibition Act, 1961. Henceforth, dowry is no longer to be treated as customary gift and if a Government servant violates the provisions of Dowry Prohibition Act, then there is a sufficient ground to institute action against him along with the legal proceedings in the statutory law.[73]

5.5 Joint Committee of Parliament Report on Dowry

In December 1980, a motion was adopted by the Indian Parliament to examine the efficacy of anti- dowry laws prescribed in the Act[74]. It resulted in the appointment of a joint committee which has submitted its report on 6 August, 1982. The report has briefly outlined the origin, growth and devastating effect of dowry as well as it has scrutinized the legal provisions and general measures to curb the dowry menace.

The prime concern of the report was the gross failure of Dowry Prohibition Act, for which the two major reasons were mentioned. Firstly, there is no specification in the statute that explains that how to prove that the valuable articles are given as dowry articles as a consideration for the marriage. Secondly, it lacks the power of enforcement because of the condition that the complaint must be filed just within a year of commission of the offence. In such a case, the aggrieved person or relatives would be reluctant to report the matter with the fear of adverse effect on the bride. It was also suggested that family courts must be set up, dowry prohibition officers shall be appointed, social organizations shall be authorized to report offences related to dowry and National Commission for Women shall be formed.[75]

5.6 Malimath Committee Report

The Committee has submitted its report in 2003 with an objective to bring reforms in administration of criminal justice.[76] It has strongly favoured the proposal to modify the nature of Section 498 A by making it a compoundable offence. The Committee observed, "A less tolerant and impulsive woman may lodge an FIR even on a trivial act. The result is that the husband and his family may be immediately arrested and there may be a suspension or loss of job. The offence alleged being non-

---

[73] P.K. Majumdar & R.P. Kataria, *Law Relating to Dowry Prohibition Cruelty & Harassment* 101 (Orient Publishing Company, New Delhi, 2014).
[74] The Dowry Prohibition Act, 1961.
[75] Ranjana Sheel, *The Political Economy of Dowry* 180-181 (Manohar Publishers, New Delhi, 1999).
[76] Government of India, Report: *Committee on Reforms of Criminal Justice System* (Ministry of Home Affairs, 2003), available at: https://mha.gov.in/sites/default/files/criminal_justice_system. pdf (Visited on January 13, 2017).

bailable, innocent persons languish in custody. There may be a claim for maintenance adding fuel to fire, especially if the husband cannot pay. Now the woman may change her mind and get into the mood to forget and forgive. The husband may also realize the mistakes committed and come forward to turn over a new leaf for a loving and cordial relationship. The woman may like to seek reconciliation. But this may not be possible due to the legal obstacles. Even if she wishes to make amends by withdrawing the complaint, she cannot do so as the offence is non-compoundable. The doors for returning to family life stand closed. She is thus left at the mercy of her natal family.

This section, therefore, helps neither the wife nor the husband. The offence being non-bailable and non-compoundable makes an innocent person undergo stigmatization and hardship. Heartless provisions that make the offence non-bailable and non-compoundable operate against reconciliations. It is therefore necessary to make this offence (a) bailable and (b) compoundable to give a chance to the spouses to come together."[77] The committee has tried to protect not only the interests of innocent husbands but also tried to give a chance of second thought to those wives who out of sudden emotion exaggerate the situation to the extent of filing false complaint but later on realize their mistake. In this way, this report has emphasized on unraveling the matrimonial discords by diluting the harshness of Section 498A.

5.7 Government Initiatives through Various Schemes and Policies

Government of India as well as various state governments have from time to time taken numerous steps for and to address various issues like women welfare, reduce the incidences of female foeticite, curb the menace of dowry and to eradicate the custom of child marriage. It is evident that directly or indirectly the custom of dowry has led to many other offences as well as actrocities against women. Many parents do not wish to have a female child due to the fear of probable burden of giving dowry in her marriage. Child marriage is another negative outcome of the dowry system. It is assumed in many communities that the amount of dowry increases with the increase in the education level and age of the girl. Therefore, very often the parents opt child marriage of their daughter to overcome this prospective dowry fear.

---

[77] Justice V.S. Malimath ,"Recommendations of the Malimath Committee on reforms of Criminal Justice System" *available at*: http://www.mha.nic.in/hindi/sites/upload_files /mhahindi/files/pdf/ criminal_justice_system (Visited on September, 03 2016).

Many other offences like cruelty, domestic violence and wife battering arise because of dowry demand or failure to fulfill such a demand by the bride or her parents. Illiteracy, financial dependence, backwardness, lack of family and societal support are some contributing factors that worsen the condition of the victims of dowry related offences to a more vulnerable level.

5.7.1 Policies and Schemes of Central Government

The Central Government has formulated some policies and schemes which either directly or impliedly help the women to fight back such circumstances. Women empowerment is another tool which has been applied and endeavored to be achieved as an alternate solution.

Ladli Yojna

The Government has started a scheme to give 1 lakh Rs. to every girl born after 1st January 2008 on attaining her the age of 18 years[78]. However it is provided that such girls must pass matric exam and get admission in 12th class. The scheme has been initiated with an objective to control female foeticite and encourage the education of girls. The scheme was specifically for those families having an annual income less than 1 lakh rupees and two girls of every family have been entitled to such benefit. But it was observed that most of the beneficiary families were interested in spending this money on the marriage of the girls rather than on their study. It has a consequential danger of adding fuel to the dowry system since the majority of the people aimed in spending the money in the marriage of the girls and finding the bridegroom easily by arranging dowry with the help of this amount.[79]

Beti Bachao Beti Padhao Programme

It has been another flagship programme as an effort of ministries of WCD[80], HFW[81] and HRD[82] to bring an improvement in sex ratio.[83] It has an objective to sensitize the people for gender parity in education, conscience building of the people

---

[78] One Stop Centre Scheme, *Ministry of Women & Child Development, available at:* https://wcd.nic. in/schemes/one-stop-centre-scheme-1(Visited on Feb17, 2019)

[79] Savita Verma, *Goverment scheme to save girls in womb a flop: Study, available at:* https://www.indiatoday. in/india/north/story/goverment-scheme-to-save-girls-in-womb-a-flop-150100-2011-12-28 (last modified Dec 28 2011)

[80] *Ibid.*

[81] *Ibid.*

[82] Beti Bachao Beti Padhao Scheme, Ministry of Women and Child Development, Government of India, *available at:* https://wcd.nic.in/schemes/beti-bachao-beti-padhao-scheme

[83] *Ibid.*

performing female foeticite and removing the inequality between the genders. The prime focus was to sensitize the prejudiced people who were against female child birth due to various negative perceptions out of which the evil of dowry was most common.[84]

Women Welfare

One Stop Centers have been established since 2015 to give medical, legal, police and mental support as well as shelter to women affected by every kind of violence including dowry related offences.[85] These OSCs[86] have been set up in 718 districts and supported approximately 1.93 lakh women. Apart from this Grievance Redresser Cell has been established to receive online grievances on women issues.[87]

Rashtriya Mahila Kosh

Economic backwardness and poverty is one of the main reasons behind the custom of dowry. Since ages, the women have been considered as a financial burden in the backward societies as she has not been able to generate any income or even to support livelihood. As a custom, the parents of these brides used to give a onetime payment as dowry, since the wife was considered as a permanent financial liability on the husband. RMK[88] society has been registered in 1993 under MWCD[89]. It aims to fulfill the credit requirement of financially helpless women to initiate various income generating activities to strengthen the socio-economic empowerment of the females.[90] It further aims to encourage women entrepreneurs to make, manufacture and sell various products made by them. Financial independence brings a ray of hope to free a huge segment of women from the age old shackles of dowry system.

Mahila Shakti Kendra Scheme

Women empowerment can play a significant role to mark a pavement in the mission of dowry eradication. MSK[91] scheme aspires to empower the women living in

---

[84] Press Information Bureau, *Beti Bachao Beti Padhao*, Ministry of Women and Child Development, *available at:* http://pib.nic.in/newsite/PrintRelease.aspx?relid=187560 (last modified Jan 17 2019)

[85] *Ibid.*

[86] One Stop Centers Scheme, Ministry of Women and Child Development, Government of India, *available at:* https://wcd.nic.in/schemes/one-stop-centre-scheme-1(Visited on Sep 17, 2019)

[87] *Ibid.*

[88] Rashtriya Mahila Kosh, *National Government Services Portal, available at:* https://services.india.gov.in/service/detail/rashtriya-mahila-kosh-1(Visited on Sep 17, 2019)

[89] Ministry of Women and Child Development

[90] Supra Note 88.

[91] Mahila Shakti Kendras, *Ministry of Women & Child Devlopment available at:* https://wcd.nic.in/schemes/mahila-shakti-kendras-msk (Visited on Oct 01, 2019)

rural areas.[92] It is also contributing in creating awareness among rural women regarding various programmes, schemes and policies formulated for the protection and welfare of women. It also sensitizes the women regarding support for women in distress, and the women who have become the victim of any kind of violence.

5.7.2 Policies and Schemes of Various State Governments

The governments of various states have also has initiated some policies and schemes which either directly or impliedly help the women to fight back such circumstances. Numerous steps have been taken for women welfare, to reduce the incidences of female foeticide, to curb the menace of dowry and to eradicate the custom of child marriage.[93]

Government of Bihar to End Dowry

A statewide campaign in Bihar was launched to abolish child marriage and dowry. It was inspired by the previous success of alcohol-free-state campaign. The proposal was to form a human chain in support of the campaign in supporting the campaign to put an end to the evil practices of child marriage and dowry in the society.[94] "Bihar ranks second in the country after neighboring Uttar Pradesh when it comes to dowry-related cases. In 2016, the number of dowry deaths registered in Bihar was 987, while the number of cases of dowry-related atrocities was 4,852."[95]

Women and Dowry related Schemes in Haryana [96]

The Government of Haryana had initiated various programmes in the year 2001 to celebrate it as women's empowerment year. A two days workshop on 'Gender and Law Enforcement Agency' had been conducted by the Haryana State Women Commission. A state level workshop on dowry prohibition was conducted at Kurukshektra by the commission itself. State level workshops on economic empowerment of women, education and entrepreneurship in women have been

---

[92] *Ibid.*
[93] Press Trust of India, *Nitish Launches Campaign to end Dowry, Child marriage, available at:* https://www.thehindu.com/news/national/other-states/nitish-launches-campaign-to-end-dowry-child-marriage/article19789076.ece (Visited on May 15, 2019)
[94] Bihar Chief Minister Nitish Kumar now vows to end dowry, *available at:* https://www.indiatoday.in/magazine/states/story/20171023-nitish-kumar-bihar-government-no-child-marriage-no-dowry-1062950-2017-10-13(lVisited on Oct 05, 2019)
[95] Nitish Kumar launches campaign to end dowry, child marriage in Bihar, *available at:* https://www.livemint.com/ (Last modified on Oct 02, 2017)
[96] Women Empowerment Year – 2001, *available at:* http://wcdhry.gov.in/women_ empowerment_year_F.html (Visited on May 15, 2019)

conducted by various governmental departments. Social Justice and Empowerment Department has conducted various awareness campaigns for the women who are suffering in difficult circumstances. The police department of Haryana has also taken an initiative and organized campaign to sensitize police personals to the needs of women with regard to their legal rights and violence against women. However, these steps were remarkable but merely celebrating 1 year as a women empowerment year cannot act as a panacea to eradicate a deep rooted evil like dowry from the society. The efforts of the government have to be continuous, consistent and effective to eradicate this evil.

Anti Dowry Schemes and Protection of Women in Karnataka.[97]

The Karnataka government has launched various schemes to protect the women from the atrocities of domestic violence and dowry. In the year 2000, *'Streeshakthi'* was launched to provide economic and social empowerment to the women by providing subsidy in bank loans and various other incentives to them. Another scheme named as *'Santhwana'* has been implemented to provide counselling, legal help, shelter and financial help to the victims of domestic violence and dowry related offences. Another scheme named as *'Stairya Nithi Yojane'* was launched in the year 2015 to provide financial help to the women who became victims of atrocities. Various district committees have been set up to review the implementation of Dowry Prohibition Act and to take further steps to eradicate the evil of dowry. A special cell was created in the year 1983 to create sensitization against social evils like dowry, domestic violence etc.

The ministry of WCD[98] has established one stop centres named as *'Sakhi'* to provide counselling, medical help, legal aid and police assistance to the women who became victims of violence.

Government Services in U.P and Dowry

The Government of U.P. implemented the project of online services in 75 districts through Citizen Service Centres (CSC). It enabled prompt, transparent, effective and efficient delivery of services to the citizen of U.P. It also offered financial assistance for women under dowry schemes, legal aid to women in dowry harassment and grant schemes for the widow's daughter marriage etc. provided the

---

[97] Bangalore Rural District, *Programmes for Women's Development, available at:*https://bangalor-erural.nic.in/en/programmes-for-womens/ (Visited on May 17, 2019)
[98] *Ibid.*

required documents such as F.I.R copy of Section 498(A), under the suit, passed allowance family; residence certificate; certificate of non re-marriage; shadow copy of bank passbook etc. were submitted. Despite such efforts, U.P. has seen maximum number of dowry deaths as well as crimes related to dowry in the year 2016. According to NCRB report, it is the state with maximum number of dowry deaths i.e. 2473 and maximum number of dowry related crimes i.e. 2867 in the year 2016.[99] Therefore, it is high time for the state government of U.P. to take certain stringent and effective measures to control the menace of dowry which is engulfing thousands of lives of helpless women every year.

'Arundhati' Scheme of Assam Government.

Assam government has introduced a unique yet controversial scheme *"Arundhiti"* while presenting the budget of 2019-20. Under this scheme, 10 grams of gold will be presented to those brides who belong to a community where there is a custom of giving gold at the time of the wedding. [100] However, it will be limited to the economically weaker sections whose income is below 5 Lakh rupees per annum, only for the first two off springs of a family and only where the bride and groom both have attained the legal age of marriage. [101] But the scheme has been criticized by many legal scholars that the scheme is promoting the custom of dowry. It is encouraging the tradition that the fathers of the brides ought to give gold and valuables in the marriage of their daughter in any case whether they are financially capable or not. However, the government is defending it as a step towards promoting *Stridhan'* rather than promoting dowry.

Gender Equality and Women Empowerment in Gujarat[102]

The women and child development department in Gujarat is endeavouring hard to initiate and promote various schemes and programmes to save the women from the atrocities of dowry. The state policy for gender inequality has been formulated which has taken various initiates in empowering the women through

---

[99] Financial Assistance for Women Under Dowry Scheme, *available at:* https://kannauj.nic.in/service/caste-certificate/ (Visited on June 20, 2019)

[100] Deendyal Singh, The Arundhati Scheme of Assam: Indulgence in the Cult of Dowry, *available at:* https://thenewleam.com/2019/03/the-arundhati-scheme-of-assam-indulgence-in-the-cult-of-dowry/(Visited on June 20, 2019)

[101] Assam's 'gold to brides' scheme welcomed by many, draws criticism too, *available at:* https://www.business-standard.com/article/news-ians/assam-s-gold-to-brides-scheme-welcomed-by-many-draws-criticism-too-119020701433_1.html (Visited on June 20, 2019)

[102] Women and Child Development Projects and Initiatives, *available at:* https://gujaratindia.gov.in/initiatives/initiatives.htm?InitiativeId=jJr8IjlsO7h8X7hPx1JgSw== (Visited on June 22, 2019)

education, entrepreneurship etc. The concept of *Nari Adalats* has been introduced on the principle of 'by women' 'for women'. There are women jurists to dispense justice in the women for the cases of divorce, dowry demands, abandonment and violence etc. It strives to provide speedy and effective justice to the women. Gujarat is facing the declining sex ratio of females, therefore, the *Beti Bachao Yogna* has been launched by the C.M. of Gujarat in the year 2005 with an objective to save girl child. Another scheme named as *kunverbai nu Mameru* scheme has been launched with an objective to provide monetary help to schedule castes for performing the marriage of their daughter.

5.8 UNICEF Strategy and Action

Child marriage is a gross violation of children rights and results into a hampered physical, emotional and mental growth of child. It not only deprives a child from his or her childhood but also snatches the educational opportunities of that child. Both boys and girls suffer the negative impact of such marriages but the gross effect has been observed much largely on the girls in comparison to boys. It ultimately results in the diminished access to their education, vast exposure to violence, hampered freedom and economic weakness. UNICEF India has observed that the problem of dowry is a major reason behind child marriages.[103] Daughters are often treated as a liability with a non existing economic role. Very often the parents feel that the amount of dowry demand increases along with the increasing age and qualification of the girl. It has further observed that although anti-dowry laws[104] are enacted since more than six decades but still the custom is common. Therefore, to get rid of this burden, many families choose the option of child marriage.

UNICEF is implementing an effective strategy towards law enforcement, women empowerment, sensitization, promoting education and women welfare schemes and programmes.[105]

---

[103] Demissew Bizuwerk, *Purulia Girls Unite Against Child Marriage*, *available at:* https://unicef.in/Story/1234/Purulia-girls-unite-against-child-marriage (Visited on June 22, 2019)
[104] Dowry Prohibition Act, 1961.
[105] UNICEF India , Major Reasons for Child Marriage , *available at:* https://www.unicef.in/Whatwedo/30/Child-Marriage (Visited on June 22, 2019)

CHAPTER 6

DOWRY PROHIBITION AND LAW – AN EMPIRICAL SURVEY

In an attempt to understand the major factors responsible for the prevalence of dowry system in society despite the existence of stringent laws, an empirical study was conducted. It was aimed at identifying the major reasons behind the giving and taking of dowry likewise; psychological, social, cultural or financial. Having regard to the widespread prevalence of this social evil, it aimed to ascertain the faith of people on laws related to dowry prohibition, police and judiciary as well as the efficacy of legal mechanism to curb the menace of this social evil. It further aimed at examining that is there any gap between actual number of dowry related cases and number of cases reported and if there is any then the major reasons due to which the victims do not report the dowry related incidences. It was attempted through this survey to enquire about the other underlying issues associated with the custom of dowry and their impact on dowry system. Keeping in mind the sensitive nature of issue of being a within family affair and therefore hesitation of people in disclosing the facts, every care was taken to introduce the issue in a gentle yet directive manner.

6.1 Empirical Survey

With regard to the objectives of empirical work and the informational needs, separate questionnaires were prepared for different categories of respondents to have in-depth view of the situation and the associated perceptions. One category of questionnaire was circulated among general public to capture their views, opinion, perception and awareness regarding the custom of dowry and the offences related to dowry. Second category of questionnaire was circulated among married women to assess their experience, perception, opinion and awareness regarding the custom of dowry and the offences related to dowry. Third category of questionnaire was circulated among Judges/Lawyers/ Police/Law Academicians to enquire about their practical experience and opinion regarding major challenges in dealing with the offences related to dowry and the lacunas in the law, societal behaviour and legal machinery to overcome the problem of widespread of this evil.

The study is based on the sample of 400 respondents which include 200 people from general public comprising of 100 respondents from district Kangra and 100 respondents from district Shimla, 100 married women comprising of 50 respondents from district Kangra and 50 respondents from district Shimla and 100 respondents from Judges/Lawyers/ Police/Law Academicians comprising of 50 respondents from district Kangra and 50 respondents from district Shimla. Data in the present study was collected through questionnaires, thereafter it was systematically arranged in SPSS (Statistical Package for Social Sciences) format, indepth discussions, analyzed and processed for final analysis.

6.2 Empirical Survey for District Shimla

Respondents - General Public

1. **What is the average amount of expenditure usually done in a marriage?**

Table: 1

Answer	Frequency	Percentage
a) Below 1 Lakh	4	4.0
b) 1 – 10 Lakh	85	85.0
c) 10-50 Lakh	8	8.0
d) Above 50 Lakh	1	1.0
e) Not Answered	2	2.0
Total	**100**	**100.0**

85% general public believe that these expenses in marriage ceremonies are in between 1 lakh to 10 lakh. 4% of general public believe that marriage ceremony expenditures remain below 1 lakh where as 8 % believe that expenditure exceeds 10 lakh and goes upto 50 lakh. Only 1% marriages are believed to have expenditure above 50 lakh.

2. **Which is the most common type of marriage that you have seen/attended in the society so far?**

Table: 2

Answer	Frequency	Percentage
a) Marriages in which not a single thing is given as dowry	11	11.0
b) huge dowry is given by the bride's parents to helplessly fulfill the demand of bridegroom / his parents	4	4.0
c) Marriages in which dowry is given and taken as a custom because both sides happily agree	67	67.0
d) Marriages in which dowry is happily given by the bride groom side for their own status	13	13.0
e) Not Answered	5	5.0
Total	**100**	**100.0**

67% people hold the opinion that they attended the marriages where dowry is given and taken as a custom because both sides happily agree. 11% people have seen marriages in which not a single thing is given as dowry. 13% people have seen such marriages where dowry is happily given by the bride groom side for their own status but 4% people have attended marriages where huge dowry is given by the bride's parents to helplessly fulfil the demand of bridegroom / his parents.

It clearly shows that the majority marriages that take place in the society are of such a kind where dowry is given and taken as a custom to which both sides happily agree. It is a completely acceptable custom in the society and therefore, steadily prevailing in the society despite the presence of numerous stringent laws which have been enacted for dowry prohibition. It becomes difficult for the legislation to implement such laws which prohibit a socially acceptable custom. Lack of social will is major impediment in the effective implementation of dowry prohibition laws.

3. **What do you think would be the effect, if parents of the bride would give nothing to the bridegroom or his family members, in connection to the marriage?**

Table: 3

Answer	Frequency	Percentage
a) No significant effect	65	65.0
b) It would become difficult for them to find a suitable match	8	8.0
c) It may lead to the maltreatment and harassment of bride after marriage	14	14.0
d) Social humiliation of bride's family and loss of status in the society.	9	9.0
e) Not Answered	4	4.0
Total	**100**	**100.0**

65% general public thinks that there would be no significant effect if parents of the bride would give nothing to the bridegroom or his family members, in connection to the marriage. 8% opine that it would become difficult for them to find a suitable match. Whereas, 14% believe that it may lead to the maltreatment and harassment of bride after marriage and 9% opine that it will lead to social humiliation of bride's family and loss of status in the society. Various variables such as age, education and occupation have no significant effect on the opinion.

Here there is a conflict in the view point of society. On one side most of them opine that there is no significant effect if no dowry is given by the parents of the bride to the bridegroom and his family but on the other side they told that dowry is given in almost all the marriages which they have attended so far. Now the question here is that if the people believe that there is no significant or negative effect of not giving dowry in the marriages then why majority of them are opting to give and take dowry in the marriages in the actual practice. There might be one of the two reasons that either the people are lying on this context or this evil is so deep rooted in the society that despite stringent laws and without any fear of any significant impact of not giving dowry, the people are blindly following this custom.

4. Do you think that the girls must get equal share in their parental property?

Table: 4

Answer	Frequency	Percentage
a) No, it creates family disputes	27	27.0
b) No, they already get dowry in their marriages	7	7.0
c) Yes, definitely	46	46.0
d) Yes, but only if they are not ready to sacrifice it for their brothers	17	17.0
e) Not Answered	3	3.0
Total	**100**	**100.0**

As far as girl's right in parental property is concerned, 46% general public agrees that girls must have the share in parental property, 27% believe that girls should not get right in the parental property as it leads to family disputes. 7% believe that contribution in dowry is enough and no further share should be given in parental property. 17% believe that, yes girls should have the share, proved they are not ready to sacrifice it for their brothers. There is no such impact of variables such as age, education, sex, income, etc on the opinion.

But if closely examine, the all four options, 56% of people have opted for either no or yes in only those circumstances where the girls themselves are not ready to sacrifice it for their brothers. Secondly, there is a huge difference between thinking that the girls must get equal share in their parental property and actually giving them equal share in the property. Because when the same question was asked by the married women, then, only 14% of them have actually received share in their parental property.[1]

So we can infer that despite various laws, practically the people are neither ready and nor even giving equal share to the females in their parental property. Dowry is also sometimes opted an escape or a substitute of this share, which is a matter of concern. Secondly, it is another example that whatever law might be enacted by the legislature, it is difficult to implement it if a contrary custom is already prevailing in the society. Social acceptability of laws is a backbone in the effective implementation of laws.

---

[1] Question 12 Questionnaire for married women(Shimla)

5.   What is the main reason behind Dowry?

Table: 5

Answer	Frequency	Percentage
a) Old age Custom and tradition	63	63.0
b) Social Pressure	13	13.0
c) Greed of the bridegroom/his parents	13	13.0
d) Parents of the bride are more interested in giving dowry	7	7.0
e) Not Answered	4	4.0
Total	**100**	**100.0**

63% general public believe that primary reason behind dowry is an old age custom and traditions. 13% people believe that social pressure is the main reason behind dowry. 13% people have opinion that the greed of the bridegroom/his parents is responsible and 7% people believe that parents of the bride are more interested in giving dowry.

The response of the respondents on the basis of Sex i.e.; Male, Female was analyzed.

Table: 5.1

What is the main reason behind Dowry?						
Variable Sex	Old age custom and tradition	Social Pressure	Greed of the bridegroom/ his parents	Parent of the bride are more interested in giving dowry	Not Answered	Total
Males	74.3%	10.0%	7.1%	4.3%	4.3%	100.0%
Females	36.7%	20.0%	26.7%	13.3%	3.3%	100.0%

But there is strong disparity among men and women in their opinion in ascertaining the main reason behind dowry. 74.3% males consider old age custom and tradition as a main reason behind dowry where as only 36.7% females agree with the same. 63.3% females believe that the other reasons like social pressure, greed or willingness of bride's parents to give dowry are more prominent reasons rather than old age customs.

It can be inferred that the males are taking the shelter of custom and tradition in justifying the dowry system whereas; the females who actually become the victims of this evil disagree with the same. They are considering the other negative reasons social pressure, greed, and willingness of bride's parents to give dowry as more prominent reasons behind this evil.

It is a high time to stop justifying this social evil under the veil of customs and to figure out the actual reasons and eradicate them to curb the menace of dowry.

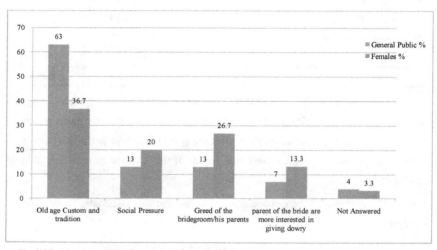

Variable 'Sex' and Chi Square value is '0.005'

Figure: 5.1

Table: 5.2

Answer	General Public %	Females %
Old age Custom and tradition	63	36.7
Social Pressure	13	20
Greed of the bridegroom/his parents	13	26.7
parent of the bride are more interested in giving dowry	7	13.3
Not Answered	4	3.3

6. **If dowry is demanded before marriage, what is the common attitude shown by the girl and her family?**

Table: 6

Answer	Frequency	Percentage
a) They try to negotiate and decrease the demand if it is beyond their financial capacity	14	14.0
b) They try to fulfill the demand if they actually like the proposal and are financially capable to fulfill the demand	36	36.0
c) They do not fulfill the demand and end up the relationship howsoever eligible the bridegroom may be	33	33.0
d) They report the matter to the police and file a case of dowry	8	8.0
e) Not Answered	9	9.0
Total	**100**	**100.0**

The cases where is dowry is demanded before marriage, 36% people believe that the family of the girl tends to fulfil the demand if they actually like the marriage proposal and are financially capable to fulfil the demand. 14% people believe that bride and her family try to negotiate and decrease the demand if it is beyond their financial capacity. But 33 % people have the opinion that they do not fulfil the demand and end up the relationship howsoever eligible the bridegroom may be. Merely, 8% opine that such cases are reported to the police and a case of dowry is filed. Various variables such as age, education and occupation have no significant effect on the opinion.

It means that majority people either tend to fulfil or negotiate and then fulfil the dowry demands. However, some people reject such demands and end up the relationship but only a negligible percentage of people report such matters to the police and file a case of dowry. It clearly indicates that there are huge chances that the numbers of the reported cases are far less than the actual number of dowry related incidents. Not merely, giving and taking dowry rather demanding dowry is also an offence but majority people do not opt to report the occurrence of this offence. This not only becomes the hindrance in the effective implementation of dowry prohibition laws but it also encourages the people to openly demand and take dowry as they know it well that the chances are very rare that someone will report the matter to the police.

7.   Is it right to take the matter of dowry in Police Stations and Courts?

Table: 7

Answer	Frequency	Percentage
a) No, dowry is a custom of marriage	7	7.0
b) No, it is personal matter of families and must be resolved through mutual discussion	29	29.0
c) Yes, otherwise it may lead to some serious offences	57	57.0
d) No, It only leads to the harassment of the families and brings no positive solution	3	3.0
e) Not Answered	4	4.0
Total	**100**	**100.0**

57% people believe that matter of dowry should be reported and taken to the courts otherwise it may lead to some serious offences subsequently. 7% people believe that matter of dowry should not be reported in police as it is a custom of marriage. 29% people believe that it is personal matter of families and must be resolved through mutual discussion. 3% people believe that it only leads to the harassment of the families and brings no positive solution and hence should not be reported.

The response of the respondents on the basis of age i.e.; < 30 Yrs, 31-40 Yrs, 41-50 Yrs, and > 50 Yrs was analyzed:

Table: 7.1

Is it right to take the matter of dowry in Police Stations and Courts?						
Variable Age	No, dowry is a custom of marriage	No, it is personal matter of families and must be resolved through mutual discussion	Yes, otherwise it may lead to some serious offences	No, It only leads to the harassment of the families and brings no positive solution	Not Answered	Total
< 30 Yrs	5.0%	15.0%	75.0%	2.5%	2.5%	100.0%
31-40 Yrs	6.9%	27.6%	55.2%	3.4%	6.9%	100.0%
41-50 Yrs	17.6%	58.8%	23.5%	0.0%	0.0%	100.0%
> 50 Yrs	0.0%	35.7%	50.0%	7.1%	7.1%	100.0%

191

There is a clear cut variation in the responses of the people who are above 41 years of age. Majority of the people below 40 years of age prefer to take the matter of dowry in police stations and courts, however, only 23.5% people between the age group of 41-50 years agree to take such matter in police station or courts. 76.5% people do not want to take such matters to the police stations or court due to some reason or another. Moreover, only 50% of the people above 50 years of age prefer to take such matters to police station or court, rest of the 50% do not prefer it. This can be identified as another major reason behind the less number of reported cases of dowry rather than actual number of cases.

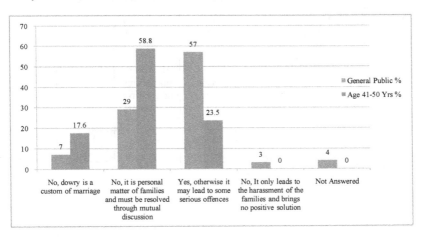

Variable 'Age' and Chi Square value is '0.049'

Figure: 7.1

Table: 7.2

Answer	General Public %	Age 41-50 Yrs %
No, dowry is a custom of marriage	7	17.6
No, it is personal matter of families and must be resolved through mutual discussion	29	58.8
Yes, otherwise it may lead to some serious offences	57	23.5
No, It only leads to the harassment of the families and brings no positive solution	3	0
Not Answered	4	0

Again there is strong disparity between the opinion of males and females. On one hand 83.3% of women believe that such matters must be taken to police stations and courts where as only 45.7% males agree to the same, 54.3% disagree to take such matters to the police stations due to some reason or another.

The response of the respondents on the basis of Sex i.e.; Male, female was analyzed:

Table: 7.3

	Is it right to take the matter of dowry in Police Stations and Courts?					
Variable Sex	No, dowry is a custom of marriage	No, it is personal matter of families and must be resolved through mutual discussion	Yes, otherwise it may lead to some serious offences	No, It only leads to the harassment of the families and brings no positive solution	Not Answered	Total
Males	8.6%	37.1%	45.7%	4.3%	4.3%	100.0%
Females	3.3%	10.0%	83.3%	0.0%	3.3%	100.0%

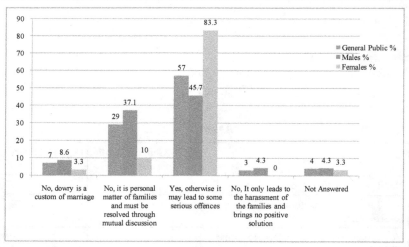

Variable 'Sex' and Chi Square value is '0.013'

Figure: 7.3

193

Table: 7.4

Answer	General Public %	Males %	Females %
No, dowry is a custom of marriage	7	8.6	3.3
No, it is personal matter of families and must be resolved through mutual discussion	29	37.1	10
Yes, otherwise it may lead to some serious offences	57	45.7	83.3
No, It only leads to the harassment of the families and brings no positive solution	3	4.3	0
Not Answered	4	4.3	3.3

Educational qualification is another factor which has an impact upon the response of the people regarding taking dowry related matters to the police station or courts. The graduates and post graduates are in the favour of the same whereas 54.5% undergraduates hesitate to take such matters to the police station or courts.

The response of the respondents on the basis of Education i.e.; Primary, Upto +2, Graduation, PG was analyzed:

Table: 7.5

Is it right to take the matter of dowry in Police Stations and Courts?						
Variable Education	No, dowry is a custom of marriage	No, it is personal matter of families and must be resolved through mutual discussion	Yes, otherwise it may lead to some serious offences	No, It only leads to the harassment of the families and brings no positive solution	Not Answered	Total
Primary	16.7%	0.0%	66.7%	0.0%	16.7%	100.0%
Upto +2	9.1%	40.9%	45.5%	0.0%	4.5%	100.0%
Graduation	0.0%	29.4%	70.6%	0.0%	0.0%	100.0%
PG	7.4%	18.5%	70.4%	3.7%	0.0%	100.0%
Not Answered	0.0%	16.7%	33.3%	33.3%	16.7%	100.0%

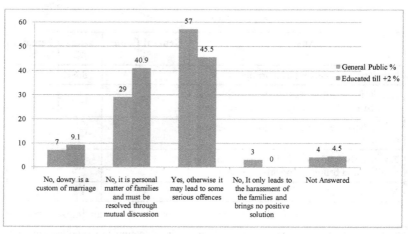

Variable 'Education' and Chi Square value is '0.001'

Figure 7.5

Table: 7.6

Answer	General Public %	Educated till +2 %
No, dowry is a custom of marriage	7	9.1
No, it is personal matter of families and must be resolved through mutual discussion	29	40.9
Yes, otherwise it may lead to some serious offences	57	45.5
No, It only leads to the harassment of the families and brings no positive solution	3	0
Not Answered	4	4.5

8. **Is it right to punish the parents of bride with imprisonment if they give the dowry as demanded by the bridegroom side?**

Table: 8

Answer	Frequency	Percentage
a) Yes	38	38.0
b) No, they are innocent/helpless	21	21.0
c) Not imprisonment but only a warning should be given	13	13.0
d) Can't say	22	22.0
e) Not answered	6	6.0
Total	**100**	**100.0**

195

38% people believe that the parents of the bride should also be imprisoned if they fulfil the dowry demands of the bridegroom and his family but 21% opined that they are helpless innocent people. 13% people believe that at least warning should be given to those parents of the bride who give/gave dowry in the marriage of their daughter/s. Various variables such as age, education and occupation have no significant effect on the opinion.

9. **Do you think that the people are ready to make a girl their daughter-in-law, who had already broken one engagement and filed a dowry case against her would be in-laws before marriage?**

Table: 9

Answer	Frequency	Percentage
a) No, not at all	22	22.0
b) Very rare	21	21.0
c) Yes, very happily	34	34.0
d) Can't say	19	19.0
e) Not answered	4	4.0
Total	100	100.0

34% people believe that they will very happily accept that girl who in past did not marry a person as he and his family had demanded dowry, rather she had filed a dowry case against them. 22% people opine that they would disagree to own such a girl as their daughter-in-law. 21% people believe that in very rare case they may accept such a girl. 19% people could not ascertain what they would do in such a situation. Various variables such as age, education and occupation have no significant effect on the opinion.

10. **If the bridegroom and his family had demanded and received huge amount of dowry in the marriage, what kind of consequences they are likely to face in general?**

Table: 10

Answer	Frequency	Percentage
a) They flaunt it in the society and most of the people get astonished by their royal wedding	40	40.0
b) Their financial status increases and they unrestrictedly enjoy the lavish gifts	22	22.0
c) A dowry case is filed against them and they are punished	14	14.0
d) They are boycotted and defamed in the society	17	17.0
e) Not answered	7	7.0
Total	**100**	**100.0**

40% people hold the opinion that bridegroom and his family flaunt in society if their royal wedding ceremony demand along with huge dowry is fulfilled by the bride's family. Along with this 22% people believe that bridegroom and family starts enjoying their increased financial status and they unrestrictedly enjoy the lavish gifts. Whereas, 14% people believe that a dowry case should be filed against them and they should be punished and 17% believe that such people should be boycotted and defamed in the society. Various variables such as age, education and occupation have no significant effect on the opinion.

11. **If a married woman reports a dowry case against her in-laws, what kind of consequences she is likely to face?**

Table: 11

Answer	Frequency	Percentage
a) She faces lots of problems in her parental house as well as outside	39	39.0
b) Society makes gossips against her and her family	28	28.0
c) She is helped and supported for being a victim of dowry	14	14.0
d) She faces harassment in the society, police station as well as court	12	12.0
e) Not answered	7	7.0
Total	**100**	**100.0**

39% people believe that woman faces lots of problems in her parental house as well as outside if she reports a dowry case against her in-laws. 28% people opine that people gossip against her and her family. But 14% people believe that such a woman gets help and support for being a victim of dowry. 12% people also opine that woman faces harassment in the society, police station as well as in the court if she reports and files dowry case. Various variables such as age, education and occupation have no significant effect on the opinion.

12. Do you know about the existing laws for dowry related offences?

Table: 12

Answer	Frequency	Percentage
a) Yes, Dowry Prohibition Act	20	20.0
b) Provisions for Dowry Death, cruelty, domestic violence etc.	10	10.0
c) Both a & b	34	34.0
d) No, not much	30	30.0
e) Not answered	6	6.0
Total	**100**	**100.0**

34% people believe that they know about Dowry Prohibition Act and Provisions for Dowry Death, cruelty, domestic violence etc. collectively. 20% people believe to have the knowledge of Dowry Prohibition Act. 10% people have understanding of provisions for dowry death, cruelty; domestic violence etc. 30% people have no knowledge of the said acts and provisions.

The response of the respondents on the basis of age i.e.; < 30 Yrs, 31-40 Yrs, 41-50 Yrs, and > 50 Yrs was analyzed:

Table:12.1

Variable Age	Yes, Dowry Prohibition Act	Provisions for Dowry Death, cruelty, domestic violence etc.	Both a & b	No, not much	Not answered	Total
< 30 Yrs	15.0%	20.0%	37.5%	25.0%	2.5%	100.0%
31-40 Yrs	20.7%	0.0%	34.5%	31.0%	13.8%	100.0%
41-50 Yrs	35.3%	0.0%	11.8%	52.9%	0.0%	100.0%
> 50 Yrs	14.3%	14.3%	50.0%	14.3%	7.1%	100.0%

Do you know about the existing laws for dowry related offences?

The middle aged people between the age group of 41-50 years deviate from the majority people who have some knowledge regarding Dowry Prohibition Laws. 52.9% of the people of this age group do not have any knowledge regarding dowry related offences and laws.

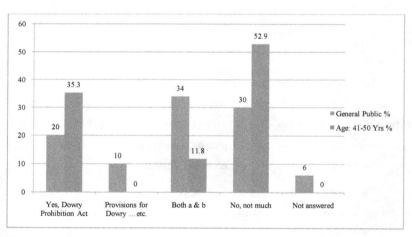

Variable 'Age' and Chi Square value is '0.049'

Figure: 12.1

Table:12.2

Answer	General Public %	Age: 41-50 Yrs %
Yes, Dowry Prohibition Act	20	35.3
Provisions for Dowry Death, cruelty, domestic violence etc.	10	0
Both a & b	34	11.8
No, not much	30	52.9
Not answered	6	0

13. **Have you ever heard/ known about any victim of dowry related offences in your surroundings or social circle?**

Table: 13

Answer	Frequency	Percentage
a) Yes, I personally know some victims	23	23.0
b) No, never	31	31.0
c) Yes, through acquaintance/ other people	6	6.0
d) Yes, but only through News papers	36	36.0
e) Not answered	4	4.0
Total	**100**	**100.0**

31% people have never received such information from their surroundings and social circle about a victim of dowry and related offences. 23% of the people personally know from their surroundings and social circle about a victim of dowry and related offences. 6% people heard about such dowry cases from acquaintance or other people and 36% people come to know about such dowry and related offenses from Newspaper etc.

14. **What is your perspective about dowry?**

Table: 14

Answer	Frequency	Percentage
a) As an act of pleasing bridegroom's family for safe keeping of their daughter	30	30.0
b) An act of show off in the society	17	17.0
c) Need of the custom, culture and tradition	28	28.0
d) Anti social and illegal act by parties performing marriage	20	20.0
e) Not answered	5	5.0
Total	**100**	**100.0**

30% general public opines that dowry is an act of pleasing bridegroom's family for safe keeping of their daughter and 17% believe it as an act of show off. 28% people believe that it is need of the custom, culture and traditions. Whereas, 20% people opine that it is an anti social and illegal act by both parties performing marriage.

The response of the respondents on the basis of Sex i.e.; Male, Female was analyzed:

Table: 14.1

	What is your perspective about dowry?					
Variable Sex	As an act of pleasing bridegroom's family for safe keeping of their daughter	An act of show off in the society	Need of the custom, culture and tradition	Anti social and illegal act by parties performing marriage	Not answered	Total
Males	27.1%	5.7%	37.1%	25.7%	4.3%	100.0%
Females	40.0%	43.3%	6.7%	6.7%	3.3%	100.0%

Males and females totally differ in their perspective about dowry. Majority of the males opine that dowry is a need of custom, culture and tradition in the society whereas, only 6.7% of females agree with the same. As majority of the females believe that either it is merely an act of show off in the society or an act to please the family of the bridegroom for the wellbeing of the bride in her matrimonial home.

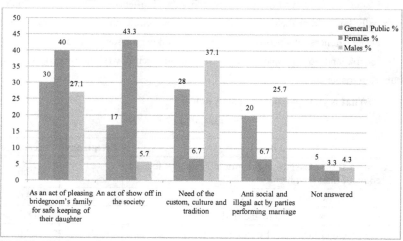

Variable 'Sex' and Chi Square value is '0.000'

Figure: 14.1

201

Table 14.2

Answer	General Public %	Females %	Males %
As an act of pleasing bridegroom's family for safe keeping of their daughter	30	40	27.1
An act of show off in the society	17	43.3	5.7
Need of the custom, culture and tradition	28	6.7	37.1
Anti social and illegal act by parties performing marriage	20	6.7	25.7
Not answered	5	3.3	4.3

15. **If the husband/in- laws, physically/mentally harass a woman for dowry, what is the feasible solution for her?**

Table: 15

Answer	Frequency	Percentage
a) She should take a divorce and start a new life	19	19.0
b) Parents ask in-laws and husband to stop harassment, as filing a case will effect readjustment in the marriage	35	35.0
c) No use of going to the police as it will result in the further harassment of that woman by the police as well as society	4	4.0
d) She should go to the police and file a complaint	37	37.0
e) Not answered	5	5.0
Total	**100**	**100.0**

37% people believe that a woman should file a police complaint in situation where she is physically/ mentally tortured for dowry. 19% people opine that a married woman should take a divorce in such a situation and should start a new life. 35% people believe that filing such complaints affect the readjustment chances in marital home and bride's parents should request for stopping the harassment in respect to dowry. 4% people opine that there is no use of going to the police as it will result in the further harassment of that woman by the police as well as society.

The response of the respondents on the basis of age i.e.; < 30 Yrs, 31-40 Yrs, 41-50 Yrs, and > 50 Yrs was analyzed:

If the husband/in- laws, physically/mentally harass a woman for dowry, what is the feasible solution for her? Table: 15.1						
Variable Age	She should take a divorce and start a new life	Parents ask in-laws and husband to stop harassment, as filing a case will effect readjustment in the marriage	No use of going to the police as it will result in the further harassment of that woman by the police as well as society	She should go to the police and file a complaint	Not answered	Total
< 30 Yrs	20.0%	27.5%	10.0%	40.0%	2.5%	100.0%
31-40 Yrs	27.6%	20.7%	0.0%	44.8%	6.9%	100.0%
41-50 Yrs	17.6%	64.7%	0.0%	17.6%	0.0%	100.0%
> 50 Yrs	0.0%	57.1%	0.0%	35.7%	7.1%	100.0%

Age has a huge impact upon determining the feasible solution for a female in case of facing harassment for dowry. The majority people below 40 years of age believe that such a woman must file a complaint in the police station against such harassment whereas, a huge percentage of the people above 40 years of the age differ in the opinion and believe that the parents of the girl must try to sort the matter within the family as filing a case will effect readjustment in the marriage. This is another reason of a lesser number of cases reported in the matters of dowry related harassment.

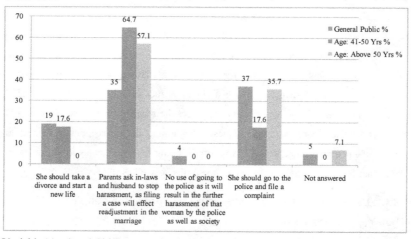

Variable 'Age' and Chi Square value is '0.034'

Figure: 15.1

203

Answer	General Public %	Age: 41-50 Yrs %	Age: Above 50 Yrs %
She should take a divorce and start a new life	19	17.6	0
Parents ask in-laws and husband to stop harassment, as filing a case will effect readjustment in the marriage	35	64.7	57.1
No use of going to the police as it will result in the further harassment of that woman by the police as well as society	4	0	0
She should go to the police and file a complaint	37	17.6	35.7
Not answered	5	0	7.1

16. **What would you do if a false case of dowry is filed against you or your family?**

Table: 16

Answer	Frequency	Percentage
a) We will end our relation with her and teach her a lesson	7	7.0
b) Negotiate and request the bride to revoke her complaint	27	27.0
c) It would be troublesome as all the laws are in the favour of women	14	14.0
d) Nothing to worry as I have full faith in police and legal system	47	47.0
e) Not answered	5	5.0
Total	**100**	**100.0**

47% of the people believe that there is nothing to worry if their daughter-in-law files a false case of dowry against them and their family as they have full faith in police and legal system. 7% people believe that they will end up the marriage and will teach a lesson to their wife/daughter-in-law if she files a false case of dowry against them and their family. 27% people also opine that in such a situation they will negotiate and request the bride to revoke her complaint. 14% people fear and find such a situation troublesome as they believe that all the laws are in the favour of women. Various variables such as age, education and occupation have no significant effect on the opinion.

17.　Is Dowry system a serious issue?

Table: 17

Answer	Frequency	Percentage
a)　Yes, very serious	78	78.0
b)　Only to some extent	12	12.0
c)　No, there are many other serious issues which need more concern	1	1.0
d)　No, it is just a integral custom of marriage	5	5.0
e)　Not answered	4	4.0
Total	**100**	**100.0**

78% people believe that dowry is a serious issue prevailing in the society whereas 12% people felt that only to some extent dowry system is a serious issue. 1% people opine that there are many other serious issues which need more concern than dowry. 5% people find dowry as an integral custom of marriage and do not find any serious issue in dowry system.

The response of the respondents on the basis of Sex i.e.; Male, Female was analyzed:

Table: 17.1

Is Dowry system a serious issue?						
Variable Sex	Yes, very serious	Only to some extent	No, there are many other serious issues which need more concern	No, it is just a integral custom of marriage	Not answered	Total
Males	70.0%	17.1%	1.4%	7.1%	4.3%	100.0%
Females	96.7%	0.0%	0.0%	0.0%	3.3%	100.0%

Gender has a strong impact on the responses given in this question. Although, 70% of the males consider dowry system as a very serious issue, even though, 30% of males still do not consider it as a serious issue. However, 100% women who have given response consider it as a very serious issue and not even a single woman contradicts it. It shows the serious impact of dowry system and its consequences on the psychology of women who are actually the victims of this social evil.

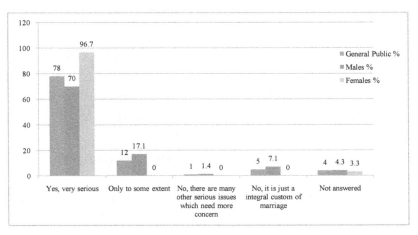

Variable 'Sex' and Chi Square value is '0.046'

Figure: 17.1

Table: 17.2

Answer	General Public %	Males %	Females %
Yes, very serious	78	70	96.7
Only to some extent	12	17.1	0
No, there are many other serious issues which need more concern	1	1.4	0
No, it is just a integral custom of marriage	5	7.1	0
Not answered	4	4.3	3.3

18. What is your opinion on anti-dowry laws?

Table: 18

Answer	Frequency	Percentage
a) Very helpful in dealing with dowry related problems	44	44.0
b) Such laws are only on papers and are totally incapable to eradicate dowry	20	20.0
c) Such laws are mostly misused to deter and falsely implicate innocent husband and in-laws.	8	8.0
d) Not much helpful in dealing with dowry related problems	24	24.0
e) Not answered	4	4.0
Total	**100**	**100.0**

44% people believe that anti dowry laws are very helpful in dealing with dowry related problems. 20% people believe that such laws are only on papers and are totally incapable to eradicate dowry. 8% people have opinion that such laws are mostly misused to deter and falsely implicate innocent husband and in-laws. 24% people do not find these laws helpful in dealing with dowry related problems. Various variables such as age, education and occupation have no significant effect on the opinion.

19.   Do you think that dowry is a major reason for not wanting a girl child?

Table: 19

Answer	Frequency	Percentage
a) Yes, certainly	23	23.0
b) No, Not at all	29	29.0
c) Yes but there are some other reasons as well	30	30.0
d) Not Sure	14	14.0
e) Not answered	4	4.0
Total	100	100.0

30% people believe that dowry is a major reason for not wanting a girl child but there are some other reasons as well for not wanting a girl child. 23% people believe that reason of not wanting a girl child is primarily due to the dowry but 29% people completely disagree with this opinion. 14% people are not sure about their opinion on this issue. Various variables such as age, education and occupation have no significant effect on the opinion.

20.   In how many years, do you think that the custom of dowry will be eradicated from the society completely?

Table: 20

Answer	Frequency	Percentage
a) Within next 5 years	11	11.0
b) Within next 10 years	11	11.0
c) More than 10 years	16	16.0
d) It will never end.	58	58.0
e) Not answered	4	4.0
Total	100	100.0

58% people believe that the practice of dowry and its menace will never end. Only 11% people believe that in next 5 years from now, menace of dowry will be completely eradicated from the society. 11% people believe that it would be possible in next 10 years. 16% people believe that eradication of menace of dowry will take more than 10 years. Various variables such as age, education and occupation have no significant effect on the opinion.

Respondents- Married Women

1. **Do you think that it becomes easy for the parents of a girl, to get a rich/well settled bridegroom by offering good dowry in the marriage of their daughter?**

Table: 1

Answers	Frequency	Percentage
a) Yes, it brings more marriage proposals	7	14.0
b) Yes, in most of the cases	4	8.0
c) No	34	68.0
d) Only in arrange marriages	5	10
Total	50	100

68% of the married women disagree with the statement that high dowry offers bring better and well settled bridegrooms for marriages. 14% women contradict and believe that better dowry offers bring better bridegrooms. 8% women believe that in most of the cases it becomes easy for the parents of a girl, to get a rich/well settled bridegroom by offering good dowry in the marriage of their daughter. But 10% women believe that this statement holds validity in cases of arrange marriages only.

The response of the respondents on the basis of Income i.e.; < 2 Lakh, 2-5 Lakh, 5-10 Lakh, > 10 Lakh was analyzed:

Table: 1.1

Do you think that it becomes easy for the parents of a girl, to get a rich/well settled bridegroom by offering good dowry in the marriage of their daughter?					
Variable Income	Yes, it brings more marriage proposals	Yes, in most of the cases	No	Only in arrange marriages	Total
< 2 Lakh	60.0%	0.0%	20.0%	20.0%	100.0%
2-5 Lakh	15.4%	0.0%	84.6%	0.0%	100.0%
5-10 Lakh	0.0%	0.0%	90.9%	9.1%	100.0%
> 10 Lakh	0.0%	100.0%	0.0%	0.0%	100.0%
Not disclosed	10.0%	15.0%	60.0%	15.0%	100.0%

There is a significant impact of self income of married women who have answered this question. The lower income group i.e. below 2 Lakhs of annual income as well as the higher income group i.e. above 10 Lakh of annual income agrees that it becomes easy for the parents of a girl, to get a rich/well settled bridegroom by offering good dowry in the marriage of their daughter. However, the middle income group i.e. from 2-10 lakh annual income in a huge majority of 87.5% strongly disagrees with this statement.

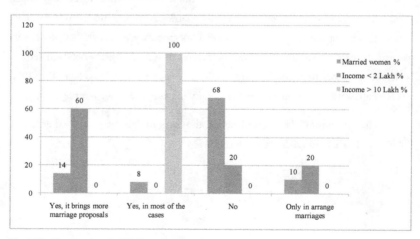

Variable 'Income' and Chi Square value is '0.003'

Figure: 1.1

209

Table 1.2

Answers	Married women %	Income < 2 Lakh %	Income > 10 Lakh %
Yes, it brings more marriage proposals	14	60	0
Yes, in most of the cases	8	0	100
No	68	20	0
Only in arrange marriages	10	20	0

2. **In your opinion, who has a better chance/eligibility to demand and get better dowry in his marriage?**

Table: 2

Answers	Frequency	Percentage
a) A government employee	9	18.0
b) A private employee	1	2.0
c) Son of a rich family with family business	10	20.0
d) None of the above, as nobody claims or demands dowry, nowadays	30	60.0
Total	**50**	**100.0**

60% women believe that nobody seeks dowry nowadays, therefore, better chance or eligibility of seeking dowry do not arise neither from Government or Private employed nor from rich business family background bridegroom. 18% women believe that a Government employed bridegrooms have better chance and eligibility to seek dowry whereas 2% women believe that private company employed bridegroom has. But at the same time 20 % of women believe that the bridegroom from a rich business family will have better chance and eligibility to seek better dowry.

3. **What is the general attitude of the people, society and relatives towards a marriage in which the parents of the bride have not given a single valuable item to their son-in-law or his family?**

Table: 3

Answers	Frequency	Percentage
a) They appreciate it	30	58.0
b) They consider it as an inferior marriage	10	20.0
c) They sympathize the family of bridegroom for not getting dowry as per custom	4	8.0
d) They show an indifferent approach	6	12.0
Total	**50**	**100.0**

58% of the married women believe that society appreciates such marriages where bride's family does not give any valuable items to bridegroom and his family in their marriages. But it is also contradicted by 20% of women as they consider it an inferior marriage. It is also observed that 8% married women still believe that people, society and relatives become sympathetic to the families of bridegroom where dowry was not given however 12 % women had indifferent approach.

The response of the respondents on the basis of age i.e.; < 30 Yrs, 31-40 Yrs, 41-50 Yrs, and > 50 Yrs was analyzed:

Table: 3.1

What is the general attitude of the people, society and relatives towards a marriage in which the parents of the bride have not given a single valuable item to their son-in-law or his family?						
Variable Age	They appreciate it	They consider it as an inferior marriage	They sympathize the family of bridegroom for not getting dowry as per custom	They show an indifferent approach	Not answered	Total
< 30 Yrs	53.3%	20.0%	0.0%	26.7%	0.0%	100.0%
31-40 Yrs	40.0%	40.0%	20.0%	0.0%	0.0%	100.0%
41-50 Yrs	60.0%	10.0%	0.0%	20.0%	10.0%	100.0%
> 50 Yrs	90.0%	0.0%	10.0%	0.0%	0.0%	100.0%

The women who belong to an age group of 30-40 years of age contradict with the majority opinion. They think that the marriage in which the parents of the bride have not given a single valuable item to their son-in-law or his family is not appreciated by the people. Such a marriage is either considered as inferior or it becomes matter of sympathy towards the family of the bridegroom for not getting dowry.

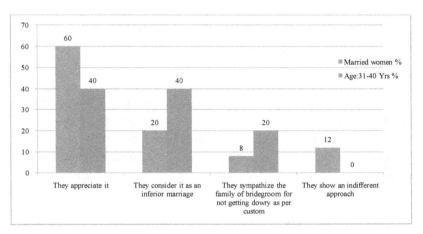

Variable 'age' and Chi Square value is '0.027'

Figure: 3.1

Table: 3.2

Answers	Married women %	Age:31-40 Yrs %
They appreciate it	60	40
They consider it as an inferior marriage	20	40
They sympathize the family of bridegroom for not getting dowry as per custom	8	20
They show an indifferent approach	12	0

4. **Do you think that the daughters like it, if their parents give gifts, valuable items, gold, cash, car etc in the marriage to their husband/in-laws?**

Table: 4

Answers	Frequency	Percentage
a) Yes, it is an integral part of our customs	4	8.0
b) No	29	58.0
c) Yes, it increases their status in family and society	6	12.0
d) It does not matter for them	11	22.0
Total	**50**	**100.0**

It has been observed that 58% of the daughters do not like if their parents give gifts, valuable items, gold, cash, car etc in their marriage neither they consider it right that such valuable article shall be given to their husband/in-laws. However 20% still like it as they believe that it is an integral part of our customs and increases their status in family and society. 22% women said that it does not matter to them in any of the situations above.

The response of the respondents on the basis of Income i.e.; < 2 Lakh, 2-5 Lakh, 5-10 Lakh, > 10 Lakh was analyzed:

Table: 4.1

Do you think that the daughters like it, if their parents give gifts, valuable items, gold, cash, car etc in the marriage to their husband/in-laws?					
Variable Income	Yes, it is an integral part of our customs	No	Yes, it increases their status in family and society	It does not matter for them	Total
< 2 Lakh	0.0%	60.0%	20.0%	20.0%	100.0%
2-5 Lakh	7.7%	69.2%	0.0%	23.1%	100.0%
5-10 Lakh	18.2%	63.6%	0.0%	18.2%	100.0%
> 10 Lakh	100.0%	0.0%	0.0%	0.0%	100.0%
Not disclosed	0.0%	50.0%	25.0%	25.0%	100.0%

The females of a self income more than 10 Lakh per annum deviate from the general opinion and agree that daughters like it if their parents give gifts, valuable items, gold, cash, car etc in the marriage to their husband/in-laws.

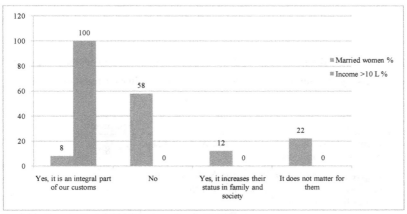

Variable 'Income' and Chi Square value is '0.042'

Figure: 4.1

Table: 4.2

Answers	Married women %	Income >10 L %
Yes, it is an integral part of our customs	8	100
No	58	0
Yes, it increases their status in family and society	12	0
It does not matter for them	22	0

5.   **In your opinion, who among the family members is more interested in demanding/ giving dowry in the marriage?**

Table: 5

Answers	Frequency	Percentage
a) The bridegroom	2	4.0
b) Parents of the bridegroom	23	46.0
c) Parents of the bride	3	6.0
d) Nobody	22	44.0
Total	**50**	**100.0**

46% of the women opine that parents of the bridegroom are most interested in the dowry however only 4% of the bridegrooms are interested in taking the dowry. 6 % of women held daughter's parents responsible for encouraging dowry in their daughter's marriage. However, 44% women believe that no one is interested in the dowry.

6. **What is the usual impact on married life of a woman when her parents give gifts, valuable items, gold, cash, car etc. to her husband or in-laws?**

Table: 6

	Answers	Frequency	Percentage
a)	It enhances the status and respect of bride and her parents in her in-laws	8	16.0
b)	It gives a temporary relief to the bride from the continuous demands from her husband/in-laws but makes them more greedy	5	10.0
c)	Most of the husbands/in-laws refuse to take it as they are against such customs	13	26.0
d)	No effect at all	24	48.0
	Total	**50**	**100.0**

48% women believe that there is no such impact on married life of a woman when her parents give gifts, valuable items, gold, cash, car etc. to her husband or in-laws. Only 16 % women believe that it enhances the status and respect of bride and her parents in her in-laws. 26% of women have come up with the thought that most of the husbands/in-laws refuse to take it as they are against such customs but 10% women have contradicted this point of view and have the opinion that it gives a temporary relief to the bride from the continuous demands of dowry from her husband/in-laws but makes them greedier. The opinion remains same across various variables such as age, education and occupation of the women.

7. **What was the approximate amount of money that was spent in your marriage celebration, ceremonies and buying gifts etc?**

Table: 7

Answers	Frequency	Percentage
a) Below 5 lakhs	27	54.0
b) 5 to 20 lakhs	19	38.0
c) 20 to 50 lakhs	3	6
d) More than 50 lakhs	1	2
Total	**50**	**100.0**

54 % of the women have told that the total expenditure that was done in their marriage was below 5 lakh where as expenditure above 5 lakh and below 20 lakh was done in 38% marriages. Only 8 % marriages incurred expenses of above 20 lakh. The opinion remains same across various variables such as age, education and occupation of the women.

8. Who had brought better gifts and dowry among all the daughter-in-laws in the family of your in-laws and their relatives?

Table: 8

Answers	Frequency	Percentage
a) I, in my marriage	6	12.0
b) Only one or two brides had brought better than mine	2	4.0
c) Most of them have brought almost same	22	44.0
d) No one had brought anything	20	40.0
Total	**50**	**100.0**

When married women were asked that who had brought better gifts and dowry among all the daughter-in-laws in the family of their in-laws, then, 44 % of the women replied that they brought almost same dowry as were brought by other brides to their in-laws whereas 12% women had opinion that they brought maximum dowry among other daughter in laws in bridegroom's family. 4 % believe that only 1 or 2 other brides brought better dowry. 40% of married women claimed to have brought nothing in the form of dowry as was also not brought by any other bride. The opinion remains same across various variables such as age, education and occupation of the women.

216

9. **What was the general conversation that took place between the two families before your marriage regarding giving gifts, shagun etc?**

Table: 9

	Answers	Frequency	Percentage
a)	The in-laws asked for the shagun, gift, gold etc merely according to their financial/social status and the employment status of bridegroom.	2	4.0
b)	No exact choice or indication was given by the bridegroom and his family but they wanted it to be a lavish affair and accepted happily whatever was given.	14	28.0
c)	The in-laws simply gave a list of names of their relatives to whom the gifts and shagun must be given as per rituals.	5	10.0
d)	The in-laws/bridegroom clearly refused to accept any cash, gold or gift in marriage.	29	58.0
	Total	**50**	**100.0**

In the discussions which were held before marriage between bride and bridegroom's family, in connection to the gifts and *shaguns*, 58% families refused to accept any cash, gold or gift in marriage. 28% women have shared that bridegroom's family wanted a lavish marriage ceremony and did not show any reluctance towards the dowry. Also, 10 % bridegroom's families shared the list of relatives to whom bride's family was expected to give gifts and shaguns and 4 % bridegroom's family asked for the shagun, gift, gold etc merely according to bride parent's financial/social status and the employment status of bridegroom.

10. **Do your parents usually give money, valuables items to you /your husband/your in-laws?**

Table: 10

	Answers	Frequency	Percentage
a)	No, not at all	24	48.0
b)	Yes, and especially when it is demanded by my husband or in-laws	-	-
c)	Yes but only if it is suggested by me	1	2.0
d)	Yes, but only at their own will	25	50.0
	Total	**50**	**100**

After the marriage of a daughter, her parents usually give money, valuables items to her/ her husband/her in-laws and 50 % women have agreed to have received such items as per the will of their parent's but asides this 48 % of women have said that they do not receive any thing after their marriage. 6 % women seek gifts as and when they themselves suggest their parents to give gifts. The variables such as age, income and education have shown no significant variation in the opinion of the women.

11. **What do you think is the main reason behind giving money, valuable items to you /your husband/your in-laws by your parents?**

Table: 11

Answers	Frequency	Percentage
a) Customs/rituals of our community	38	76.0
b) Demand/Pressure of husband or in-laws	2	4.0
c) It helps in maintaining social status as well as my happiness and good relations with husband and in-laws	3	6.0
d) My requests	4	8.0
e) Not Answered	3	6.0
Total	**50**	**100.0**

76% of the women have opinion that major reason behind the dowry is the customs and rituals of the society. Only 6 % women correlate the dowry with the social status, happiness and ground of amicable relations with husband and in-laws. Merely, 4% women have opined dowry culture as pressure or demand from bridegroom's side. 8 % of women believe that bride does themselves insist their parents for giving dowry. The opinion of the women remains same across various variables such as age, education, occupation and income.

12. **Had your parents given/shall give you any share in your parental property?**

Table: 12

Answers	Frequency	Percentage
a) Yes, definitely	7	14.0
b) No, it is for my brothers	23	46.0
c) Yes, but they are not happily willing	1	2.0
d) No, they have already done enough for me, so I refused	19	38.0
Total	**50**	**100.0**

When rights in parental property come into the consideration of the married women, 46% women consider their male sibling's right over parental property. 38 % of the women refused to take their legal share in the parental property as they believe that their parents have already done enough for them. Only 14% women have agreed to have received or to receive share in the parental property. 2% women believe that they received their share but their parents were not willing and happy to give share to their married daughter. However, women across various educational background, age, income and occupation have no impact on the opinion.

13.   Have you ever heard any of the following sentences from your husband or his relatives in general?

- Some other bride has brought more valuable items, gold, cash in her marriage than you.
- The gifts, valuable items, gold, *shagun* given by your parents is not up to the mark
- Your parents should have given a bike/ car/ a more expensive car / more gold etc in your marriage
- Your husband deserves much more than the gifts, valuable items, gold, shagun given by your parents to him.

Table: 13

Answers	Frequency	Percentage
a) Sometimes	4	8.0
b) Always	-	-
c) Only once	-	-
d) No, never	46	92.0
Total	**50**	**100.0**

92% of married women have refused that they had ever heard any of the sarcastic remarks from their husband or his relatives in general. Only 8% have admitted that they have heard such remarks sometimes. But a hesitation has been observed in many women to speak up the truth when such a direct question regarding their family matter is asked and another surprising fact was that 46% of these women have admitted that they have received mental harassment related to dowry from their husband or his relatives.

14. **Have you ever faced any kind of physical harassment by your husband or his relatives for demanding dowry from you/your parents?**

Table: 14

Answers	Frequency	Percentage
a) No	26	52
b) Yes, but only once or twice	-	-
c) Yes, very often	1	2.0
d) Not physical but there is mental harassment	23	46.0
Total	**50**	**100.0**

52 % married women have said that they never faced any kind of physical harassment by her husband or his relatives in respect to dowry demands, however, 46 % women have agreed to have received mental harassment which is related to dowry. Only, 2 % women get physically harassed repeatedly for dowry. However, women across various educational background, age, income and occupation have no impact on the opinion.

15. **What would you do if your husband /your in-laws would demand or compel you/your parents to give gifts, valuable property, gold, cash, car etc to them in connection to your marriage?**

Table: 15

Answers	Frequency	Percentage
a) I will request my parents to fulfill their demand as much as possible	-	-
b) I will not agree to fulfill such demands	33	66.0
c) I will try to compromise with mutual understanding	8	16.0
d) I will file a complaint against them in the Police Station	9	18.0
Total	**50**	**100.0**

66% married women said that they will not fulfill the demands if their husband / in-laws would demand or compel them or their parents to give gifts, valuable property, gold, cash, car etc to them in connection to your marriage. 16 % women said that they will try to resolve by mutual understanding whereas 18 % women consider filing a Police complaint on such dowry demands. No woman was willing to request her own parents to fulfill the dowry demands. The opinion of the women remains unchanged across various variables such as age, income, occupation and education.

16. **Is it easy/ feasible for a married woman to file a complaint in the police station if her husband/in-laws tortures her for dowry?**

Table: 16

Answers	Frequency	Percentage
a) Yes, it will improve the behavior of her in-laws	6	12.0
b) No, it will degrade her position in her in-laws and society	7	14.0
c) Only if she is ready to break her marriage	6	12.0
d) Yes, law will definitely help her	31	62.0
Total	**50**	**100.0**

62% of the women believe in the Law and will file a complaint in the police station if her husband/in-laws tortures her for dowry. 26% women have opinion that such an action will degrade the relations further and such action should be taken only when a women is ready to break the marriage. However, 12 % women believe that reporting such demands of dowry in police results in improved behaviour of the in-laws. There is no effect of variables such as age, education and occupation on the opinion.

17. **What are the chances of escape/survival of a woman if the in-laws/ husband try to kill her for dowry within the four walls of house?**

Table: 17

Answers	Frequency	Percentage
a) It depends on her luck	4	8.0
b) Very low as she is helpless among their majority	11	22.0
c) Very high, she is strong enough to fight back	21	42.0
d) Good enough, neighbors and relatives provide help in such cases	13	26.0
Total	**50**	**100.0**

There is mixed opinion among women as 42 % women believe that woman is strong enough as she can fight back and escape if the in-laws/ husband try to kill her for dowry within the four walls of house but 22 % women believe that her chances to survive in such a situation is very low. 8 % women left it on their fate and 26% have opinion that neighbors and relatives will help in escaping her from such a situation. The opinion of the women remains unchanged across various variables such as age, income, occupation and education.

18. What are the necessary changes that must be brought to make a woman feel comfortable in raising her voice against dowry related offences and torture?

Table: 18

Answers	Frequency	Percentage
a) The society shall become positive towards such women	6	12.0
b) The women shall be imparted more education and employment	10	20.0
c) The police and legal system shall become supportive and take these offences seriously	9	18.0
d) All of the above	25	50.0
Total	**50**	**100.0**

All the women have strongly felt that there is a strong need to bring certain necessary changes in Law, society as well as police administration to provide a minimum level of comfort to the female victims of dowry in order to raise their voice against dowry related offences. 50 % women felt that all of the above measures should be taken collectively to empower women to raise and handle instances of dowry demand and torture. 12% women believe that society should become more positive towards the women. 20 % women believe that imparting more education and employment opportunities will help woman. 18 % believe that police and legal system should deal such dowry instances more seriously.

Respondents- Police, Lawyers, Judges, Law- Academicians

1. **How many cases of Dowry have you dealt so far?**

Table: 1

Answer	Frequency	Percentage
a) Less than 20	33	66.0
b) 20 to 50	12	24.0
c) 50 to 100	2	4.0
d) More than 100	3	6.0
Total	**50**	**100**

66% people from the profession of Police/Lawyer/Judge/academicians believe that they have dealt with less than 20 dowry cases till time. 24% professionals have dealt 20-50 dowry cases. 4% have dealt 50-100 cases and 6% professional have dealt with more than 100 dowry related cases. . There is no significant change on the opinion across variables such as age, occupation, sex, and education.

2. **What do you think are the factors responsible for the continuance of offences related to dowry despite stringent laws?**

Table: 2

Answer	Frequency	Percentage
a) Most of the offences likewise; demanding dowry, cruelty, domestic violence etc are not reported properly	15	30.0
b) Social recognition of dowry as a custom	24	48.0
c) Ineffective police/legal mechanism	5	10.0
d) Any Other	6	12.0
Total	**50**	**100.0**

48% professionals opine that social recognition of dowry as a custom is the prime reason of continuation of offence of dowry. 30% professionals (Police/Lawyer/Judge/academicians) believe that factors responsible for the continuance of offences related to dowry despite stringent laws is that such cases are not reported properly. 10% believe that ineffective police/legal mechanism is responsible whereas 12% opine that some other reasons are responsible. . There is no significant change on the opinion across variables such as age, occupation, sex, and education.

3. **Do you think that there is any difference between the actual number and the reported number of incidents of dowry related offences?**

Table: 3

Answer	Frequency	Percentage
a) Yes, huge	26	52.0
b) Yes but not much	17	34.0
c) No, not at all	7	14.0
d) It can't be ascertained	-	-
Total	**50**	**100.0**

52% professionals (Police/Lawyer/Judge/academicians) believe that there is a huge difference in the total number of dowry incidences to the total number of cases which get reported. 34% professionals also find that there is difference but do not much difference. Whereas, 14% believe that such reported and actual cases are equal.

4. **In your opinion, how many cases of Domestic violence are related to Dowry?**

Table: 4

Answer	Frequency	Percentage
a) 0 to 25 %	22	44.0
b) 25 to 50 %	17	34.0
c) 50 to 75%	7	14.0
d) 75 to 100%	4	8.0
Total	**50**	**100.0**

44% professionals (Police/Lawyer/Judge/academicians) believe that up to 25% of the domestic violence cases are primarily related to the dowry whereas 34% professionals believe that 25-50% domestic violence cases are related to the dowry. 14% opine that 50-75% cases of domestic violence is due to the dowry and 8% believe that 75-100% cases of domestic violence occur due to the dowry. . There is no significant change on the opinion across variables such as age, occupation, sex, and education.

224

5. **Do you think that the people file a complaint for giving or taking of Dowry?**

Table: 5

Answer	Frequency	Percentage
a) Yes, in most of the cases	7	14.0
b) In very few cases	28	56.0
c) In almost half of the cases	4	8.0
d) No, not at all	11	22.0
Total	**50**	**100.0**

56% professionals believe that very few cases of dowry get reported. 14% professionals (Police/Lawyer/Judge/academicians) believe that in most cases, people file a complaint if dowry is demanded and is given or taken. 8% opine that that almost half of such cases get reported whereas, 22% believe that people do not file a complaint where dowry is demanded and is given and taken.

6. **The people of which category are more likely involved in dowry related offences?**

Table: 6

Answer	Frequency	Percentage
a) Educated and high-class	9	18.0
b) Uneducated and backward	6	12.0
c) Both the categories	32	64.0
d) Any Other	3	6.0
Total	**50**	**100.0**

64% professionals believe that both i.e. educated, high class and uneducated, backward are equally involved the dowry related offences. 18% professionals (Police/Lawyer/Judge/academicians) believe that educated and high-class people are more likely to be involved in the dowry related offences whereas 12% believe that uneducated and backward are more involved in the dowry related offenses. There is no significant change on the opinion across variables such as age, occupation, sex, and education.

7. **What are the reasons behind the non-compliance of the laws related to dowry prohibition, by the society?**

Table: 7

Answer	Frequency	Percentage
a) Acceptance of dowry as a custom	27	54.0
b) Social pressure of giving and taking Dowry	16	32.0
c) Lack of faith on legal system	2	4.0
d) Any other	5	10.0
Total	**50**	**100.0**

54% professionals (Police/Lawyer/Judge/academicians) believe that acceptance of dowry as a custom is the main reason behind the non-compliance of the laws related to dowry prohibition. 32% opine that social pressure of giving and taking dowry is the root cause whereas 4% believe that people do not adhere dowry prohibition laws as they lack faith on legal system. Opinion remains same across various variables such as age, experience, sex and occupation.

8. **Is there any abuse or misuse of the dowry prohibition laws?**

Table: 8

Answer	Frequency	Percentage
a) Yes, most of the cases are false	18	36.0
b) Misuse is not common but lack of implementation is a problem	18	36.0
c) Only few implications are false, rest are genuine	13	26.0
d) No, Not at all	1	2.0
Total	**50**	**100.0**

It is noticeable that 36% professionals (Police/Lawyer/Judge/academicians) opine that in most of the cases; there is abuse/ misuse of the Dowry Prohibition Laws. 36% professionals opine that misuse is not common but lack of implementation is a problem. 26% believe that only few implications are false, rest are genuine whereas, 2% believe that such laws are not misused at all.

The response of the respondents on the basis of Occupation i.e.; Police, Judge, Lawyer, Academicians was analyzed:

Table: 8.1

Is there any abuse or misuse of the dowry prohibition laws?					
Variable Occupation	Yes, most of the cases are false	Misuse is not common but lack of implementation is a problem	Only few implications are false, rest are genuine	No, Not at all	Total
Police	33.3%	50.0%	16.7%	0.0%	100.0%
Judge	33.3%	58.3%	8.3%	0.0%	100.0%
Lawyer	57.9%	5.3%	31.6%	5.3%	100.0%
Academicians	7.7%	53.8%	38.5%	0.0%	100.0%

Majority of the lawyers deviate from the general opinion as 57.9% believe that most of the dowry cases are false whereas only 33.3% police as well as Judges believe that most of the dowry related cases are false. It can be inferred that there are chances that the lawyers of those accused who are falsely implicated understand the helplessness and genuineness of their client as usually the clients speak up the truth privately to their own lawyer. But due to the polar opinion of police and Judges that the misuse is not common or most of the implications are genuine, such accused get helplessly dragged and suffer the severe consequences of misuse of dowry prohibition laws.

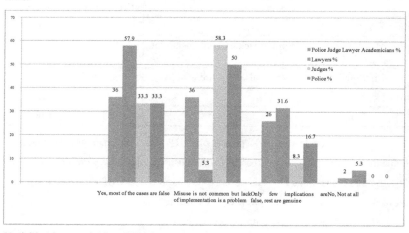

Variable 'Occupation' and Chi Square value is '0.037'

Figure: 8.1

Table 8.2

Answer	Police Judge Lawyer Academicians %	Lawyers %	Judges %	Police %
Yes, most of the cases are false	36	57.9	33.3	33.3
Misuse is not common but lack of implementation is a problem	36	5.3	58.3	50
Only few implications are false, rest are genuine	26	31.6	8.3	16.7
No, Not at all	2	5.3	0	0

9. **Do you think that the existing Anti-Dowry laws are practically capable to curb the evil of dowry from society?**

Table: 9

Answer	Frequency	Percentage
a) Only up to some extent	19	38.0
b) No, these laws are complicated/ outdated	10	20.0
c) Yes, but it is difficult to get justice over long period of time	14	28.0
d) Yes	6	12.0
e) Not Answered	1	2.0
Total	**50**	**100.0**

38% professionals (Police/Lawyer/Judge/academicians) believe that existing Anti-Dowry laws practically help to only to a small extent to curb the evil of dowry from society whereas 20% believe that these laws are outdated/ complicated. 28 % opine that such laws are helpful but it is difficult to get justice over long period of time. 12% opine that such laws are helping in controlling the menace of dowry. . There is no significant change on the opinion across variables such as age, occupation, sex, and education.

10. **Do you find any lacuna in the functioning of police in dealing with the cases related to dowry prohibition?**

Table: 10

Answer	Frequency	Percentage
Yes, many	17	34.0
Very few	20	40.0
Can't say	12	24.0
No, not at all	1	2.0
Not Answered	-	-
Total	**50**	**100.0**

40% professionals find very few drawbacks in the functioning of police in dealing with the cases related to dowry prohibition. 34% professionals (Police/Lawyer/Judge/academicians) find many drawbacks in the functioning of police in dealing with the cases related to dowry prohibition. 24% have no certain opinion but 2% believe that there is no drawback in the functioning of police in dealing with the cases related to dowry prohibition.

The response of the respondents on the basis of Occupation i.e.; Police, Judge, Lawyer, Academicians was analyzed:

Table: 10.1

Do you find any lacuna in the functioning of police in dealing with the cases related to dowry prohibition?					
Variable Occupation	Yes, many	Very few	Can't say	No, not at all	Total
Police	16.7%	66.7%	0.0%	16.7%	100.0%
Judge	16.7%	66.7%	16.7%	0.0%	100.0%
Lawyer	31.6%	31.6%	36.8%	0.0%	100.0%
Academicians	61.5%	15.4%	23.1%	0.0%	100.0%

The academicians completely deviate from the majority answer as 61.5% of them strongly believe that there are many lacunas in the functioning of the police in dealing with the cases related to dowry prohibition. It indicates that practically there are lesser chances of improvement in the functioning of police in the near future as the lawyers, Judges and the police itself do not agree that there are many lacunas in the functioning of police, although these three categories are only having the practical control over this improvement. However, the academicians do not have any direct control over the functioning of police. Another possibility is that the academicians take a theoretical perception which is otherwise quite different from the practical situation.

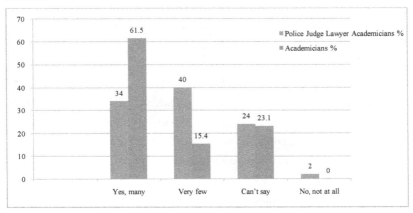

Variable 'Occupation' and Chi Square value is '0.016'

Figure: 10.1

Table: 10.2

Answer	Police Judge Lawyer Academicians %	Academicians %
Yes, many	34	61.5
Very few	40	15.4
Can't say	24	23.1
No, not at all	2	0

11. **Is there any hesitation observed in the behavioural pattern of victim/her family before filing a complaint of dowry related offences?**

Table: 11

Answer	Frequency	Percentage
a) Yes, most of the times	35	70.0
b) Sometimes	12	24.0
c) Only if the cases are false	2	4.0
d) No	1	2.0
e) Not Answered	-	-
Total	**50**	**100.0**

70% professionals (Police/Lawyer/Judge/academicians) believe that they have observed hesitation in behavioural pattern of victim/her family before filing a complaint of dowry related offences while 24% believe that it is observed sometimes. 4% opine that only in false cases behaviour pattern shows hesitation. 2% opine that no such hesitation is observed in behaviour of victim and her family. . There is no significant change on the opinion across variables such as age, occupation, sex, and education.

12. **What is the general concern of victim/her family before filing a complaint of dowry related offences?**

Table: 12

Answer	Frequency	Percentage
a) Getting justice	7	14.0
b) Worried for break-up of Marriage	31	62.0
c) Revenge	6	12.0
d) Any other	6	12.0
Total	**50**	**100.0**

62% professionals (Police/Lawyer/Judge/academicians) opine that people are worried for break-up of marriage before filing a dowry related offence complaint. 14% professionals (Police/Lawyer/Judge/academicians) believe that general concern of a victim and her family before filing a complaint of dowry related offences is to get justice whereas. 12% opine that revenge is the main reason to file a dowry related complaint. 12% opine that any other concern is there. . There is no significant change on the opinion across variables such as age, occupation, sex, and education.

13. **What is the general attitude of complainants while filing a complaint of dowry towards the Husband/ in-laws of victim?**

Table: 13

Answer	Frequency	Percentage
a) Eager to compromise	9	18.0
b) Fearful of their anger/ breaking of marriage	23	46.0
c) Revengeful	13	26.0
d) Any other___	5	10.0
Total	**50**	**100.0**

46% professionals (Police/Lawyer/Judge/academicians) believe that while filing a complaint of dowry towards the husband and in-laws of victim, the complainants are fearful of their anger and breaking of marriage. 18% professionals opine that complainants are eager to compromise while filing a complaint of dowry towards the husband and in-laws of victim.. 26% professionals believe that complainants become revengeful while filing the complaint. . There is no significant change on the opinion across variables such as age, occupation, sex, and education.

14. **Do you think that it is easy to find genuine witnesses in the case of dowry death?**

Table: 14

Answer	Frequency	Percentage
a) Yes, people take it very sensitively	1	2.0
b) No, it is within the four walls where victim is all alone	32	64.0
c) The neighbors are usually reluctant to give any statement against the in-laws of the victim	15	30.0
d) Any other_____	2	4.0
Total	**50**	**100**

64% professionals (Police/Lawyer/Judge/academicians) believe that finding a witness is not possible in dowry death cases as such acts of bride killing are done within the premises of home and victim is all alone. 2% professionals

(Police/Lawyer/Judge/academicians) believe that it is easy to find genuine witnesses in dowry death cases because people take it very seriously whereas. 30% professional opine that neighbors are usually reluctant to give any statement against the in-laws of the victim. There is no significant change on the opinion across variables such as age, occupation, sex, and education.

15. **What are the chances of escape/survival of a woman if the in-laws/ husband try to kill her for dowry within the four walls of house?**

Table: 15

	Answer	Frequency	Percentage
a)	It depends on her luck	12	24
b)	Very low as she is helpless among their majority	29	58
c)	Very high, she is strong enough to fight back	0	0
d)	Good enough, neighbors and relatives provide help in such cases	9	18
	Total	**50**	**100**

58% professionals (Police/Lawyer/Judge/academicians) believe that chances of escape/survival of a woman if the in-laws/ husband try to kill her for dowry within the four walls of house is very low as she is helpless among their majority. 24% professionals opine that the chances of escape/survival of a woman if the in-laws/ husband try to kill her for dowry within the four walls of house depend on her luck.. None of the professional believes that there are strong chances of survival. 18% professionals believe that neighbours and relatives extend help in such cases and therefore good chances of survival are there.

16. **What are the common challenges faced while investigating/dealing with the offences of cruelty and domestic violence?**

Table: 16

	Answer	Frequency	Percentage
a)	It is difficult to collect evidence	15	30.0
b)	The victims change/ revoke their statements due to family pressure	25	50.0
c)	Most of the cases are false	6	12.0
d)	There is no major challenge	4	8.0
	Total	**50**	**100**

50% opine that the common challenges faced while investigating/dealing with the offences of cruelty and domestic violence is that victims change/ revoke their statements due to family pressure. 30% professionals (Police/Lawyer/ Judge/ academicians) believe that common challenges faced while investigating/dealing with the offences of cruelty and domestic violence is the difficulty to collect the evidence. 12% believe that most of these cruelty and domestic violence cases are false where as 8% believe that there is no major challenge in such investigations.

The response of the respondents on the basis of Occupation i.e.; Police, Judge, Lawyer, Academicians was analyzed:

Table: 16.1

What are the common challenges faced while investigating/dealing with the offences of cruelty and domestic violence?					
Variable Occupation	It is difficult to collect evidence	The victims change/ revoke their statements due to family pressure	Most of the cases are false	There is no major challenge	Total
Police	0.0%	100.0%	0.0%	0.0%	100.0%
Judge	83.3%	16.7%	0.0%	0.0%	100.0%
Lawyer	10.5%	47.4%	26.3%	15.8%	100.0%
Academicians	23.1%	61.5%	7.7%	7.7%	100.0%

The Judges have an entirely different view point than the majority opinion as 83.3% Judges opine that the major challenge in dealing with the offences of cruelty and domestic violence is that it is difficult to collect evidence. Surprisingly, 100% police officials answered that the victims change/revoke their statements due to family pressure. It clearly indicates that the police officials mostly face this problem that the complainants change their statement in the court from the original statement which they have given in the police station and consequently the judges fail to get sufficient evidence to give the decision. It is the major reason due to which the administration of justice in the cases related to dowry, cruelty and domestic violence has become extremely difficult.

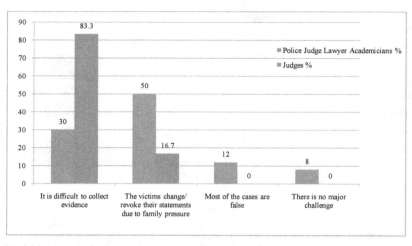

Variable 'Occupation' and Chi Square value is '0.000'

Figure: 16.1

Table: 16.2

Answer	Police Judge Lawyer Academicians %	Judges %
It is difficult to collect evidence	30	83.3
The victims change/ revoke their statements due to family pressure	50	16.7
Most of the cases are false	12	0
There is no major challenge	8	0

17.   **Do you think that the people hesitate in approaching the police stations and courts to seek justice in dowry-related offences**

Table: 17

Answer	Frequency	Percentage
a) No	2	4.0
b) Yes , they lack faith	6	12.0
c) Yes, they feel uncomfortable due to social pressure	34	68.0
d) Both b & c	8	16.0
Total	**50**	**100**

68% professionals (Police/Lawyer/Judge/academicians) opine that people hesitate in approaching the police stations and courts to seek justice in dowry-related offences as they feel uncomfortable due to social pressure. 4% professionals (Police/Lawyer/Judge/academicians) believe that people do not hesitate in approaching the police stations and courts to seek justice in dowry-related offences whereas 12% professionals opine that people hesitate as they lack faith.. 16% believe that people lack faith and are also under social pressure and hence hesitate to report such dowry related instances. . There is no significant change on the opinion across variables such as age, occupation, sex, and education.

18. **What are the necessary changes that must be brought to make a woman feel comfortable in raising her voice against dowry related offences and torture?**

Table: 18

Answer	Frequency	Percentage
a) The society should become positive towards such women	10	20.0
b) The women should be provided better opportunities of education and employment	19	38.0
c) The police and legal system should become more supportive	16	32.0
d) Any other_____		
Total	**50**	**100**

It is sure that certain changes must be brought to make a woman feel comfortable in raising her voice against dowry related offences and torture and 38% professionals (Police/Lawyer/Judge/academicians) opine that women should be provided better opportunities of education and employment and according to 20% professionals (Police/Lawyer/Judge/academicians), society should become positive towards such women who face physical and mental harassment in respect to dowry. 32% believe that the police and legal system should become more supportive.

The response of the respondents on the basis of Sex i.e.; Male, Female was analyzed:

Table: 18.1

What are the necessary changes that must be brought to make a woman feel comfortable in raising her voice against dowry related offences and torture?					
Variable Sex	The society should become positive towards such women	The women should be provided better opportunities of education and employment	The police and legal system should become more supportive	Any other_____	Total
Male	27.8%	25.0%	36.1%	11.1%	100.0%
Female	0.0%	71.4%	21.4%	7.1%	100.0%

It is a matter of surprise that the difference of gender has brought a variation even in the reply of law professionals. Majority of the males opine that the necessary changes to make women comfortable in raising their voice against dowry related offences are either the positive attitude of the society or the police/legal system should become more supportive. Whereas, 71.4% of the females completely disagree with the same and believe that better opportunities of education and employment should be provided to the women to make them comfortable in reporting or raising their voice in such cases. It means that the gender has a strong impact on the opinion of the professionals as well. On one side where the male professionals are ready to take the responsibility on their own shoulders and favour societal sensitization for providing justice in such cases, on the other side, female professionals discard this dependability and favour the strengthening of women.

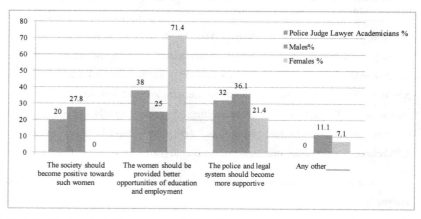

Variable 'Sex' and Chi Square value is '0.015'

Figure: 18.1

237

Table: 18.2

Answer	Police Judge Lawyer Academicians %	Males %	Females %
The society should become positive towards such women	20	27.8	0
The women should be provided better opportunities of education and employment	38	25	71.4
The police and legal system should become more supportive	32	36.1	21.4
Any other_____	0	11.1	7.1

Which of these items shall be given by the parents of the bride to the bridegroom and his family in connection to their daughter's marriage?

Respondents- General Public – Shimla

Table: 1

List ----General Public—Shimla	YES	NO
1. Shagun/Cash to the bridegroom	90	9
2. Shagun/Cash to the parents of bridegroom	56	39
3. Shagun/Cash to the close relatives of the bridegroom	40	56
4. Shagun/Cash to the other relatives of the bridegroom	31	64

As far as *Shagun* is concerned in the marriage ceremonies, 90% general public believe that it should be given to the bridegroom, 56% believe that *Shagun* should be given to the parents of the bridegroom, 40% believe that it should be given to the close relatives of bridegroom and 31% believe that *Shagun* also be given to the other relatives of the bridegroom.

Table: 2

List ----General Public—Shimla	YES	NO
1. Gold/silver to the bridegroom	61	37
2. Gold/silver to the parents of the bridegroom	17	77
3. Gold/silver to the close relatives of the bridegroom	4	92
4. Gold/silver to the other relatives of the bridegroom	3	93

As far as Gold/Silver is concerned in the marriage ceremonies, 61% general public believe that it should be given to the bridegroom, 17% believe that Gold/Silver should be given to the parents of the bridegroom, 4% believe that it should be given to the close relatives of bridegroom and 3% believe that *Shagun* also be given to the other relatives of the bridegroom

Table: 3

List ----General Public—Shimla	YES	NO
1. Gifts to the bridegroom	80	16
2. Gifts to the parents of the bridegroom	48	45
3. Gifts to the close relatives of the bridegroom	32	64
4. Gifts to the other relatives of the bridegroom	15	81

80% general public opines that gifts should be given to the bridegroom. 48% believe that gifts should also be given to the parents of the bridegroom. 32% public believes that close relatives of bridegroom should also receive the gifts and15% opine that other relatives should also receive gifts in the marriage.

Table: 4

List ----General Public—Shimla	YES	NO
1. Clothes to the bridegroom	85	12
2. Clothes to the parents of the bridegroom	60	36
3. Clothes to the close relatives of the bridegroom	34	62
4. Clothes to the other relatives of the bridegroom	11	83

Exchange of clothes in marriages is old age custom and 85% general public believes that clothes should be given to the bridegroom. 60% believe that clothes should also be given to the parents of the bridegroom. 34% people believe that relatives & 11% believe that other relatives of bridegroom should also receive the clothes in the marriage

Table: 5

List ----General Public—Shimla	YES	NO
1. FD/Cheque	13	83
2. TV/LED	47	49
3. Fridge	45	51
4. Washing Machine	44	53
5. AC/Cooler	19	76
6. Almirah	56	42
7. Double Bed	51	45
8. Sofa set/ Centre Table/ Chairs/ etc.	49	48
9. Dining Table	22	72
10. Car	6	89
11. Bike/Scooter/Scooty	8	86
12. Flat/ House etc	4	91
13. Land/ Property etc	4	92
14. Any other item	17	76

Approximately 50% people believe that articles such as TV, Fridge, Washing machine, Air conditioner, cooler, Almirah, Double bed, Sofa set etc. should be included in the list of items of the marriage. Whereas, less than 15% people opine that articles such as car, scooter, Bike, Flat, property, land, FD/cheque and other items should be given in the marriages.

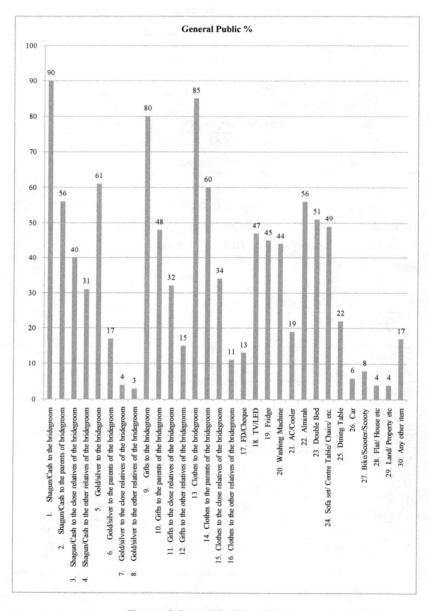

Figure: 5 General Public – Shimla

Which of these items were given by your parents to the bridegroom and his family in connection to your marriage?

Respondents- Married Women

Table: 1

List ----Married Women	YES	NO
1. Shagun/Cash to the bridegroom	39	11
2. Shagun/Cash to the parents of bridegroom	25	25
3. Shagun/Cash to the close relatives of the bridegroom	17	33
4. Shagun/Cash to the other relatives of the bridegroom	13	37

As far as *Shagun* is concerned in the marriage ceremonies, 78% married women believe that it should be given to the bridegroom, 50% believe that *Shagun* should be given to the parents of the bridegroom, 34% believe that it should be given to the close relatives of bridegroom and 26% believe that *Shagun* also be given to the other relatives of the bridegroom.

Table: 2

List ----Married Women	YES	NO
1. Gold/silver to the bridegroom	36	14
2. Gold/silver to the parents of the bridegroom	11	39
3. Gold/silver to the close relatives of the bridegroom	2	48
4. Gold/silver to the other relatives of the bridegroom	1	49

As far as Gold/Silver is concerned in the marriage ceremonies, 72% married women believe that it should be given to the bridegroom, 22% believe that Gold/Silver should be given to the parents of the bridegroom, 4% believe that it should be given to the close relatives of bridegroom and 2% believe that gold/silver also be given to the other relatives of the bridegroom.

Table: 3

List ----Married Women	YES	NO
1. Gifts to the bridegroom	35	15
2. Gifts to the parents of the bridegroom	24	26
3. Gifts to the close relatives of the bridegroom	15	35
4. Gifts to the other relatives of the bridegroom	5	45

70% married women opine that gifts should be given to the bridegroom. 48% believe that gifts should also be given to the parents of the bridegroom. 30% believes that close relatives of bridegroom should also receive the gifts and 10% opine that other relatives should also receive gifts in the marriage.

Table: 4

List ----Married Women	YES	NO
1. Clothes to the bridegroom	44	6
2. Clothes to the parents of the bridegroom	38	12
3. Clothes to the close relatives of the bridegroom	25	25
4. Clothes to the other relatives of the bridegroom	8	42

Exchange of clothes in marriages is old age custom and 88% married women believe that clothes should be given to the bridegroom. 76% believe that clothes should also be given to the parents of the bridegroom. 50% believe that close relatives & 16% believe that other relatives of bridegroom should also receive the clothes in the marriage.

Table: 5

List ----Married Women	YES	NO
1. FD/Cheque	8	42
2. TV/LED	15	35
3. Fridge	16	34
4. Washing Machine	18	32
5. AC/Cooler	2	48
6. Almirah	26	24
7. Double Bed	32	18
8. Sofa set/ Centre Table/ Chairs/ etc.	32	18
9. Dining Table	17	33
10. Car	1	49
11. Bike/Scooter/Scooty	1	49
12. Flat/ House etc	1	49
13. Land/ Property etc	4	46
14. Any other item	3	47

Around 20% married women have shown interest towards household articles such as TV, Fridge, Washing machine, Dining table etc but towards furniture such as Almirah, Double bed and Sofa set , around 30% women believe that such articles should be included in the list of items to given in the marriages.

Surprisingly, only 8% believe that FD/Cheque should be given in the marriages. Almost all married women believe that car, scooter, bike, Flat, house, Land, property should not be given to the bridegroom in the marriage.

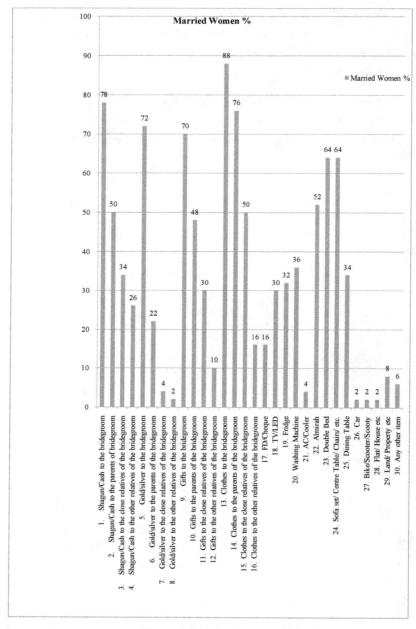

Figure: 5 Married Women

Comparison of list items between General Public and Married Women in district Shimla

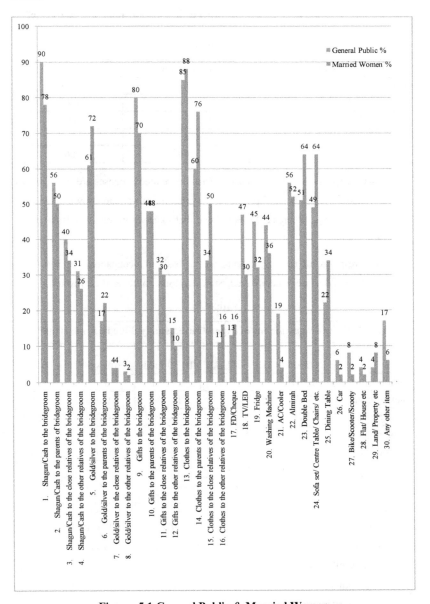

Figure: 5.1 General Public & Married Women

246

6. 3 Empirical Survey for District Kangra

Respondents- General Public

1.   What is the average amount of expenditure usually done in a marriage?

Table: 1

Answer	Frequency	Percentage
a) a) Below 1 Lakh	20	20.0
b) b) 1 – 10 Lakh	64	64.0
c) c) 10-50 Lakh	15	15.0
d) Not Answered	1	1.0
Total	**100**	**100.0**

64% people believe that marriage ceremony related expenses are in between 1 lakh to 10 lakh. 20% of general public believe that marriage ceremony expenditures remain below 1 lakh. Whereas, 15 % believe that expenditure exceeds 10 lakh and goes upto 50 lakh.

The response of the respondents on the basis of occupations ie; Self Emp, Govt Service, Pvt Service, Unemployed, Student, House Wife, Retired was analyzed:

Table: 1.1

What is the average amount of expenditure usually done in a marriage?				
	Below 1 Lakh	1 – 10 Lakh	10-50 Lakh	Not Answered	Total
Self Emp	13.3%	66.7%	20.0%	0.0%	100.0%
Govt Service	3.8%	80.8%	15.4%	0.0%	100.0%
Pvt Service	25.0%	53.6%	21.4%	0.0%	100.0%
Unemployed	50.0%	50.0%	0.0%	0.0%	100.0%
Student	54.5%	45.5%	0.0%	0.0%	100.0%
House Wife	18.8%	68.8%	12.5%	0.0%	100.0%
Retired	0.0%	100.0%	0.0%	0.0%	100.0%
Not Answered	0.0%	0.0%	0.0%	100.0%	100.0%

Students have an entirely different point of view regarding the expenditure which is done in marriage. Primarily the reason could be their younger age and lack of experience. Another possibility is that the young generation is deviating from the unnecessary pomp and show done in the marriages, which is a good sign for eradicating dowry in the upcoming future.

247

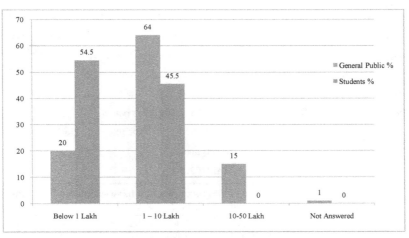

Variable-'Occupation' and Chi Square value is '0.00.'

Figure: 1.1

Table: 1.2

Answer	General Public %	Students %
Below 1 Lakh	20	54.5
1 – 10 Lakh	64	45.5
10-50 Lakh	15	0
Not Answered	1	0

2. **Which is the most common type of marriage that you have seen/attended in the society so far?**

Table: 2

Answer	Frequency	Percentage
a) Marriages in which not a single thing is given as dowry	17	17.0
b) huge dowry is given by the bride's parents to helplessly fulfill the demand of bridegroom / his parents	11	11.0
c) Marriages in which dowry is given and taken as a custom because both sides happily agree	59	59.0
d) Marriages in which dowry is happily given by the bride groom side for their own status	12	12.0
e) Not Answered	1	1.0
Total	**100**	**100.0**

59% people hold the opinion that they attended the marriages where dowry is given and taken as a custom because both sides happily agree. 17% have seen marriages in which not a single thing is given as dowry. 12% people have seen such marriages where dowry is happily given by the bride groom side for their own status but 11% people have attended marriages where huge dowry is given by the bride's parents to helplessly fulfill the demand of bridegroom / his parents.

The response of the respondents on the basis of income i.e. : No Income, < 2 Lakh, 2-5 Lakh, 5-10 Lakh, > 10 Lakh, was analyzed:

Table: 2.1

Which is the most common type of marriage that you have seen/attended in the society so far?						
Variable Income	Marriages in which not a single thing is given as dowry	huge dowry is given by the bride's parents to helplessly fulfill the demand of bridegroom / his parents	Marriages in which dowry is given and taken as a custom because both sides happily agree	Marriages in which dowry is happily given by the bride groom side for their own status	Not Answered	Total
No Income	21.7%	17.4%	56.5%	4.3%	0.0%	100%
< 2 Lakh	28.6%	35.7%	28.6%	7.1%	0.0%	100%
2-5 Lakh	5.9%	0.0%	88.2%	5.9%	0.0%	100%
5-10 Lakh	17.6%	2.9%	55.9%	23.5%	0.0%	100%
> 10 Lakh	0.0%	16.7%	83.3%	0.0%	0.0%	100%
Not Disclosed	16.7%	0.0%	50.0%	16.7%	16.7%	100%

Majority of the people below the income of 2 lakh have seen mostly those type of marriages in which huge dowry is given by the bride's parents to helplessly fulfill the demand of bridegroom / his parents which is different from the general opinion. It shows that even the low income group people become the helpless victim of dowry system and unwillingly give huge in marriages.

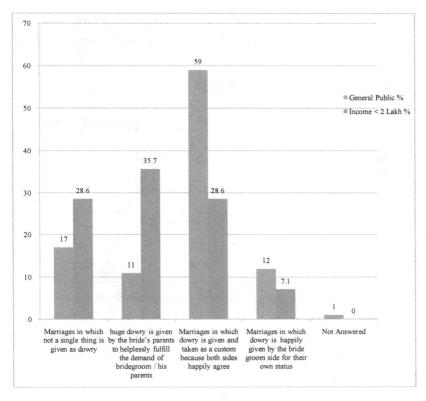

Variable 'Income' and Chi Square value is '0.001'

Figure: 2.1

Table: 2.2

Answer	General Public %	Income < 2 Lakh %
Marriages in which not a single thing is given as dowry	17	28.6
huge dowry is given by the bride's parents to helplessly fulfill the demand of bridegroom / his parents	11	35.7
Marriages in which dowry is given and taken as a custom because both sides happily agree	59	28.6
Marriages in which dowry is happily given by the bride groom side for their own status	12	7.1
Not Answered	1	0

3. **What do you think would be the effect, if parents of the bride would give nothing to the bridegroom or his family members, in connection to the marriage?**

Table: 3

Answer	Frequency	Percentage
a) No significant effect	50	50.0
b) It would become difficult for them to find a suitable match	11	11.0
c) It may lead to the maltreatment and harassment of bride after marriage	25	25.0
d) Social humiliation of bride's family and loss of status in the society.	12	12.0
e) Not Answered	2	2.0
Total	**100**	**100.0**

50% general public thinks that there would be no significant effect if parents of the bride would give nothing to the bridegroom or his family members, in connection to the marriage. 11% opine that it would become difficult for them to find a suitable match. Whereas, 25% believe that it may lead to the maltreatment and harassment of bride after marriage and 12% opine that it will lead to social humiliation of bride's family and loss of status in the society.

The majority of the people otherwise opine that there would be no significant effect but if we closely monitor the rest three options which tend to put some or other negative impact on the bride if no dowry is given in her marriage. It means the ratio is exactly equal i.e. 50% of those people who believe that there would be no significant effect and 50% of those people who believe that there would be some kind of negative impact of not giving dowry.

The response of the respondents on the basis of education i.e.; Primary, Upto +2, Graduation, PG, was analyzed:

What do you think would be the effect, if parents of the bride would give nothing to the bridegroom or his family members, in connection to the marriage?					
Variable Education	No significant effect	It would become difficult for them to find a suitable match	It may lead to the maltreatment and harassment of bride after marriage	Social humiliation of bride's family and loss of status in the society.	Not Answered
Primary	100.0%	0.0%	0.0%	0.0%	0.0%
Upto +2	42.9%	14.3%	21.4%	21.4%	0.0%
Graduation	45.5%	9.1%	33.3%	9.1%	3.0%
PG	58.3%	11.1%	22.2%	8.3%	0.0%
Not Answered	0.0%	0.0%	0.0%	0.0%	100.0%

Majority of the graduates and under graduates believe that there would be some negative impact on the bride if no dowry is given in her marriage.

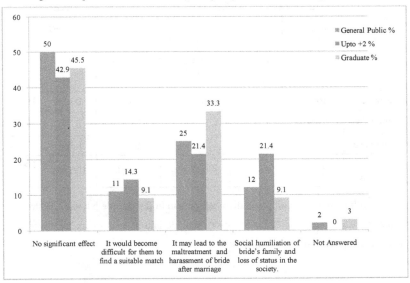

Variable 'education' and Chi Square value is '0.00'

Figure: 3.1

Answer	General Public %	Upto +2 %	Graduate %
No significant effect	50	42.9	45.5
It would become difficult for them to find a suitable match	11	14.3	9.1
It may lead to the maltreatment and harassment of bride after marriage	25	21.4	33.3
Social humiliation of bride's family and loss of status in the society.	12	21.4	9.1
Not Answered	2	0	3

The response of the respondents on the basis of marital status i.e.; Married, Unmarried, Divorced was analyzed:

Table: 3.3

What do you think would be the effect, if parents of the bride would give nothing to the bridegroom or his family members, in connection to the marriage?						
Variable Marital Status	No significant effect	It would become difficult for them to find a suitable match	It may lead to the maltreatment and harassment of bride after marriage	Social humiliation of bride's family and loss of status in the society.	Not Answered	Total
Married	50.7%	15.5%	26.8%	7.0%	0.0%	100%
Unmarried	51.9%	0.0%	18.5%	25.9%	3.7%	100%
Divorced	0.0%	0.0%	100.0%	0.0%	0.0%	100%
Not Answered	0.0%	0.0%	0.0%	0.0%	100.0%	100%

Although there is only one divorced person in the sample but she has strongly stated that not giving anything in dowry will definitely lead to maltreatment and harassment of bride after marriage.

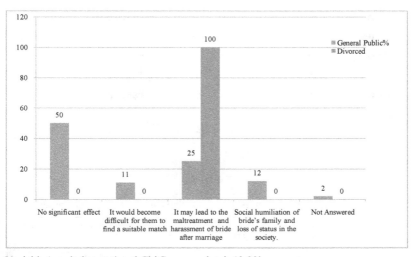

Variable 'marital status' and Chi Square value is '0.00'

Figure: 3.3

Table: 3.4

Answer	General Public%	Divorced
No significant effect	50	0
It would become difficult for them to find a suitable match	11	0
It may lead to the maltreatment and harassment of bride after marriage	25	100
Social humiliation of bride's family and loss of status in the society.	12	0
Not Answered	2	0

4. **Do you think that the girls must get equal share in their parental property?**

Table: 4

Answer	Frequency	Percentage
a) No, it creates family disputes	21	21.0
b) No, they already get dowry in their marriages	6	6.0
c) Yes, definitely	49	49.0
d) Yes, but only if they are not ready to sacrifice it for their brothers	22	22.0
e) Not Answered	2	2.0
Total	**100**	**100.0**

As far as girl's right in parental property is concerned, 49% general public agrees that girls must have the share in parental property. 21% believe that girls should not get right in the parental property as it leads to family disputes. 6% believe that contribution in dowry is enough and no further share should be given in parental property. 22% believe that, yes girls should have the share, provided they are not ready to sacrifice it for their brothers.

The response of the respondents on the basis of education status i.e.; Primary, Upto +2, Graduation, PG was analyzed:

Table: 4.1

Do you think that the girls must get equal share in their parental property?					
Variable Education	No, it creates family disputes	No, they already get dowry in their marriages	Yes, definitely	Yes, but only if they are not ready to sacrifice it for their brothers	Not Answered
Primary	0.0%	0.0%	0.0%	100.0%	0.0%
Upto +2	21.4%	10.7%	39.3%	28.6%	0.0%
Graduation	30.3%	9.1%	42.4%	15.2%	3.0%
PG	13.9%	0.0%	66.7%	19.4%	0.0%
Not Answered	0.0%	0.0%	0.0%	0.0%	100.0%

100% people who are uneducated or only educated at primary level believe that the girl should only get an equal share in the parental property if in case they are not ready to sacrifice it for their brothers. It shows that the illiteracy leads to a conservative view point in giving the share of property to the daughters despite stringent laws.

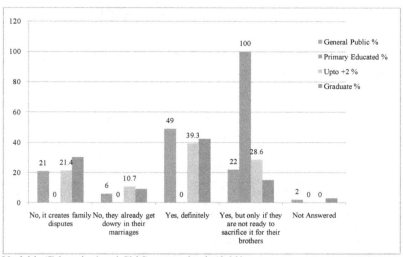

Variable 'Education' and Chi Square value is '0.00'

Figure: 4.1

Table: 4.2

Answer	General Public %	Primary Educated %	Upto +2 %	Graduate %
No, it creates family disputes	21	0	21.4	30.3
No, they already get dowry in their marriages	6	0	10.7	9.1
Yes, definitely	49	0	39.3	42.4
Yes, but only if they are not ready to sacrifice it for their brothers	22	100	28.6	15.2
Not Answered	2	0	0	3

5.   What is the main reason behind Dowry?

Table:5

Answer	Frequency	Percentage
a) Old age Custom and tradition	66	66.0
b) Social Pressure	14	14.0
c) Greed of the bridegroom/his parents	9	9.0
d) parent of the bride are more interested in giving dowry	10	10.0
e) Not Answered	1	1.0
Total	**100**	**100.0**

66% general public believes that primary reason behind dowry is an old age custom and traditions. 14% people believe that social pressure is the main reason behind dowry. 9% people have opinion that the greed of the bridegroom/his parents is responsible and 10% people believe that parents of the bride are more interested in giving dowry.

6. **If dowry is demanded before marriage, what is the common attitude shown by the girl and her family?**

Table: 6

Answer	Frequency	Percentage
a) They try to negotiate and decrease the demand if it is beyond their financial capacity	17	17.0
b) They try to fulfill the demand if they actually like the proposal and are financially capable to fulfill the demand	45	45.0
c) They do not fulfill the demand and end up the relationship howsoever eligible the bridegroom may be	26	26.0
d) They report the matter to the police and file a case of dowry	10	10.0
e) Not Answered	2	2.0
Total	**100**	**100.0**

The cases where is dowry is demanded before marriage, 45% people try to fulfill the demand if they actually like the marriage proposal and are financially capable to fulfill the demand. 17% people believe that bride and her family try to negotiate and decrease the demand if it is beyond their financial capacity. But 26 % people have the opinion that they do not fulfill the demand and end up the relationship howsoever eligible the bridegroom may be. Merely, 10% opined that such cases are reported to the police and a case of dowry is filed.

7.   Is it right to take the matter of dowry in Police Stations and Courts?

Table: 7

Answer	Frequency	Percentage
a) No, dowry is a custom of marriage	11	11.0
b) No, it is personal matter of families and must be resolved through mutual discussion	22	22.0
c) Yes, otherwise it may lead to some serious offences	58	58.0
d) No, It only leads to the harassment of the families and brings no positive solution	7	7.0
e) Not Answered	2	2.0
Total	**100**	**100.0**

58% people believe that matter of dowry should be reported and taken to the courts otherwise it may lead to some serious offences subsequently. 11% people believe that matter of dowry should not be reported in police as it is a custom of marriage. 22% people believe that it is personal matter of families and must be resolved through mutual discussion. 7% people believe that it only leads to the harassment of the families and brings no positive solution and hence should not be reported.

Majority of the married people do not think that it is right to take the matter of dowry in police station and courts due some reason or other. It clearly indicates that the married people who are in actual either the direct victims or offenders in dowry related offences; they are not willing to report these offences. This could be the other major reason of lesser number of reported cases of dowry than the actual cases of dowry.

8.   Is it right to punish the parents of bride with imprisonment if they give the dowry as demanded by the bridegroom side?

Table: 8

Answer	Frequency	Percentage
a) Yes	26	26.0
b) No, they are innocent/helpless	40	40.0
c) Not imprisonment but only a warning should be given	23	23.0
d) Can't say	8	8.0
e) Not answered	3	3.0
Total	**100**	**100.0**

40% opine that the parents of the bride should not be imprisoned if they fulfill the dowry demands of the bridegroom and his family as they are helpless innocent people. 26% people believe that the parents of the bride should also be imprisoned if they fulfill the dowry demands of the bridegroom and his family. 23% people believe that at least warning should be given to those parents of the bride who give/gave dowry in the marriage of their daughters. 8% people could not give their opinion.

The response of the respondents on the basis of Education status i.e.; Primary, Upto +2, Graduation, PG was analyzed:

Table:8.1

Is it right to punish the parents of bride with imprisonment if they give the dowry as demanded by the bridegroom side?						
Variable Education	Yes	No, they are innocent/ helpless	Not imprisonment but only a warning should be given	Can't say	Not answered	Total
Primary	100.0%	0.0%	0.0%	0.0%	0.0%	100.0%
Upto +2	17.9%	42.9%	28.6%	10.7%	0.0%	100.0%
Graduation	33.3%	39.4%	12.1%	12.1%	3.0%	100.0%
PG	22.2%	41.7%	30.6%	2.8%	2.8%	100.0%
Not Answered	0.0%	0.0%	0.0%	0.0%	100.0%	100.0%
Total	26.0%	40.0%	23.0%	8.0%	3.0%	100.0%

100% people who are uneducated or only educated at primary level answer that it is right to punish the parents of bride with imprisonment if they give the dowry as demanded by the bridegroom side. It shows that the educated class opines against the current existing punishment in the Dowry Prohibition Act, 1961 for giving dowry. However, uneducated class is still unable to understand the sensitivity of this lacuna.

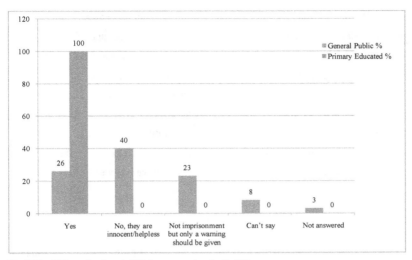

Variable 'Education' and Chi Square value is '0.00'

Figure: 8.1

Table: 8.2

Answer	General Public %	Primary Educated %
Yes	26	100
No, they are innocent/helpless	40	0
Not imprisonment but only a warning should be given	23	0
Can't say	8	0
Not answered	3	0

9. **Do you think that the people are ready to make a girl their daughter-in-law, who had already broken one engagement and filed a dowry case against her would be in-laws before marriage?**

Table: 9

Answer	Frequency	Percentage
a) No, not at all	13	13.0
b) Very rare	55	55.0
c) Yes, very happily	16	16.0
d) Can't say	14	14.0
e) Not answered	2	2.0
Total	**100**	**100.0**

55% people believe that in very rare case they may accept such a girl as their daughter-in-law who in past did not marry a person as he and his family had demanded dowry, rather she had filed a dowry case against them. 13% people opine that they would disagree to own a girl as their daughter-in-law who in past did not marry a person as he and his family had demanded dowry, rather she had filed a dowry case against them.. Only 16% people believe that they will very happily accept that girl. 14% people could not ascertain what they would do in such a situation.

10. If the bridegroom and his family had demanded and received huge amount of dowry in the marriage, what kind of consequences they are likely to face in general?

Table: 10

Answer	Frequency	Percentage
a) They flaunt it in the society and most of the people get astonished by their royal wedding	43	43.0
b) Their financial status increases and they unrestrictedly enjoy the lavish gifts	22	22.0
c) A dowry case is filed against them and they are punished	22	22.0
d) They are boycotted and defamed in the society	11	11.0
e) Not answered	2	2.0
Total	**100**	**100.0**

43% people hold the opinion that bridegroom and his family flaunt in society if their royal wedding ceremony demand along with huge dowry is fulfilled by the bride's family. Along with this 22% people believe that bridegroom and family starts enjoying their increased financial status and they unrestrictedly enjoy the lavish gifts. Whereas, 22% people believe that a dowry case should be filed against them and they should be punished and 11% believe that such people should be boycotted and defamed in the society.

11. **If a married woman reports a dowry case against her in-laws, what kind of consequences she is likely to face?**

Table: 11

Answer	Frequency	Percentage
a) She faces lots of problems in her parental house as well as outside	34	34.0
b) Society makes gossips against her and her family	24	24.0
c) She is helped and supported for being a victim of dowry	22	22.0
d) She faces harassment in the society, police station as well as court	18	18.0
e) Not answered	2	2.0
Total	**100**	**100.0**

34% people believe that woman faces lots of problems in her parental house as well as outside if she reports a dowry case against her in-laws. 24% people opine that people gossip against her and her family. But 22% people believe that such a woman gets help and support for being a victim of dowry. 18% people also opine that woman faces harassment in the society, police station as well as in the court if she reports and files dowry case.

12. **Do you know about the existing laws for dowry related offences?**

Table: 12

Answer	Frequency	Percentage
a) Yes, Dowry Prohibition Act	23	23.0
b) Provisions for Dowry Death, cruelty, domestic violence etc.	10	10.0
c) Both a & b	45	45.0
d) No, not much	19	19.0
e) Not answered	3	3.0
Total	**100**	**100.0**

45% people believe that they know about Dowry Prohibition Act and Provisions for Dowry Death, cruelty, domestic violence etc. collectively. 23% people believe to have the knowledge of Dowry Prohibition Act. 10% people have understanding of provisions for dowry death, cruelty; domestic violence etc. 19% people have no knowledge of the said acts and provisions.

The response of the respondents on the basis of Education status i.e.; Primary, Upto +2, Graduation, PG was analyzed:

Table: 12.1

Do you know about the existing laws for dowry related offences?						
Variable Education	Yes, Dowry Prohibition Act	Provisions for Dowry Death, cruelty, domestic violence etc.	Both a & b	No, not much	Not answered	Total
Primary	0.0%	0.0%	0.0%	100.0%	0.0%	100.0%
Upto +2	21.4%	10.7%	35.7%	32.1%	0.0%	100.0%
Graduation	30.3%	15.2%	42.4%	12.1%	0.0%	100.0%
PG	19.4%	5.6%	58.3%	11.1%	5.6%	100.0%
Not Answered	0.0%	0.0%	0.0%	0.0%	100.0%	100.0%

100% people who are uneducated or only educated at primary level are completely unaware about the existing laws for dowry related offences. It means the government should formulate some policies and programmes to sensitize and educate the illiterate people about the existing laws for dowry related offences.

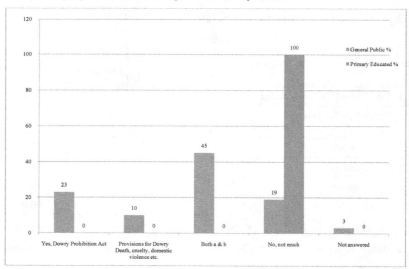

Variable 'Education' and Chi Square value is '0.00'
Figure: 12.1

Answer	General Public %	Primary Educated %
Yes, Dowry Prohibition Act	23	0
Provisions for Dowry Death, cruelty, domestic violence etc.	10	0
Both a & b	45	0
No, not much	19	100
Not answered	3	0

13. **Have you ever heard/ known about any victim of dowry related offences in your surroundings or social circle?**

Table: 13

Answer	Frequency	Percentage
a) Yes, I personally know some victims	20	20.0
b) No, never	20	20.0
c) Yes, through acquaintance/ other people	24	24.0
d) Yes, but only through News papers	34	34.0
e) Not answered	2	2.0
Total	**100**	**100.0**

34% people come to know about dowry and related offenses from Newspaper etc. 20% of the people personally know from their surroundings and social circle about a victim of dowry and related offences but 20% people have never received such information from their vicinity. 24% people heard about such dowry cases from acquaintance or other people and But if we closely monitor the option (a) & option (c), it indicates that 44% of the people know the victims of the dowry in their close circle or vicinity. It means that we cannot agree that there is either no or very less number of incidences of dowry related offences in district Kangra. However, it might be possible that most of such cases are not reported properly.

14.   What is your perspective about dowry?

Table: 14

Answer	Frequency	Percentage
As an act of pleasing bridegroom's family for safe keeping of their daughter	27	27.0
An act of show off in the society	24	24.0
Need of the custom, culture and tradition	22	22.0
Anti social and illegal act by parties performing marriage	25	25.0
Not answered	2	2.0
Total	**100**	**100.0**

27% general public opines that dowry is an act of pleasing bridegroom's family for safe keeping of their daughter and 24% believe it as an act of show off. 22% people believe that it is need of the custom, culture and traditions. Whereas, 25% people opine that it is an anti social and illegal act by both parties performing marriage. It means that 78% of people consider dowry as an act of show off or an anti social and illegal practice or an act of pleasing bridegroom's family for the safety of bride in her matrimonial home. It implies that the nature of this custom has completely changed from the historic times. In nowadays, it has taken a form of evil and has no more remained a need of custom, culture and tradition.

The response of the respondents on the basis of education status i.e.; Primary, Upto +2, Graduation, PG was analyzed:

Table: 14.1

What is your perspective about dowry?						
Variable Education	As an act of pleasing bridegroom's family for safe keeping of their daughter	An act of show off in the society	Need of the custom, culture and tradition	Anti social and illegal act by parties performing marriage	Not answered	Total
Primary	0.0%	0.0%	100.0%	0.0%	0.0%	100.0%
Upto +2	35.7%	14.3%	17.9%	32.1%	0.0%	100.0%
Graduation	36.4%	27.3%	15.2%	21.2%	0.0%	100.0%
PG	13.9%	30.6%	27.8%	25.0%	2.8%	100.0%
Not Answered	0.0%	0.0%	0.0%	0.0%	100.0%	100.0%

However, 100% people who are uneducated or only educated at primary level still treat it as a need of the custom, culture and tradition. It means the government should formulate some policies and programmes to sensitize and educate the illiterate people about the evils of dowry system.

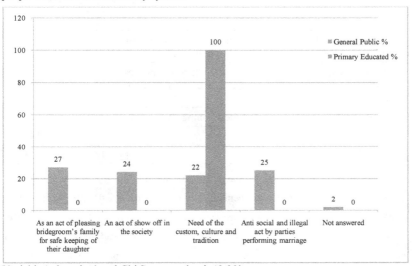

Variable 'education' and Chi Square value is '0.00'

Figure: 14.1

Table: 14.2

Answer	General Public %	Primary Educated %
As an act of pleasing bridegroom's family for safe keeping of their daughter	27	0
An act of show off in the society	24	0
Need of the custom, culture and tradition	22	100
Anti social and illegal act by parties performing marriage	25	0
Not answered	2	0

15. **If the husband/in- laws, physically/mentally harass a woman for dowry, what is the feasible solution for her?**

Table: 15

Answer	Frequency	Percentage
a) She should take a divorce and start a new life	30	30.0
b) Parents ask in-laws and husband to stop harassment, as filing a case will effect readjustment in the marriage	25	25.0
c) No use of going to the police as it will result in the further harassment of that woman by the police as well as society	2	2.0
d) She should go to the police and file a complaint	41	41.0
e) Not answered	2	2.0
Total	**100**	**100.0**

41% people believe that that a woman should file a police complaint in situation where she is physically/ mentally tortured for dowry. 30% people opine that a married woman should take a divorce in such situation and should start a new life. 25% people believe that filing such complaints affect the readjustment chances in marital home and bride's parents should request for stopping the harassment in respect to dowry. 2% people opine that there is no use of going to the police as it will result in the further harassment of that woman by the police as well as society.

16. **What would you do if a false case of dowry is filed against you or your family?**

Table: 16

Answer	Frequency	Percentage
a) We will end our relation with her and teach her a lesson	13	13.0
b) Negotiate and request the bride to revoke her complaint	13	13.0
c) It would be troublesome as all the laws are in the favour of women	22	22.0
d) Nothing to worry as I have full faith in police and legal system	50	50.0
e) Not answered	2	2.0
Total	**100**	**100.0**

50% of the people believe that there is nothing to worry as they have full faith in police and legal system. 13% people believe that they will end up the marriage and will teach a lesson to their wife/daughter-in-law if she files a false case of dowry against them and their family.13% people also opine that in such a situation they will negotiate and request the bride to revoke her complaint. 22% people fear and find such a situation troublesome as they believe that all the laws are in the favour of women.

The response of the respondents on the basis of occupation status i.e.; Self Emp, Govt Service, Pvt Service, Unemployed, Student, House Wife, Retired was analyzed

Table 16.1

What is your perspective about dowry?						
Variable Occupation	We will end our relation with her and teach her a lesson	Negotiate and request the bride to revoke her complaint	It would be troublesome as all the laws are in the favour of women	Nothing to worry as I have full faith in police and legal system	Not answered	Total
Self Emp	20.0%	20.0%	13.3%	46.7%	0.0%	100.0%
Govt Service	11.5%	7.7%	26.9%	53.8%	0.0%	100.0%
Pvt Service	10.7%	14.3%	14.3%	60.7%	0.0%	100.0%
Unemployed	50.0%	0.0%	0.0%	50.0%	0.0%	100.0%
Student	9.1%	9.1%	63.6%	18.2%	0.0%	100.0%
House Wife	12.5%	18.8%	12.5%	50.0%	6.3%	100.0%
Retired	0.0%	0.0%	0.0%	100.0%	0.0%	100.0%
Not Answered	0.0%	0.0%	0.0%	0.0%	100.0%	100.0%

63.6% students believe that it would be troublesome as all the laws are in the favour of women and only 18.2% have full faith in police and legal system. It is a matter of concern that our younger generation is losing faith in police and legal system regarding misuse of dowry related laws.

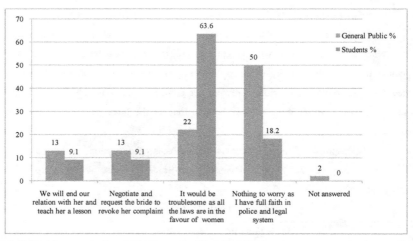

Variable 'Occupation' and Chi Square value is '0.00'

Figure: 16.1

Table: 16.2

Answer	General Public %	Students %
We will end our relation with her and teach her a lesson	13	9.1
Negotiate and request the bride to revoke her complaint	13	9.1
It would be troublesome as all the laws are in the favour of women	22	63.6
Nothing to worry as I have full faith in police and legal system	50	18.2
Not answered	2	0

17. **Is Dowry system a serious issue?**

Table: 17

Answer	Frequency	Percentage
a) Yes, very serious	73	73.0
b) Only to some extent	16	16.0
c) No, there are many other serious issues which need more concern	6	6.0
d) No, it is just a integral custom of marriage	3	3.0
e) Not answered	2	2.0
Total	**100**	**100.0**

73% people believe that dowry is a serious issue prevailing in the society whereas 16% people felt that only to some extent dowry system is a serious issue. 6% people opine that there are many other serious issues which need more concern than dowry. 3% people find dowry as a integral custom of marriage and do not find any serious issue in dowry system.

18.   What is your opinion on anti-dowry laws?

Table: 18

Answer	Frequency	Percentage
a) Very helpful in dealing with dowry related problems	48	48.0
b) Such laws are only on papers and are totally incapable to eradicate dowry	22	22.0
c) Such laws are mostly misused to deter and falsely implicate innocent husband and in-laws.	15	15.0
d) Not much helpful in dealing with dowry related problems	14	14.0
e) Not answered	1	1.0
Total	**100**	**100.0**

48% people believe that anti dowry laws are very helpful in dealing with dowry related problems. 22% people believe that such laws are only on papers and are totally incapable to eradicate dowry. 15% people have opinion that such laws are mostly misused to deter and falsely implicate innocent husband and in-laws. 14% people do not find these laws helpful in dealing with dowry related problems.

The response of the respondents on the basis of Education status i.e.; Primary, Upto +2, Graduation, PG was analyzed:

Table: 18.1

What is your opinion on anti-dowry laws?						
Variable Education	Very helpful in dealing with dowry related problems	Such laws are only on papers and are totally incapable to eradicate dowry	Such laws are mostly misused to deter and falsely implicate innocent husband and in-laws.	Not much helpful in dealing with dowry related problems	Not answered	Total
Primary	100.0%	0.0%	0.0%	0.0%	0.0%	100.0%
Upto +2	50.0%	21.4%	7.1%	21.4%	0.0%	100.0%
Graduation	45.5%	27.3%	15.2%	12.1%	0.0%	100.0%
PG	47.2%	19.4%	22.2%	11.1%	0.0%	100.0%
Not Answered	0.0%	0.0%	0.0%	0.0%	100.0%	100.0%

The educated class i.e. graduates and post graduates in majority lack faith in the efficacy of Anti-Dowry Laws for some reason or another. There is a possibility that the anti dowry laws lack practibility and it has reduced the social acceptance of these laws in the educated class.

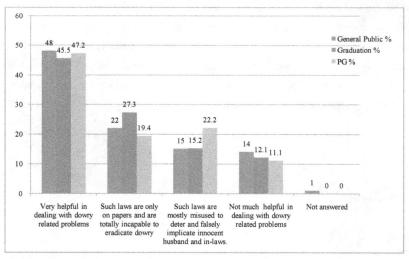

Variable 'Education' and Chi Square value is '0.00'

Figure: 18.1

271

Table: 18.2

Answer	General Public %	Graduate %	PG %
Very helpful in dealing with dowry related problems	48	45.5	47.2
Such laws are only on papers and are totally incapable to eradicate dowry	22	27.3	19.4
Such laws are mostly misused to deter and falsely implicate innocent husband and in-laws.	15	15.2	22.2
Not much helpful in dealing with dowry related problems	14	12.1	11.1
Not answered	1	0	0

The response of the respondents on the basis of Marital status i.e.; Married, Unmarried, Divorced was analyzed:

Table: 18.3

What is your opinion on anti-dowry laws?						
Variable Marital status	Very helpful in dealing with dowry related problems	Such laws are only on papers and are totally incapable to eradicate dowry	Such laws are mostly misused to deter and falsely implicate innocent husband and in-laws.	Not much helpful in dealing with dowry related problems	Not answered	Total
Married	45.1%	26.8%	15.5%	12.7%	0.0%	100.0%
Unmarried	59.3%	7.4%	14.8%	18.5%	0.0%	100.0%
Divorced	0.0%	100.0%	0.0%	0.0%	0.0%	100.0%
Not Answered	0.0%	0.0%	0.0%	0.0%	100.0%	100.0%

54.9 % of married women lack faith in the efficacy of Anti-Dowry Laws for some reason or another. There is a possibility that the anti dowry laws lack practibility and it has reduced the faith of these laws in the married women

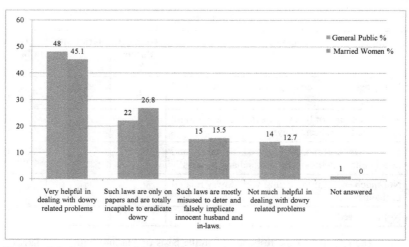

Variable 'Marital status' and Chi Square value is '0.00'

Figure: 18.3

Table: 18.4

Answer	General Public %	Married Women %
Very helpful in dealing with dowry related problems	48	45.1
Such laws are only on papers and are totally incapable to eradicate dowry	22	26.8
Such laws are mostly misused to deter and falsely implicate innocent husband and in-laws.	15	15.5
Not much helpful in dealing with dowry related problems	14	12.7
Not answered	1	0

19. Do you think that dowry is a major reason for not wanting a girl child?

Table: 19

Answer	Frequency	Percentage
a) Yes, certainly	17	17.0
b) No, Not at all	20	20.0
c) Yes but there are some other reasons as well	49	49.0
d) Not Sure	11	11.0
e) Not answered	3	3.0
Total	**100**	**100.0**

49% people believe that dowry is a major reason for not wanting a girl child but there are some other reasons as well for not wanting a girl child. 17% people believe that reason of not wanting a girl child is primarily due to the dowry but 20% people completely disagree. 11% people are not sure about their opinion on this issue.

20. **In how many years, do you think that the custom of dowry will be eradicated from the society completely?**

Table: 20

Answer	Frequency	Percentage
a) Within next 5 years	8	8.0
b) Within next 10 years	22	22.0
c) More than 10 years	26	26.0
d) It will never end.	43	43.0
e) Not answered	1	1.0
Total	**100**	**100.0**

43% people believe that the practice of dowry and its menace will never end. Only 8% people believe that in next 5 years from now, menace of dowry will be completely eradicated from the society. 22% people believe that it would be possible in next 10 years. 26% people believe that eradication of menace of dowry will take more than 10 years. The uneducated or the less educated people in majority believe that the custom of dowry will be eradicated from the society completely within 10 years or more. But the well educated class of people strongly believes that it will never end. It means that either there are lacunas in the legal system related to dowry prohibition laws and their implementation, which the educated people can precisely understand or lack of social will among the educated class is the major impediment in the effective implementation of the dowry prohibition laws.

The response of the respondents on the basis of Education status i.e.; Primary, Upto +2, Graduation, PG was analyzed:

Table: 20.1

Variable Education	Within next 5 years	Within next 10 years	More than 10 years	It will never end.	Not answered	Total
Primary	0.0%	0.0%	100.0%	0.0%	0.0%	100.0%
Upto +2	3.6%	39.3%	21.4%	35.7%	0.0%	100.0%
Graduation	15.2%	24.2%	9.1%	51.5%	0.0%	100.0%
PG	5.6%	8.3%	41.7%	44.4%	0.0%	100.0%
Not Answered	0.0%	0.0%	0.0%	0.0%	100.0%	100.0%

In how many years, do you think that the custom of dowry will be eradicated from the society completely? (header spanning the table)

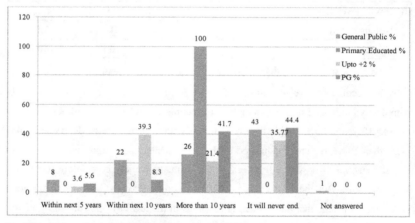

Variable 'Education' and Chi Square value is '0.00'

Figure: 20.1

Table: 20.2

Answer	General Public %	Primary Educated %	Upto +2 %	PG %
Within next 5 years	8	0	3.6	5.6
Within next 10 years	22	0	39.3	8.3
More than 10 years	26	100	21.4	41.7
It will never end.	43	0	35.77	44.4
Not answered	1	0	0	0

Respondents- Married Women

1. **Do you think that it becomes easy for the parents of a girl, to get a rich/well settled bridegroom by offering good dowry in the marriage of their daughter?**

Table: 1

Answers	Frequency	Percentage
a) Yes, it brings more marriage proposals	3	6.0
b) Yes, in most of the cases	8	16.0
c) No	37	74.0
d) Only in arrange marriages	2	4.0
Total	**50**	**100.0**

74% of the married women disagree with the statement that high dowry offers bring better and well settled bridegrooms for marriages. However, 22% women contradict and believe that in most of the cases lucrative dowry offers bring better bridegrooms and marriage proposals. 4% women believe that such practices hold significance in arrange marriages only. The women from various educational background, occupation and income slabs have same point of view.

2. **In your opinion, who has a better chance/eligibility to demand and get better dowry in his marriage?**

Table: 2

Answer	Frequency	Percentage
a) A government employee	7	14.0
b) A private employee	3	6.0
c) Son of a rich family with family business	14	28.0
d) None of the above, as nobody claims or demands dowry, nowadays	26	52.0
Total	**50**	**100.0**

52% women believe that nobody seeks dowry nowadays, therefore, better chance or eligibility of seeking dowry do not arise neither from Government or Private employed nor from rich business family background bridegroom. 14% women believe that a Government employed bridegrooms have better chance and eligibility to seek dowry whereas 6% women believe that private company employed bridegroom has. But at the same time 28 % of women believe that the bridegroom from a rich business family will have better chance and eligibility to seek better dowry

The response of the respondents on the basis of education status i.e.; Primary, Upto +2, Graduation, PG was analyzed:

Table: 2.1

In your opinion, who has a better chance/eligibility to demand and get better dowry in his marriage?					
Variable Education	A government employee	A private employee	Son of a rich family with family business	None of the above, as nobody claims or demands dowry, nowadays	Total
Upto +2	21.4%	0.0%	28.6%	50.0%	100.0%
Graduation	0.0%	6.7%	6.7%	86.7%	100.0%
PG	22.2%	5.6%	38.9%	33.3%	100.0%
Not Answered	0.0%	33.3%	66.7%	0.0%	100.0%

However the women who belong to the highly qualified segment i.e. graduates and above, strongly deviate from the majority opinion and belief that sons of rich family have a better eligibility to demand and get more dowry in marriage. Only 33.3% of these women believe that nobody demands dowry nowadays. Rest 66.7% of these women believe that in one sphere or another, the well settled bridegrooms possess better chance/eligibility to demand and get more dowry.

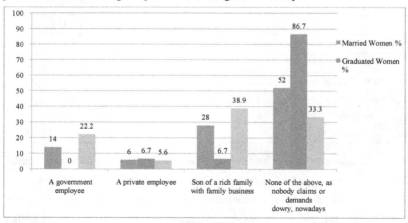

Variable 'Education' and Chi Square value is '.021'

Figure: 2.1

277

Table: 2.2

Answer	Married Women %	Graduated Women %	PG Women %
A government employee	14	0	22.2
A private employee	6	6.7	5.6
Son of a rich family with family business	28	6.7	38.9
None of the above, as nobody claims or demands dowry, nowadays	52	86.7	33.3

3. **What is the general attitude of the people, society and relatives towards a marriage in which the parents of the bride have not given a single valuable item to their son-in-law or his family?**

Table: 3

Answer	Frequency	Percentage
a) They appreciate it	21	42.0
b) They consider it as an inferior marriage	16	32.0
c) They sympathize the family of bridegroom for not getting dowry as per custom	7	14.0
d) They show an indifferent approach	6	12.0
Total	**50**	**100.0**

42% of the married women believe that society appreciates such marriages where bride's family does not give any valuable items to bridegroom and his family in their marriages. But it is also contradicted by 32% of women, irrespective of their age, education and occupation, as they consider it an inferior marriage. It is also observed that 14% married women still believe that people, society and relatives become sympathetic to the families of bridegroom where dowry was not given however 12 % women had indifferent approach. These observations remain similar across various variables such as age, education and occupation of the women.

4. **Do you think that the daughters like it, if their parents give gifts, valuable items, gold, cash, car etc in the marriage to their husband/in-laws?**

Table:4

Answer	Frequency	Percentage
a) Yes, it is an integral part of our customs	9	18.0
b) No	27	54.0
c) Yes, it increases their status in family and society	7	14.0
d) It does not matter for them	7	14.0
Total	**50**	**100.0**

It has been observed that 54% of the daughters do not like if their parents give gifts, valuable items, gold, cash, car etc in their marriage neither they consider it right that such valuable article shall be given to their husband/in-laws. However 32% still like it as they believe that it is an integral part of our customs and increases their status in family and society. 14% women said that it does not matter to them in any of the situations above.

The response of the respondents on the basis of income of husband i.e.; < 2 Lakh, 2-5 Lakh, 5-10 Lakh, 10-15 Lakh, > 15 Lakh was analyzed:

Table: 4.1

Do you think that the daughters like it, if their parents give gifts, valuable items, gold, cash, car etc in the marriage to their husband/in-laws?					
Variable Income of husband	Yes, it is an integral part of our customs	No	Yes, it increases their status in family and society	It does not matter for them	Total
< 2 Lakh	23.5%	58.8%	17.6%	0.0%	100.0%
2-5 Lakh	71.4%	14.3%	0.0%	14.3%	100.0%
5-10 Lakh	0.0%	64.3%	21.4%	14.3%	100.0%
10-15 Lakh	0.0%	66.7%	0.0%	33.3%	100.0%
> 15 Lakh	0.0%	25.0%	25.0%	50.0%	100.0%

However, the women whose husbands are having an annual income of 2-5 lakhs differ in the opinion as 71.4% of these women think that the girls like it if their parents give gifts, valuable items, gold, cash, car etc in the marriage to their husband/in-laws.

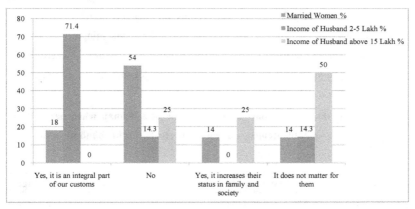

Variable 'income' and Chi Square value is '.010'

Figure: 4.1

Table: 4.2

Answer	Married Women %	Income of Husband 2-5 Lakh %	Income of Husband above 15 Lakh %
Yes, it is an integral part of our customs	18	71.4	0
No	54	14.3	25
Yes, it increases their status in family and society	14	0	25
It does not matter for them	14	14.3	50

5.   **In your opinion, who among the family members is more interested in demanding/ giving dowry in the marriage?**

Table: 5

Answer	Frequency	Percentage
a) The bridegroom	1	2.0
b) Parents of the bridegroom	28	56.0
c) Parents of the bride	10	20.0
d) Nobody	11	22.0
Total	**50**	**100.0**

56% of the women opine that parents of the bridegroom are most interested in the dowry however only 2% of the bridegrooms are interested in taking the dowry. 20% of women held daughter's parents responsible for encouraging dowry in their daughter's marriage. However, 22% women believe that no one is interested in dowry. The opinion remains same across various variables such as age, education and occupation of the women.

6. **What is the usual impact on married life of a woman when her parents give gifts, valuable items, gold, cash, car etc. to her husband or in-laws?**

Table: 6

Answer	Frequency	Percentage
a) It enhances the status and respect of bride and her parents in her in-laws	13	26.0
b) It gives a temporary relief to the bride from the continuous demands from her husband/in-laws but makes them more greedy	14	28.0
c) Most of the husbands/in-laws refuse to take it as they are against such customs	11	22.0
d) No effect at all	11	22.0
e) Not Answered	1	2.0
Total	**50**	**100**

Only 26% women believe that it enhances the status and respect of bride and her parents in her in-laws when her parents give gifts, valuable items, gold, cash, car etc. to her husband or in-laws 22% women believe that there is no such impact on married life of a woman when her parents give gifts, valuable items, gold, cash, car etc. to her husband or in-laws.. 24% of women have come up with the thought that most of the husbands/in-laws refuse to take it as they are against such customs but 28% women have contradicted this point of view and have the opinion that it gives a temporary relief to the bride from the continuous demands of dowry from her husband/in-laws but makes them greedier. The opinion remains same across various variables such as age, education and occupation of the women.

7. **What was the approximate amount of money that was spent in your marriage celebration, ceremonies and buying gifts etc?**

Table: 7

Answer	Frequency	Percentage
a) Below 5 lakhs	32	64.0
b) 5 to 20 lakhs	14	28.0
c) 20 to 50 lakhs	2	4.0
d) More than 50 lakhs	1	2.0
e) Not Answered	1	2.0
Total	**50**	**100.0**

64 % of the women have told that the total expenditure that was done in their marriage was below 5 lakh where as expenditure above 5 lakh and below 20 lakh was done in 28% marriages. Only 6 % marriages incurred expenses of above 20 lakh.

8. **Who had brought better gifts and dowry among all the daughter-in-laws in the family of your in-laws and their relatives?**

Table: 8

Answer	Frequency	Percentage
a) I, in my marriage	4	8.0
b) Only one or two brides had brought better than mine	4	8.0
c) Most of them have brought almost same	25	50.0
d) No one had brought anything	15	30.0
e) Not Answered	2	4.0
Total	**50**	**100.0**

When married women were asked that who had brought better gifts and dowry among all the daughter-in-laws in the family of their in-laws, then 50 % of the women opine that they brought almost same dowry as were brought by other brides to their in-laws 8% women had opinion that they brought maximum dowry among other daughter in laws in bridegroom's family. 8 % believe that only 1 or 2 other brides brought better dowry. 30 % of married women claimed to have brought nothing in the form of dowry as was also not brought by any other bride.

The response of the respondents on the basis of husband income i.e.; Self Emp/Business, Govt Service, Pvt Service, Retired was analyzed:

Table: 8.1

Who had brought better gifts and dowry among all the daughter-in-laws in the family of your in-laws and their relatives?						
Variable Husband income	I, in my marriage	Only one or two brides had brought better than mine	Most of them have brought almost same	No one had brought anything	Not Answered	Total
Self Emp/Business	17.6%	17.6%	35.3%	29.4%	0.0%	100.0%
Govt Service	0.0%	6.7%	53.3%	33.3%	6.7%	100.0%
Pvt Service	7.1%	0.0%	78.6%	14.3%	0.0%	100.0%
Retired	0.0%	0.0%	0.0%	75.0%	25.0%	100.0%

It shows that 70% of the total women as well as other women in their family have brought dowry in one form or another in their marriage. However, apparently it is presumed that the custom of dowry is not much prevalent in Himachal Pradesh. But here the responses tell a different story. It may be concluded that the custom is prevalent but the people are not ready to directly admit its prevalence in their society. However, the women of old age whose husbands are retired vary in the response as 75% of these women clearly answered that no one had brought anything as dowry. It also shows that the custom of dowry in the district Kangra of Himachal Pradesh was not much prevalent in the olden times in comparison to the present times.

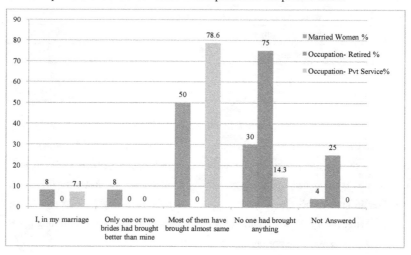

Variable 'husband income' and Chi Square value is '.039'

Figure: 8.1

283

Table: 8.2

Answer	Married Women %	Occupation- Retired %	Occupation- Pvt Service%
I, in my marriage	8	0	7.1
Only one or two brides had brought better than mine	8	0	0
Most of them have brought almost same	50	0	78.6
No one had brought anything	30	75	14.3
Not Answered	4	25	0

9. **What was the general conversation that took place between the two families before your marriage regarding giving gifts, shagun etc?**

Table: 9

Answer	Frequency	Percentage
a) The in-laws asked for the shagun, gift, gold etc merely according to their financial/social status and the employment status of bridegroom.	3	6.0
b) No exact choice or indication was given by the bridegroom and his family but they wanted it to be a lavish affair and accepted happily whatever was given.	19	38.0
c) The in-laws simply gave a list of names of their relatives to whom the gifts and shagun must be given as per rituals.	13	26.0
d) The in-laws/bridegroom clearly refused to accept any cash, gold or gift in marriage.	14	28.0
e) Not Answered	1	2.0
Total	**50**	**100.0**

In before marriage discussions held between bride and bridegroom's family about the gifts and, 38% women have shared that bridegroom's family wanted a lavish marriage ceremony and did not show any reluctance towards the dowry. Also, 26 % bridegroom's families shared the list of relatives to whom bride's family was expected to give gifts and shaguns. Only 28% families refused to accept any cash, gold or gift in marriage. The variables such as age, income and education have shown no significant variation in the opinion of the women. 6% asked for the shagun, gift, gold etc merely according to their financial/social status and the employment status of bridegroom.

10.   Do your parents usually give money, valuables items to you /your husband/your in-laws?

Table: 10

Answer	Frequency	Percentage
a) No, not at all	17	34.0
b) Yes, and especially when it is demanded by my husband or in-laws	2	4.0
c) Yes, but only if it is suggested by me	3	6.0
d) Yes, but only at their own will	28	56.0
Total	50	100

After the marriage of a daughter, her parents usually give money, valuables items to her /her husband/her in-laws and 56% women have agreed to have received such items as per the will of their parent's but asides this 34% of women have said that they do not receive any thing after their marriage. 6% women seek gifts as and when they themselves suggest their parents to give gifts and only 4% women seek gifts from their parents when demand comes from their husband or in-laws. The variables such as age, income and education have shown no significant variation in the opinion of the women.

11.   What do you think is the main reason behind giving money, valuable items to you /your husband/your in-laws by your parents?

Table:11

Answer	Frequency	Percentage
a) Customs/rituals of our community	39	78.0
b) Demand/Pressure of husband or in-laws	1	2.0
c) It helps in maintaining social status as well as my happiness and good relations with husband and in-laws	5	10.0
d) My requests	4	8.0
e) Not Answered	1	2.0
Total	50	100.0

78% of the women have the opinion that major reason behind the dowry is customs and rituals of the society. Only 10 % women correlate the dowry with the social status, happiness and ground of amicable relations with husband and in-laws.

Merely, 2 % women have opined dowry culture as pressure or demand from bridegroom's side. 8 % of women believe that bride does themselves insist their parents for giving dowry.

12.   Had your parents given/shall give you any share in your parental property?

Table: 12

Answer	Frequency	Percentage
a) Yes, definitely	7	14.0
b) No, it is for my brothers	15	30.0
c) Yes, but they are not happily willing	-	-
d) No, they have already done enough for me, so I refused	28	56.0
Total	**50**	**100.0**

When rights in parental property comes into the consideration of the married women, 56 % of the women refused to take their legal share in the parental property as they believe that their parents have already done enough for them. Additionally, 30% women consider their male sibling's right over parental property. Only 14% women have agreed to have received or to receive share in the parental property. However, women across various educational background, age, income and occupation have no impact on the opinion.

13.   Have you ever heard any of the following sentences from your husband or his relatives in general?

- Some other bride has brought more valuable items, gold, cash in her marriage than you.

- The gifts, valuable items, gold, *shagun* given by your parents is not up to the mark

- Your parents should have given a bike/ car/ a more expensive car / more gold etc in your marriage

- Your husband deserves much more than the gifts, valuable items, gold, shagun given by your parents to him.

Answers	Frequency	Percentage
e) Sometimes	7	14.0
f) Always	2	4.0
g) Only once	1	2.0
h) No, never	40	80.0
Total	50	100.0

80% of married women have refused that they had ever heard any of the sarcastic remarks from their husband or his relatives in general. Only 14% have admitted that they have heard such remarks sometimes. 4% of the married women accepted it as always. But a hesitation has been observed in many women to speak up the truth when such a direct question regarding their family matter is asked and another surprising fact was that 26% of these women have admitted that they have received mental harassment related to dowry from their husband or his relatives and even 8% of them have admitted that they have faced physical violence as well.

14.   Have you ever faced any kind of physical harassment by your husband or his relatives for demanding dowry from you/your parents?

Table: 14

Answer	Frequency	Percentage
a) No	33	66.0
b) Yes, but only once or twice	3	6.0
c) Yes, very often	1	2
d) Not physical but there is mental harassment	13	26.0
Total	50	100.0

66 % married women have said that they never faced any kind of physical harassment by her husband or his relatives in respect to dowry demands, however, 26 % women have agreed to have received mental harassment which is related to dowry. Only, 1 % women get physically harassed repeatedly for dowry. However, women across various educational background, age, income and occupation have no impact on the opinion.

15. **What would you do if your husband /your in-laws would demand or compel you/your parents to give gifts, valuable property, gold, cash, car etc to them in connection to your marriage?**

Table: 15

Answer	Frequency	Percentage
a) I will request my parents to fulfill their demand as much as possible	1	2.0
b) I will not agree to fulfill such demands	32	64.0
c) I will try to compromise with mutual understanding	9	18.0
d) I will file a complaint against them in the Police Station	7	14.0
e) Not Answered	1	2.0
Total	**50**	**100.0**

64% married women said that they will not fulfill the demands if their husband / in-laws would demand or compel them or their parents to give gifts, valuable property, gold, cash, car etc to them in connection to your marriage. 18 % women said that they will try to resolve by mutual understanding whereas only 14 % women consider filing a Police complaint on such dowry demands. No woman was willing to request her own parents to fulfill the dowry demands. The opinion of the women remains unchanged across various variables such as age, income, occupation and education.

16. **Is it easy/ feasible for a married woman to file a complaint in the police station if her husband/in-laws tortures her for dowry?**

Table: 16

Answer	Frequency	Percentage
a) Yes, it will improve the behavior of her in-laws	9	18.0
b) No, it will degrade her position in her in-laws and society	6	12.0
c) Only if she is ready to break her marriage	3	6.0
d) Yes, law will definitely help her	31	62.0
e) Not Answered	1	2.0
Total	**50**	**100.0**

62% of the women believe in the Law and will file a complaint in the police station if her husband/in-laws tortures her for dowry. 18 % women have opinion that such an action will degrade the relations further and such action should be taken only when a women is ready to break the marriage. However, 18 % women believe that reporting such demands of dowry in police results in improved behavior of the in-laws. There is no effect of variables such as age, education and occupation on the opinion.

17. **What are the chances of escape/survival of a woman if the in-laws/ husband try to kill her for dowry within the four walls of house?**

Table: 17

Answer	Frequency	Percentage
a) It depends on her luck	4	22.0
b) Very low as she is helpless among their majority	11	34.0
c) Very high, she is strong enough to fight back	17	34.0
d) Good enough, neighbors and relatives provide help in such cases	17	2.0
e) Not Answered	1	2
Total	**50**	**100**

There is mixed opinion among women as 34 % women believe that woman is strong enough as she can fight back and escape if the in-laws/ husband try to kill her for dowry within the four walls of house but 34 % women believe that her chances to survive in such a situation is very low. 22 % women left it on their fate and only 2 % have opinion that neighbours and relatives will help in escaping her from such a situation.

18. **What are the necessary changes that must be brought to make a woman feel comfortable in raising her voice against dowry related offences and torture?**

Table: 18

Answer	Frequency	Percentage
a) The society shall become positive towards such women	4	8.0
b) The women shall be imparted more education and employment	11	22.0
c) The police and legal system shall become supportive and take these offences seriously	1	2.0
d) All of the above	33	66.0
e) Not Answered	1	2.0
Total	**50**	**100**

All the women have strongly felt that there is a strong need to bring certain necessary changes in Law, society as well as police administration to provide a minimum level of comfort to the female victims of dowry in order to raise their voice against dowry related offences. 66 % women felt that all of the above measures should be taken collectively to empower women to raise and handle instances of dowry demand and torture. 8 % women believe that society should become more positive towards the women. 22 % women believe that imparting more education and employment opportunities will help woman. 2 % believe that police and legal system should deal such dowry instances more seriously.

Respondents- Police, Lawyers, Judges, Law- Academicians

1.   How many cases of Dowry have you dealt so far?

Table: 1

Answer	Frequency	Percentage
e) Less than 20	27	54.0
f) 20 to 50	14	28.0
g) 50 to 100	3	6.0
h) More than 100	6	12.0
Total	**50**	**54.0**

54% people from the profession of Police/Lawyer/Judge/academicians believe that they have dealt with less than 20 dowry cases till time. 28% professionals have dealt 20-50 dowry cases. 6% have dealt 50-100 cases and 12% professional have dealt with more than 100 dowry related cases.

2.   What do you think are the factors responsible for the continuance of offences related to dowry despite stringent laws?

Table: 2

Answer	Frequency	Percentage
e) Most of the offences likewise; demanding dowry, cruelty, domestic violence etc are not reported properly	21	42.0
f) Social recognition of dowry as a custom	26	52.0
g) Ineffective police/legal mechanism	3	6.0
h) Any Other	0	0
Total	**50**	**100.0**

52% professionals opine that social recognition of dowry as a custom is the prime reason of continuation of offence of dowry. 42% professionals (Police/Lawyer/Judge/academicians) believe that factors responsible for the continuance of offences related to dowry despite stringent laws is that such cases are not reported properly whereas. 6% believe that ineffective police/legal mechanism is responsible.

The response of the respondents on the basis of Occupation i.e.; Police, Judge, Lawyer, Retired was analyzed:

Table: 2.1

What do you think are the factors responsible for the continuance of offences related to dowry despite stringent laws?				
Variable Occupation	Most of the offences likewise; demanding dowry, cruelty, domestic violence etc are not reported properly	Social recognition of dowry as a custom	Ineffective police/legal mechanism	Total
Police	80.0%	20.0%	0.0%	100.0%
Judge	50.0%	0.0%	50.0%	100.0%
Lawyer	31.6%	63.2%	5.3%	100.0%

The opinion of police and judges is completely different from the majority opinion. 80% of Police officials and 50% of judges believe that the major factor responsible for the continuance of dowry related offences is that such cases are not reported properly. And the other 50% of the judges believe that the ineffective police/legal mechanism is responsible. Whereas, only lawyers are in majority who believe that social recognition of dowry as a custom is mainly responsible behind increase in dowry related offences.

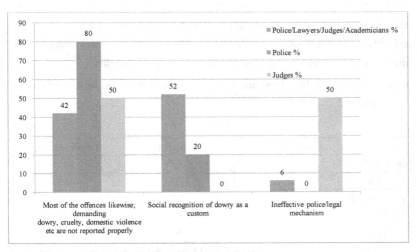

Variable 'Occupation' and Chi Square value is '.004'

Figure: 2.1

Answer	Police/Lawyers/ Judges/ Academicians %	Police %	Judges %
Most of the offences likewise; demanding dowry, cruelty, domestic violence etc are not reported properly	42	80	50
Social recognition of dowry as a custom	52	20	0
Ineffective police/legal mechanism	6	0	50

3. **Do you think that there is any difference between the actual number and the reported number of incidents of dowry related offences?**

Table: 3

Answer	Frequency	Percentage
e) Yes, huge	29	58.0
f) Yes but not much	14	28.0
g) No, not at all	1	2.0
h) It can't be ascertained	6	12.0
Total	**50**	**100.0**

58% professionals (Police/Lawyer/Judge/academicians) believe that there is a huge difference in the total number of dowry incidences to the total number of cases which get reported. 28% professionals also find that there is difference but do not much difference. Whereas, 2% believe that such reported and actual cases are equal and 12% opine that it cannot be ascertained. There is no significant change on the opinion across variables such as age, occupation, sex, and education.

4. **In your opinion, how many cases of Domestic violence are related to Dowry?**

Table: 4

Answer	Frequency	Percentage
e) 0 to 25 %	17	34.0
f) 25 to 50 %	20	40.0
g) 50 to 75%	10	20.0
h) 75 to 100%	3	6.0
Total	**50**	**100.0**

40% professionals believe that 25-50% domestic violence cases are related to the dowry. 34% professionals (Police/Lawyer/Judge/academicians) believe that up to

25% of the domestic violence cases are primarily related to the dowry. 20% opine that 50-75% cases of domestic violence is due to the dowry and 6% believe that 75-100% cases of domestic violence occur due to the dowry.

The response of the respondants on the basis of Occupation i.e.; Police, Judge, Lawyer, Retired was analyzed

Table: 4.1

In your opinion, how many cases of Domestic violence are related to Dowry?					
Variable Occupation	0 to 25 %	25 to 50 %	50 to 75%	75 to 100%	Total
Police	50.0%	10.0%	20.0%	20.0%	100.0%
Judge	0.0%	0.0%	50.0%	50.0%	100.0%
Lawyer	31.6%	50.0%	18.4%	0.0%	100.0%

There is a huge difference in the response of police, Judges and lawyers with each other. Only the reply of the lawyers is similar to the majority opinion that 25-50% cases of domestic violence are related to dowry. The experience of police and Judges is entirely opposite to each other. 50% of police officials believe that only 0-25% cases of domestic violence is related to dowry whereas, 100% of the judges believe that most of the domestic violence cases are related to dowry. Out of these, 50% Judges believe that 50-75% cases of domestic violence are related to dowry and other 50% Judges believe that 75-10% cases of domestic violence are related to dowry.

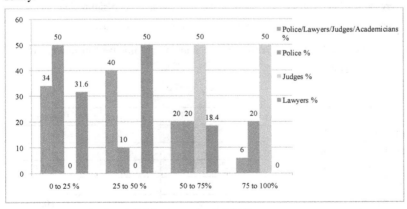

Variable 'Occupation' and Chi Square value is '.005'

Figure: 4.1

294

Table: 4.2

Answer	Police/Lawyers/ Judges/Academicians %	Police %	Judges %	Lawyers %
0 to 25 %	34	50	0	31.6
25 to 50 %	40	10	0	50
50 to 75%	20	20	50	18.4
75 to 100%	6	20	50	0

5. **Do you think that the people file a complaint for giving or taking of Dowry?**

Table: 5

Answer	Frequency	Percentage
e) Yes, in most of the cases	5	10.0
f) In very few cases	30	60.0
g) In almost half of the cases	4	8.0
h) No, not at all	11	22.0
Total	**50**	**100.0**

60% professionals (Police/Lawyer/Judge/academicians) believe that very few cases of dowry get reported. 10% professionals believe that in most cases people file a complaint if dowry is demanded and is given or taken. 8% opine that that almost half of such cases get reported whereas, 22% believe that people do not file a complaint where dowry is demanded and is given and taken. There is no significant change on the opinion across variables such as age, occupation, sex, and education.

6. **The people of which category are more likely involved in dowry related offences?**

Table: 6

Answer	Frequency	Percentage
e) Educated and high-class	5	10.0
f) Uneducated and backward	7	14.0
g) Both the categories	38	76.0
h) Any Other	0	0
Total	**50**	**100.0**

76% professionals (Police/Lawyer/Judge/academicians) believe that both i.e. educated, high class and uneducated, backward are equally involved in dowry related offences. 10% professionals believe that educated and high-class people are more likely to be involved in the dowry related offences whereas 14% believe that uneducated and backward are more involved in the dowry related offenses.

7. **What are the reasons behind the non-compliance of the laws related to dowry prohibition, by the society?**

Table: 7

Answer	Frequency	Percentage
e) Acceptance of dowry as a custom	26	52.0
f) Social pressure of giving and taking Dowry	19	38.0
g) Lack of faith on legal system	5	10.0
h) Any other	0	0
Total	50	100.0

52% professionals (Police/Lawyer/Judge/academicians) believe that acceptance of dowry as a custom is the main reason behind the non-compliance of the laws related to dowry prohibition. 38% opine that social pressure of giving and taking dowry is the root cause whereas 10% believe that people do not adhere dowry prohibition laws as they lack faith on legal system. Opinion remains same across various variables such as age, experience, sex and occupation. There is no significant change on the opinion across variables such as age, occupation, sex, and education.

8. **Is there any abuse or misuse of the dowry prohibition laws?**

Table: 8

Answer	Frequency	Percentage
e) Yes, most of the cases are false	18	36.0
f) Misuse is not common but lack of implementation is a problem	9	18.0
g) Only few implications are false, rest are genuine	21	42.0
h) No, Not at all	2	4.0
Total	50	100.0

42% believe that only few implications are false in relation to dowry related cases and rest are genuine. It is noticeable that 36% professionals (Police/Lawyer/

Judge/academicians) opine that in most of the cases; there is abuse/ misuse of the Dowry Prohibition Laws. 18% professionals opine that misuse is not common but lack of implementation is a problem, 4% believe that such laws are not misused at all.

9.   **Do you think that the existing Anti-Dowry laws are practically capable to curb the evil of dowry from society?**

Table: 9

Answer	Frequency	Percentage
f) Only up to some extent	26	52.0
g) No, these laws are complicated/ outdated	3	6.0
h) Yes, but it is difficult to get justice over long period of time	12	24.0
i) Yes	7	14.0
j) Not Answered	2	4.0
Total	**50**	**100.0**

52% professionals (Police/Lawyer/Judge/academicians) believe that existing Anti-Dowry laws practically help to only to a small extent to curb the evil of dowry from society whereas 6% believe that these laws are outdated/ complicated. 24 % opine that such laws are helpful but it is difficult to get justice over long period of time. 7% opine that such laws are helping in controlling the menace of dowry.

10.   **Do you find any lacuna in the functioning of police in dealing with the cases related to dowry prohibition?**

Table: 10

Answer	Frequency	Percentage
f) Yes, many	26	52.0
g) Very few	14	28.0
h) Can't say	5	10.0
i) No, not at all	4	8.0
j) Not Answered	1	2.0
Total	**50**	**100.0**

52% professionals (Police/Lawyer/Judge/academicians) find many drawbacks in the functioning of police in dealing with the cases related to dowry prohibition. 28% professionals find very few drawbacks in the functioning of police in dealing with the cases related to dowry prohibition. 10% have no certain opinion but 8% believe that there is no drawback in the functioning of police in dealing with the cases related to dowry prohibition. There is no significant change on the opinion across variables such as age, occupation, sex, and education.

11. **Is there any hesitation observed in the behavioral pattern of victim/her family before filing a complaint of dowry related offences?**

Table: 11

Answer	Frequency	Percentage
f) Yes, most of the times	29	58.0
g) Sometimes	14	28.0
h) Only if the cases are false	5	10.0
i) No	1	2.0
j) Not Answered	1	2.0
Total	**50**	**100.0**

58% professionals (Police/Lawyer/Judge/academicians) believe that they have observed hesitation in behavioral pattern of victim/her family before filing a complaint of dowry related offences while 28% believe that it is observed sometimes. 10% opine that only in false cases behavior pattern shows hesitation. 2% opine that no such hesitation is observed in behavior of victim and her family. There is no significant change on the opinion across variables such as age, occupation, sex, and education.

12. **What is the general concern of victim/her family before filing a complaint of dowry related offences?**

Table: 12

Answer	Frequency	Percentage
e) Getting justice	20	40.0
f) Worried for break-up of Marriage	24	48.0
g) Revenge	6	12.0
h) Any other	0	0
Total	**50**	**100.0**

48% professionals (Police/Lawyer/Judge/academicians) opine that people are worried for break-up of marriage before filing a complaint of dowry related offences.

40% professionals believe that general concern of a victim and her family before filing a complaint of dowry related offences is to get justice whereas. 12% opine that revenge is the main reason to file a dowry related complaint. There is no significant change on the opinion across variables such as age, occupation, sex, and education.

13. **What is the general attitude of complainants while filing a complaint of dowry towards the Husband/ in-laws of victim?**

Table: 13

Answer	Frequency	Percentage
e) Eager to compromise	16	32.0
f) Fearful of their anger/breaking of marriage	17	34.0
g) Revengeful	15	30.0
h) Any other___	2	4.0
Total	**50**	**100.0**

34% professionals (Police/Lawyer/Judge/academicians) believe that the complainants are fearful of the anger of husband and in-laws of victim and fear about breaking of marriage. 32% professionals (Police/Lawyer/Judge/academicians) opine that complainants are eager to compromise while filing a complaint of dowry towards the husband and in-laws of victim. 30% professionals believe that complainants become revengeful while filing the complaint. There is no significant change on the opinion across variables such as age, occupation, sex, and education.

14. **Do you think that it is easy to find genuine witnesses in the case of dowry death?**

Table: 14

Answer	Frequency	Percentage
e) Yes, people take it very sensitively	14	28.0
f) No, it is within the four walls where victim is all alone	22	44.0
g) The neighbors are usually reluctant to give any statement against the in-laws of the victim	14	28
h) Any other_____	0	0
Total	**50**	**100**

44% professionals (Police/Lawyer/Judge/academicians) believe that finding a witness is not possible as such acts of bride killing are done within the premises of home and victim is all alone. 28% professionals (Police/Lawyer/Judge/academicians) believe that it is easy to find genuine witnesses in dowry death cases because people take it very seriously. 28% professional opine that neighbors are usually reluctant to give any statement against the in-laws of the victim.

The response of the respondents on the basis of Occupation i.e.; Police, Judge, Lawyer, Retired was analyzed:

Table: 14.1

Do you think that it is easy to find genuine witnesses in the case of dowry death?				
Variable Occupation	Yes, people take it very sensitively	No, it is within the four walls where victim is all alone	The neighbors are usually reluctant to give any statement against the in-laws of the victim	Total
Police	0.0%	80.0%	20.0%	100.0%
Judge	0.0%	100.0%	0.0%	100.0%
Lawyer	36.8%	31.6%	31.6%	100.0%

The opinion of lawyers is entirely different in comparison to police and Judges in the availability of genuine witnesses in the cases of dowry death. Majority of the lawyers think that such witnesses can be easily found whereas; all of the Judges and the police take a contrary view. Surprisingly, not a single Judge or a police official agrees that such witnesses are genuine or can be easily found. It clearly shows that even if the lawyers produce such witnesses of dowry death in the court, police officials question their credibility and the Judges do not rely upon them.

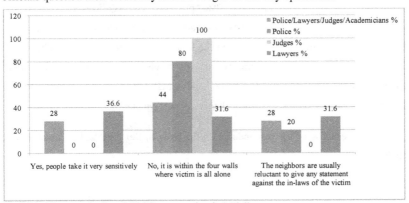

Variable 'Occupation' and Chi Square value is '.026'

Figure: 14.1

300

Table: 14.2

Answer	Police/Lawyers/ Judges/ Academicians %	Police %	Judges %	Lawyers %
Yes, people take it very sensitively	28	0	0	36.6
No, it is within the four walls where victim is all alone	44	80	100	31.6
The neighbors are usually reluctant to give any statement against the in-laws of the victim	28	20	0	31.6

15. **What are the chances of escape/survival of a woman if the in-laws/ husband try to kill her for dowry within the four walls of house?**

Table: 15

Answer	Frequency	Percentage
e) It depends on her luck	11	22
f) Very low as she is helpless among their majority	26	52.0
g) Very high, she is strong enough to fight back	6	12.0
h) Good enough, neighbors and relatives provide help in such cases	7	14.0
Total	**50**	**100**

52% professionals believe that there are very low survival chances if the in-laws/ husband try to kill her for dowry within the four walls of house as she is helpless among their majority. 22% professionals (Police/Lawyer/ Judge/ academicians) opine that the chances of escape/survival of a woman if the in-laws/ husband try to kill her for dowry within the four walls of house depend on her luck. 12% believe that there are strong chances of survival because woman is strong enough to fight back. 14% professionals believe that neighbors and relatives extend help in such cases and therefore good chances of survival are there.

The response of the respondents on the basis of Sex i.e.; Males, females was analyzed:

Table: 15.1

Variable Sex	It depends on her luck	Very low as she is helpless among their majority	Very high, she is strong enough to fight back	Good enough, neighbors and relatives provide help in such cases	Total
Males	33.3%	42.4%	12.1%	12.1%	100.0%
Females	0.0%	70.6%	11.8%	17.6%	100.0%

What are the chances of escape/survival of a woman if the in-laws/ husband try to kill her for dowry within the four walls of house?

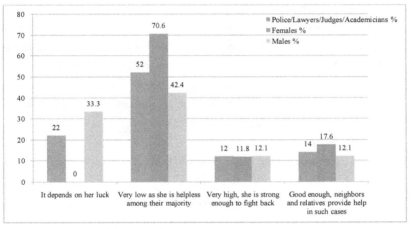

Variable 'Sex' and Chi Square value is '.054'

Figure: 15.1

Table: 15.2

Answer	Police/Lawyers/ Judges/ Academicians %	Females %	Males %
It depends on her luck	22	0	33.3
Very low as she is helpless among their majority	52	70.6	42.4
Very high, she is strong enough to fight back	12	11.8	12.1
Good enough, neighbours and relatives provide help in such cases	14	17.6	12.1

302

16. What are the common challenges faced while investigating/dealing with the offences of cruelty and domestic violence?

Table: 16

Answer	Frequency	Percentage
e) It is difficult to collect evidence	17	34.0
f) The victims change/ revoke their statements due to family pressure	28	56.0
g) Most of the cases are false	4	8.0
h) There is no major challenge	1	2.0
Total	**50**	**100**

56% professionals (Police/Lawyer/Judge/academicians) opine that common challenges faced while investigating/dealing with the offences of cruelty and domestic violence is that the victims change/ revoke their statements due to family pressure. 34% professionals (Police/Lawyer/Judge/academicians) believe that common challenges faced while investigating/dealing with the offences of cruelty and domestic violence is the difficulty to collect the evidence. 8% believe that most of these cruelty and domestic violence cases are false where as 2% believe that there is no major challenge in such investigations. There is no significant change on the opinion across variables such as age, occupation, sex, and education.

17. Do you think that the people hesitate in approaching the police stations and courts to seek justice in dowry-related offences

Table: 17

Answer	Frequency	Percentage
e) No	6	12
f) Yes , they lack faith	12	24.0
g) Yes, they feel uncomfortable due to social pressure	28	56.0
h) Both b & c	4	8.0
Total	**50**	**100**

56% professionals (Police/Lawyer/Judge/academicians) opine that people hesitate in approaching the police stations and courts to seek justice in dowry-related offences as they feel uncomfortable due to social pressure 12% professionals believe that people do not hesitate in approaching the police stations and courts to seek justice in dowry-related offences whereas 24% professionals opine that people hesitate as they lack faith.. 8% believe that people lack faith and are also under social pressure

303

and hence hesitate to report such dowry related instances. There is no significant change on the opinion across variables such as age, occupation, sex, and education.

18. **What are the necessary changes that must be brought to make a woman feel comfortable in raising her voice against dowry related offences and torture?**

Table: 18

Answer	Frequency	Percentage
e) The society should become positive towards such women	16	32
f) The women should be provided better opportunities of education and employment	19	38.0
g) The police and legal system should become more supportive	13	26
h) Any other_____	0	0
Total	**50**	**100**

It is sure that certain changes must be brought to make a woman feel comfortable in raising her voice against dowry related offences and torture and according to 38% professionals (Police/Lawyer/Judge/academicians), women should be provided better opportunities of education and employment. 32% professionals believe that society should become positive towards such women who face physical and mental harassment in respect to dowry. 26% believe that the police and legal system should become more supportive.

The response of the respondents on the basis of occupation i.e.; Police, Judge, Lawyer was analyzed:

Table: 18.1

What are the necessary changes that must be brought to make a woman feel comfortable in raising her voice against dowry related offences and torture?					
Variable Occupation	The society should become positive towards such women	The women should be provided better opportunities of education and employment	The police and legal system should become more supportive	Any other_____	Total
Police	20.0%	50.0%	10.0%	20.0%	100.0%
Judge	0.0%	0.0%	100.0%	0.0%	100.0%
Lawyer	36.8%	36.8%	26.3%	0.0%	100.0%

Majority of the professionals believe that to make women comfortable in raising their voice against dowry related offences; either the society should become more positive or the women should be educated and given employment. But there is a 100% deviation in the opinion of Judges as 100% of the Judges believe that there is no flaw in society rather the police and legal system should become more supportive. It shows that it is not only the society or the helplessness of the women which is responsible for not reporting dowry related offenses rather the police and legal system should also take the responsibility to improve their attitude instead of shifting the blame on the society and the educational and financial strength of women.

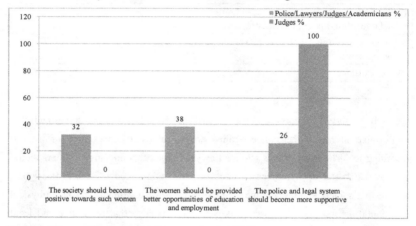

Variable 'Occupation' and Chi Square value is '.015'

Figure: 18.1

Table: 18.2

Answer	Police/Lawyers/Judges /Academicians %	Judges %
The society should become positive towards such women	32	0
The women should be provided better opportunities of education and employment	38	0
The police and legal system should become more supportive	26	100

Which of these items shall be given by the parents of the bride to the bridegroom and his family in connection to their daughter's marriage?

Respondents- General Public

Table: 1

List ----General Public—Kangra	YES	NO
1. Shagun/Cash to the bridegroom	70	30
2. Shagun/Cash to the parents of bridegroom	53	47
3. Shagun/Cash to the close relatives of the bridegroom	40	60
4. Shagun/Cash to the other relatives of the bridegroom	26	74

As far as *Shagun* is concerned in the marriage ceremonies, 70% general public believe that it should be given to the bridegroom, 53% believe that *Shagun* should be given to the parents of the bridegroom, 40% believe that it should be given to the close relatives of bridegroom and 26% believe that *Shagun* also be given to the other relatives of the bridegroom.

Table: 2

List ----General Public—Kangra	YES	NO
1. Gold/silver to the bridegroom	40	60
2. Gold/silver to the parents of the bridegroom	29	71
3. Gold/silver to the close relatives of the bridegroom	11	89
4. Gold/silver to the other relatives of the bridegroom	7	93

As far as Gold/Silver is concerned in the marriage ceremonies, 40% general public believe that it should be given to the bridegroom, 29% believe that Gold/Silver should be given to the parents of the bridegroom, 11% believe that it should be given to the close relatives of bridegroom and 7% believe that Gold/Silver also be given to the other relatives of the bridegroom

Table: 3

List ----General Public—Kangra	YES	NO
1. Gifts to the bridegroom	43	57
2. Gifts to the parents of the bridegroom	35	65
3. Gifts to the close relatives of the bridegroom	20	80
4. Gifts to the other relatives of the bridegroom	7	93

43% general public opines that gifts should be given to the bridegroom. 35% believe that gifts should also be given to the parents of the bridegroom. 20% public believes that close relatives of bridegroom should also receive the gifts and 7% opine that other relatives should also receive gifts in the marriage.

Table: 4

List ----General Public—Kangra	YES	NO
1. Clothes to the bridegroom	51	49
2. Clothes to the parents of the bridegroom	42	58
3. Clothes to the close relatives of the bridegroom	23	77
4. Clothes to the other relatives of the bridegroom	16	84

Exchange of clothes in marriages is old age custom and 51% general public believes that clothes should be given to the bridegroom. 42% believe that clothes should also be given to the parents of the bridegroom. 23% people believe that relatives & 16% believe that other relatives of bridegroom should also receive the clothes in the marriage.

Table: 5

List ----General Public—Kangra	YES	NO
1. FD/Cheque	5	95
2. TV/LED	13	87
3. Fridge	15	85
4. Washing Machine	12	88
5. AC/Cooler	7	93
6. Almirah	22	78
7. Double Bed	27	73
8. Sofa set/ Centre Table/ Chairs/ etc.	24	76
9. Dining Table	11	89
10. Car	6	94
11. Bike/Scooter/Scooty	6	94
12. Flat/ House etc	4	96
13. Land/ Property etc	11	89
14. Any other item	11	89

Less than 15% general public has shown interest towards household articles such as TV, Fridge, Washing machine, Air conditioner, Dining table etc but towards furniture such as Almirah, Double bed and Sofa set , around 25% people believe that such articles should be included in the list of items to given in the marriages.

Surprisingly, only 5% believe that FD/Cheque should be given in the marriages. Only 6% believe that car, scooter and bike should be given where as 11% opines that land, property and other items should be given in the marriage.

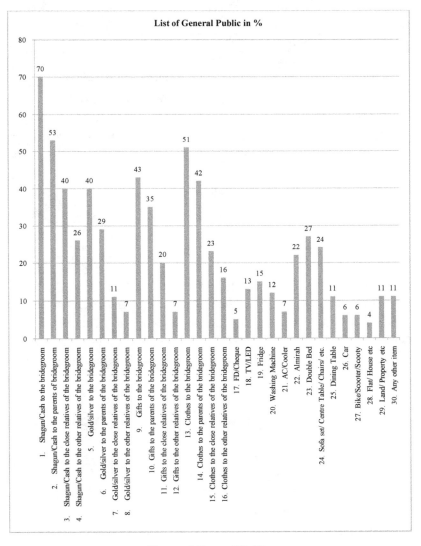

Figure: 5 General Public

Which of these items were given by your parents to the bridegroom and his family in connection to your marriage?

Respondents- Married Women

Table:1

List ----Married Women---Kangra	YES	NO
1. Shagun/Cash to the bridegroom	40	10
2. Shagun/Cash to the parents of bridegroom	37	13
3. Shagun/Cash to the close relatives of the bridegroom	33	17
4. Shagun/Cash to the other relatives of the bridegroom	23	27

As far as *Shagun* is concerned in the marriage ceremonies, 80% married women believe that it should be given to the bridegroom, 74% believe that *Shagun* should be given to the parents of the bridegroom, 66% believe that it should be given to the close relatives of bridegroom and 46% believe that *Shagun* also be given to the other relatives of the bridegroom.

Table: 2

List ----Married Women---Kangra	YES	NO
1. Gold/silver to the bridegroom	39	11
2. Gold/silver to the parents of the bridegroom	29	21
3. Gold/silver to the close relatives of the bridegroom	8	42
4. Gold/silver to the other relatives of the bridegroom	2	48

As far as Gold/Silver is concerned in the marriage ceremonies, 78% married women believe that it should be given to the bridegroom, 58% believe that Gold/Silver should be given to the parents of the bridegroom, 16% believe that it should be given to the close relatives of bridegroom and 4% believe that gold/silver also be given to the other relatives of the bridegroom.

Table: 3

List ----Married Women---Kangra	YES	NO
1. Gifts to the bridegroom	28	22
2. Gifts to the parents of the bridegroom	22	28
3. Gifts to the close relatives of the bridegroom	11	39
4. Gifts to the other relatives of the bridegroom	8	42

56% married women opine that gifts should be given to the bridegroom. 44% believe that gifts should also be given to the parents of the bridegroom. 22% believes that close relatives of bridegroom should also receive the gifts and 7% opine that other relatives should also receive gifts in the marriage.

Table: 4

List ----Married Women---Kangra	YES	NO
1. Clothes to the bridegroom	39	11
2. Clothes to the parents of the bridegroom	38	12
3. Clothes to the close relatives of the bridegroom	29	21
4. Clothes to the other relatives of the bridegroom	17	33

Exchange of clothes in marriages is old age custom and 78% married women believe that clothes should be given to the bridegroom. 76% believe that clothes should also be given to the parents of the bridegroom. 58% believe that close relatives & 16% believe that other relatives of bridegroom should also receive the clothes in the marriage.

Table: 5

List ----Married Women---Kangra	YES	NO
1. FD/Cheque	4	46
2. TV/LED	10	40
3. Fridge	9	41
4. Washing Machine	5	45
5. AC/Cooler	4	46
6. Almirah	18	32
7. Double Bed	23	27
8. Sofa set/ Centre Table/ Chairs/ etc.	16	34
9. Dining Table	3	47
10. Car	0	50
11. Bike/Scooter/Scooty	1	49
12. Flat/ House etc	0	50
13. Land/ Property etc	1	49
14. Any other item	6	44

Less than 10% married women have shown interest towards household articles such as TV, Fridge, Washing machine, Air conditioner, Dining table etc but towards furniture such as Almirah, Double bed and Sofa set , around 20% women believe that such articles should be included in the list of items to given in the marriages.

Surprisingly, only 4% believe that FD/Cheque should be given in the marriages. Almost all married women believe that car, scooter, bike, Flat, house, Land, property should not be given to the bridegroom in the marriage.

310

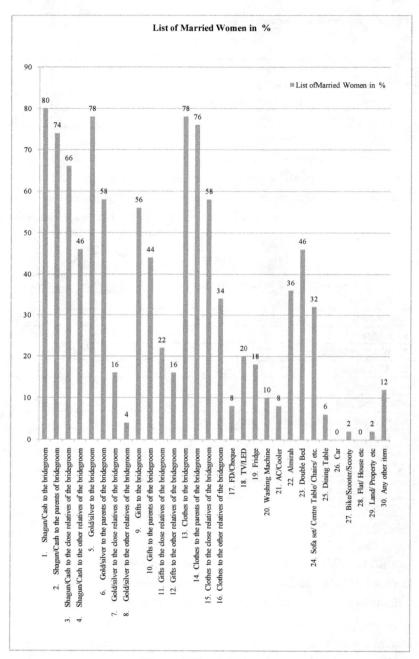

Figure: 5 Married Women

311

Comparison of list items between General Public and Married Women in district Kangra.

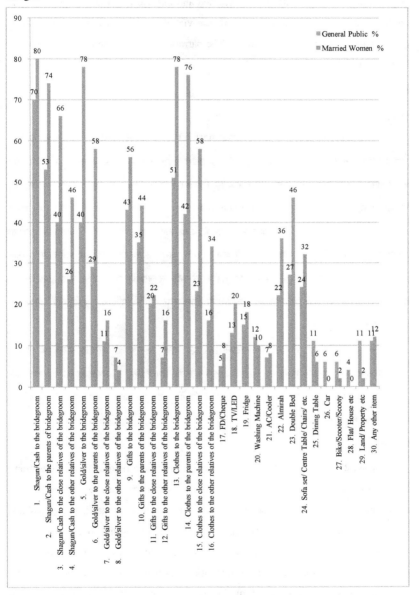

Figure: 5.1 General Public & Married Women

6.4 Narrative Study

Two married females were identified and interviewed, who alleged to be the victim of dowry related offences. Both the victims had faced physical as well as mental harassment for dowry demand. The narrations of the victims are explained in their own words respectively:

6.4.1 Narration of First Victim

Hindi

मैं 27 वर्ष की हूँ और मैंने 10 + 2 तक पढ़ाई की हैं। मैं फैशन डिज़ाइनिंग करती हूँ और मेरी आय 1 लाख प्रति वर्ष से भी कम है। मेरी शादी 19 अप्रैल 2019 को हुई व मेरे पति की मोबाइल फोन की दुकान है। शादी की रात ही पति ने मुझे कमरे से बाहर निकाल दिया। म फैशन डिज़ाइनिंग के लिए कालेज़ जाती थी तो पति ने मुझे बस का किराया या कोई भी अन्य खर्च देने से साफ इन्कार कर दिया। वो बस यही ताना देता था कि तेरे बाप ने दहेज में कुछ नहीं दिया। मेरे पिता ने अपनी हैसीयत के हिसाब से मुझे, मेरे पति, सास ससुर आदि को कपड़े, गहने, शगुन आदि सब दिया था। दहेज का सामान भी था जैसे कि अलमारी, टी. वी. फ्रिज, बैड आदि। मेरे पति ने मुझ से पत्नी जैसा कोई सम्बन्ध नहीं रखा। उसने 2 – 3 बार मुझ पर हाथ भी उठाया। मेरे सास ससुर भी मेरे पति को कभी नहीं समझाते हैं उल्टा मुझे ही दहेज के ताने देते हैं।

मैंने देखा कि मेरे पति के मेरी जेठानी के साथ गलत सम्बन्ध हैं। ऐतराज़ करने पर वो मुझे दहेज के ताने देता था और हाथ उठाता था। 4 महीने में ही तंग आकर मैं अपने मायके आ गयी और पति पर मुकदमा दायर कर दिया। मामला अब कोर्ट में हैं। मेरे दहेज का सारा सामान अभी भी मेरे पति व ससुराल वालों के पास ही है।

English

I am 27 years old. I have passed 10+2. I am in the field of fashion designing and my annual earning is less than 1 lakh rupees. I got married on 19th April 2019 and my husband has a mobile phone shop. On the first night after marriage my husband expelled me out of his room. During this period, I was going to college but my husband clearly refused to give me any sort of bus fare or any other expense of my college. The reason that he gave me in taunting was that my father has not given any dowry. However, as per means of my father, he had given clothes, ornaments as well as *shagun* to me, my husband and my in-laws. He has also given some other dowry

313

items like Almirah, TV, Fridge, Double bed etc. The consummation of marriage never took place between us at the discretion of my husband. He had also beaten me twice or thrice during this period. After some days, I observed that my husband has some illicit relation with the wife of his elder brother. Any objection from side always resulted in my beating by my husband. After harassment of 4 months, I returned back to my parental house. Now I have filed a court case against my husband. My dowry articles are still lying at my in-laws house.

Analysis of the Narrative

- In this case the victim has been a newly married female who has suffered the dowry related harassment from the very first day of her marriage. She is neither much educated nor financially much capable. Her father has given cash, clothes, ornaments as well as other dowry items like almirah, TV, fridge, double bed, etc. as dowry in her marriage. Despite receiving dowry, her husband has given her verbal, mental as well as physical harassment and expected more dowry. She was compelled to leave her matrimonial home merely within four months of her marriage by subjecting her to dowry related harassment. With the help of this case various aspects have come to light:

- Dowry is openly given and taken in the marriages despite dowry prohibition laws.

- The parents of the girl try to give as much dowry as possible to the maximum of their financial capacity.

- Even after receiving ample dowry, the greed of bridegroom and his expectations for more dowries usually increase. He becomes fearless in asking more dowries and non fulfillment of such demands may result in mental and physical torture to the wife.

- Less educated and financially dependent dowry victims have only one alternative to return to their parent's house after leaving the matrimonial home because of dowry related harassment.

- It takes a long legal battle to get back the dowry articles given in the marriage in such dowry related disputes.

6.4.2 Narration of Second Victim

Hindi

मैं 38 वर्ष की एक शादी शुदा महिला एवम् गृहिणी हूँ। मेरी शैक्षिक योग्यता एम.ए. बी.एड. है। मेरी शादी को 14 वर्ष हो चुके हैं व मैं अपने ससुराला में रहती हूँ। मेरी शादी 2005 में हुई थी। उस वक्त मेरे पति का निजी व्यवसाय था मगर हाल ही में उन्हें सरकारी नाकरी मिली है।

हमारी शादी में मेरे पिता ने अपनी हैसीयत के मुताबिक सारा दहेज दिया जैसे कि मुझे कपड़े, गहने, रुपया, पति व सास ससुर को कपड़े, गहने, रुपया, टी.वी., फ्रिज, अलमारी, डबल बैड इत्यादि सब सामान दिया। शादी के 1-2 महीने तक तो सब ठीक रहा मगर उसके बाद मेरे पति ने मुझे दहेज के लिए प्रताड़ित करना शुरु कर दिया। वो चाहते थे कि उनकी दुकान के लिए, मेरे पिता उन्हें 2 लाख रुपये दें। मेरे पिता की आर्थिक स्थिति इतना पैसा देने या कर्जा लेने की नहीं थी। मेरे पति इसी मांग को पूरा करने के लिए मुझे मानसिक प्रताड़ना देने लगे। वो मुझे मारते पीटते भी थे। वो यह दबाव बनाने लगे कि मेरे पिता अपनी ज़मीन बेच कर उन्हें पैसे दें। यह मेरे पिता की ज़मीन थी जिस में मेरा या मेरे पति का कानूनी रूप से कोई हिस्सा नहीं था। मेरे सास-ससुर या ननदों ने मुझे कभी परेशान नहीं किया, न ही कोई मांग की। वो मेरे पति को भी समझाने का प्रयास करते थे मगर मेरे पति सुनने को तैयार ही नहीं थे। इस बीच, इस शादी से हमारी एक बेटी भी हुई, मेरे पति मुझे या उस बेटी के खर्च के लिए कभी एक पैसा नहीं देते थे। 2009 में मेरे पति कुछ समय के लिए दिल्ली जाकर काम करने लगे। यह वहां जिस घर में रहते थे उनके परिवार को भी खर्च देते थे मगर मुझे नहीं। अपने और अपनी बेटी के खर्च को चलाने के लिये मैंने मनरेगा मे मज़दूरी शुरु कर दी। मेरे पिता भी कुछ मद्द कर दिया करते थे। दिल्ली से लौट आने पर पति का अत्याचार और बढ़ गया। यह रोज़ शराब पीकर घर आते थे और मार पिटाई करते थे। यह मेरे पिता पर दबाव बनाने लगे कि वो इन्हें कर्जा लेकर पैसे दिलवा दें। मेरे पिता का मानना था कि इनकी शराब का रोज का खर्च ही 500 रुपये था तो यह सारे पैसे बर्बाद कर देंगे।

एक दिन, दहेज की मांग के लिए मुझे पीटते हुए मेरे पति ने मेरी बाजू तोड़ दी। इनके खिलाफ धारा 498A के अंतर्गत मामला दर्ज हुआ पर कुछ न्याय नहीं मिला। इस बीच कोर्ट से मुझे खर्चा लगा दिया पर मेरे पति ने वो कभी नहीं दिया। मेरे पास बार-बार कोर्ट जाने के पैसे नहीं होते थे। इस बीच मेरी सास की भी मृत्यु हो गयी। अब मैं अपनी बेटी और ससुर के साथ रहती हूँ। मेरी बेटी आठवीं कक्षा में है मगर उसे उच्च शिक्षा दिलवाने के लिए मेरे पास पैसे नहीं है। आजकल नौकरी भी तो नहीं मिलती। मेरे पति का कहना है कि जब मेरे ससुर भी मर जायेंगे तो वो मुझे और बेटी को सड़क पर भीख मांगने हुए देखना चाहता है। अब उसने मेरे खिलाफ तलाक का मामला दर्ज कर दिया है। मेरे पास कोर्ट कचहरी

जाने के लिए पैसे नहीं होते। इतने साल हो गए मुझे कोई न्याय नहीं मिला। हमारे क्षेत्र में मुझ जैसी बहुत सी महिलाएं हैं जो दहेज से प्रताड़ित हैं पर अधिकतर पढ़ी-लिखी नहीं हैं, दूसरा इस उम्र में घर छोड़ कर कहाँ जावेंगी। कोर्ट जाकर भी बस पैसे ही खर्च होते हैं, मगर मामला लटकता रहता है। आप भी वकील हैं। आप मेरी मदद कर सको तो बड़ी कृपा होगी। मैं तो बहुत निराश हो चकी हूँ।

English Translation

I am 38 years old married lady and a housewife. My educational qualification is M.A., B Ed. I got married 14 years ago and presently live with my in-laws. When I got married in year 2005, my husband was doing his own business but recently he got Government job.

My father gave me dowry as per his means, like clothes, ornaments, money to me as well as to parents-in-law and my husband too. Other items like Fridge, Almirah, double bed etc. were also given. Everything was normal in initial 1-2 months but after that my husband started thrashing me for dowry. He wanted me to bring 2 Lac rupees from my father for his shop. My father was not capable of giving money due to his own financial constraints. My husband constantly tortured me for the fulfillment of his demand and even started beating me. He started compelling me to ask my father to sell his land and give money to my husband, although neither me nor my husband had any legal right on this land. During this period, my father-in-law or my mother-in-law never harassed me for anything rather they always tried to advise their son not to behave like this but he paid no heed to them. It was during this period that I gave birth to a baby girl. My husband has never given a penny to me or our daughter to meet our daily expenses. In the year 2009, he went to Delhi for some job. He used to give money to the family of his landlords for their expenses but he never gave me a penny during that period. In order to meet my expenses and to look after my daughter, I started working in MNREGA. After some time he returned back from Delhi, hence his cruelty and tyranny started increasing day by day. He came home drunk and would beat me daily compelling me to ask my father to give loan of 2 lac rupees. My father had lost confidence in him as he used to spend at least 500 rupees daily on alcohol, hence would waste this entire amount. One day during this physical violence, he broke my arm. I registered a complaint against him under

Section 498A but of no use, I have not got any justice. In the meantime, court ordered him to pay maintenance to me but it was never paid by him. I am not financially capable to incur the expenditure of court case. In the meanwhile, my mother-in-law also died and presently I am living with my daughter and father-in-law. My daughter is studying in 8th standard but I know that I am unable to bear expenses of her higher education. My husband ruthlessly says he would like to see both of us as beggars once my father-in-law will die. Now he has also filed a case of Divorce against me and I am very helpless without money to fight this legal battle. Many years have passed but I am still unable to get justice. It is not only my case, similar other cases are there in our area and most of the females are uneducated. They are bearing it helplessly as they find no place to go at this stage of life. So far as justice at court is concerned, one has to spend lots of money and still matter remains pending for years. You are also a Lawyer, please help me. I shall be grateful to you otherwise I have totally lost all the hope.

Analysis of the Narrative

The victim in this case has suffered dowry related harassment as well as she had been several times subjected to cruelty by her husband in a long time span of fourteen years of her married life. Her father has given cash, clothes, ornaments as well as other dowry items like almirah, TV, fridge, double bed, etc. as dowry in her marriage. She started suffering huge violence merely after two months of her marriage by her husband as he was demanding two lakh of rupees for his business. Her father was financially not capable to fulfill this demand; therefore, her husband started compelling her father to sell his land. However no harassment has been ever done by her in-laws. Her husband never gave any expense to her or to their daughter who was born out of this wedlock. Her husband has even gone to the extent of breaking her arm while committing physical violence upon her for dowry. With the help of this case various aspects have come to light:

- The dowry victim was uneducated and she had to even work as a labour in MNREGA to meet her own and her daughter's expenses.
- She has registered a complaint against her husband under Section 498A of IPC but has never got any justice.

317

- Due to her financial constraints, she is not able to pursue the legal battle against her husband to get justice.
- In a huge financial difficulty, she had to spend a lot of money but the case is still pending in the court since many years.
- There are many uneducated females who are suffering the similar agony of getting victimized for dowry related offences but they are bearing it helplessly without reporting such cases in the police station.
- The major reason behind for not reporting dowry related cases in the police station is illiteracy, financial incapability, delayed justice in court cases and the helplessness of many victims who find no place to go at this stage of their life after filing dowry related cases against their husbands or in-laws.

6.5 Findings

On the basis of analytical evaluation of data, narrative and discussions various conlusions can be drawn as under:

6.5.1 Extent of existence and prevalence of dowry system

- **The amount of expenditure usually done in marriages**

  The average expenditure done in marriages assumed by the people in district Shimla and Kangra is between 1-10 lakh. However on analysing the list of items which should be given or were actually given by the bride's side to the bridegroom and his family cost far more than 10 lakh. The actual average expenditure done in marriages reported by the married women in both the districts is between 5 to 20 lacks. Only a small category of women have reported it above twenty lacks. The expenditure which has been done in these marriages is neither too low to assume that no dowry was given nor too high to assume that the dowry which was given was entirely beyond the financial capacity of parents of the brides.

- **Extent of marriages in which dowry is demanded**

  There is a difference in the attitude of bridegroom's family in demanding dowry or a lavish marriage in district Shimla and district Kangra. Majority of the people from bridegroom's side clearly refused to accept any dowry from the bride's side in district Shimla. Whereas, in district Kangra most of the people from bridegroom's side either demand a lavish marriage or give a list of their relatives to whom gifts, *shaguns* etc. are to be given.

- **Extent of marriages in which dowry is actually given**

But the study has clearly indicated another aspect that still there is a huge gap in the actual number of cases related to giving and taking of dowry or dowry related harassment and the reported number of cases related to dowry. All three categories of respondents have somehow accepted that neither district Shimla nor district Kangra is untouched by the prevalence of dowry system. Most of the women have accepted that they themselves as well as the other daughter in laws in their families have brought dowry in their marriages. But the women of old age in district Kangra have denied of bringing any kind of dowry. Therefore, it is clear that the dowry custom is prevalent but the people are not directly admitting its prevalence. However, it was not as much prevalent in the older times in comparison to the modern times.

- **Valuable gifts or dowry are given by the parents of married women even after marriage**

Most of the parents of the married women usually give money and valuable items to their daughters, son-in-laws and the in-laws of their daughters even after so many years of their daughter's marriage. Although, it is mostly given by them at their own will. However a majority of women dislike receiving such gifts, valuable items, gold, dowry etc. from their parents However, the low income group women in district Kangra and the high income group women in district Shimla completely deviate from the general opinion as they like receiving such items. It clearly shows that financial needs in the poor class women and an urge to gather more and more wealth in the rich class women has also contributed in the practice of dowry. Such women themselves endeavour to get wealth in the form of dowry from their parents.

6.5.2 Factors responsible for continuance practice of dowry despite stringent laws

- **Main reason behind prevalence of dowry system**

It has been observed that in majority of the marriages, dowry is given and taken as a custom because both sides happily agree. It is a very small percentage of marriages in which dowry has not been given. Despite being prohibited under the legislation, it is openly demanded, given and taken in both the districts. Surprisingly, the numbers of cases reported in the state of Himachal Pradesh are very less. It clearly shows that there is a huge difference in the actual and the reported incidences of giving and taking of dowry.

Majority of the women opine that the customs and rituals of the society are the major reason behind the prevalence and widespread of the dowry system. Majority of the people as well as legal professionals opine that social recognition of the dowry as a custom is the major factor responsible for the continuance of dowry related offences despite stringent laws. However, police and judges in district Kangra consider that since dowry related cases are not reported properly, therefore, it primarily contributes in the increase of such offences.

The prevalence of dowry system is so deep rooted in the society that majority of the people believe that this custom will never end. All the categories of people, whether educated, uneducated, rich or poor, all are in a similar way involved in dowry related offences. It means there is no significant effect of education or financial status on the practice and prevalence of dowry.

- **Usual Impact of giving/not giving dowry in a marriage**

There is no significant effect as such reported by the married women on the married life of those women who have brought a huge dowry in their marriages. Therefore, it is the matter of surprise as well as irony that still the parents of bride give more and more dowry to their daughters for their better and happy married life. A significant number of the married women have opined that the marriages in which the dowry is not given are appreciated. However this opinion is stronger in district Shimla in comparison to district Kangra.

But a major deviation has been observed in the women of an age group of 30-40 years as they have opined that such marriages are considered to be very inferior in family and society.It shows that the prevalence of the dowry and its significance as a status symbol has been increased in last few years in district

Shimla. Hence the impact of diminishing matriarchal setup and rising patriarchal setup in this district can be traced in the increasing social inclination towards the custom of dowry.

- **Attitude of parents of bride on giving dowry**

It has been observed that in majority of the marriages, dowry is given and taken as a custom because both sides happily agree. It is a very small percentage of marriages in which dowry has not been given. Despite being prohibited under the legislation, it is openly demanded, given and taken in both the districts. A general pattern has been observed that until and unless the dowry demands reach beyond the capacity of the bride's parents, such demands are happily fulfilled.

- **Attitude of parents of bridegroom on taking dowry**

It has been clearly admitted by the married women that the parents of the bridegroom are most interested in receiving the dowry in their son's marriage. In most of the marriages they either give list of their relatives to whom gifts and shagun are to be given by the bride's side or they ask to make the marriage a very lavish affair. Only a very few number of married women had told that their in-laws clearly refused to take dowry, cash or gifts in any form.

- **Attitude of society towards marriages in which dowry is given and taken**

Whenever a huge amount of dowry is demanded and received by the bridegroom and his family despite being prohibited by law, they hardly face any criticism or humiliation by the society. Rather such dowry articles are openly exhibited, flaunted and people get astonished by their royal wedding. The matter of irony is that after receiving huge amount of dowry, the financial status of the bridegroom's side enhances and they unrestrictedly enjoy the lavish gifts instead of any penal consequences.

- **Attitude of bride and bridegroom on giving and taking dowry**

Most of the women do not agree to fulfil or to let their parents fulfil any demand of dowry if it would have ever been done by their husband or in-laws. The majority of the women dislike receiving gifts, valuable items, gold, dowry etc.

321

from their parents in their marriage.

It is a surprising response that negligible percentages of bridegrooms are themselves interested in receiving dowry The number of such bridegrooms is even lesser that the number of those parents of bride who are most interested in giving dowry. It clearly shows that the husband of the bride who is supposed to be most benefitted stakeholder from this custom of dowry is not the actual person responsible for the prevalence of this custom.

6.5.3 Difference between actual and the reported incidence of dowry and its reasons

- **Difference in actual and the reported incidence of dowry**

Despite being prohibited under the legislation, dowry is openly demanded, given and taken in both the districts. Surprisingly, the numbers of cases reported in the state of Himachal Pradesh are very less. It clearly shows that there is a huge difference in the actual and the reported incidences of giving and taking of dowry.

Most of the women have accepted that they themselves as well as the other daughter in laws in their families have brought dowry in their marriages. But the women of old age in district Kangra have denied of bringing any kind of dowry. Therefore, it is clear that the dowry custom is prevalent but the people are not directly admitting its prevalence. However, it was not as much prevalent in the older times in comparison to the modern times.

- **Existence of dowry related violence**

A considerable number of women in district Shimla have admitted that they have faced mental harassment from their husband or in-laws for the demand of dowry. A small number of women have admitted that they have faced some mental or physical harassment from their husband or in-laws for demanding dowry in district Kangra. But a hesitation has been observed in many women to disclose such a personal information and family matter.

There is a significant difference in the actual number of dowry related offences and the reported number of offences. The total number of reported cases of dowry

322

related offences is very low in the state of Himachal Pradesh. But after the field survey it has been clearly shown that most of the people know many victims of dowry related offences in their close circle or vicinity especially in district Kangra. The number of people who personally know many victims of dowry related offences is comparatively low in district Shimla.

- **Reluctance of people to report dowry related matters in police station**

The percentage of number of cases related to dowry dealt by lawyers, police and judges is quite low in both the districts. There is slight increase in district Kangra in compassion to district Shimla but it is otherwise considerably low. It clearly indicates that dowry related cases are very rarely reported in police stations and courts.

Until and unless the physical and psychological harassment of a woman exceeds the limits of her patience and tolerance, such cases are neither taken as crime nor are reported. Majority of the married people do not think that it is right to take the matter of dowry in police station and courts due to some reason or other. It clearly indicates that the married people who are in actual either the direct victims or offenders in dowry related offences; they are not willing to report these offences.

But again the survey conducted in the district Shimla had a strong variation in the opinion of males and females. Majority of the females are strong and courageous enough to believe that such matters must be reported in the police station. However, majority of the males disagree to the same. The educated people are in more favour of taking such matters to the police stations whereas, the lesser educated or uneducated people are against it.Most of the married women find it feasible to file a complaint in the police station against any kind of torture done in connection to the dowry demand. Again, the young people of district Shimla are more willing to report dowry related cases in the police stations in comparison to times. The old and middle aged people are reluctant for the same. It may bring an increase in the reporting of dowry related cases in the upcoming times.

- **Major Reasons behind not reporting the dowry related matters in police station or courts**

  People do not accept those girls as their daughter-in-law, who had broken their engagement or marriage and filed a dowry case against her in-laws before or after marriage. Many people hesitate in approaching the police stations and courts to seek justice in dowry related offences because they feel uncomfortable due to societal pressure.

  The victim of dowry related offences and her family members are more concerned for the breakdown of marriage rather than focusing upon getting justice. This concern is more prominently seen in district Shimla than district Kangra. The victims of dowry related offences are very fearful from their husband and in-laws of their anger or of the fact that they may breakdown the marriage. In district Shimla this concern of victims is higher whereas in district Kangra most of the victims are very eager to compromise with their husband or in-laws even after filing complaint of dowry.

6.5.4 Efficacy of laws related to dowry prohibition

- **Awareness of people regarding legislations and statutes related to dowry prohibition and offences related to dowry**

  The awareness regarding the existing laws on the offences related to dowry is another area of concern. In district Kangra, the uneducated and less educated people were completely unaware about these existing laws and in district Shimla, the middle aged people were quite unaware regarding these laws.

- **Feasibility of law for the implementation and practice**

  There are still many lacunas in the existing anti dowry laws like impracticability and some procedural lacunas like a prolonged time period for getting justice.

  Majority of the people believe that the laws are incapable to end this. It is a gross failure of laws related to dowry that even after more than 58 years of continuous legislative efforts of eradicating dowry, the people do not believe that this custom will ever come to an end.

- **Changes demanded by people in law and society**

  All the women of both the districts admitted that there is a strong need to bring certain changes in law and society to curb the offences related to dowry. Majority of the women primarily focus upon the women empowerment as a most essential need of hour.

  Providing better opportunities of education and employment to the women is the most necessary change to be brought in the society. It will make women more comfortable in raising their voice against dowry related offences and torture.

- **Major lacunas in the Dowry Prohibition Act**

  A major lacuna in the Dowry Prohibition Act lies in the provision related to the punishment for giving dowry. It has been debated a number of times that the parents of the bride are innocent as they become helpless over the demands of groom's side. Moreover, once they will give dowry, they themselves will hesitate to report the matter with a fear of getting punished. The public also had a same view point that giving of dowry must not be penalized with imprisonment and at the most a warning may suffice. The educated class opines against the current existing punishment in the Dowry Prohibition Act, 1961 for giving dowry. However, uneducated class is still unable to understand the sensitivity of this lacuna.

6.5.5 Reasons behind the non- compliance of society towards the laws related to dowry prohibition.

- **Attitude of people towards dowry system**

  Most of the people consider dowry system a very serious issue in both the districts. But in district Shimla, gender has a strong impact on the attitude regarding the seriousness and concern towards dowry system. Not even a single woman has deviated from the majority opinion that dowry system has become a serious issue in present times.

- **Reluctance among people to abide by the laws related to dowry prohibition**

  Anti-dowry laws have failed to inculcate faith in the common man. More than half of the population of general public criticizes these laws for being incapable to eradicate dowry, for being misused and for not being practically much helpful in dealing with dowry related issues. The highly educated class in majority lack faith in the efficacy of these laws. These laws are impractical and therefore, the social acceptance for these laws has been reduced.

There is a mixed response upon the efficacy of anti dowry laws to curb the menace of dowry in both the districts. But in district Kangra, the variables like education and marital status had a strong impact on the difference in opinion. The highly educated people of district Kangra totally lack faith in the efficacy of anti dowry laws. Moreover, majority of the married women also lack faith in the efficacy of anti dowry laws.

The acceptance of dowry as an integral custom is a major reason behind the non-compliance of laws related to dowry prohibition. Apart from that, social pressure of giving and taking dowry is another major reason.

- **Impact on the family life of women depending upon the amount of dowry given and taken in their marriage**

No significant effect has been accepted by the married women that depend upon the amount of dowry given and taken in their marriage. Another reason which is wrongly presumed behind giving dowry by the parents of bride is that it becomes difficult to find a suitable match for their daughter without giving any dowry. Majority of the people in both the districts have clearly negated it as a reason behind giving dowry. Even the married women in majority have also denied that giving dowry enhances the chances of finding a suitable match. There is a conflict in the view point of society. On one side most of them opine that there is no significant effect if no dowry is given by the parents of the bride to the bridegroom and his family but on the other side they told that dowry is given in almost all the marriages which they have attended so far.

6.5.6 Prevalence of dowry system and its impact on other offences against women

- **Impact of dowry system on growing incidences of female foeticide**

The prevalence of dowry system is responsible either directly or indirectly for female foeticide and female infanticide. Undoubtedly there are some reasons as well but still it has a close proximity in forming the opinion of the people that girl child is a burden and a boy child is an asset. Most of the people agree that dowry is one of the major reasons for not wanting a girl child. However, they do not consider it as an only reason and opine that besides dowry, there are some other reasons as well for not wanting a girl child.

- **Impact of dowry system on subjecting the women to cruelty or domestic violence**

The number of cases of domestic violence which are related to dowry is very limited. So we cannot say that dowry is a prime reason for domestic violence in this area. Providing better opportunities of education and employment to the women is the most necessary change to be brought in the society. It will make women more comfortable in raising their voice against dowry related offences and torture.

- **Impact of dowry system on practical implementation of law related to property rights of daughters**

In both the districts, majority of the people are reluctant for some or another reason to give equal share to the girls in their parental property. In district Kangra, illiteracy has a huge impact on the attitude of the people in this regard. Illiteracy or a very low education level leads to a conservative approach in giving share in the property to the daughters. Now it is a contributing factor in the existence of dowry system. The age old notion of compensating the share in estate of father by giving dowry in the marriage of daughter has still an impact in the modern world. Law has given equal property rights and inheritance rights to the daughters but the patriarchal mind set has never ever led to the implementation of the same.

The married women do not get share in their parental property in any of the district. Only negligible number of married females gets any share in their parental property. Surprisingly there is no effect of education, financial status or age on the probability of getting such share.

6.5.7 Efficacy of legal and police machinery in dealing with dowry related offences

- **Extent of faith of people on police and courts to get justice in dowry related offences**

The general public and married women in both the districts have verbally shown the faith on police and courts to get justice in dowry related offences. But as told by the Police, lawyers and judges, the actual filing of complaint for giving or taking dowry is very rare in police stations or courts. Most of the times, lots of hesitation is observed in the victim or her family before or while filing a complaint of dowry related offences.

- **Accessibility and approachability of Legal and police machinery to get justice in dowry related offences**

    The law professionals in district Kangra admit that there are many lacunas in the functioning of police in dealing with the cases related to dowry prohibition. However, in district Shimla they believe that there are negligible or very few lacunas in the functioning of the police.

    All the judges in district Kangra had strongly admitted that it is not just the societal pressure that makes women uncomfortable in raising their voice against dowry related offences. In fact the police and legal system should become supportive to make the victims of dowry related offences more comfortable in raising their voice.

- **Major obstacles in effective functioning of legal and police machinery in dealing with dowry related offences**

    The chances of escape or survival of woman who has been attacked by her husband or in-laws in order to kill her for dowry is very rare. Since she is helpless among their majority and all alone within the four walls of house, her chances of escape is almost negligible.

    It is surprising that most of the married women consider that the chances of survival or escape of a female is very high if her husband or in-laws attempt to kill her within the four walls of the house for dowry.

    Moreover, it is sometimes difficult to find evidence and witnesses in the case of cases of dowry deaths. The opinion of lawyers is entirely different in comparison to police and Judges in the availability of genuine witnesses in the cases of dowry death. Majority of the lawyers think that such witnesses can be easily found whereas; all of the Judges and the police take a contrary view. Surprisingly, not a single Judge or a police official agrees that such witnesses are genuine or can be easily found. It clearly shows that even if the lawyers produce such witnesses of dowry death in the court, police officials question their credibility and the Judges do not rely upon them.

It is also difficult for the judges to get proper evidence in the cases of cruelty and domestic violence. The police officials face a huge problem in prosecuting the offenders as the victims of cruelty and domestic violence change or revoke their statement in the court due to family pressure.

- **Main challenges through which the legal and police machinery come across while dealing with dowry related offences**

The major challenge faced by the prosecution is to get genuine witnesses and proper evidence. Most of the law professionals opine that since such an offences committed within the four walls of an enclosed house where the victim is all alone, therefore, it is not easy to find witnesses. Another challenge that comes before the police and courts while dealing with the offences of cruelty and domestic violence is that the victims change or revoke their statements due to family pressure.

6.5.8 Extent of Abuse and misuse of the dowry prohibition laws

- **Scope and extent of misuse of dowry prohibition laws by the women**

There is a mixed response related to the misuse and abuse of dowry prohibition laws. Several times these laws are misused for falsely implicating the innocent people but it cannot be alleged that most cases related to dowry are false.

Majority of the lawyers deviate from the general opinion as 57.9% believe that most of the dowry cases are false whereas only 33.3% police as well as Judges believe that most of the dowry related cases are false. It can be inferred that there are chances that the lawyers of those accused who are falsely implicated understand the helplessness and genuineness of their client as usually the clients speak up the truth privately to their own lawyer. But due to the polar opinion of police and Judges that the misuse is not common or most of the implications are genuine, such accused get helplessly dragged and suffer the severe consequences of misuse of dowry prohibition laws.

- **General attitude of people towards the misuse of dowry prohibition laws**

Majority of the people do not have any fear of any misuse of anti dowry laws against them. They have full faith in police and legal system and hence do not worry of getting falsely implicated or roped in any dowry related offence. But a deviation has been seen in the opinion of younger generation in district Kangra. Most of the youth believed that misuse of dowry prohibition laws is common and troublesome as all the laws are in the favour of women only.

6.6 Hypothesis

Explanatory result:

The present study is based on the hypothesis that-

Lack of social will is an impediment in the effective implementation of laws relating to dowry prohibition and as well leads to the misuse of the laws.

The first part of hypothesis that lack of social will is the major impediment in the effective implementation of dowry prohibition laws, stands proved on the evaluation of certain questions responded by the general public, married women as well as police, lawyers, judges and academicians. As answered in question 2 of the questionnaire given to the general public, 67% of the people in district Shimla and 59 % of the people in district Kangra have attended the marriages where dowry is given and taken as a custom because both sides happily agree. It clearly indicates that despite the presence of numerous stringent laws on dowry prohibition, it is completely acceptable practice in this society and therefore, steady prevailing. In other responses like question 10, the people who receive huge dowry in the marriage do not face any negative consequences on the society rather they flaunt the lavish dowry and their social status is increased. In further responses like in question 11, it has been observed that the women who report any dowry related harassment; they face huge difficulties posed by in-laws and society. Majority of the people consider social acceptance of dowry as a custom and believe that it will never end. However, it has been also observed that in comparison to district Shimla, there is much more social acceptance of dowry in district Kangra and it is evaluated on the basis of certain responses like only 28% of in-laws in district Kangra have refused to accept any dowry whereas 58% of in-laws in district Shimla have refused to accept any dowry. More number of married women in district Kangra have accepted that the bridegroom's family shared the list of names of those relatives to whom bride's family was expected to give gifts and *shaguns*, than district Shimla.

Various responses of police, lawyers, judges and academicians of law are also in conformity with the first part of the hypothesis. Majority of them consider that social recognition of dowry as a custom is the prime reason behind the continuance of offence of dowry and non-compliance of the laws related to dowry prohibition. However, very few cases of dowry get reported as there is a strong hesitation observed in the victim and her family in filing a complaint against dowry related offences. These respondents have further answered that the major concern of victim and her family while filing dowry related complaints is the fear of breakdown of marriage. Such victims feel uncomfortable due to social pressure in approaching the police stations and courts to seek justice in dowry related offences.

The second part of the hypothesis stands disproved that the lack of social will also leads to the misuse and abuse of laws related to dowry prohibition.

After the evaluation of question 16 asked from general public that what could they do if a false case of dowry is filed against them or their family, it has become clear that majority of the people do not worry at all in such a situation. The reason reported in both the districts was that they have full faith in the police and legal system against any kind of misuse or false implication in dowry related laws. Very few people answered that they fear and consider such situation troublesome as they believed that all the laws are in favour of women. Further, in question 18, while giving the opinion on anti-dowry laws, a very few people from both the districts have answered that such laws are mostly misused to deter and falsely implicate the innocent husbands and in-laws. Some of them agree that such laws are only on papers and are totally incapable to eradicate dowry and others find it helpful in dealing with dowry prohibition laws. In question 8 of the questionnaire circulated among police, lawyers, judges and academicians of law, only 36% of respondents answered that there is misuse and abuse of dowry prohibition laws, rest 64% of the respondents do not believe that the misuse and abuse of dowry prohibition laws is common. Further by evaluating question 12, 13 and 16 of this questionnaire, it is inferred that due to social and family pressure, it is not easy for the females to file dowry related complaints in police stations. Even the genuine victims hesitate to file such complaints and fear of the breakdown of the marriage, their common approach is more inclined in reaching to a compromise and in-laws rather than getting justice. Moreover, the general public has also shown reluctance in making such females their daughter-in-laws who have ever filed a dowry related complaint against their in-laws or future in-laws. Therefore, we cannot assume that in such a society where the genuine reporting of cases is very less, on such a sensitive matrimonial dispute, social will is leading to a greater abuse or misuse of dowry prohibition laws.

CHAPTER 7
CONCLUSION AND SUGGESTIONS

The institution of marriage originated as a need of companionship and lineage. Gradually it brought certain customs and rituals while performing this ceremony of marriage. The custom of dowry began with the institution of marriage. The initial idea behind the advent of this custom was to give gifts, ornaments and wealth to the bride and bridegroom as a token of love, affection and blessings by the father of the bride. Later on it also started serving as a tool of financial support to the newly married couple in their new household. At that time there were no property rights or share in the parental property were given to the daughters. Hence it was also considered as a financial security as well as full and final payment of a kind of share in the father's wealth to the daughter. Practically speaking, it was somehow more convenient for the father and brothers of brides to give dowry as a wealth in the marriage of their daughter. Being a voluntary and discretionary amount it was usually far lesser than the share of sons in the father's property.

7.1 Conclusion

The socio-culture role of the women was also responsible for the rise and growth of dowry system. In those civilizations where the socio-culture role of women was merely confined to the household chores like cooking, bringing up children etc, those women were financially totally depended upon the husband and in-laws. Therefore, the fathers of brides used to give dowry impliedly as a compensation for bearing the expenses of their daughter to the rest of the life.[1]

With the passage of time, the custom of dowry has become so popular and an integral part of the marriage. It gradually got associated with the social status and esteem of bride's father in the society. Therefore, the bride's side started doing pomp and show in the marriages and giving more and more dowry sometimes even beyond their financial capacity. The greed of bridegroom's side also ignited and they started demanding dowry as a matter of societal right. It became a shortcut of getting wealth in a quick and easier form by getting one's son married. It resulted into the increase in pressure on the bride's father and family. The girl's began to be treated as burden and

---

[1] P.K. Majumdar & R.P. Kataria, *Law Relating to Dowry Prohibition Cruelty & Harassment* 7 (Orient Publishing Company, New Delhi, 3rd edn., 2014).

a common term was used for them i.e. '*Paraya Dhan*' (someone else's wealth).[2] People started wanting male child not merely for lineage but also with an underlying desire of collecting wealth in his marriage. It further strengthened the patriarchal setup and male chauvinism.

As soon as dowry had become an integral part of marriage, thereafter the expectations of bridegroom's side started increasing. They started expressly demanding dowry as a condition precedent of tying the nuptial knot. Non fulfilment of demand of dowry began to often resulting into breaking the engagements or even leaving the wedding ceremony in between before '*saptpadi*'. Discontentment regarding insufficient dowry even resulted into maltreatment, harassment, mental or physical torture to the married women in their matrimonial homes. The ugliest consequences of non fulfilment of the dowry demands led to the most heinous forms of crime like bride burning and dowry killings.

The custom had taken a form of social evil leading to various kinds of atrocities on brides and psychological harassment of their parents. Therefore, the need of enacting certain legislation to curb this evil was realized by the state. The enactments which were enacted during British era likewise "*Sind Deti Leti* Act, 1939"[3], "Hindu Law of Inheritance Act, 1929", "Hindu Women's Right to Property Act, 1937"[4] were completely incapable of eradicating dowry practice. Many other social evils like '*Sati Pratha*', '*Devdasi*', prohibition of widow remarriage etc. have emerged, flourished but subsequently eroded with the passage of time and legislative efforts.[5] To the contrary, the evil of dowry has not only strengthened with the passage of time but also gave birth to several new offences within the framework of the marriage like cruelty, dowry death, domestic violence etc.[6] Indirectly, it also contributed in increasing female foeticide and female infanticide to some extent.

---

[2] Zeba Hasan, "Blasphemy of Dowry in India and an Insurgence of an Artist: Neelima Sheikh Against the System", 2 *ESJ* 400 (2014) *available at*: https://eujournal.org/index.php/esj/article/ viewFile/3734/3587(Visited on October 12, 2016).

[3] The Sindh Deti-Leti Act, 1939 *available at*: http://sindhlaws.gov.pk/setup/publications/PUB-14-000155.pdf(Visited on May 22, 2019).

[4] As referred in Dr. Shipra Kaushal, *Gender Inequality Illustrated through A Legal Perspective on Female Foeticide* 165 (Satyam Law International, New Delhi, 2014)

[5] India Today, "The abolished 'Sati Pratha': Lesser-known facts on the banned practice", *Available at*: https://www.indiatoday.in/education-today/gk-current-affairs/story/sati-pratha-facts-275586-2015-12-04 (Last Modified on December 4, 2015, 11:23 AM)

[6] P.K. Rana, "Critical Analysis on Criminalization against Burning of Widows" 3 *IJL* 19 (2017) *available at*: http://www.lawjournals.org/download/84/3-1-12-944.pdf

After independence, "The Dowry Prohibition Act, 1961" was enacted and it strived hard to eradicate this evil.[7] Some amendments were also done time to time, to increase the efficacy of this enactment. Undoubtedly, the enactment of this Act was a positive step to curb the menace of dowry and to prohibit a deep rooted social evil. But unfortunately, all went in vein as the Act had failed in bringing the desired results.[8]

Apart from that various other provisions were introduced in the penal laws like the offence of cruelty, dowry death, abetment to suicide, criminal breach of trust etc. These provisions have been given the biting teeth through the insertions of presumptions to shift burden of proof on the accused in the evidence law. To provide relief in the cases of wife bettering, a separate Act, "The Protection of Women from Domestic Violence Act, 2005" had been enacted.[9]

Various bodies like National Commission for Women[10], Law Commission of India[11] as well as certain committees like Malimath Committee[12] have time to time suggested many changes and recommendations in the laws to increase the effectiveness and implementation of these laws. But surprisingly the suggestions given by National Commission of Women in 2005 were neither taken seriously and nor were adopted at all. The prime inclination of these recommendations was towards making the dowry related laws, especially the offence of dowry death more stringent. It has been suggested to treat this offence equivalent to murder, enhance the minimum punishment, and even enhance the time limit of seven years time span after marriage.

Not only through the legislations but also through various policies and schemes, the central governments as well as various state governments have endeavoured to eradicate the evil of dowry and to control the menace of dowry related

---

[7] See, The Dowry Prohibition Act, 1961

[8] Suman Nalwa and Hari Dev Kohli, *Law Relating to Dowry, Dowry Death, Cruelty to Women & Domestic Violence 26* (Universal Law Publication Co., New Delhi, 2013).

[9] See Section 3(b) and Section 31(3), The Protection of Women from Domestic Violence Act, 2005.

[10] Annual Report, National Commission for Women, 1996-97, 1-2 referred in Sadhna Arya, "The National Commission for Women: A Study in Performance" 22 available at: http://www.cwds. ac.in/wp-content/uploads/2016/11/NCWreport.pdf.

[11] Law Commission of India, 91st Report on Dowry Deaths and Law Reform: Amending The Hindu Marriage Act, 1955, The Indian Penal Code 1860 and The Indian Evidence Act, 1872, (August, 1983) *available at:* http://lawcommissionofindia.nic.in/51-100/Report91.pdf *(Visited on January 11, 2017).*

[12] Government of India, Report: *Committee on Reforms of Criminal Justice System* (Ministry of Home Affairs, 2003), available at: https://mha.gov.in/sites/default/files/criminal_justice_system. pdf *(Visited on January 13, 2017).*

offences. The schemes like '*Ladli Yojna*' and '*Beti Bachao Beti Padhao* Programme' have been introduced with an objective to save girl child birth and to promote the education of girls.[13] *Ladli Yojna* was a scheme of giving one lakh rupees to the girls who were born after 1st January 2008 in a family having an annual income below one lakh rupees on attaining the age of 18 years for education.[14] But it has a consequential danger of adding fuel to the dowry system as most of the families are interested in using this money to gather dowry for the marriage of these girls rather than on their study.

'One stop centre' have been established in more than 700 districts to give medical, legal, police as well as psychological support to the women affected by any kind of violence including dowry related offences[15]. Undoubtedly, it is a commendable initiative because the major concern for a dowry victim is of shelter and support. The one who has come out of her matrimonial relation and took a stand against her own husband and in-laws becomes all alone. Many times it has been observed that either due to societal pressure or due to other personal reasons, the parents of such dowry victims are not even able to support them completely. In such a situation, these One Stop Centres provide shelter and support to these victims. Another challenge faced by the dowry victims is the attitude and cooperation of police towards them. The One Stop Centres provide the required assistance and support in the entire process from filing an FIR to the whole court procedure. India has a conservative social setup where a bride is usually taught by her parents that the matrimonial home is a place where a bride goes in her palanquin and comes out only in her funeral bier. The problem is that in such a conservative society, the victims of dowry related offences are not courageous enough to go and report the matters of dowry related harassment against them. Especially when the harassment is merely verbal or psychological and there is no physical assault, neither the victim nor her parents are interested to take such petty family issues to police stations or even to the One Stop Centres.

---

[13] Beti Bachao Beti Padhao Scheme, Ministry of Women and Child Development, Government of India, *available at:* https://wcd.nic.in/schemes/beti-bachao-beti-padhao-scheme

[14] Savita Verma, *Goverment scheme to save girls in womb a flop: Study, available at:* https://www.indiatoday. in/india/north/story/goverment-scheme-to-save-girls-in-womb-a-flop-150100-2011-12-28 (last modified Dec 28 2011)

[15] One Stop Centre Scheme, *Ministry of Women & Child Development, available at:* https://wcd.nic. in/schemes/one-stop-centre-scheme-1(Visited on Feb17, 2019)

But the question is that whether these efforts suffice the objectives with which these legislations have been enacted. Merely by making the laws more and more stringent and enhancing the punishment cannot result in an effective implementation. Because it is not only the fear of stringent laws but also a common willingness of people to abide by such laws that makes the implementation of the laws effective. Secondly, the enhanced punishment or the strict laws can only work if the cases are well reported, witnesses and evidence are available and the victims are fearless to stand and fight for justice. But in dowry related offences, the above discussed factors are the major challenges in the effective implementation of laws.

7.1.1 Loopholes in the Dowry Prohibition Act

The Dowry Prohibition Act, 1961 has been operative from more than fifty eight years but there is no decline in dowry related crimes.[16] NCRB has recorded a tremendous growth in the dowry related violence especially from the last few decades.[17] It clearly indicates that there are certain lacunas in this Act which are creating hindrance to its effective implementation.

The key postulates of this act prohibit and penalize all the acts of giving and taking dowry, demanding dowry and even abetment for giving or taking dowry. The Act envisages the appointment of 'Dowry Prohibition Officers' as well as establishment of Advisory boards for advising and assisting these officers. But the problem is that in most of states, no separate appointments of DPOs have been done. The other state officers like sub divisional magistrates, superintendents of police, probation officers etc. have been given the charge of Dowry Prohibition Officers.

The provisions for appointment of DPOs under the Act were inserted with an objective of effective implementation of this Act. If no separate and dedicated officers would be appointed, then such DPOs will probably be an eye wash and formality. Another concern is that by giving the additional charge of DPOs to the already existing officers will again result in pendency of cases and hence a delayed justice.

Definition of dowry is not exhaustive enough to cover all kinds of dowry demands. It has been observed very commonly that sometimes the parents of the

---

[16] *Supra* note 7.
[17] National Crime Records Bureau, Report: *Crime in India, 2016 Statistics* (Ministry of Home Affairs, October, 2017) 4 *available at*: http://ncrb.gov.in/StatPublications/CII/CII2016/pdfs/ NEWPDFs/ Crime%20in%20India%20-%202016%20Complete%20PDF%20291117.pdf (Visited on January 11, 2019).

bridegroom do not demand anything directly but pressurize the bride's parents to perform a very lavish marriage.[18] They often say that they do not want dowry but marriage must be extremely lavish and of very high status. Now the demand for the so called 'lavish marriage' is not included in the term dowry. But many times it not only becomes a heavy financial expense on the bride's side and even puts them under debts or a compulsion to pay huge loans afterwards. The species of these 'lavish marriages' is quite similar to dowry in terms of motive and consequences. Therefore, it is still a grey area in the definition of 'dowry'.

The Act has made compulsory for the bride and bridegroom to maintain the list of the presents given to them in the marriage.[19] It must be separately maintained and duly signed by the parties. But there is no practical implementation and no genuine maintenance of such lists takes place in actual. This rule is mostly ignored in the marriages as the people do not take it seriously.

The Dowry Prohibition Act prescribes certain persons of bodies who may file a complaint in case of an offense under this Act. Such complaints can be filed either by the aggrieved person, or a parent or a relative of such person or any recognized welfare organization. Secondly, the punishment of five years is also prescribed for the person who has given dowry. Thirdly, every offence under this Act is non-bailable and non-compoundable at any stage of trial. It can be clearly seen that the provisions of the Act itself have created certain practical challenges in the implementation of the Act. For an instance, if the parents of the aggrieved person have given dowry at the initial stage, they will hesitate to report matter to the authorities afterwards. Because they have given the dowry and therefore they are also liable for the punishment under this Act. Another drawback is that no third person for example a neighbour or anyone else in public who is aware of a dowry transaction in any marriage cannot file the complaint. It mitigates the chances of reporting the dowry related matters. Another crucial aspect observed in the survey is that most of the victims of dowry related matters are more interested in reaching to a compromise with husband and in-laws rather than punishing them. Therefore, the non-bailable and non-compoundable nature

---

[18] Section 2, The Dowry Prohibition Act, 1961, (For details, See at *Supra* Chapter 3)
[19] The Dowry Prohibition (Maintenance of the Lists of Presents to the Bride and Bridegroom) Rules, 1985, also see, Rule 2 (2), The Dowry Prohibition (Maintenance of the Lists of Presents to the Bride and Bridegroom) Rules, 1985.

of offences may lead to reluctance in filing the complaint as it will end the chances of compromise.

7.1.2 Procedural Shortcomings in Effective Functioning of Dowry Prohibition Laws

Dowry death is the most brutal form of dowry related offences. Nothing can be more agonising for a female that the person, who has taken a pledge to protect her throughout her life, kills her for an illegitimate demand of money or valuables. It is an offence under Indian Penal Code and the punishment is minimum seven years and maximum life imprisonment. Only a married female can be a victim whose death has been occurred in abnormal circumstances or by burns or bodily injury within seven years of her marriage. It has to be proved that she has been subjected to the cruelty soon before her death in connection to the demand of dowry. The provision has given teeth by the insertion of presumption under Indian Evidence Act that if all the essentials of dowry death are fulfilled then the burden of the proof will shift upon the accused and the court will presume the accused guilty until and unless the contrary is proved by the defence side.

But the major procedural challenge that comes across in most of the cases of dowry death is the procuring of evidence. The offence is usually committed within the four walls of matrimonial house of the victim. The victim is all alone among the majority of her husband and his relatives who are usually the culprits or the mute spectators of the crime.[20] It creates the difficulty for the prosecution to find the genuine witnesses of the crime. Several times, the circumstantial evidence is also tampered by the accused or their family members to escape the chances of prosecution. The victim is not taken to the hospital on time which not only mitigates her chances of survival but also minimize the chances of recording of her dying declaration. The forensic evidence may play a vital role in establishing the guilt for example presence of kerosene on body, clothes or surroundings, injuries of strangulation or any physical struggle on the body of the victim, finger prints, signs of smothering, signs of poisoning, introspection of viscera etc.[21] But such evidence is

---

[20] K.D.Gaur, *Commentary on the Indian Penal Code* 960 (Universal Law Publishing, 2013).
[21] Afzal Haroon, "A Study of Epidemiological Profile of Dowry Death Victims in Aligarh" 3 IABMCR 7 (2017) *available at:* https://pdfs.semanticscholar.org/ b1aa/ed70a31 e3cb 856b0ee2507 c851ed25538a6d.pdf?_ga=2.20997243.1143021006.1578113541-1292684471.1578113541(Visited on March10, 2019).

likely to be destroyed as it could be easily done by the culprits in their own home where victim is all alone in their trap. Moreover, the forensic laboratories or the forensic experts in India are not as advanced as are required in today's modern world.

The offence of cruelty in the Indian Penal Code is invoked when a woman is subjected to any kind of mental or physical harassment by her husband or his relatives for demand of dowry or causing any injury to her life, limb or health or sufficient to drive her to commit suicide. It is a cognizable, non-bailable and non-compoundable offence.[22] Very often the question is raised to make the offence non-cognizable and compoundable .The Law Commission of India in its reports as well as the report given by the Malimath Committee also suggested making the offence compoundable.[23] But the view point is discarded on the grounds that it will dilute the provision and hence defeat its objective. The violence done to a woman in her own matrimonial house cannot be taken with a non serious approach because of the mere fact that it is done by her own husband or in-laws. Undoubtedly on ethical and legal grounds the gravity of the offence cannot be ignored. But on practical grounds, the non-compoundable nature of this offence seems to be a major obstacle in the smooth implementation of this provision. The violence done to a woman and that too for dowry is completely unacceptable. But it cannot rule out the will of the victim who is after all the wife of the offender, sometimes even the mother of offender's children. This non-compoundable nature of the offence leaves no probability of compromise between the both spouses, howsoever regretful the husband might be and howsoever willing the wife might be. The only option left for the victim to reach to the compromise is only through the route of Section 482 of Criminal Procedure Code in the High Court.[24] Being a very tedious, time consuming and expensive process, it is of course not a very good option. It has been widely observed in the survey that most of the victims of cruelty are more interested in reaching to a compromise with the husband rather than penalizing him. It has been also reported by the police, lawyers and Judges that the victims of dowry related offences and cruelty hesitate to file a complaint as they have strong fear of breakdown of marriage. It is most likely

---

[22] Section 498A, The Indian Penal Code, 1860.
[23] *Supra* note 12.
[24] Section 482- Saving of inherent powers of High Court. Nothing in this Code shall be deemed to limit or affect the inherent powers of the High Court to make such orders as may be necessary to give effect to any order under this Code, or to prevent abuse of the process of any Court or otherwise to secure the ends of justice., The Criminal Procedure Code, 1973.

impossible that once the husband or in-laws would undergo the imprisonment, they will accept the victim again in that matrimonial relationship. Those victims who are financially dependent, psychologically weak or socially alone, their own life become miserable after filing such a complaint. The provision has been made to provide justice to the victim and not to leave her in a state of helplessness. Therefore, before emphasising upon the stringent aspect of this provision, the practical aspect must be taken into the consideration.

7.1.3 No Share in the Property to the Daughters is another Cause of Dowry Prohibition

In India, initially there was no concept of giving share to the daughters in their parental or ancestral property. There were times when not even the property rights were given to the women. Gradually, several legislations were formulated time to time under personal laws and other laws to give not only the property rights but also the right of inheritance to the daughters.[25] This right prevails even after the marriages of the daughters. But the biggest irony of the fate is that despite the legislations, neither the parents or brothers are ready to give share in property to the daughters nor the daughters are interested to claim this share. Ultimately the result is that almost nil percentage of married women is taking their legitimate share in their ancestral or parental property.[26]

In olden times, the custom of dowry also evolved as a result of absence of right of share in father's property.[27] Dowry was seen as compensation or a full and final payment in lieu of the share of daughter in her father's property. Not only in India but in other countries like China, the fathers and brothers used to give dowry in the marriage of their daughter as an alternate to her share in property. It served a dual purpose firstly, to give a discretionary amount of dowry which was usually far lesser than the share in the property; secondly, giving dowry in the marriage of the daughter was the best way to flaunt wealth and status in the society.[28] In the modern India the law has given the right to take share in the parental property but nothing has changed in actual practice. The daughters are not at all exercising this right; the fathers are

---

[25] The Hindu Succession Act, 1956 *available at*: http://egazette.nic.in/WriteReadData/1956/E-2173-1956-0038-99150.pdf (Visited on April 24, 2018).

[26] John L. McCreery, "Women's Property Rights and Dowry in China and South Asia" 15, No. pp. 163-174 (1976) *available at:* http://www.jstor.org/stable/3773327 (Visited on July 22, 2017).

[27] *Ibid.*

[28] *Id.* at 170.

giving dowry in the marriages of their daughter with the mentality that at least something is given to the daughters from their wealth. Moreover, the custom of dowry is also serving a purpose of giving some financial security to the daughters, especially where such females are not financially independent. Therefore, a denial to the adherence of laws providing property rights to the daughters in the parental property is also a major factor promoting the system of dowry.

7.1.4 Lack of Social Will as a major Impediment in the Implementation of Dowry Prohibition Laws

The custom of dowry and offences related to dowry are an age old concept. But with the passage of time, instead of getting diminished and therefore loosing the significance, these offences have become an area of a major concern. The pomp and show in the marriages is increasing day by day, dowry is openly given, taken and demanded in marriages and leading to a huge mockery of law. The offences related to dowry are on constant increase, leaving a devastating effect on the victim as well as on the society. While examining the major factors responsible for the prevalence of dowry system and related offences, some contributing factors like loop holes in dowry related laws, historical impact, weak governmental policies and schemes etc. are widely discussed. But the major cause or the most prominent reason behind the prevalence of dowry system and increasing dowry related offences is the social acceptability of this custom.[29] Lack of social will is the major impediment in the effective implementation of laws relating to dowry prohibition.[30]

The giving and taking of dowry is inherently deep rooted in the mind set of people that either they do not realise their natural customization to the practice or they do not want to accept their inclination towards this custom. In majority of the marriages, dowry is given and taken as a custom because both sides happily agree.[31] It is a very small percentage of marriages in which dowry is not given. Despite being prohibited under the legislation, it is openly demanded, given and taken.

However the actual number of cases reported is quite lesser than the actual number of incidences of dowry demand and harassment.[32] The number of dowry related offences which are reported is quite low in the state of Himachal Pradesh in

---

[29] See *Supra* Chapter 6 for detailed Empirical Survey.
[30] *Ibid.*
[31] *Supra* Chapter 6.
[32] *Ibid.*

comparison to the other states like U.P., Bihar, Andhra Pradesh, Karnataka, Odisha, West Bengal etc.[33] Undoubtedly, the severe incidents of dowry deaths and brutal tortures of females for dowry is uncommon in H.P. unlikely the other states. But the study has clearly indicated another aspect that still there is a huge gap in the actual number of cases related to giving and taking of dowry or dowry related harassment and the reported number of cases related to dowry.

All three categories of respondents have somehow accepted that neither district Shimla nor district Kangra is untouched by the prevalence of dowry system. A common pattern of behaviour has been observed throughout the study that the conduct of the people towards giving and taking dowry, reporting such matters in the police station and believing on the legal machinery is entirely different from their verbal statements. It clearly reflects that a major segment of society verbally condemns dowry system and expresses faith in legal machinery, however in actual practice; they give and take dowry under the veil of gifts, blessings, affection, etc.[34] Until and unless the dowry demands reach beyond the capacity of the bride's parents, such demands are happily fulfilled.

Majority of the married people do not think that it is right to take the matter of dowry in police station and courts due some reason or other. There is a further approach that till the physical and psychological harassment of a woman exceeds the limits of her patience and tolerance, such cases are neither taken as crime nor are reported.

7.1.5 Misuse and Abuse of Anti-Dowry Laws

The misuse or abuse of anti-dowry laws does not seem to very common in the district Kangra and District Shimla through the analysis of primary data. Neither the general public has a fear of any false implication in dowry related matters by their wives and daughter-in-laws nor have the married women shown any tendency in unnecessarily roping innocent family members in dowry related offences.[35] Somehow the legal professionals have acknowledged the misuse and abuse of anti-dowry laws upto some extent.

---

[33] Supra note 17 at 32.
[34] See *Supra* Chapter 6 for detailed Empirical Survey.
[35] *Ibid.*

However through the secondary data of NCRB and through analysis of various judicial pronouncements of Supreme Court of India like *of Sushil Kumar Sharma v. Union of India*[36], *Preeti Gupta*[37] *and Rajesh Sharma*[38], it cannot be denied that there are several instances of the exaggerated versions and tendency of over-implication by women of dowry related allegations on the innocent husbands or their relatives. A less tolerant impulsive woman may lodge an FIR even on a trivial act.[39] The result is that the husband and his family may be immediately arrested and there may be a suspension or loss of job. The offence alleged being non-bailable, innocent persons languish in custody. The laws suffer from the following shortcomings for which they are likely to be misused:

- There is a slight gender bias in the laws as it does not recognize cruelty and domestic violence against men. The police in India generally do not register complaints of extortion or violence against men in a domestic relationship, but registering a complaint under 498A (where a woman is the aggrieved party) is widespread.

- Corruption in the police force, which often does no investigation before arresting innocent people.

- Often gifts offered by the bride's parents to win over the bridegroom are channelized into a dowry tunnel.[40]

- There is no provision for penalties or punishment for false complaints or perjury.

Need of the hour is to reconsider the fact that 498A was intended to be used a shield and not an assassin weapon. There is no question of investigating agency and Courts casually dealing with the allegations. They cannot follow any straitjacket formula in the matters relating to dowry tortures, deaths and cruelty. It cannot be lost sight of that ultimate objective of every legal system is to arrive at truth, punish the guilty and protect the innocent. There is no scope for any pre-conceived notion or view. It is to be noted that the role of the investigating agencies and the courts is that of watch dog and not of a bloodhound. It should also be an effort of judiciary to see

---

[36] 2005 (6) SC 266
[37] *Preeti Gupta & Anr* v. *State of Jharkhand* (2010) 7 SCC 667
[38] *Rajesh Sharma* v. *State of UP* (2018) 10 SCC 472
[39] Supra note 12.
[40] "Dowry Law in India", *available at: http*//delhijustice.com/The Dowry Prohibition Act1961.html (visited on March 9, 2016)

that an innocent person is not made to suffer on account of unfounded, baseless and malicious allegations.

7.2 Suggestions

7.2.1 Suggestions related to the Dowry Prohibition Act

1. The definition of the term 'dowry' under Section 2 shall also include any demand of pressurising the either side to arrange a lavish marriage with huge pomp and show as a condition precedent for marriage.[41]

2. There shall not be any restriction on a third party other than the aggrieved person or aggrieved person's relatives or a welfare organization.[42] It will help in overcoming the problem of very lesser number of reported cases of dowry in comparison to actual number of dowry related incidences.

3. The appointment of Dowry Prohibition Officers under "The Dowry Prohibition Act, 1961" must not be done as a formality by giving additional charge to the other state officers.[43] These officers must be separately and specifically appointed to deal with dowry related matters. Proper training must be given to these officers to deal dowry related matters with sensitivity and judicious mind in an expeditious way.

4. There must be a proper check to ensure the maintenance of list of the presents given to the bride and groom in their marriage in accordance to the manner and procedure prescribed under law. This might be done by making it compulsory to produce the duly signed copy of this list as a requirement of registration of marriage. It will ensure the practical implementation of law related to the maintenance of lists, which is merely on paper till date.

5. There is a need to revisit the cognizable and non-compoundable nature of all offences covered under Dowry Prohibition Act.[44] The offences related to demand of dowry or giving or taking of dowry shall be made compoundable with the permission of court at least in the situations where the marriage has already taken place and where no violence has been done to the aggrieved. It will safeguard the interest of the aggrieved if the offenders are extremely regretful and the

---

[41] Supra note 18.
[42] Section 7, The Dowry Prohibition Act, 1961, (For details, See at *Supra* Chapter 3)
[43] Section 8B, The Dowry Prohibition Act, 1961, (For details, See at *Supra* Chapter 3)
[44] See *Supra* Chapter 6 for detailed Empirical Survey.

aggrieved is more interested in reaching to a compromise rather than punishing the wrong doer.

7.2.2 Suggestion Related to Criminal Law

1. In case of dowry death, the offences usually committed within the four walls of an enclosed house where the victim is all alone, therefore, it is difficult to get proper evidence and genuine witnesses. The cases where the prosecution fails to prove the essentials of dowry death beyond reasonable doubt merely due to insufficient evidence or lack of evidence, the court must not order an acquittal. It has been mentioned by the report of Malimath Committee as well, that the cases in which improper investigation has been done or there is non-production of evidence, the court must not act as a mute spectator.[45] For meeting the ends of justice, the court must direct for reinvestigation and give another chance and some further time to the prosecution side to produce the relevant evidence.

2. The forensic evidence may play a vital role in arranging the circumstantial evidence in the cases of dowry death as well as suicide.[46] There is strong need of setting up of technologically advanced forensic laboratories in India. Usually the police constables collect the samples from the crime scene. Such persons are not trained to collect the samples without causing any harm to the samples in an accurate way. The samples for minute forensic tests must be collected by the forensic experts.

3. The offence of cruelty may be made non-compoundable with the permission of court.

7.2.3 Suggestions Related to Social Change

1. The society must adopt a positive approach towards the genuine complainants of dowry related offences. Such females either unmarried or divorcee, must not be avoided to be chosen as a wife or daughter-in-law merely for the reason they have previously filed a complaint against dowry related offences.

2. The society must treat the offenders who have committed the dowry related offences with the same hatred and stigma like the offenders of any other offence.

---

[45] *Supra* note 12.
[46] O. P. Murty, "Dowry Crimes Investigation"4 *IJLTLM* 13(2002) *available at:* https://www.researchgate.net/publication/260955963_Dowry_crimes_investigation (Visited on August 10, 2017).

It is the responsibility of people of not to encourage the taking of huge dowry by showing an astonishment towards the increased wealth of the people by taking dowry.

3.   The extra ordinary pomp and show in the marriages sets an example in the society to arrange lavish marriages. Till the time, such marriages would be treated as a status symbol; the dowry system will never come to an end. The youth must take a responsibility on their shoulder to refrain from unnecessary show off in the marriages.

4.   Any kind of physical or mental harassment to a female in connection to the dowry is an offence. The people in the society bear a responsibility to object, report and give statement in case of witnessing any such incident. It must not be considered as a personal family matter of the offenders or victim as a crime must not be ignored under the veil of personal family matter.

5.   The people, especially the neighbours must not hesitate to record the statement as a witness of dowry death, in case they have seen any kind of suspicious activity or violence committed with the victim by her husband or relatives.

6.   The marriages conducted in a very simple manner and in which no dowry is given or taken must not be treated as inferior. Rather such kind of marriages must be appreciated whole heartedly in the society and embraced as an example.

7.2.4 Suggestions related to Sensitization for Dowry Prohibition

1.   The lack of social will is one of the major reasons that people are not abiding the dowry related laws. Merely making the laws more and more stringent shall not solve the purpose until and unless people are sensitized towards the existing dowry related laws and convinced to positive adherence for these laws.

2.   It is the responsibility of the government, judiciary, police, legal professionals as well as educated class to contribute in sensitizing the people towards the significance of anti dowry laws and make them aware towards the evil consequences of the dowry system on the people.

3.   It is a matter of great irony that numerous insurance policies, investment schemes target a huge segment of society on the idea of saving money for a daughter's marriage since her birth takes place in the family. Undoubtedly it is giving an

indirect but clear message that a daughter's father has to save surplus money throughout years so that he can perform such marriage. It is indirectly promoting pomp and show as well as dowry system. The government has to scrutinize such minute details, wherever any advertisement or promotion somehow showcase or encourage dowry system and put a reasonable check on the same.

4. It has been observed that sometimes policies or schemes of government also contribute an unintentional promotion of dowry system. For example '*Arundhati*' scheme of Assam government which was presented in the budget of 2019-20 was also indirectly encouraging the custom of dowry.[47] It was held under this scheme that 10 grams of gold will be presented to the brides of economically weaker section in their marriage where there is a custom of giving gold in wedding. Such schemes neither be framed nor be implemented as it encourages the tradition that the fathers are ought to give gold and valuables in any case whether they are financially capable or not.

5. There are still a good number of marriages that take place without any dowry. Recently in West Bengal, a bridegroom who was a school teacher has strictly refused to take any kind of dowry in his marriage. He was surprised by his in-laws by gifting a huge pile of books of approximately 1 lac rupees.[48] In another example, the CM of Bihar, Mr. Nitish Kumar randomly surprised a couple by attending their marriage on the node of information that it was completely a dowryless marriage and Mr. Kumar wanted to encourage the families as an appreciation.[49] The marriages which take place without any dowry must be highly appreciated, publicised and rewarded with honour to give a strong message in the society.

6. Numerous seminars and conferences are organized by government agencies, welfare organizations, universities as well as educational institutes to create

---

[47] Assam's 'gold to brides' scheme welcomed by many, draws criticism too, *available at:* https://www.business-standard.com/article/news-ians/assam-s-gold-to-brides-scheme-welcomed-by-many-draws-criticism-too-119020701433_1.html (Visited on June 20, 2019)

[48] Priyanshi Mathur, "Bride's Family Surprises Groom With 1000 Books Worth Rs 1 Lakh After He Refuses To Take Dowry" *India Times, available at:* https://www.indiatimes.com/trending/human-interest/bride-s-family-surprises-groom-with-1000-books-worth-rs-1-lakh-after-he-refuses-to-take-dowry-367765.html(Visited on December 23, 2019)

[49] Rohit Kumar Singh , "Couple Get Surprise Visit from Bihar Chief Minister for Opting for No-Dowry Marriage", *India Today, available at:* https://www.indiatoday.in/india/story/for-refusing-dowry-couple-get-surprise-visit-from-bihar-chief-minister-on-wedding-day-1093148-2017-11-24 (Last modified on November 24, 2017)

awareness regarding the social evils of which dowry system is also one. But these seminars and conferences are confined to the academicians, professionals and educated group only. There is no participation or presence of general public which actually requires such kind of awareness as well as sensitisation. Therefore, it is suggested to invite general public to attend such events through advertising on mass level.

7. Few senior secondary schools were also visited while conducting the survey in this study. It is observed that the young students are not accustomed with a predetermined mindset for favouring dowry system. Therefore, through a regular literacy camps in schools and colleges, we can save our youth to develop an inclination towards dowry system. They must be made aware with the disastrous consequences of the menace of dowry in the society in the form of various dowry related crimes. It will be a slow and steady process to completely eradicate this deep rooted evil and its acceptability in the upcoming societies.

7.2.5 Suggestions Related to Prevent the Misuse and Abuse of Anti-Dowry Laws

1. To avoid misuse of anti-dowry laws and give real implementation of these enactments, there must be some provision of punishment for false and forged complaints. Criminal charges should be brought against all authorities those are collaborating with falsely accusing women and their parental families.

2. Police should seriously scrutinize the complaint related to dowry matters before registering the case. Arrest warrant should be issued only against the main accused and only after cognizance has been taken. Innocent family members of the bridegroom should not be arrested.

3. Family counseling centre should be established across the country to help the falsely implicated aggrieved families. For facilitating amicable settlement, to envisage a better and more results against Matrimonial cruelty, extensive role should be played by Legal Services.

4. The provision of Cruelty shall be made gender neutral to satisfy the changing dimensions of society. Mental cruelty has been vaguely defined in the Act, which leaves scope of misuse. The definition of cruelty should be clearly elaborated to remove the loopholes.

5. The offence under section 498-A should be made compoundable.[50] If the wife realizes that she has done wrong and wants to come back to her matrimonial home she must get a chance to compromise.

6. Human rights violations must be checked as in most cases involving non-resident Indians, their passports are impounded and they are restricted from traveling outside the country.

7.2.6 Other suggestions to curb the Menace of Dowry

Media, Newspapers and nowadays even social media plays a very significant role in forming public opinion. However, it has been observed that a subject like dowry system and related offences have become an outdated topic for discussion or debate in these agencies. Undoubtedly the custom is age old but has neither eradicated nor eroded with the passage of time, rather is the menace of this evil increasing day by day. It has not only given rise to some serious dowry related offences like dowry death, cruelty, abetment to suicide etc. but is also responsible for some recently fast growing issues like female foeticide, disturbed sex ratio and domestic violence on women. Therefore, the press, media as well as social media must condemn this social evil and its consequences by conducting discussions and debates.

The media plays a wrong role in hugely publicizing the fat weddings, the celebrity marriages done with huge pomp and show. Surprisingly, the details of expenses on decoration, exact expenditure spent on wedding rings, ornaments and clothes as well as the extraordinary lavish gifts given to the bridegroom and his family by the bride's side are not only discussed by the media but also compared with the other fat weddings. It is giving an extremely wrong social message towards the promotion of dowry.

The offenders of the dowry related offences must be publically criticized on media and social media to discourage this custom in the society. Since this evil has a strong proximity with the social acceptance, the people still consider giving huge dowry as a status symbol as well as taking huge dowry as an enhancement of financial status in the society. Therefore, by strongly condemning the people who practice dowry system and commit dowry related offences, we can end the social acceptability of this custom.

---

[50] *Supra* note 22.

Another serious concern which must be taken into the consideration by the law implementing bodies is the practical non adherence to the one and a half decade amended property right of daughters. It is a matter of huge pain that it took more than fifty years to enact equal rights on parental property for the daughters and still after that the law has merely remained on the papers.[51] Neither the parents, nor the brothers are giving and nor even the married daughters themselves are practically taking any share in the parental property. Dowry still exists as compensation or an alternate to the share in such property. Strict yet positive and encouraging steps must be taken to ensure the effective implementation of law related to property rights of daughters.

Dowry is such a custom of society which is continuously prevailing but no educated Indian would expressly accept or own up it with pride, although most of the people still adhere to this disreputable practice. The dowry system continues to be given and taken in all forms of the society; educated or uneducated, rich or poor, rural or urban etc. Apparently, the educated and high class people flaunt their eminence by discarding this social evil in their verbal and public discussions but practically the practice of dowry persists to be an integral part of the negotiations that are done in their family marriages. In Indian customs, dowry was given in a marriage for the security of the girl and it was considered as a blessing for her. But it has been observed that the husband and in-laws were torturing the bride for bringing more and more dowry and harass her to take cash from her parental house. In the wake of seeing this legislature has time to time enacted and amended numerous laws to shield the brides from worst impact of this custom. It has to be seen that such laws must solve the purpose of protection of women from harassment rather than benefitting the women to misuse it for harassing men and taking revenge by exploiting them through false implications.

There are many conflicting interests associated with the dowry related offences; firstly the possibility of tying the knots of broken family relationship, secondly, saving the children of the couple from trauma if any, thirdly, to assure that the offenders must be punished for their deeds. Apart from that, the wife or the would-be bride as a victim has a justified right to get justice for the agony which she has undergone and the mental harassment she has suffered When poor or middle class parents cannot give their daughters an expected dowry in such situations, very often

---

[51] See *Supra* Chapter 6 for detailed Empirical Survey.

the bride suffers cruelty and harassment after her marriage for not bringing expected dowry. Even many times, such cruelty results in brutal dowry deaths. The socio-cultural reasons are undoubtedly responsible for the failure of the law to combat the problem but another aspect is that there are still some drawbacks in the substantive provisions related to dowry prohibition. The procedural aspects like that of difficulty in gathering the evidence for convicting the main culprit further contribute in creating impediments in effective implementation of dowry prohibition laws. The cases of dowry deaths or suicide, where the brides opt to end their lives rather than reporting such cases to the police are a question on the lack of faith on legal framework for dowry prohibition and lacunas of Anti-Dowry laws.

Each citizen must attempt to be refreshed with the existing Acts and statutes passed by the legislature and should appropriately use them when there is a critical need to practice their rights. At the same time, law making and law implementing agencies must focus upon legislating and amending dowry related laws in such a way that these laws must get the acceptability of society. The sensitization of the masses will further act as an effective tool to combat the increase in dowry related offences. It is a collective responsibility of legislature, government, police machinery, judiciary as well as whole society to ensure that the sanctity of the institution of marriage, beauty of union of two individuals as well as their families through this pious ceremony of marriage and joy of the birth of a daughter as an epitome of goddess *'Lakshmi'* must not be overshadowed by merely an evil custom of 'Dowry'.

SUMMARY

"Dowry Prohibition and Law: A Socio-Legal Study"

The custom of dowry originated with the institution of marriage and ultimately changed to an evil practice which gave birth to several offences like; offences related to dowry, cruelty, abetment to suicide and dowry deaths, female foeticide, domestic violence etc. The custom of dowry was present in several countries and under various civilizations since inception. But its origin from ancient times to medieval times, its growth during British era and rise after independence has created a huge menace in India. Various laws are enacted in India to curb the menace of dowry like; Dowry Prohibition Act, 1961, provisions related to dowry in; Indian Penal Code, Criminal Procedure Code, Indian Evidence Act, Hindu Law and Domestic Violence Act. But the latest data of the NCRB, many landmark judgments as well as the empirical survey have indicated that these laws are unable to curb its menace. The present study has shown that lack of social will is the major impediment in the effective implementation of laws related to dowry prohibition. The research is based on review of existing literature, statutes, reports, policies etc and the empirical survey in district Kangra and district Shimla of Himachal Pradesh. The various other lacunas in the laws, functioning of police and other practical challenges in administration of justice in dowry related cases are also discussed. The various suggestions to overcome the impediments and lacunas in the effective implementation of laws related to dowry prohibition are given.

SUMMARY

"Dowry Prohibition and Law: A Socio-Legal Study"

The custom of dowry originated with the institution of marriage and ultimately changed to an evil practice which gave birth to several offences like; offences related to dowry, cruelty, abetment to suicide and dowry deaths, female foeticide, domestic violence etc. The custom of dowry was present in several countries and under various civilizations since inception. But its origin from ancient times to medieval times, its growth during British era and rise after independence has created a huge menace in India. Various laws are enacted in India to curb the menace of dowry like; Dowry Prohibition Act, 1961, provisions related to dowry in; Indian Penal Code, Criminal Procedure Code, Indian Evidence Act, Hindu Law and Domestic Violence Act. But the latest data of the NCRB, many landmark judgments as well as the empirical survey have indicated that these laws are unable to curb its menace. The present study has shown that lack of social will is the major impediment in the effective implementation of laws related to dowry prohibition. The research is based on review of existing literature, statutes, reports, policies etc and the empirical survey in district Kangra and district Shimla of Himachal Pradesh. The various other lacunas in the laws, functioning of police and other practical challenges in administration of justice in dowry related cases are also discussed. The various suggestions to overcome the impediments and lacunas in the effective implementation of laws related to dowry prohibition are given.

CPSIA information can be obtained
at www.ICGtesting.com
Printed in the USA
BVHW091115210123
656727BV00013B/1573